'NO CAR, NO RADIO, NO LIQUOR PERMIT'

Impoverished children prior to the enactment of Ontario Mothers' Allowance, 1913 (*City of Toronto Archives DPW 32–246*).

'NO CAR, NO RADIO, NO LIQUOR PERMIT'

The Moral Regulation of Single Mothers in Ontario, 1920–1997

Margaret Jane Hillyard Little

OXFORD
UNIVERSITY PRESS

OXFORD
UNIVERSITY PRESS

Oxford University Press
70 Wynford Drive, Don Mills, Ontario M3C 1J9
http://www.oupcan.com

Oxford New York
Athens Auckland Bangkok Bogotá Buenos Aires Calcutta
Cape Town Chennai Dar es Salaam Delhi Florence Hong Kong Istanbul
Karachi Kuala Lumpur Madrid Melbourne Mexico City Mumbai
Nairobi Paris São Paulo Singapore Taipei Tokyo Toronto Warsaw

and associated companies in
Berlin Ibadan

Oxford is a trademark of Oxford University Press

Canadian Cataloguing in Publication Data

Little, Margaret Jane, 1958–
No car, no radio, no liquor permit

Includes bibliographical references and index.
ISBN 0-19-541150-1

1. Single mothers – Ontario – Conduct of life – History – 20th century.
2. Mothers' pensions – Ontario – History – 20th century. I. Title.

HV700.C3L57 1998   362.83'9282'097130904   C98-930932-0

Cover design: Sonya Thursby
Text design: Max Gabriel Izod
Cover illustrations: City of Toronto Archives DPW 32-326;
courtesy of the Multicultural History Society of Ontario/Rev.
Ma T.K. Wou Collection; private collection

2 3 4 — 01 00

This book is printed on permanent (acid-free) paper ∞.
Printed in Canada

Contents

List of Tables

Abbreviations and Acronyms

AO	Archives of Ontario
CAP	Canada Assistance Plan
CAS	Children's Aid Society
CCCW	Canadian Council on Child Welfare
CHST	Canada Health and Social Transfer
COMSOC	Ministry of Community and Social Services
CPEA	County of Prince Edward Archives, Picton
CYC	Company of Young Canadians
DBW	D.B. Weldon Library, Western Regional Collection, London
ECL	Elgin County Library, St Thomas
ERO	Eligibility review officers
ESI	Employment Support Initiatives
FBA	Family Benefits Act
GWA	General welfare assistance
JSM	Just Society Movement
ILP	Independent Labour Party
LIFT	Low Income Families Together
LIPI	Low Income People Involvement
LPV	Lang Pioneer Village, Keene
LRR	City of London Records Retention
MTRA	Metropolitan Toronto Records and Archives
NA	National Archives, Ottawa
NAPO	National Anti-Poverty Organization
NCW	National Council of Women
NDA	Norwich and District Archives
OAP	Old Age Pensions
OCAP	Ontario Coalition Against Poverty
OMA	Ontario Mothers' Allowance
OWC	Ontario Workers' Compensation
PCMA	Peterborough Centennial Museum and Archives
RPA	Region of Peel Archives
SARB	Social Assistance Review Board
SARC	Social Assistance Review Committee
SCA	Simcoe County Archives, Minnesing
SIU	Special Investigation Unit
STEP	Supports to Employment Program
TLC	Trades and Labour Congress
TLCW	Toronto Local Council of Women
WIN	Work Incentive Program

Acknowledgements

Recently a reporter asked me, 'How did you get from the farm to here?' With a lot of help is the simplest answer. Certainly this book is the culmination of years of support from family, friends, and fellow activists.

First, this book would not have been possible without the enthusiasm and advice of a great number of archivists. While examining documents at small county and local archives, I was treated to cups of tea, home-made fudge, a dozen cobs of fresh corn, and many a tale about local history. I wish to thank Ralph Coram and Stormie Stewart of the Ontario Archives; Mary Jo Moore and Joyce Pettigrew of Norwich and District Archives; and the staff and volunteers at Elgin County Library, Lang Pioneer Village, County of Prince Edward Archives, and the Western Regional Collection, D.B. Weldon Library for their generosity in this regard. I am grateful for the financial support of the Jean Royce Scholarship, Queen's University; the Marta Danlewycz Memorial Award from the Canadian Research Institute for the Advancement of Women; and the Advisory Research Council grant from Queen's University. My research assistants, Jonathan Greene and Tonya Lailey, hired during the last hours of this project, scrambled to find every last newspaper clipping and every historical photograph to make this complete. I am grateful to Euan White, Phyllis Wilson, and especially Valerie Ahwee, of Oxford University Press, for their patience, enthusiasm, and support for this book.

I have been very fortunate to encounter a number of gifted and challenging teachers along the way. Frustrated as a journalist that I could not write about 'the big questions', Doreen Barrie urged me to go back to school. I am grateful for her confidence in my ability. The residents at Bridge House, Kingston, a shelter for women, introduced me to the struggles of low-income single mothers. By welcoming me into their lives, they taught me far more than they realize. During my doctoral program, when I reached a critical fork in the road, Michael Kaufman came along and convinced me that it was indeed possible to be both an academic and an activist. I continue to look to him as an example of how to do meaningful work. Jim Struthers is another who has quietly encouraged me during our coffee breaks at the archives. Mariana Valverde introduced me to the concept of moral regulation and provided endless encouragement and insightful comments. Leo Panitch never failed to challenge me intellectually, balancing his scrupulous editorial skills with a contagious enthusiasm for the project.

During the research and early stages of writing this book I was a member of two lively study groups: the Toronto Gender History Group and the Toronto Sex History Group. Along with intellectual stimulation, they gave me food, drink, and amusing gossip to brighten the days. Many thanks to Mary Louise Adams, Debi Brock, Lykke de la Cour, Karen Dubinsky, Nancy Forestell, Julie Guard, Kate

McPherson, Lynne Marks, Cecilia Morgan, Suzanne Morton, Becki Ross, and Carolyn Strange. After I left Toronto, Ian Morrison served as my very own study group and willingly provided me with the latest information and commentary on welfare changes.

A number of antipoverty groups kept me grounded in the 'here and now'. Bread Not Circuses, a coalition that formed to protest against the Toronto Olympic bid, introduced me to the Toronto antipoverty community and demonstrated that politics can be great fun. Josephine Grey of Low Income Families Together encouraged me to join their board of directors and become even more involved in the everyday concerns of single mothers. John Clarke and the Ontario Coalition Against Poverty always invited me to participate in their boisterous events. Running in an anti-Olympic race, marching through Rosedale, protesting and being removed from the Ontario legislature all renewed my energy and commitment to this project.

I am truly fortunate to have the very best of friends who help to sustain me when the going gets tough. Many of them have provided me with a roof over my head, good food, and a listening ear. I wish to thank the Oak Street Co-op staff and members, especially Brynne Teall, Jennifer Ramsay, Michael Shapcott, Nicole and Malcolm Shapcott Ramsay, Carolyn Whitzman, and, most importantly, Janet Borowy, for they were there when this project began. Throughout the writing and editing years the following friends have shown immense tolerance and provided numerous social diversions: Jacquie Buncel, Lykke de la Cour, Karen Dubinsky, Nancy Forestell, David Kidd, Eleanor and Grace McDonald, Ruth Mott, Becki Ross, Judith Weisman, and Sandy Whitworth. Lynne Marks deserves special mention for she is indeed a very special friend who has offered more than her share of advice and support.

I cannot begin to express my gratitude to my family—both biological and chosen. It was my father who told me and my two sisters, 'If you were sons, I'd give you the farm. But you are my daughters, so I'll give you education.' Clearly I got more than my fair share of the farm. My parents have supported me in every possible way. My mother, who was a beneficiary of Ontario Mothers' Allowance as a child, taught me to believe in myself above all else. And my father and I have shared a love of politics, albeit from different philosophical positions. We have argued passionately about politics ever since I can remember. My most important thanks goes to Rose-Marie Kennedy. I met this poet/activist/intellectual at the critical moment: the editing stage. Her sharp analytical and writing skills were forced to the test for she read and commented on every comma, every phrase, every argument. She and her parents, Patricia and Bernard, provided me with a house by the ocean in Frogmarsh, Newfoundland, where I could watch herring hogs and pick blueberries when I just could not write one more word.

Finally, I would like to dedicate this book to all the single mothers on welfare I have met. I am humbled by their courage, outraged by the injustice they continually face, and honoured that they invited me into their homes and into their lives.

'A WELFARE WOMAN'S SONG'
by Carole Silliker, 1969[1]

My children go to school each day
In ragged hand me down
I just ran out of powdered milk
And I am breaking down
I told my social worker
We just cannot get by
But she said this is all you get
And then she said goodbye

And every place I tried to work
I had to please the boss
Refused them and got fired
But it made the welfare cross
And just like all the other girls
My husband was no good
So here I am on welfare
And living by their rules

Chorus: I'm a woman on welfare
And depressed all the time
I haven't got a damned red cent
And nothing that is mine
If we don't slowly starve to death
Then something sure is wrong
I want the whole wide world to hear
A welfare woman's song

With luck I'll find a boyfriend
Who'll try to help us out
But he cannot afford us all
He'll break without a doubt
And lord I drink a lot
To ease the pain of being poor
But then I get the Children's Aid
A knockin' on my door

They sit there in their party clothes
And say the kids look bad
I try to make them understand
I gave them all I had
They said they'd take them all away
If I didn't settle down
I told them all where they could go
Cause hell is where they're bound

Introduction

An examination of the historical development of Ontario Mothers' Allowance (OMA), from its enactment in 1920 to its dissolution in 1997, provokes theoretical questions regarding the nature of the welfare state generally and its specific relationship to poor single mothers. The welfare state 'represents perhaps the single most important transformation of every-day social life in the past 50 years yet it remains virtually unexamined.'[2] Rarely is the welfare state studied for its own particular features; instead it is used as a test case to explain larger phenomena (such as industrialization, capitalism, patriarchy, or federalism).[3] With a few exceptions, much of welfare state scholarship has involved pan-historic, cross-cultural comparisons to address these metatheoretical questions.[4]

This study of Ontario Mothers' Allowance began from quite a different starting-point. Rooted in the specificities of time, place, and policy, this inquiry emerged from community work with poor single mothers and their concerns. More than a decade ago I volunteered at Bridge House, a shelter in Kingston, Ontario, for women, many of whom were OMA recipients.[5] I watched them fret about accepting a coffee or beer at the local bar, or permitting a male friend to walk them home. I was outraged by the minute ways in which social workers and neighbours intruded into their lives. I was appalled by how they even self-censored their days and nights, all in an attempt to guarantee the continuance of the monthly OMA cheque, a cheque that did not begin to meet their subsistence needs. This Bridge House experience had a profound impact on my personal, political, and intellectual life. Since then I have been active in a number of antipoverty groups and have conducted workshops and research projects with and about poor women.[6] Through these political activities I began to ask questions about the nature of our welfare state and its impact on poor women's lives.

Contrary to popular opinion, single mothers are not a new phenomenon. There have always been widows, husbands who deserted their wives and children, mothers who bore and raised children outside the bounds of heterosexual marriage. But at the turn of the century this group was perceived as a new social problem, requiring new societal remedies. And this group has continued during the last century to be viewed as both the cause and effect of larger moral concerns.

Despite their prevalence, poor women, particularly single mothers, have rarely been studied. Feminist contributions to social science have tended to focus on the lives of working-class, middle-class, or bourgeois women. This is partly a result of limited sources, but it is also a reflection of poor women's invisibility in our society generally. It is important to recognize that the treatment of single mothers reflects societal values on mothering and marriage for all women. 'A lack of social support for single mothers makes marriage coercive. If mothers must be supported by men to be good mothers, then it would appear that good mothering is dependent on women being dependent.'[7] The status of single mothers (including their access to jobs, education, and child care) indicates a society's and a government's commitment both to women's economic independence and to children's welfare.

This lack of attention to poor women and single mothers is reflected in the welfare state literature. There have been few studies of early welfare policies, many of which involved women as initiators, administrators, and recipients. Only recently have American and European feminists begun to examine the variety of early maternalist policies enacted at the turn of the century (i.e., mothers' allowance, child care provisions, and protective labour legislation).[8]

As one of the first welfare policies, mothers' allowance provides an important site to begin a re-examination of the Canadian welfare state. Along with a number of other Western industrialized nations, most Canadian provinces enacted legislation to provide aid to needy widows in the early twentieth century. Over time this policy expanded to include a variety of impoverished single mothers. Despite its important history, this policy has been virtually ignored by Canadian scholars.[9]

This study of the historical development of Ontario Mothers' Allowance attempts to fill a gap in the existing mothers' allowance and welfare state literature in a number of ways. As the project unfolded, three large theoretical questions emerged. Why did mothers' allowance become one of the first social assistance programs in the country? What are the predominant characteristics of both past and present OMA policy? And, finally, how does our exploration of the historical development of OMA help to provide a better understanding of the nature of the welfare state generally? Based on the historical evidence provided by subsequent chapters, the remainder of this Introduction will explore these three questions.

HOW CAN WE BEGIN TO UNDERSTAND THE ORIGINS OF ONTARIO MOTHERS' ALLOWANCE?

An examination of the origins of Ontario Mothers' Allowance requires an exploration of neglected fields within welfare state theory. Most welfare state scholars focus on national and universal income security and contributory social programs, such as family allowance, unemployment insurance, and universal health care. These programs, generally introduced during or immediately following the Second World War, account for the lion's share of government social spending. Their introduction represented important victories in the fight against poverty and economic security and provided citizens with a new sense of social rights. Comparatively, earlier welfare policies such as OMA have received, for the most part, little examination even though they set the stage for the modern era in social welfare.[10]

Few welfare state analyses have adequately explored the origins of a welfare policy. Policies are not created in a vacuum. To understand the origins
of a specific policy, it is important to locate the emergence of historical
actors, their interests, and the alliances they formed. An attention to historical actors also challenges our understanding of where the political arena is
constituted.[11] Most policy studies have granted attention to the 'public' or
political sphere, often to the exclusion of activities in the 'private' sphere.
The historical development of OMA illustrates the importance of bourgeois
women's activities, often outside the traditional spheres of political and economic power.

As Chapter 1 will demonstrate, the enactment of OMA represents a
major victory for bourgeois women to influence the political arena. But
why was it bourgeois women rather than labour, religious, or other societal
groups who became the leaders in child and maternal welfare reform? Part
of the answer lies in the changing family form, the rising importance of the
middle class, and an accompanying maternal ideology. Economically, the
turn of the century was a period of rapid industrialization, urbanization,
and immigration that had a dramatic impact on the familial unit and
women's place within it. As the bourgeois family changed from a self-sufficient productive unit to one increasingly dependent on the external and
predominantly male wage, the status of women and children also altered.[12]

With the separation of home from work, and the removal of at least bourgeois women from productive activities, a new definition of motherhood
emerged. These women were economically dependent upon their husbands'
wages and were often hesitant to critique women's oppression within the
family. Instead, they used their position as mothers to assert a position for
themselves in the public sphere.[13] They espoused a maternal ideology that
reflected their own class and race privilege and simultaneously their gender
subordination. They believed domestic responsibilities to be essential to
women and to the social order more generally. They strongly advocated the
family form of the male breadwinner with dependent wife and children, an
ideal to which few working-class families were able to adhere. And they also
asserted that their experience as mothers made them uniquely suited to help
others, particularly less fortunate mothers and children.

For the most part, these women were Protestant Euro-Canadians who
were concerned about the rapid influx of other ethnic groups and wanted
to preserve their racial group's social position. Through charity work these
middle-class reformers were able to promote Protestant Euro-Canadian
values of cleanliness and morality among other ethnic groups. But this help
for the subordinate classes and races was rarely an attempt to assimilate
them. Rather, this charity work ensured the long-standing superiority of a
gendered and race-specific middle class.

One of the first focuses of charity work involved the plight of single
mothers and children. Until the introduction of OMA, single mothers were
often forced to place their children in orphanages that were indirectly

funded and periodically monitored by the state. At the turn of the century these orphanages were overflowing with unwanted children. One solution to this increasing number of unwanted children would have been the construction of more orphanages. Why did the state reject this previous solution and instead establish a direct welfare payment program?

In order to answer this question, we need to pay more attention to the role of OMA advocates. There has been enormous debate about the motivations of these bourgeois women lobbyists. Did they desire a cross-class alliance of women? If so, why did they support a policy that was moralistic, financially inadequate, and that perpetuated women's economic dependence? These questions have provoked considerable debate in the American welfare state literature. Most notably, Theda Skocpol argues that these women lobbyists did attempt a cross-class alliance and a more generous policy than the one that resulted, but others assert that these women were never really able to transcend their own class privilege.[14]

This book provides new evidence to add to this debate. As Chapter 1 illustrates, these women lobbyists supported a bourgeois notion of motherhood. They advocated payments that were well below those granted to soldiers' wives through the Canadian Patriotic Fund. And once these meagre allowances were established, they made little attempt to improve them. In fact, despite the minimal allowance rates, these lobbyists remained adamant that poor single mothers should not work. They also upheld a morality that was bourgeois. Questions of morality dominated this campaign and lobbyists were gravely concerned about what types of single mothers should be considered morally worthy to receive the allowance. At no time did these women consult or otherwise engage with poor women during the campaign. Consequently, these bourgeois women were the advocates of a policy that would be both inadequate and moralistic.

But despite these important weaknesses, mothers' allowance represented a significant departure from previous legislation. It was the first policy to involve regular and direct state payments to citizens. How did this new type of social expenditure become acceptable? It was in good part a result of bourgeois charity women's lobby effort. These women proposed a policy that would involve both private and public welfare responsibility. Since only the most worthy single mothers, namely widows, would receive mothers' allowance, many fatherless children would remain under the care of private charities. Even the mothers' allowance recipient would be closely monitored by private charities, thereby reducing state administrative costs and responsibilities. At the same time, the enactment of mothers' allowance could provide a new arena for bourgeois women to assert their moral/cultural authority. Some charity women acted as 'poverty experts', advising and influencing state policy for the first time. A few secured their professional status as paid social workers through the introduction of mothers' allowance. Thus the introduction of OMA suggested that charity women might expand their role and influence in society.[15]

Why was there little opposition to a policy that appeared to enhance bourgeois women's authority? During the same period members of the women's suffrage movement who also employed a maternalist argument met considerable resistance. Perhaps this is because charity and social work were already considered a female domain whereas suffrage and party politics were understood as a male arena. Suffrage would involve a dispersion or sharing of power between men and women, whereas the introduction of mothers' allowance did not appear to interfere with male authority. As such the lobby for mothers' allowance did not threaten the dominant gender, class, or race interests and therefore did not meet strong opposition.

This attempt to understand the origins of OMA reveals the inadequacies of conventional welfare state theories. Frances Fox Piven and Richard Cloward's argument that welfare policies are introduced to appease the masses during periods of great unemployment and civil disaffection, expressed in the streets or at the polls, does not fit OMA developments.[16] While there was considerable economic dislocation at the turn of the century, it did not include mass unemployment and dramatic civil disorder. Similarly, the radical feminist claim that the welfare state is patriarchal and oppressive to all women does not address the important role women played in the initiation of OMA.[17] And, finally, a state-centred approach that focuses attention on formal political institutions cannot help us to understand why the major impetus for OMA came not from politicians and civil servants but from private charity. I argue that the origins of OMA must include a more precise understanding of the complex class, race, and gender interests of the welfare reformers. In negotiating a new position for themselves within the public sphere, these bourgeois women utilized conventional gender and family arrangements, which were oppressive to most women, to assert their particular class and race advantage. Through their articulation of a maternal ideology, they achieved new political and economic power while distinguishing themselves from the very people they sought to 'help'. Consequently, attention to the intersection of class, race, and gender interests helps to explain why this policy did not represent a step towards social equality where all would have rights to public welfare. Although mothers' allowance provided new protection for a few poor single mothers and new recognition for middle-class women, it reinforced a notion of motherhood that not only emphasized gender differences but was also based on a Protestant Euro-Canadian middle-class model. Motherhood defined as full-time care of children was not possible for a large number of ethnic-minority, working-class, and poor women. Despite this reality, few bourgeois women reformers advocated a more generous policy that would meet the real needs of these poor single mothers. This legacy of the policy's initiation would be felt for many years to come.

WHAT ARE THE PREDOMINANT CHARACTERISTICS OF OMA POLICY?

After seventy-seven years, welfare designated specifically for single mothers was disbanded in November 1997. Despite numerous amendments to the OMA policy during its history, there were a few general characteristics that persisted. One such trait was the inadequate nature of the allowance throughout the years. While this allowance granted women some economic independence from a male partner, its inadequacy ensured that this option never became too appealing. But mothers' allowance was not the only policy that was minimal in nature; so was general welfare. This trait was inherited from the Poor Law belief that minimal welfare for the poor was necessary to protect the work ethic. Most welfare policies in industrialized countries specifically designated for the poor have remained well below the subsistence level. This is in contrast to contributory policies such as Workers' Compensation and unemployment insurance. Either workers who have 'contributed to society' through their labour are assumed to be more worthy of welfare benefits than the poor, or the poor have less economic and political clout than workers to demand more substantial welfare programs.

Associated with a minimal allowance was the government's continued reluctance to promote economic independence for single mothers. Initially this policy helped to restrict women's participation in the workforce. Around the turn of the century the state enacted a number of laws that distinguished male from female labour. These laws protected women as active or potential reproducers and introduced limitations on their hours and type of work. In doing so, women became an economic liability to employers and were effectively ghettoized into a low-paid, sex-segregated job sector that was exempted from this protective legislation.[18] The introduction of OMA helped to support this general trend. Through mothers' allowance the unpaid work of motherhood helped to provide a more stable and healthy future workforce. At the same time, these recipients were encouraged to do some paid work that did not interfere with their mothering responsibilities. As such, these women became part of a reserve army of labour characterized by seasonal, part-time, service, and small-business work with few (if any) benefits. This reserve army helped to guarantee a continuing source of cheap (female) labour that curbed workers' demands for better wages. This pattern continues today. Although single mothers on welfare are permitted to train for full-time work, this education is directed towards the low-wage sector. There is very little opportunity for a single mother on welfare to rise beyond the working poor. One of the few ways to escape this impoverishment is to find another male breadwinner.

While at face value the policy appeared to provide women with the possibility of economic independence, the meagre rates ensured that it did not significantly challenge the family wage structure of male breadwinner with dependent wife and children. This family structure is at the centre of most welfare policies of this century. Government payments to unemployed men attempted to replace wages and hence preserve their male breadwinner status and simultaneously keep their wives and children at home. Similarly, mothers' allowance 'aimed to prevent its recipients from being too comfortable on their own'.[19] Only wives who had lost their husbands were presumed to need state aid; all others were assumed to be sheltered from economic hardship through the family unit. As with most other welfare policies, mothers' allowance was premised on the need to compensate men's wages rather than meet the actual needs of women and children.

In supporting this family form and sexual division of labour, the policy established contradictory expectations for poor single mothers. Recipients could not adequately fulfil both their family and labour force responsibilities as these roles were fundamentally incompatible. Throughout the history of the policy, administrators have tended to blame working mothers if their children misbehave. Simultaneously, full-time mothers were urged to participate in the labour force. This demonstrates the policy's ambivalence regarding single mothers and paid work. The current push towards full-time employment without the necessary child care and support services in place or an adequate job market exacerbates these contradictions. Throughout the history of the policy, OMA administrators chose to ignore the fact that raising children and providing for children are conflicting responsibilities for poor single mothers.

As demonstrated earlier, seemingly benign welfare policies such as OMA have helped to reinforce the importance of masculine labour and authority within the family and the labour force. Those women who challenged their prescribed role received subsistence benefits and stigmatization. This kept unmarried motherhood and the breakup of the two-parent family from appearing too attractive to others. While OMA increased some women's ability to leave their partners, it promoted the subordination of women to men in the workforce and in the home.

Perhaps OMA's most significant trait was the intrusive and intensive moral scrutiny of applicants and recipients. The fact that this policy and its administration were saturated with questions of morality has not been adequately addressed. Throughout the history of OMA moral issues dominated the activities of the administrators and various societal leaders. Case files, annual reports, and interviews clearly demonstrated the minute ways in which social workers and neighbours scrutinized the lives of OMA recipients.

This moral investigation of welfare recipients has not been adequately explored by most welfare scholars. Generally, moral concerns regarding the poor are associated with charity work prior to the twentieth century. Many assume that this type of moral scrutiny withered with the emergence of the welfare state.[20] But the history of OMA suggests that moral questions continue to dominate some areas of welfare legislation. In this respect, we have much to learn from Philip Corrigan, Derek Sayer, Bruce Curtis, Mariana Valverde, and Lorna Weir, who have explored what they term the *moral regulation* of citizens. There is much debate among those who utilize the term 'moral regulation'. Corrigan and Sayer in their innovative book, *The Great Arch*, examine the formation of the English state through its activities, forms, routines, rituals, and regulations. Not only do they examine the processes by which the state organizes social life, they also study the relationship between the rulers, the ruled, and the procedures that ensure this relationship. They observe how these state practices become a project of normalizing or rendering natural certain behaviours, family forms, and sexual practices while marginalizing others. They perceive the state's involvement in this moral regulation as ongoing, not merely imposing a dominant ideology as a *fait accompli* but continuously regulating the formation of identities and subjectivities of citizens. In short, they look at the cultural content of state institutions and state activities, arguing that capitalism requires not only workers but moral workers, workers who participate willingly in unequal relationships with their bosses, families, and neighbours.[21]

Other moral regulation scholars include a more Foucauldian understanding of moral culture. Whereas Corrigan and Sayer are most concerned about how moral regulatory practices reinforce class interests, Valverde and Weir have applied this model to questions of gender, race, and sexuality. They explore the process by which multiple discourses, generated by both the state and civil society, define and produce morality.[22]

In the case of OMA, moral regulation can be seen to reinforce not merely class but also gender, race, and sexual inequalities. Until recently, the policy promoted single mothers and their children as a reserve army of labour, but not all aspects of this policy were always beneficial for bourgeois economic interests. There were other less costly and less cumbersome bureaucratic processes to ensure that the poor subdued workers' demands for better wages and remained a ready reserve army of labour. Also, the investigation of minute aspects of a single mother's life—which included her dress, language, attitude, and behaviour—could not be justified in purely economic terms. These intrusive procedures suggest that gender, race, and sexual definitions of morality often predominated in the everyday administration of this policy.

These administrative processes and the definition of morality changed over time. In the case of OMA, initially only widows were considered morally worthy for the allowance, but over time a variety of single mothers, including unwed and cohabiting women, became eligible to apply. Although this policy continued to involve intensive investigation of applicants' lives, the definition of what was 'morally worthy' altered over time. Until the mid-1990s the policy had consistently expanded its definition of deservedness. During the final years of OMA this moral terrain shifted once again and the policy began to restrict its eligibility criteria.

By highlighting the moral investigative processes of a policy, one is better able to understand the complex and interdependent relationship between the regulator and the regulated. There has been little attempt in traditional welfare studies to address adequately this relationship. Social control scholars tend to grant the regulators absolute power and focus attention on those who are regulated, but moral regulation students argue that this process is more one of preserving and shaping rather than suppressing. They suggest that there is a relationship developed over time between the regulator and the regulated that must be explored. For instance, in addressing the question of origins, it became clear to me that those who initiated and administered OMA did not have absolute or even secure power but were attempting to preserve and reinforce their own socio-economic position through this policy during a period of social turmoil. Instead of assuming regulators to be powerful, moral regulation scholars examine the contestation of different definitions of morality and the alliances formed.[23]

An examination of the regulator, the regulated, and the regulations also helps one appreciate the resistance to change. As mentioned earlier, regulators or administrators could be replaced by other moral experts. As a result, the regulators depended on these recipients for a job and for their socio-economic position, which in turn granted the recipients a degree of bargaining power over the regulators. Since so many OMA regulations were arbitrarily applied, this negotiation process was ongoing. At the same time, it is important to remember that the recipient's negotiating power was limited, given that she had little to bargain with and could easily be replaced by another more needy and worthy applicant. These regulations to some degree bound both parties over time to a certain relationship that was not easily altered.[24]

In sum, moral regulation provides us with another lens through which to examine the complexities of welfare policy. This model cannot *explain* the conditions observed, but it can help to highlight relationships and regulations that many take for granted. In doing so moral regulation presents welfare state scholars with an important tool with which we can better understand the cultural activities of the state and other social agencies. Given current trends, it is probable that moral regulation will become even more useful in examining contemporary welfare activity. With the erosion of the welfare state and the increased importance of private welfare agencies in making up the loss, new moral concerns are being raised. This environment has renewed an interest in the moral scrutiny of applicants. Moral regulation will help to elucidate the punitive nature of many of these public and private welfare activities.

HOW DOES OMA'S HISTORICAL DEVELOPMENT HELP US TO KNOW MORE ABOUT THE WELFARE STATE GENERALLY?

An analysis of Ontario Mothers' Allowance reveals the importance of a gender analysis in the field of welfare state scholarship. Generally, welfare state theorists have been inattentive to gender questions and Canadian scholars have been particularly slow to take up the feminist challenge in comparison to our American and European colleagues.[25] Questions of

Canadian federalism, region, and class have tended to obscure the gender dimensions of many welfare policies, which has resulted in a number of omissions at various levels of welfare analysis. First, certain policies directed towards women (especially poor women), such as OMA, have been virtually ignored by welfare scholars. Second, certain political actors, such as women charity workers at the turn of the century, have rarely been considered in any examination of welfare policy origins. Third, these female actors have been involved in a variety of activities in the social/cultural arena that have often been deemed apolitical and thereby neglected. And, finally, women's work in connection with welfare policies is often unacknowledged. For example, women are the main workers within the welfare system, yet they remain for the most part in the poorly paid, lower echelon jobs. An examination of the historical development of OMA reveals that once gender is included as a category of analysis, new types of political actors, new political arenas, and new styles of political activities must be addressed.

This case-study also reveals the need for a structural analysis of gender inequality. The 'add women and stir' approach that acknowledges new political actors, activities, and arenas does not explain how the state both reflects and reinforces gender inequalities. Feminist scholars have begun to critique previous structural analyses of the state and offer alternative explanations. Feminist scholars have argued that the welfare state is gendered in structure and that many of its policies help to reinforce an entire system of women's oppression. Many socialist feminists have suggested that the welfare state has promoted the family wage model of the male breadwinner and the dependent wife and children. They believe this helps explain some of the more contradictory aspects of welfare policies, for example, why many programs discourage women's economic independence.[26] Others emphasize the transition from private patriarchy to a capitalist patriarchal state. They claim that this patriarchal state, based on a distinction between public (male) and private (female) life, has limited women's socio-economic power in the public sphere.[27] More recently, feminists have suggested that the welfare state is structured along two distinct tiers, each with different ideologies, clienteles, principles of entitlement, and administrative styles. One tier, based on the traditional Elizabethan Poor Law notion of welfare as a privilege, is characterized by minimal benefits, intrusive regulation of the recipients' lives, and the majority of recipients being women. The second tier is characterized by more generous benefits, automatic payment, the belief that this provision is a right rather than a privilege, and the majority of the recipients being men.[28] Those characterized by the first tier, such as OMA, have often been initiated by women's charity organizations, whereas the second tier has tended to be a compromise between capital and labour.

Feminist scholars disagree about women's relationship to the state, but each of these structuralist arguments has uncovered new dimensions of the problem. Some feminist historians, however, have found these structural analyses somewhat limiting in their explanatory power. Because structural arguments focus on the rationale of a welfare policy for a particular group in power, they are not able to adequately explain contradictions. As such, this approach sometimes tends to encourage views of women as passive victims or targets of policies and obscures the agency of women as initiators and clients. Attention to the struggles of class, gender, or race might help to explain some of the contradictions of welfare policies. For example, the role of women during the initiation of OMA is at least partially explained by the class, gender, and race struggles at the turn of the century. As a result, structural analyses do not remain infallible to historical and political evidence, but they do provide some appreciation for certain long-standing features of welfare programs.

What most of these structural analyses reveal is the fact that the state, particularly the welfare state, is rarely (if ever) neutral to women. Instead, the welfare state has played a contradictory role as a site of both women's liberation and ongoing oppression.[29] Women have a particularly close relationship to the welfare state for they make up both the majority of workers and clients. Welfare policies, such as mothers' allowance, help reproduce gender inequities within the home and society generally. In fact, women as lobbyists helped to create this unequal welfare state structure. And women as state workers reinforce these gender inequities through the everyday administration of these policies. At the same time, these welfare programs also grant some women independence from men, both as state workers and as recipients. Structural analyses that include questions of contradiction and agency promote a better understanding of the complex relationship between women and the welfare state.

Such theoretical questions informed this attempt to understand better the day-to-day reality of poor single mothers. The stories of their lives during the last seventy-seven years are compelling. Whether told by the OMA administrators or by the mothers themselves, these accounts speak of the profound way that the welfare state and various social agencies intrude in the lives of the poor. They describe a welfare system that is morally judgemental rather than benevolent, and they also demonstrate that this moral and financial scrutiny of poor single mothers is intensifying.

SOURCES FOR THE STUDY OF ONTARIO MOTHERS' ALLOWANCE

The book is chronological in structure, beginning with the lobby for OMA (Chapter 1), then examining policy changes throughout eight decades of administration (chapters 2 to 6) and the contemporary struggles of single mothers (Chapter 7), and culminating with an exploration of current trends and issues (Conclusion). In addition to the chronological chapters, other aids are provided for the reader. Tabulated statistical data are presented in some chapters. A chronology of amendments to the act is in the Appendix.

Historians have utilized case files to explore, among other things, the production of 'truth'. Influenced by post-modernism, some historians have become increasingly concerned about the fragmentary and incomplete nature of case files as a window into the real lives of people. This is particularly difficult when one is trying to interpret the experiences of those who are the subjects of these case files.

I utilized a variety of sources to explore the policy's origins, historical development, and contemporary nature. My use of case files is of particular significance to this study. While there is now an emerging body of literature on the history of this policy in Europe and the United States, none of these scholars has had access to case files. After a thorough search of provincial and municipal archival holdings, I was fortunate to locate case files from the city of London; three counties in southern Ontario (Elgin, Lincoln, and Oxford); and a scattering of problem or sample cases from throughout the province. In total, this provided 9.5 cubic feet of case files spanning OMA administration from 1920 to 1955 (see Appendix). These case files include minute details of these mothers' lives—following them from the time they wrote out their application, through the schooling of their children, the tabulation of their accumulating debts, etc. As such, they enable us to examine how this new relationship between social worker and client was established and simultaneously contested.

The use of these OMA case files provided a number of challenges. For a variety of reasons these case files are fragmented and often distorted in the stories they tell. The OMA case records are uneven in the amount of evidence they contained, depending mainly on the thoroughness of the individual investigator. Also, bureaucratic errors could result in loss of evidence when information was sent to and from various interested parties. The voices of the investigators dominate the papers. Even when the investigator is attempting to represent the views of the mother, the investigator's opinions shine through. Fortunately, many case records contain letters from the mothers to OMA officials or to community leaders to seek help with their particular case and are generally written in a humble, pleading tone. Such correspondence cannot be unquestioningly taken as the mother's true feelings about her experiences with OMA administration. The letters the mothers wrote directly to the premier or the prime minister are generally more assertively written. While neither type of letters can be considered representative of a single mother's experience with the policy, the subject matter of the letters can give one some sense of what the mother believed was negotiable, given the discretionary nature of OMA administration generally.

While it is impossible to determine the extent to which this is a representative sample, these case files do provide a window into the early administration of the policy and the lives of the recipients. The case files from London give us an opportunity to examine the policy's workings in an urban, predominantly Protestant Euro-Canadian setting. Those from Elgin and Oxford counties illustrate the everyday experiences of poor single mothers in the rural, livestock, and tobacco counties where the residents were predominantly Protestant Euro-Canadian or German Mennonite.

Lincoln County was mainly a fruit- and vegetable-producing area in the Niagara region and populated by Protestant Euro-Canadians, Italians, and southern Europeans.

Given that the caseworkers' opinions, comments, and evidence dominated the case files, it is often difficult to hear the muted voices of the single mothers, yet there is evidence to suggest that clients were not passive victims of this welfare policy. Instead, the vast majority of single mothers actively sought out this state aid. They argued their case before the welfare worker or 'investigator', as they were called. These clients also appealed for outside support when necessary. Despite their limited resources, they used tremendous ingenuity to protect and nurture their children. This contestation and cooperation of investigator and client will be given particular focus.

The OMA case records represented a tremendous improvement in record keeping from nineteenth-century charity work. The 1920s were a period of consolidation for welfare workers, and the Canadian Association of Social Workers was founded in 1928 to organize and regulate these new professionals.[30] Social workers expounded on the usefulness of case work to carefully and 'objectively' detail the lives of the less fortunate, and the formal OMA application forms and quarterly investigative reports were at least partly in response to this new scientific era. This contrasted with nineteenth-century welfare, which was generally conducted by volunteer and/or untrained labour whose record keeping was haphazard and inconsistent. Earlier record keeping tended to be in the form of ledger books in which the barest outlines describing the family were handwritten on three or four lines of the ledger. Emphasis tended to be more on the number of families aided and the amount or type of help given, but few details were recorded.

These case files are rich in information about an individual single mother's situation. The application form marked the first official interaction between the investigator and the single mother. A standard application form of four pages contained information about the date of application; the ages of the mother, father, and children; the number of children; the place of birth and racial origin; reasons for application; the financial circumstances (including any jobs held by family members); and names of three referees.

Page two of the form was generally reserved for financial questions. The mother would be asked to list her sources of income (profits from business, the sale of produce, the rent of property; from savings or insurance, pension or annuity, or workers' compensation; interest on investments; income from boarders, lodgers, or other sources, and the total per month) and her expenses (rent, taxes, principal, interest, house insurance, light and water, fuel, cleaning materials, food, recreation, clothing, life insurance, sundries, and the total for the month).

The fourth and final page was blank and reserved for the investigator's comments. Generally, the investigator's personal subjective opinions rather than 'objective' data characterized the comments on this page. In this section the investigator commented freely upon the mother's moral worthiness for the allowance. These comments often displayed class arrogance and insensitivity. In this initial stage of the process, the mother's voice was almost completely silent. Her sole contribution was to provide her signature at the bottom of the form.

Attached to many application forms were lengthy follow-up notes from the investigator and letters from the community to support or condemn the applicant. The subsequent documentation of the case provided less quantitative details and even more opportunity for subjective determinations. Also included in many case files were interagency memoranda, letters and queries from the clients, as well as correspondence from neighbours, store owners, clergy, doctors, charity leaders, and other interested people.

Whereas the mothers' voices were often muted by the case file documentation, interviews with current OMA recipients provided an opportunity to hear directly from the clients. These interviews were conducted with sixty-one OMA recipients in six different areas of the province between 1990 and 1996. These interviews did not attempt to represent all clients' experience of the policy. The interviews were conducted with single mothers who had already formed groups for the purpose of social and/or political activity, and included clients from urban and rural, eastern, western, northern, and southern areas of the province. The majority of the clients interviewed were anonymous, in keeping with their wishes. (For further discussion of these interviews, see Chapter 7.)

In addition, a small number of community legal workers, social workers, and antipoverty activists were also interviewed. These interviews were conducted merely to supplement or clarify the evidence provided by the single mothers. Finally, a few civil servants who had been involved in the administration of OMA over a number of years were also interviewed in an attempt to understand better the internal workings of government and the rationale behind certain policy amendments.

This combination of qualitative and quantitative evidence derived from both the perusal of historical documents and 'hands-on' interviews with current administrators, activists, and recipients resulted in a wealth of research findings.[31] The contemporary evidence helped me to ask new questions about the past. For instance, did some single mothers strategize over coffee in the 1920s and 1930s as some do today even though there is no historical record of this? Did others put on a humble performance only for the benefit of the OMA administrator to get what they needed, as a number of current OMA recipients do? Similarly, questions about recent policy decisions sent me back to the earlier documents and discussions to understand the reasoning behind them.

None of the sources enables me to tell the complete history of this policy and its impact on the lives of poor single mothers, but this book does attempt to provide a starting-point from which to begin an analysis of single motherhood and poverty. Today single mothers are increasingly under attack. Welfare policy amendments that improved the lives of single mothers are now being rolled back or rewritten. In order to assess the impact of these current changes, we need to understand how this policy was developed, how it was administered, and how it affected the daily lives of single mothers. Only then can we support single mothers in their struggle for economic security and dignity.

Chapter 1

Maternal Origins: 'God Could Not Be Everywhere, So He Made Mothers'[1]

The Ontario Mothers' Allowance lobby emerged out of an international child-saving movement, led by middle-class social reformers, which spread throughout the industrialized world, promoting protective labour legislation and welfare reforms. Aware of these international events, Ontario social reformers promoted their own welfare agenda. White bourgeois women, who had not yet achieved full political rights, played a leading and instrumental role both in the international movement and in Ontario. Other middle-class representatives, including church and charity leaders, judges and medical professionals, joined the Ontario campaign. Finally, organized labour also entered the debate, albeit late. Although the labour representatives had a distinctive economic analysis of poverty, they, like the middle-class reformers, embraced both racist and maternalist assumptions about worthiness. Lobbyists expressed racist fears about the overpopulation of 'foreigners' and were adamant that ethnic minorities should not be eligible for public help. Similarly, all the lobbyists, including organized labour, endorsed a maternalist philosophy. This ideology, which extolled the virtues of domesticity, unified the campaign and provided new opportunities in the 'public' sphere for middle-class women while simultaneously limiting the opportunities for less fortunate mothers. Over a period spanning more than three decades, the lobby gained momentum. Following continuous and overwhelming pressure, the Ontario government established an inquiry into the question in 1919. All ninety-three speakers at the inquiry unanimously endorsed the establishment of a mothers' allowance policy. A year later, the government enacted one of the first and most popular welfare measures in Ontario's history. This chapter will examine the context in which this lobby developed, the positions of the historical actors as they emerged, the alliances they formed, and the government's response.[2]

SETTING THE WELFARE SCENE

Nineteenth-century welfare in Ontario was characterized by three important features that have cast a long shadow over welfare debates well into the twentieth century. First, welfare took the form of a haphazard *mélange* of public and private administration with no organization or government body assuming full responsibility. Except for local governments, the state resisted direct disbursements to the needy and instead helped to finance and regulate institutions such as orphanages, houses of industry, and prisons. Other types of welfare varied by community, but generally took the form of haphazard distribution of food and clothes.[3] Second, both public and private welfare administrators believed that welfare should distinguish between the deserving and the undeserving poor, providing a minimal existence for the former and denying the latter. All able-bodied men were considered undeserving and were refused any type of relief except under very strict conditions, most notably rigorous work tests that proved the individual was willing and able to work, but simply could not find any employment. In keeping with the popular Malthusian ideas of the time, the undeserving poor were left to fend for themselves, allowing nature to take its course. Those who deserved help included the old, the sick, the infirm, and widows. During this era poverty was considered both a moral and an economic weakness, with emphasis on the former. As a result, even the most destitute were considered suspect and had to prove continuously that they were morally deserving. It was generally believed that the worthy poor required constant guidance to improve their moral life and strengthen their work habits. Third, welfare administrators adhered to the principle of 'less eligibility'; it was believed that assistance should always remain well below the lowest wage, thus ensuring that welfare would not be too appealing. The assumption was that citizens would not willingly work if given the alternative of receiving adequate welfare assistance.[4]

The lobby and subsequent enactment of OMA marked both change and consistency in previous welfare practices. The majority of OMA lobbyists favoured a policy that would be a joint public-private welfare venture, distinguish between the deserving and undeserving poor, provide minimal benefits, and morally regulate the recipients. These characteristics were similar to those of early nineteenth-century welfare. At the same time, mothers' allowance permitted the state to make direct payments to the poor and to be involved in the moral regulation of the poor in a more direct, continuous, and intrusive manner than previously.

To understand why the state was urged to take on this role, one must appreciate the dramatic economic and social changes at the turn of the century. This period was one of rapid urbanization, industrialization, and large-scale immigration. Ontario cities expanded rapidly as the young and able-bodied left farms and sought industrial jobs. Men, women, and children were forced to work long days at unhealthy and dangerous jobs. This had a profound impact on family life. Between 1870 and 1901 the province's birth rate declined by 44 per cent. During this period Ontario had the lowest fertility rate in the country.[5] Simultaneously, the number of family breakdowns escalated. Economic dislocation dissolved many families. The number of widowed, deserted, and unwed mothers increased, as did the accounts of neglected and delinquent children. Dangerous working conditions resulted in incapacitation or early deaths for many male breadwinners. Communicable disease, such as tuberculosis and influenza, claimed the lives of both adults and children.[6] The First World War only exacerbated these health concerns. At one point during the war, 68 per cent of the applicants for enlistment were rejected, the vast majority for health reasons.[7]

The migration of thousands of immigrant workers, predominantly from southern and eastern Europe, also greatly altered the social and economic fabric of the province. Fears, prejudices, and emotions ran high as a result. There were concerns that ethnic-minority immigrants and French Canadians had higher fertility rates and would exceed the predominantly Protestant Euro-Canadian population. The First World War losses of Protestant Euro-Canadian soldiers on the battlefield only exacerbated these fears, and indeed these events did alter the racial composition of both the province and the country. From 1871 to 1921 those of British origin declined from 60 to 40 per cent of the country's population. Protestant Euro-Canadian citizens demanded that the state intervene to save this group from potential 'race suicide'.[8]

Class relations were also destabilized by these changes. Industrialization prompted the emergence of the middle class, who were eager to solidify their new-found socio-economic position, but their declining birth rate in relation to the working class caused them considerable anxiety. They believed this could lead to 'degeneration' or a deterioration in the moral fibre of the province's citizens. There was also a fear that the working class

Many social reformers argued that mothers' allowance would ensure that a single mother would not have to seek paid work (*National Archives C30948*).

was growing in strength as workers attempted to unite to protest their working conditions. In 1872 the Trade Union Act legalized union activity, and by the mid–1880s the Trades and Labour Congress of Canada, the official voice of Canadian workers, was established with the majority of its members from Ontario.

War losses, declining birth and fertility rates, rapid immigration, industrialization, and urbanization all led to a changing role for the charities and the emergence of an organized movement to demand state reform. The very nature of charitable work transformed from haphazard hand-outs to a coordinated system during this period. Just before the war, private charities began to coordinate their efforts and simultaneously an emerging group of middle-class social reformers began to lobby for increased government involvement. Historical sociologist Mariana Valverde explains this transition:

> The traditional means of relieving poverty was largely individual and impulsive, and its purpose was to relieve the immediate need of the recipient while earning virtue points for the giver. Organized charity . . . sought to eliminate both the impulsive and the individual elements of giving. [Organized charity leaders] . . . sought to rationalize and often curtail the material aid, focusing instead on 'training' the poor in habits of thrift, punctuality, and hygiene.[9]

The Canadian social reform movement that emerged was a loose collection of groups and individuals drawn mainly from the Protestant Euro-Canadian religious, professional, and business groups that made up the growing middle class. Middle-class women played a leadership role in many of their lobbies for social reform, but this movement also included shifting alliances with farm and labour organizations on certain issues. Because of these tenuous connections, members of these organizations would support an issue such as female suffrage or protective legislation for a variety of disparate reasons.[10]

One issue that most social reformers could agree upon was the alleviation of poverty. As self-proclaimed experts in the daily care of the poor, these social reform leaders coordinated their efforts with a burgeoning group of middle-class professionals (i.e., educators, doctors, nurses, and community workers). They conducted investigations to seek out the very roots of poverty in the belief that they would then be able to cure the disease.[11]

But unlike nineteenth-century welfare workers, these new poverty experts appealed to the state. They became political lobbyists, using their studies of the poor to demand social reform from various levels of government. As they promoted their expertise, they simultaneously helped to reorganize class, gender, and race relations during a turbulent social period. As part of an emerging middle class, these poverty experts were involved in a process of creating and reaffirming their own social position while distinguishing themselves from those they studied and 'helped'. While both middle-class men and women were involved in social reform work, their positions were distinguished by gender. Often denied leadership in churches and other social organizations, middle-class women were able to assert a new role for themselves in society as moral reformers. Promoting a maternal ideology that purported the moral superiority of Protestant Euro-Canadian women, this select group of women established themselves as rescuers, reformers, and even experts while consciously or unconsciously reducing others to objects of philanthropic concern.[12]

State solutions became more appealing as previous solutions faltered under the weight of increased poverty. Administrators of orphanages admitted that they were disillusioned with this solution to poor children's care. 'The insufficiency of institutional life, the stigma later attached to the institutional child, the over-crowding of our institutions, and the increasing cost of their upkeep' worried social reformers. And they became alarmed at the vast numbers of single mothers who placed their children in orphanages to seek paid work. A 1918 study of 2,000 institutionalized children in Toronto revealed that 'one-half were there because of illness or desertion of a parent, one-quarter because of the death of a parent, and less than 10 per cent because of emotional or physical neglect. Only one per cent were true orphans.' The expense associated with this institutionalized care was also a concern. Institutionalization was a 'most extravagant way of dealing with the children', said Ontario's superintendent of prisons and charities. It was generally agreed that care in the home with a government allowance would provide both superior care and be less costly.[13]

Until the First World War, the provincial government's main response to these growing social problems was to establish a number of inquiries. These inquiries and subsequent government reports reflected many of the opinions advocated by social reformers and set the tone for the OMA lobby. For example, the 1897 provincial inquiry into the criminal system reported that immigrant youths and children of poor parenting, particularly children of needy widows, conducted the most crimes. A decade later the Select Committee on Child Labour documented the fact that increasingly younger children were working long hours in unsafe workplaces. The commissioners suggested that the state should consider supporting poor families whose children under fourteen were forced to enter the workforce because of economic need.[14]

Two other provincial inquiries during the early twentieth century raised concerns about the plight of poor single mothers. Commissioners of the inquiry on employment conditions in 1916 were troubled by the number of women, including mothers, who worked outside the home. Support for a mothers' pension came from the Reverend Peter Bryce of Earlcourt Methodist Church and from the Trades and Labour Congress of Canada.[15] The inquiry did not take up this suggestion, but instead recommended domestic training for all women: 'the conclusive reason for universal domestic training is that home occupations are the ultimate employment for all but a comparatively small percentage of women.'[16] As such, the commission introduced the radical belief that government should take some responsibility for supporting mothers, but their solution reinforced the belief that women's first duty was in the home.

A final provincial inquiry that included the issue of single motherhood was the study of the 'feeble-minded' in 1919. 'Feeble-minded' was a term widely employed at the turn of the century to categorize and segregate those who were considered of low intellect, psychologically damaged, or morally deviant. This commission included unwed mothers in this category and argued that 'feeble-minded' women should be institutionalized to prevent them from reproducing other feeble-minded citizens. This notion that unwed mothers were 'feeble-minded' and required different government treatment from other more worthy single mothers would re-emerge during the OMA lobby.[17]

While these provincial inquiries highlighted the issue of single motherhood, they led to only limited welfare reforms. For the most part, the provincial government continued to direct money towards the maintenance of institutions, asylums, hospitals, schools, and refuges rather than initiating welfare payments directly to citizens in need, but four pieces of legislation enacted during this period opened the door for a new type of public welfare. The Children's Act, which established the Children's Aid Society, was introduced in 1893. This act granted the state the right to remove children from parents or guardians who failed to meet the economic or moral standards imposed by the government and to prescribe

At the turn of the century, social reformers became concerned about 'street Arabs', children who lived on the streets. Some of these children were abandoned by poor single mothers who could not afford to feed and clothe their offspring (*National Archives C4228, John J. Kelso Collection/William James*).

serious penalties for the neglect and mistreatment of children. The act also provided temporary shelters for children until they were placed in foster homes. Also, a voluntary committee, including a number of charity women, would visit and oversee the operation of both the shelters and the foster homes. In doing so, this act opened the door for greater state involvement in the regulation of moral behaviour. At the same time it established a joint public–private welfare structure that acknowledged and reinforced the special contribution of middle-class women to welfare issues.[18]

The other three pieces of legislation involved direct public welfare payments to citizens. The Ontario Workmen's or Workers' Compensation Act of 1914 was the first piece of social insurance that provided compulsory income protection against work-related injuries or death. It also defined compensation as a right rather than an act of charity, in the sense that it provided automatic cash payments to compensate for loss of the breadwinner's income.[19]

The First World War provided the occasion to establish war pensions and veterans' allowances. Through the War Pensions Act of 1916, the federal government administered payments to disabled soldiers, their families, and the widows and orphans of men killed in battle. Similar to Workers' Compensation, these pensions were defined as a right rather than a charity for those who had suffered as a result of war service to the nation. In the same year the government introduced veterans' allowances to supplement a soldier's pay for his dependants. Unlike war pensions, veterans' allowances were administered through a joint charity-state operation. The Canadian Patriotic Fund (CPF), a nationalist charity organization, administered the fund while federal, provincial, and municipal government grants supplemented these allowances. Initially this provided a monthly income of $30, not including assigned pay, to a soldier's dependant, plus an amount ranging from $3 to $7.50 per child, depending on age. This was a rather large sum of money, especially compared to relief payments of the day, but the CPF insisted 'that the soldier's wife should be entitled to enough money to live decently without having to go out to work as someone's maid'.[20]

The Children's Act, Workers' Compensation, war pensions, and veterans' allowances all signalled a significant break from past welfare practices. The Children's Act granted the provincial government an interventionist moral role in citizens' homes. And the latter three policies marked the first time in Canadian history that federal and provincial governments became involved in direct payments to citizens. These legislative reforms helped to create the possibility for Ontario Mothers' Allowance.

THE ONTARIO MOTHERS' ALLOWANCE LOBBY

Few other issues could capture the attention of such a broad spectrum of public opinion as the plight of single mothers and their children. Representatives of churches, charities, the medical profession, women's organizations, and labour were all concerned about the impoverished lives of many mothers. As they articulated their views on mothers' allowance, these historical actors promoted, consciously or unconsciously, their own particular understanding of how the world should be ordered. In doing so, they helped to reorganize class, gender, and race relations during a turbulent era when much was at stake. It was not merely a question of imposing one's views upon others less powerful. Rather, each group attempted to assert a foothold into societal order with their claims to authoritative knowledge. In doing so, they were involved in an ongoing process of *asserting themselves* and simultaneously *distinguishing themselves* from others they studied, guided, or 'helped'.[21]

This section will explore the historical actors as they emerge upon the political scene and lay a claim to their particular 'expert' opinion on the subject. While many of these spokespeople supported mothers' allowance

It was living conditions like this that prompted Toronto social reformers to take a leading role in campaigning for Ontario Mothers' Allowance (*City of Toronto Archives DPW 32–320*).

for distinct reasons, what is also evident was the degree of consensus that was built over three decades of lobbying. A maternalist theme predominated much of the OMA debate and helped to consolidate the lobby effort. Both male and female lobbyists promoted the notion of gender difference, advocating that women's 'natural' role in life was that of care-giver while men were 'naturally' economic providers. Women's experiences as care-givers made them uniquely able to nurture both their families and society at large. Thus, women were perfectly situated to lead certain social and political campaigns that would help or improve society. While this maternalist ideology was gendered, it was also racist. These mothers' allowance advocates purported the moral superiority of Protestant Euro-Canadian women over all other ethnic-minority groups.

John J. Kelso, the founder of the Children's Aid Society, was the first to initiate debate in Ontario. He was internationally known as a mothers' allowance advocate and was invited to speak at numerous social reform events throughout North America. He was well placed to establish himself as an expert on child and maternal poverty. During the 1880s and early 1890s, a number of social reformers led by Kelso organized first the Toronto Humane Society, followed by the Children's Aid Society of Toronto, the Children's Fresh Air Fund, and the Santa Claus fund for poor children. In 1893 Kelso was appointed superintendent of neglected and dependent children in Ontario, a position he occupied for forty-one years under eight governments.[22]

As superintendent, Kelso frequently encountered widowed mothers who were forced to work to support their families. Many of these women could not make ends meet and asked Kelso to place their children in foster homes. He was reluctant to accept children in these circumstances, and advocated the need for Workers' Compensation for widows whose breadwinners had died in work-related accidents. In his 1895 report to the Ontario legislature, he expanded this notion by advocating assistance for other needy widows:

> Widows applying for release from parental responsibility through poverty, should be assisted to keep the home together rather than encouraged to part with their offspring. The aim of the Society through all its work should be to elevate home life and strengthen and ennoble family ties.[23]

In his report a year later, Kelso pursued the matter once again:

> There are poor, but respectable mothers who require help and this should be given them in their own homes, either by the municipality or Church organizations, so that the home may not be broken up. It is no real charity or help to a poor mother to close up her home and send her children, one to this institution and one to that, thus robbing both of the ties and influences that are after all the only thing worth living for.[24]

In his subsequent reports to the provincial government from 1897 to 1900 he continued to advocate financial aid for single mothers.[25] He was a

prominent member of the American-based National Conference of Charities and elected vice-president in 1902. He gave numerous public addresses on the importance of mothers' allowance at this conference and other charitable events across the continent.[26] Kelso also had a flair for writing and promoted his cause with many compelling anecdotes about the 'unwashed, unschooled street arabs' that were frequently distributed in magazines and pamphlets throughout North America. In a pamphlet published in 1904, he outlined his scheme in more detail: 'Some day we will have a system whereby respectable mothers on whom the care and maintenance of children devolve, will be allowed a pension so that they can stay at home and give them proper attention.'[27] Seven years later in 1911 the first mothers' allowance policy in North America was enacted in Missouri.

During the OMA lobby effort Kelso and other Children's Aid Society (CAS) representatives expressed very strong opinions regarding how such a policy should be developed. Having cared for many needy children, they presented themselves as experts on the causes of poverty and the best means to administer welfare. They endorsed mothers' allowance as part of a maternalist project that would keep mothers at home with their children. They believed strongly that there was a connection between delinquency and working single mothers, a theme that other proponents of OMA would also endorse. Kelso argued that anywhere between 40 to 100 per cent of children raised by working single mothers were delinquents.[28]

It is important to note that while Kelso advocated mothers' allowance, he opposed such social reforms as community provision of child care for employed mothers. He believed child care was 'fundamentally wrong' and urged social workers 'not [to] give it too much prominence' in reform debates.[29] In doing so, Kelso affirmed women's maternal role within the home and the traditional division of labour between men and women and simultaneously rejected policies such as child care that would challenge this.

These CAS representatives strongly advocated the need for close moral supervision of allowance recipients. At the turn of the century it was generally accepted that institutionalized children were neglected children. As Kelso argued, 'Our most hopeless criminals are these young men who at an early age were placed in public institutions and grew up without family ties. Driftwood—tossed hither and thither and never finding a secure abiding place.'[30] The CAS was established to alleviate this social problem—to help place orphans in moral homes that would be carefully monitored by moral experts. From their own experience as CAS workers, these representatives recommended weekly investigations and strict supervision as 'absolutely necessary'.[31] Also in keeping with a moral agenda, the CAS representatives differentiated between worthy mothers who could be guided and unworthy ones who were beyond reform. As a result, they recom-

Opposite: Mother and children in the backyard, William Street, Toronto, 1914 (*City of Toronto Archives DPW 32–326*).

mended the allowance for needy widows and deserted mothers, but flatly denied unwed mothers. Unwed mothers were considered unfit and the CAS recommended that their children be immediately removed from these homes and placed with foster parents.[32] Although this position was argued solely on the basis of morality, it also helped to guarantee a future for the CAS and its workers.

The CAS representatives favoured an administrative structure not unlike their own organization. Their organization was a joint public-private welfare venture; although it received public funds and some state regulation, for the most part it was considered a private association staffed predominantly by volunteer charity workers. Similarly, they believed mothers' allowance should also be administered by the voluntary sector with government merely facilitating this initiative.[33]

Whereas the CAS initiated the idea for mothers' allowance, it was women's organizations under the umbrella of the National Council of Women (NCW) that spearheaded and dominated the provincial lobby. The NCW members were early activists in the mothers' allowance campaign who discussed this legislation as early as 1899. After several unsuccessful petitions to government, the Toronto chapter of the NCW created its own mothers' allowance program in 1914. This pilot project was instrumental in the creation of a unified mothers' allowance movement that swept the province and demanded government action. This project also helped to solidify the NCW's position as a moral authority on the needs of the poor.

A woman and children in the early 1900s, Toronto (*National Archives C4256, John J. Kelso Collection/ William James*).

Given their concern with numerous social issues, it is not surprising that NCW members were early activists in the mothers' allowance campaign. According to historical record, Kelso discussed the possibility of such legislation with the NCW as early as 1899. In 1904 Kelso provided pamphlets for the NCW on child and maternal welfare that were distributed to all the locals, and he became a regular guest speaker on the subject at national and local meetings of the council.[34]

Within the decade the NCW emerged as the leader in the lobby for mothers' allowance legislation in Canada. In 1913 the council members pressured both the federal and the Ontario governments to provide mothers' allowances. In response the federal government appointed a special committee in 1913 to look into mothers' pensions, but did not pursue the matter further.[35]

Frustrated by the lack of government action, the Toronto Local Council of Women (TLCW) established its own mothers' allowance in 1914. This initiative was virtually unprecedented in the international mothers' allowance lobby and very influential in the Ontario campaign.[36] While several American states implemented the legislation, the TLCW members decided that they could no longer await government approval of the policy but would establish their own payment to needy widows. They decided to conduct the project for a one-year trial period to prove 'and so engage the sympathy and co-operation of the public that the [Ontario] Government will make permanent arrangement for it'.[37] 'Private philanthropy', they believed, 'must always point the way for state legislation in matters pertaining to charities or pensions.'[38]

The project began in January 1914 with Mrs W.E. Struthers as supervisor. Mrs Struthers was previously a social service worker on the East Side of New York City and the head of a nursing school.[39] Given that the council was entering the domain of private charities, it sought the approval of the Social Service Commission, a board composed largely of representatives of private charities in the city, charged with the coordination and administration of poor relief.[40] The commission had some reservations and approved the initiative, provided it terminated in one year and met the following conditions:

1. The amount to be collected from the public is not to exceed $10,000.
2. The number of cases assisted during the year shall be limited.
3. The fund shall be for the benefit of mothers with one or more children.
4. The amount to be given shall not exceed $10 per month for the mother and $10 per month for each child, the maximum amount to be paid in any case being $40 per month.
5. Children over fourteen years of age shall be excluded from the benefit of the fund.
6. All cases (with full information) shall be submitted to the Commission for their approval before the assistance shall be given.
7. Direct supervision of the conditions in each home to be benefited by the fund shall be exercised by the Local Council of Women.[41]

By May 1914 the fund was well under way, with the council preparing to determine which families would be considered most worthy for the aid. Families were chosen from 'a lengthy list of children whose mothers' poverty made it necessary for them to leave school in order to earn [money]'. All requests were thoroughly investigated 'as to their worthiness and their necessity' before proceeding.[42] During the lifetime of the project, a total of six widows and twenty-two children were supported. According to the TLCW minutes, the homes were visited by Mrs Struthers:

> . . . she visited the pensioned families at irregular intervals, advising as the best means of maintaining the health of the children and the mother and empha-sizing at all times the fact that the mother's duty was to remain at home and to care for the children. Suggestions were made, in a friendly manner, as to the best outlay of the pension money and a statement was required from the mothers showing their approximate expenditures each month, under the headings, food, clothing, fuel and so forth.[43]

Generally, the fund was considered extremely beneficial; as one mother explained in a letter of thanks to the council, 'You will never know the blessing of full rent, instead of taking it to the landlord in five instalments.'[44]

This initiative operated on a shoestring budget. The TLCW constantly had to appeal to other charity and women's organizations, including the Patriotic Fund, Woman's Art Association, Trafalgar Daughters, and the Beaches Patriotic League, in order to provide the families with a steady allowance. As well as donations, the TLCW created a postcard campaign, and other organizations donated proceeds from plays and concerts. In 1917 when the fund was in debt after three years of operation, the council was forced to terminate the experiment even though the provincial govern-ment had failed to establish a mothers' allowance policy.[45]

This three-year pilot project was very influential in the OMA lobby and subsequent policy development. From this initiative the TLCW members gained concrete evidence of the conditions of needy single mothers that helped to establish them as experts for the remainder of the OMA lobby. In turn, the public policy, once enacted, closely emulated the philosophy and administration of this earlier project.

As experts in family poverty, members of the NCW and their local chap-ters spent many meetings discussing the details of the policy they advocat-ed. For the most part, NCW members favoured a policy that would include detailed investigations and moral guidance of recipients, similar to the TLCW initiative. Only the local councils of Victoria and Vancouver opposed such moral regulation, but they were in the minority. The NCW over-whelmingly approved of an act that would include a stipulation regarding unworthy conduct, as long as the woman was granted 'due warning'.[46]

The NCW members supported more restrictive eligibility than the CAS had advocated. Whereas the CAS representatives had suggested the inclusion of deserted cases, the NCW wished to restrict mothers' allowance solely to widows. The TLCW initiative had only financed widows, and this remained the position of the NCW generally. Some NCW members feared that any inclusion of deserted mothers would 'make it easy for them [wives] . . . to leave their husbands for trifling causes.' Instead of the allowance, the NCW members advocated increased legal penalties for deserting fathers. Occasionally, NCW chapters took action on their own, prosecuting the deserter for non-support. As for unwed mothers, the NCW generally believed that a mother with one child should seek support from the father, while unwed mothers with more than one child should be institutionalized because these women were thought to have 'weak intellects'.[47]

The position expressed by the NCW regarding mothers' allowance was in keeping with their middle-class maternalist goals. While these women advocated economic support for needy widows, they did so in a manner that did not challenge traditional gender roles. The NCW members as a rule did not promote political and economic equality between the sexes. Regarding political rights, the NCW had been hesitant to enter the suffrage debate. Initially, these women hoped to establish a 'Parliament of Women' outside the legislature, where all views could be heard and emphasis would be on change through persuasion rather than direct participation in the political process. Eventually they entered the debate, but they did so in maternalist terms, arguing that the vote would help to ensure the enactment of mothers' allowance. 'Woman's place is in the home', said one NCW newsletter, 'and it takes a vote to keep her there.'[48]

As for economic rights, the NCW members advocated a number of improvements in women's working conditions, but these campaigns for protective legislation (from separate lavatories in the workplace, to seats for shop-girls, to female standards inspectors) were advocated to ensure that women's primary role was motherhood. They, like Kelso, were opposed to long-term child care that would have provided the possibility of greater economic independence than mothers' allowance. Also, long-term child care directly challenged the traditional division of labour both inside and outside the home, whereas mothers' allowance promoted traditional maternal values.[49]

Religious leaders were already prominent in social reform politics and brought this expertise to the OMA lobby. During the early 1900s the Protestant churches played a leadership role in organizing disparate reform organizations, including labour, farm, and women's groups, into the Social Service Council of Canada. In 1914, a year after the council was formed, it called an emergency conference to discuss these escalating social and moral problems. During the 1914 meeting a number of leading child welfare experts were invited to speak, including John Kelso, Helen MacMurchy, and Rose Henderson, a well-known socialist and feminist. The conference delegates passed a resolution that the federal government adopt a policy to help 'widows, deserted wives and other needy mothers on whom devolves the responsibility of providing for their children'. To demonstrate their support, the council sent this resolution to the NCW.[50]

Reverend Peter Bryce of Earlscourt Methodist Church in downtown Toronto was a well-known social reformer, a founding member of the Social Service Council, and one of the leading religious advocates for mothers' allowance. His church was located in 'shacktown', a downtown community of Toronto that was predominantly settled by impoverished British immigrants. Along with publisher and fellow Methodist Joseph Atkinson, Bryce created the *Toronto Star*'s Santa Claus Fund. His Sunday school was the largest in Canada, servicing more than 2,000 children, and his Earlscourt Children's Home was also one of the largest Protestant orphanages and day care facilities within the city. The demand for Bryce's services exemplified the growing demand for government action. Whereas religious leaders in the nineteenth century had looked to their congregations to help the poor, Bryce and other ministers of the early twentieth century turned to the state for help.

Bryce was instrumental in creating an alliance between the Social Service Council and the NCW in order to promote a mothers' allowance policy. Given that both the NCW and the council supported an allowance that endorsed maternalist and moral principles, it is not surprising that this association developed and eventually dominated the debate. Bryce was often a guest speaker on the subject at NCW events, and it was he who was chosen to lead the Committee on Mothers' Allowance, the final lobby effort that persuaded the Ontario government to act.

Bryce and other religious leaders advocated mothers' allowance in maternal and moral terms. They were concerned about the moral impoverishment of poor children and believed that a full-time mother could provide the necessary guidance. One minister clearly articulated this position in his support for mothers' allowance:

> We [the clergy] feel the greatest function performed for society is motherhood and that provision ought to be made so that every child should have the opportunity of, at least, a normal start, *morally*, physically and intellectually [my emphasis].

To this minister, 'even . . . a fourth rate mother' was better than any type of institutional care for children.[51] Given their fundamental belief in the moral superiority of mothers, religious leaders were more generous in their eligibility criteria than most other lobbyists. Like the CAS, they advocated the inclusion of widows and deserted wives, but religious leaders went even further and recommended the allowance for families with temporarily incapacitated husbands.[52]

Similar to both the CAS and NCW representatives, religious leaders advocated a joint public-private administrative structure. One minister suggested that half of the provincial commission overseeing the policy should be women. 'You could count on the hard-hearted man to keep them [the women] right', he suggested. And another minister believed that church ladies should be invited to visit the recipients.[53]

Charity representatives were the only OMA lobbyists who were initially somewhat hesitant in their support for the policy. Until the turn of the century charities played a leading role in welfare, particularly in urban centres. The provincial government had generally restricted its welfare involvement to funding various public institutions that did not interfere with charity's direct relief activities. As such, charitable leaders were able to claim themselves as welfare experts and moral guardians of the poor. To meet the growing demand for their services in the early 1900s, charities attempted to coordinate their activities within various urban centres. Through these organizations, charitable leaders were able to develop a relatively coherent position on social reform. Mothers' allowance, if implemented, would open the door to increased state involvement and potentially challenge these charitable leaders' social and moral authority. At the same time, these private welfare organizations were finding it difficult to cope with the increasing demands on their services. Thus, some representatives of private charities were initially ambivalent about the mothers' allowance lobby.

There are two examples of this hesitancy to endorse mothers' allowance. First, the Social Service Commission of Toronto was reluctant to authorize the TLCW mothers' allowance pilot project and established a number of conditions that both limited the scope of the project and ensured a role for charity workers.[54] Another example occurred in 1917 when one representative of an orphaned girls' home said she feared that mothers' allowance would threaten to close her home.[55] The majority of charities, however, supported the proposal. Some hoped that mothers' allowance would relieve them of the overwhelming demand for their services.[56] By the end of the TLCW initiative, the Social Service Commission of Toronto supported the lobby and conducted a survey of needy widows for the Ontario government in 1917. During this survey a number of local charitable organizations (including the Canadian Patriotic Fund, the Canadian Club, several infants' homes, and various private charities) were contacted; all but one endorsed the proposal.[57]

While supporting mothers' allowance, these charity leaders were careful to position themselves within a changing welfare system. They endorsed a policy that reflected many of the characteristics of previous charity work. For instance, they promoted a policy that included close moral supervision of the recipients. One charity leader argued that food 'should be sent to the home every day, so much bread, so much meat and vegetables to be cooked. . . .'[58] All the charity leaders believed that volunteer charity workers were the best suited for this type of supervision. They also recommended volunteer charity workers as members of local mothers' allowance boards. They advocated eligibility criteria that clearly distinguished between the worthy and the unworthy. The majority of charity representatives only endorsed mothers' allowance for widows and argued forcefully against the inclusion of deserted and unwed mothers.[59]

These charity leaders were also adamantly opposed to financially supporting ethnic-minority mothers, as demonstrated by one representative of an infants' home:

> . . . we have not found that the foreigner has any idea of stigma being attached to putting his child into other people's care. We find our sturdy immigrants from Scotland and England don't take their children except in cases of necessity. Any legislation about paying out to foreign mothers would have to be carefully guarded.[60]

According to these charity advocates, those mothers who were excluded or required close supervision would be the responsibility of volunteer charity workers. These leaders were aware that outright opposition to the proposal was politically dangerous. Their American counterparts had opposed the scheme earlier, which brought them an unprecedented amount of public criticism. Instead, Canadian charity leaders became involved in the campaign and ensured that the proposal and its administration would follow traditional notions of charity.

It is difficult to assess what effect the initial ambivalence of some charity leaders had on the OMA lobby. Canadian social work scholar Dennis Guest believes that mothers' allowance legislation was more quickly adopted in Manitoba (1916), Saskatchewan (1917), and Alberta (1919) than in Ontario (1920) because private charities were less influential in the West. With the relative absence of charities to provoke opposition, women's groups in the West were able to petition their provincial governments directly and demand that the state intervene to support needy single mothers. Given that the Ontario lobby included some of the leading North American figures in the debate and the effectiveness of the TLCW initiative, it does suggest that the reluctance of some charity leaders may have provided the Ontario government with an opportunity to resist this powerful lobby effort for three and a half decades.[61]

There were a number of middle-class professionals who also joined the OMA lobby. Social work, legal, medical, and academic professionals all positioned themselves as experts during this debate. The majority of these professionals adhered to maternalist values, but couched these assumptions within their particular areas of expertise. It was particularly significant that social workers were attempting to achieve professional status during this period. In May 1920, at the first annual meeting of the Canadian Conference of Public Welfare, social workers expressed concern about the public's perception of their work:

> The loud voices of ill-informed persons may still be heard in the market places declaiming that the social worker is a dreamer and a theorist, an impractical person of superficial education. The male social worker, pictured by this individual, has long hair, baggy trousers, weak eyes and large spectacles. If the social worker be a woman, she is depicted as having short hair, a pronounced nose and a severe expression.[62]

During the mothers' allowance lobby social workers were attempting to change this public image and simultaneously promote their status. They did so by condemning the sentimental work of volunteer charity workers and distinguishing themselves as highly trained specialists using scientific principles and management. With these scientific skills the social worker could examine the causes of poverty, 'diagnose the cases', and be able to 'cure' the problem. The poor could be scientifically studied and rehabilitated. Consequently, social workers and the Canadian Council on Child Welfare advocated that OMA should be administered by professionals and should involve careful and continuous scrutiny of the poor.[63] Through this scientific investigation of the poor, these social workers would bolster the family and women's traditional role within it. Thus, professional social workers endorsed maternalist values through their scientific work.

Legal representatives also promoted maternalist views within their area of expertise. Throughout North America legal representatives, especially juvenile court magistrates, played a persuasive role in the mothers' allowance campaigns. These legal experts employed their unquestioned legal authority to legitimize further maternalist views. They argued that there was a strong association between working mothers and juvenile delinquency, and advocated mothers' allowance as a measure to keep mothers in the home and reduce juvenile delinquency. Based on this assumption, the Ontario government examined 250 files of the juvenile court in Toronto, but was unable to find a connection. Despite this, the opinions of these juvenile court officials were generally accepted as fact during the OMA lobby.[64]

Single mothers in rural Ontario, like this mother and her children near Napanee in 1917, often experienced poverty in isolation (*National Archives PA123675, John J. Kelso Collection*).

In a similar fashion, medical professionals based their support for mothers' allowance on expert medical evidence. Infant mortality had been a concern of social reformers at the turn of the century, and both doctors and nurses played an increasing role as experts in this debate. During the OMA lobby both doctors and nurses asserted a strong relationship between working mothers and infant mortality. If mothers were to stay home and nurse their babies, fewer children would die, medical experts argued. They believed that 'hundreds, probably thousands of children are weaned because the mother has to go to work to earn a living'. These same medical experts did not support child care in the factory with nursing breaks, which France had implemented. In keeping with maternalist values, they strongly rejected the French model and asserted that maintaining mothers at home was the only solution to the province's health concerns.[65]

Other professionals were more blatant in their maternalist views, such as antifeminist McGill professor Stephen Leacock. He, along with a number of 'red tory' conservatives, advocated mothers' allowance on the following grounds:

> Social policy should proceed from the fundamental truth that women are and must be dependent. . . . To expect a woman, for example, if left by the death of her husband with young children without support, to maintain herself by her own efforts, is the most absurd mockery of freedom ever devised.[66]

The framework for the debate over mothers' allowance was well established by the time organized labour entered the fray. In 1912, following almost two decades of discussion by women's, religious, and charitable organizations, labour leaders began to argue among their own ranks for the creation of such a policy. Although organized labour demonstrated a different understanding of the causes of poverty and promoted a more generous policy, they endorsed the maternalist and racist philosophy of the other social reformers.

The Ontario workforce changed significantly during this period. With increasingly mechanized production methods, a number of workers' jobs and crafts became obsolete while others were transformed. The job market became increasingly competitive as new, less skilled immigrant and women workers entered the workplace. These female workers were primarily single women and those referred to as the 'unfortunates', who included widows, deserted, divorced, and separated mothers and wives of unemployed men.[67] During the war, female labour participation in Ontario more than doubled.[68] As their numbers increased, women workers made greater demands for better wages and working conditions, but for a number of reasons their voices were often muted. First, the nature of women's work tended to be transient, unskilled, and isolated. Second, women had the added responsibility of housework and child care. Finally, male workers were often resistant to working women's demands. These three factors combined to create extraordinary barriers to working women's organizing during this period.[69] As a result, working women and their advocates often chose the path of least resistance—supporting women through traditional familial structures.

During this turbulent period, labour organizations were generally opposed to women working except when absolutely necessary. Trade unions were overwhelmingly male in membership and their position on women's issues often reflected this. In the late nineteenth century the Trades and Labour Congress (TLC) had a platform of principles that included the 'abolition of . . . female labour in all branches of industrial life, such as mines, workshops, factories, etc.'[70] Even during the war some vocal male unionists insisted that women should be employed only as a last resort.[71] The TLC promoted equal pay for women and men doing the same jobs during the war years, but this was 'primarily in the hope of ending competition from cheap female labour'.[72]

Following the war, unions made few attempts to protect women's jobs. As historian Jim Naylor explains:

> No concerted effort came from any quarter to defend women's rights to the jobs they had held during the war. Many unionists were pleased to see the departure of women from their industries, and the few proponents of women's employment in such sectors were powerless to act.[73]

Many of the leading labour proponents advocated a family model that promoted men as the breadwinners and women as dependent wives and mothers. Working-class women's interests were promoted *within* the family rather than alongside their working-class brothers on the factory floors. Following the war, the provincial government, with labour's support, did everything possible to ensure a smooth transition to this family form by opening an employment bureau to find jobs for returned soldiers. Pamphlets from this bureau that were directed to the female worker stated the government's position quite explicitly:

> Who has the job you have before you took it?
> Was it a soldier?
> Then to him you owe the opportunity you had to gain a new experience, and some extra money.
> To his bravery and self sacrifice you owe the fact that you were able to work in peace and security.
> Now he has come back.
> He must have work to support himself and those dependent upon him.
> What is your duty?
> *There is only one answer to that question. Of course you will go back to your home in order that the man may have a job* [my emphasis].[74]

These economic considerations affected labour's support of mothers' allowance. Rose Henderson, a member of the Independent Labour Party of Ontario (ILP) and a social worker for the Montreal juvenile court, persuasively introduced the topic at the 1912 Trades and Labour Congress. The convention endorsed mothers' allowance along with resolutions in support of compulsory education, the abolition of prison labour, female industrial labour, and child labour for those under fourteen, all of which would have reduced competition in the labour market.[75]

In 1914 the TLC representative at the Social Service Council of Canada conference endorsed the resolution for mothers' allowance and began to join middle-class social reformers to lobby various levels of government. A year later the TLC made two efforts to lobby the federal government to establish a national mothers' allowance policy.[76] And when the Committee on Mothers' Allowance was formed in 1918 three union officials were represented.

For the most part, mothers' allowance advocates were enthusiastic that labour had joined the campaign. Labour and religious leaders had worked on a number of social issues in the past through the Social Service Council,[77] but the relationship between the NCW and labour was less than amicable. The TLC federal government lobby in 1915 outraged NCW leaders because they were not consulted. As one prominent NCW member wrote:

> You will see by the enclosed that the Trades and Labour Congress are to present Mothers' Pensions to Sir Robert Borden, on January the 15th. Knowing that the National Council of Women have had this reform before them for 3 years, I feel that they should have a representative, a good speaker, who can go fully in[to] the question. . . . It seems to me, that if we do not have a representative before the Trades and Labour Council, they will receive all the credit, as others have done in the past. After the women have worked for years up comes a body of men and reaps all our sowing. . . .[78]

And in 1919 the ILP women debated at their provincial convention whether they should affiliate with the NCW, given the latter's close ties with business organizations such as the Canadian Manufacturers' Association.[79]

Labour differed from other OMA lobbyists regarding their understanding of poverty. For them, poverty was not a result of individual weakness as most of the other lobbyists suggested. Instead, it was a result of low wages, intense job competition, and the exploitation of women's and children's labour. Consequently, labour believed mothers' allowance could have clear economic benefits for the working class, and its advocates often linked the issue to low wages, as Rose Henderson explained at the 1912 TLC convention:

> [The] average wage in Canada is a little over $400 for the male workers and for women approximately $200 per annum. With such low wages it is almost impossible for the worker to pay union dues, much less Insurance dues. Industrial accidents are on the increase.[80]

Labour advocates also believed that mothers' allowance would reduce the number of working-class children who were forced either to live in institutions or become a source of cheap labour because their families could not afford to feed and clothe them. It was clear that labour advocates believed that mothers' allowance would reduce the competition for jobs. As the TLC president, Tom Moore, argued: 'The removal of the necessity of these mothers and children to seek industrial employment has enlarged the opportunity of work for others and made somewhat easier the maintenance of higher standards of working conditions.'[81] A cartoon in the *Industrial Banner*, Ontario's regional labour paper, also clearly reinforced this view. The cartoon depicted a woman looking at a notice posted at a factory that read:

> Notice
> Widows
> With Dependent
> Children
> No Longer Needed
> To Work Here.
> Government
> Pensions
> Will Enable Them
> To Devote Themselves
> To Their Homes and
> Little Ones.

A child is tugging at her skirt saying, 'Come on home mother, and look after us. You don't have to work in the factory now.'[82]

Mothers' allowance was not the only social policy that labour advocated at this time. Whereas social reformers preferred limited state involvement in welfare activities and promoted the continued role of charitable work, the labour movement advocated an expansion of state services to alleviate structural inequities. Labour rejected the social reform notion that an expanded welfare state would encourage the poor to be lazy and immoral, as Rose Henderson illustrates in her appeal:

> . . . Is there any reason why our widowed mothers with young children should not be pensioned? Thirty-three bishops and archbishops in the House of Lords in England draw large pensions for practically doing nothing but opposing progressive measures introduced for the amelioration of the lot of the poor. Would anyone suggest that these noble lords were being pauperized by their pensions?[83]

The Ontario labour movement had successfully achieved the enactment of state-administered Workers' Compensation in 1914. The TLC regarded mothers' allowance and Old Age Pensions as a joint welfare platform and did not separate the two legislative proposals until 1915.[84] For the most part, the labour movement perceived mothers' allowance as similar to these other rights-based welfare reforms, as TLC president Tom Moore stated:

> Organized labour has always emphasized that these payments should not be considered as charity or relief, but as a payment to which the mother is rightly *entitled* in order to enable her to properly perform the important duty of raising her family under such conditions as will give them an equal chance with other citizens of this country.[85]

Other OMA lobbyists generally perceived the allowance as a privilege rather than a right.

This rights-based understanding of welfare led labour to call for a more inclusive mothers' allowance policy than the other advocates. Although there was some debate within the labour movement, generally labour representatives favoured the inclusion of widows and deserted, divorced, and unwed mothers. The Street Railway Men in Toronto proposed that only widows be eligible, as the majority of middle-class social reformers argued. The TLC advocated the inclusion of both deserted and unwed mothers. Tom Moore argued: 'The child has no choice as to whether it is born in the home of the unmarried or the married mother' and many illegitimate children grew up to 'become some of the brightest citizens of this and other countries . . . I don't think we should allow sentiment to enter into it.' Hamilton labour leader Walter Rollo contended that 'the Act should be made as wide as possible and should cover every case.' And the District 18 United Mine Workers of American called for a universal mothers' allowance policy, arguing that *all* married women and children, regardless of their financial circumstances, should be eligible.[86]

Labour spokespeople also suggested a more representative administrative structure than the other OMA advocates. Both the TLC and the ILP opposed the appointment of judges, municipal politicians, and others merely because of their social position. Rollo of the TLC argued that someone 'from the same class as the widows . . . who has had to go through hardships' should be appointed, although he added that this person should be an intellectual.[87]

But labour representatives did not substantially distinguish themselves from the other lobbyists in three important areas. While labour advocates supported the principle of mothers' allowance, they were often uncertain about the particulars of everyday administration and deferred to the social reformers as the experts. Rollo's submission at the Hamilton inquiry illustrates this point:

> While the TLC have not been brought in direct touch with the needs for Mothers' Pensions, still we believe that the principle of such legislation is sound . . . the TLC could [not] give any direct evidence as to the need, as they do not come in direct contact with it in the way that women . . . do, who have given a great deal of their time and money in trying to relieve cases of distress.[88]

Labour agreed with the other lobbyists that OMA recipients would require supervision. Supervision is generally associated with charity-style welfare rather than rights-based policies, implying that the poor are inadequately prepared for life and require guidance. There is an inherent contradiction in labour's call for a rights-based policy and the desire for supervision. Labour's advocacy for supervision was, however, somewhat distinct from that proposed by social reformers. At the Hamilton inquiry Mr A. Griffiths of the ILP suggested that this supervision be more professionally organized than the charity work of the past:

There certainly would have to be supervision and paid supervision. . . . I think they [Victoria Order of Nurses] could do that work, and that the mothers would not look on it as supervision. . . . If she didn't spend it satis-factorily, or if the children were not brought up satisfactorily, the machinery we have now would handle that matter. . . . I think in Hamilton District we have had some splendid work done by the women workers, but sometimes there have been busybodies who went around and the mother finally told them to keep out.[89]

Second, organized labour expressed racist sentiments in their lobby for mothers' allowance. While generally advocating a more inclusive mothers' allowance policy, labour advocates demanded citizenship restrictions. Concerned about increasing job competition from 'dangerous foreigners', the TLC argued against their inclusion in the allowance, otherwise 'there might be a possibility of loading the Country up with deserted children from other nationalities. . . .'[90]

Third, both male and female labour representatives endorsed the mater-nalist underpinnings of this policy, as did other lobbyists. The president of the TLC affirmed that a woman's place was in the home: 'Thousands of mothers, whose *real duty lay at home,* were compelled to compete for jobs in the factories and workshops . . .' [my emphasis].[91] And Rose Henderson believed that returning women to their maternal role in the home would reduce juvenile delinquency. Mothers' allowance would permit poor women to remain at home and strengthen the family ties. In Henderson's view, these family ties, 'deeply embedded as they are in the laws of nature and life, are the greatest source of the strength, morality and stability of the social order, and should not be broken'.[92] Thus, she contended that moth-ers' allowance would promote women's 'natural' role within the family and also morality and social stability—values that the middle-class social reform-ers held dear.[93] This willingness to define women as mothers rather than workers limited labour's ability to envision a welfare policy that would cre-ate long-term financial security for all workers, regardless of their gender.

THE LOBBY INTENSIFIES: THE COMMITTEE ON MOTHERS' ALLOWANCE

In 1918, following more than three decades of debate, the major mothers' allowance lobbyists coalesced and established a Toronto-based committee to pursue their legislative goal. The Committee on Mothers' Allowance rep-resented a wide cross-section of middle-class social reformers and labour interests, as this membership list indicated:

Bureau of Municipal Research, Catholic Charities, Children's Aid Society, Inspector of the Feeble-Minded, Jewish Synagogue, Juvenile Court, Machinists' Union, Memorial Institute, National Council of Women, Neighbourhood Workers' Association, Personal Service Club, Public Health Nurses, Separate Schools, Social Service Club, Social Service Council of Ontario, Toronto Department of Public Health, Toronto Local Council of

Women, Toronto Social Service Commission, Toronto Police Department of Morality, Toronto Trades and Labour Council, Trades and Labour Council, and the Toronto Women's Council.[94]

Chaired by Reverend Peter Bryce, this committee included many long-time social reformers such as John Kelso, Helen MacMurchy, and F.N. Stapleford. The committee represented a turning-point in the mothers' allowance lobby. Whereas previously these historical actors had worked together in a haphazard fashion, participated on a joint project, or belonged to more than one particular association, the committee coordinated their efforts. As such, the committee was able to place new, more forceful pressure upon the provincial government. Committee members wrote articles for the press, criticizing the Ontario government for its reluctance to introduce the policy.[95] The committee produced and widely distributed a petition along with a detailed report outlining the preferred policy and administrative structure. This report and its recommendations became the basis of the provincial government inquiry into mothers' allowance in 1919 and the subsequent policy that was introduced a year later.

The committee's report and the subsequent provincial inquiry hearings demonstrated that the majority of mothers' allowance lobbyists had solidified their position, which was articulated through the predominance of three important themes. The most central theme was the unanimous endorsement of maternalism. All of these lobbyists, including representatives of various labour organizations, endorsed a maternalist ideology that was firmly rooted in middle-class experience and aspirations. This maternalist ideology extolled the virtues of domesticity while simultaneously legitimating a new 'public' or political role for certain women. They endorsed protective legislation and mothers' allowance while rejecting other policies such as child care; thus they helped to improve the conditions of poor women's lives, but did not support policies that would have dramatically altered gender relations. With regard to mothers' allowance, most of the lobbyists agreed that women should be well represented on the local boards and should be the administrators who would visit the homes, but they also argued that men, as the more hard-headed rationalists, should also be included in mothers' allowance administration. As such, middle-class men and women remained the 'experts' on how to 'help' the poor. Women's position within society remained defined by their mothering ability. Both social reformers and labour advocates promoted a familial model characterized by a male breadwinner and dependent wife and children. For instance, these lobbyists clearly opposed collective child care, which would have freed poor women to engage in full-time employment, while they promoted mothers' allowance. This maternalist stance provided limited opportunity for the development of policy options that would have granted needy single mothers a greater degree of economic independence from both men and the state.

Second, this lobby effort promoted Protestant Euro–Canadian values at the expense of all other ethnic-minority groups. This was a period of intensified immigration and popular concern that other racial groups would overwhelm the 'founding' Protestant Euro–Canadian group. Many social reformers adhered to a eugenics doctrine that feared that ethnic-minority groups would reproduce faster than Protestant Euro–Canadians, leading to social degeneration. There was also a general belief that immigrants were lazy and quick to become dependent upon welfare. The Canadian immigration law permitted new immigrants to be deported if they became dependent upon hand-outs during their first three years in the country. In keeping with this sentiment, all of the OMA lobbyists clearly articulated their opposition to new immigrants or non-British subjects receiving the allowance.

Finally, the majority of OMA lobbyists adopted a unified moral position. The principal lobbyists were representatives of women's organizations, charities, and churches who presented themselves as the moral guardians of poor women. Many of these advocates were extensively involved in the moral regulation of poor citizens at the turn of the century and strongly advocated that this be continued in any new policy. They believed that poverty entailed much more than economic need; rather, impoverishment was based on moral weakness and required constant and vigilant moral guidance. This was reflected in their differentiation between different groups of single mothers. They advocated mothers' allowance for widows since they were poor through no fault of their own, whereas deserted mothers were considered morally dubious and unwed mothers were flatly morally unacceptable. Most believed that it would be better to put up illegitimate children for adoption as their original familial environment would not lend itself to proper moral training. As these distinctions between single mothers were made, a 'widow discourse' emerged that made the widow synonymous with the virtuous mother while insidiously reducing all other single mothers to the immoral. This discourse worked to intensify the stigmatization of other single mothers; the emphasis on the widow's innocence simultaneously insinuated the guilt of others.[96]

Those who did not agree with the importance of moral regulation or the moral distinctions between types of single mothers did not effectively challenge it. Labour advocates, for instance, called for a more inclusive policy but often deferred to the social reformers as the experts in everyday welfare administration. Also, labour representatives did not directly oppose the moralism associated with welfare work. With no clear opposition, moralism predominated both the OMA lobby and the subsequent policy.

One voice is noticeably absent from this powerful coalition. Not one needy single mother was encouraged to become part of this lobby effort. There is scant evidence on whether single mothers themselves wanted mothers' allowance legislation. Poor single mothers did not lobby for this legislation, nor is there any evidence of other lobbyists attempting to include them in any political alliance. The majority of the historical actors showed no discomfort in speaking on behalf of this unrepresented group.[97] Despite this omission, the government could no longer ignore this powerful coalition of OMA lobbyists.

PROVINCIAL GOVERNMENT RESPONSE

Premier William Hearst's Conservative government was a reluctant convert to mothers' allowance. In 1917 the government conducted a study examining mothers' allowance policies in other countries. The subsequent report recommended further study. The establishment of the Toronto-based Committee on Mothers' Allowance in 1918 spurred the government to study the issue yet again. Along with local pressure, the Ontario government was aware that mothers' allowance legislation had already been enacted in Manitoba (1916), Saskatchewan (1917), and Alberta (1919), and that there was a strong campaign pressuring the British Columbia government to do likewise. Similar legislation had been enacted in New Zealand (1912), Denmark, and the city of New Glasgow, Scotland. In the US, twenty states had adopted mothers' allowance between 1911 and 1913, and twenty more did so prior to 1920. On 16 January 1919, in response to these local, national, and international events, the Ontario government announced an inquiry to 'investigate fully the question of mothers' [allowances] . . . with a view to recommending a scheme'.[98] This inquiry, headed by Dr W.A. Riddell, deputy minister of labour, examined legislation enacted in other countries, assessed the amount of need, and held four public hearings throughout the province on the issue.[99]

The two major components of the inquiry were data collection and public hearings. The point of the data collection was to assess authoritatively the amount of need in the province. As a result of national registration for the war, government officials knew with a fair degree of accuracy both the number and the location of widows with children in the province. More than 400 widowed women selected from this registry were visited by 'special investigators' from the inquiry to determine their need. As a result of these investigations, it was determined that eighty of the 400 families (or one-fifth of the total) would be eligible for some form of mothers' allowance. Given that there were approximately 16,000 widows in the province, it was estimated that 3,200 families would require the allowance.[100]

The public hearings permitted the government to assess the amount of support for such legislation. The response from the public hearings illustrated that the lobbyists had indeed developed an overwhelming consensus. All of the lobbyists urged the government to act immediately and provide an allowance for dependent mothers.[101] This extensive support for mothers' allowance was also evidenced by the numerous supportive resolutions sent to the government. In sum, thirty-four resolutions were received from such disparate groups as the Charities of the Jewish Church, the Lincoln County Board of Agriculture, the United Women Voters, and many city councils, women's groups, charities, and churches.[102]

The inquiry issued the Riddell Report, which was sympathetic but conservative in its recommendation of a mothers' allowance policy. The report was preoccupied with the cost of such a program. It is striking that the lobbyists, for the most part, did not venture an opinion on the costs of the program or on the amount of the allowance. Despite the numerous studies these lobbyists used to illustrate infant mortality rates, maternal health concerns, and familial breakdown, they produced no evidence of the financial need of poor families or any estimates of the benefit level required to ensure that single mothers could remain at home to care for their children. These lobbyists were concerned about moral rather than economic impoverishment. Consequently, there was very little discussion of benefit levels for worthy single mothers. When they did express an opinion of benefits levels, these lobbyists assumed that the rate should be similar to that of the war pensions. The Riddell Report itself did not follow this route. Without knowing the extent of financial need, the report recommended that the allowance be similar to institutional costs of keeping a child, which was estimated at 33¢ a day or $120 annually per child. This amount was considerably below that of war pensions. For instance, a soldier's widow with three children would receive $70 a month from war pensions, whereas the report recommended that a mothers' allowance recipient with the same number of children should only receive $30 a month.[103] The report did not clarify whether this amount was considered adequate or whether a mother would be expected to work.

The entire report was based on this minimal allowance. It carefully calculated that the government would spend $1 million just in providing an allowance to all needy widows. And it warned: 'Every extension of the application of the Act to the wives of the incarcerated insane, the permanently incapacitated, the temporarily incapacitated, prisoners in penal institutions, deserted wives, unmarried mothers, etc., means, accordingly, an increase in cost.'[104]

In an effort to control costs, the report recommended very restrictive eligibility criteria. According to the report, OMA recipients should be British subjects, have two or more children, and be widowed, wives of the incarcerated insane, or wives of permanently incapacitated husbands. All deserted, unwed, and other needy mothers would be completely excluded. As the report noted:

> In these recommendations as above you will notice a certain conservatism.
> We have eliminated as applicants,
>
> 1. All classes of Mothers but three;
> 2. All families with only one child;
> 3. All children over 14 years of age;
> 4. All Non-British families ... [reducing] the final total estimate [of costs to] $716,097.[105]

Riddell defended this restrictive eligibility. '[A] solid foundation, well-laid is the best assurance of really adequate administration and to secure this at the beginning of so new an undertaking, the doors should not be thrown open wide to all classes of applicants.'[106]

The report, while conservative, did reflect the majority opinions of the OMA lobbyists in several important ways. Regarding eligibility, there was general agreement concerning citizenship, desertion, unwed motherhood, and imprisoned fathers. All of the lobbyists had advocated that non-British subjects should be excluded from the policy, which the report recommended. Most advocates were also reluctant to include deserted mothers in the legislation. Either there was a tendency to blame deserted wives for their predicament or, as Riddell himself suggested at the Hamilton public hearing, it was thought that including deserted mothers would make desertion too tempting and encourage husbands and fathers to be irresponsible.[107] The majority of OMA lobbyists agreed that a safer route would be for the government to establish tougher legislation to prevent the father from deserting and to enforce child support if the father did so. Walter Rollo, as the TLC representative, was one of the few who advocated that deserted mothers be included, but only once every effort had been made to have the father pay.[108] Similarly, no one except for one labour advocate had recommended the inclusion of unwed mothers. Neither did the report. With regard to imprisoned fathers, most of those who spoke on their behalf preferred some scheme of paid labour for prisoners in which the fathers' pay would be sent home to support the family.[109] Labour opposed this scheme, believing it could undermine their demands for better wages and instead argued that this group should be eligible for mothers' allowance.[110] Again the report ignored labour's position and argued that the wives of imprisoned fathers should be excluded.

The administrative structure recommended by the report also reflected the majority of the lobbyists, particularly the views of charity, religious, and women's leaders. In an effort not to antagonize these groups, the report recommended a joint public-private welfare scheme that would include a role for the 'public spirited and socially minded men and women ready and anxious to give their services'. The report recommended that the local boards include representatives from women's organizations, municipal councils, and the provincial government, and that each be granted a per diem allowance. Also in keeping with the concerns of charity, religious, and women's leaders, the report recommended intensive and frequent investigation of the recipients.[111]

The report did differ from the consensus of the lobby regarding mothers with one child. During the 1919 public hearings W.A. Riddell attempted to dissuade lobbyists from including mothers with one child, suggesting that these women could become live-in domestic servants instead.[112] In his report, Riddell strengthened his position by claiming that the government would save $847,200 by excluding mothers with one child. He believed this exclusion would reduce the number of OMA recipients by half.[113] None of the lobbyists had distinguished between the number of children a needy mother had. In this regard, the report clearly favoured the interests of taxpayers over the opinions of the OMA lobbyists.

In August 1920 a Mothers' Allowance Act, very much in keeping with the report's recommendations, was passed and Ontario became the fifth province to provide monthly allowances to needy mothers. The features of this legislation reflected the consensus that had developed during the three-and-a-half decades of debate. Consequently, the policy was moralistic, maternalist, miserly, and racist. As subsequent chapters will illustrate, this would have grave implications for the lives of Ontario Mothers' Allowance recipients.

Chapter 2

Building the Infrastructure:
The First Decade of Ontario Mothers' Allowance

Following one of the most unexpected electoral upsets in Ontario political history, Premier Ernest Drury and his minority United Farmers of Ontario (UFO) government enacted mothers' allowance legislation on 4 June 1920, a mere three months following the opening of the legislature. In doing so, Ontario became the fifth province in Canada to enact mothers' allowance legislation, following the lead of the Western provinces: Manitoba (1916), Saskatchewan (1917), Alberta (1919), and British Columbia (1920). Several industrialized countries had already passed a similar policy, including forty of the forty-eight states south of the border.[1] As we have seen in Chapter 1, Sir William Hearst's Conservative government conducted two inquiries on the subject in 1917 and 1919, followed by a sympathetic report, and began to draft legislation before the election. The Ontario Mothers' Allowance lobby effort, which intensified following the war and included a wide array of societal leaders, could hardly be ignored forever. Drury and the UFO had not advocated mothers' allowance as part of their electoral platform, but the Independent Labour Party of Ontario, under the direction of Walter Rollo, had promised both mothers' allowance and old age pension. The ILP's support was crucial to the UFO's minority government and mothers' allowance helped to cement this alliance.[2] Once enacted, there was much administrative preparation involved in the establishment of this policy. This chapter explores the features of OMA's administrative structure during the policy's first decade.

The OMA's administrative structure reveals that the UFO government attempted to balance the concerns of the OMA lobbyists and those of the taxpayers. This policy was introduced at the least possible cost to taxpayers and the government. Closely following the recommendations of the Riddell Report, particularly the financial assessment, the UFO government announced a policy with restrictive eligibility criteria. This was in keeping with the general philosophy of the Drury government. The UFO had achieved electoral success partly as a result of farmers' concerns with growing urbanization and the depopulation of rural areas. As a Simcoe County farmer and pro-temperance advocate, Drury often spoke nostalgically of a return to 'the good old days'. Drury considered himself a social reformer, particularly in the area of child welfare, but much of his social legislation reflected a desire to return to Victorian values. He created an adoption act that made adoption easier and less costly, and a Parents' Maintenance Act that forced older children to provide for their needy parents and, moreover, made it an offence for fathers to desert their children. Regarding illegitimate children, he established legislation that compelled fathers to assume financial responsibilities for illegitimate children and allowed these children to be legitimized by the subsequent marriage of the parents. All of this legislation had a similar goal: to uphold the heterosexual family unit by reinforcing family responsibilities and, as a last resort, to provide limited state aid.[3]

Despite the conservative nature of the Ontario Mothers' Allowance policy, the Drury government was able to meet a number of diverse interests. With the 1919 election, women became voters alongside men and politicians wanted to secure the female vote by appealing to women's particular interests. OMA could enhance the value of motherhood that maternal feminists endorsed. For labour, OMA could offer wives and children some security if the male breadwinner died, thus making it unnecessary for some women and children to work full time. Also, this legislation could provide an increased role for social workers as they struggled to gain professional status and expertise. At the same time, it would provide continued work for a number of charities—charitable workers could help those who were excluded from the policy and provide volunteer help and advice to the OMA administration.

The popularity of this legislation, combined with the economic boom of the 1920s, allowed the Drury government to venture one step further into the field of public welfare. Mothers' allowance signalled a departure from previous welfare practices in the sense that the provincial state was willing to provide a fixed sum of money on a monthly basis for some needy mothers. As a result, at least some mothers would not need to depend on the 'whims' of private charities or municipal relief, or be forced to place their offspring in orphanages or foster homes. Also, this policy ensured that some needy children and mothers would not have to engage in full-time wage labour to help sustain the family. Thus, a new level of economic security, however minimal, was established.

This allowance also indicated a greater role for the state as moral guardians of its citizens. Whereas charities and private associations had dominated the field of moral authority in the nineteenth century, both the provincial and federal state became increasingly involved in this arena at the turn of the century. To gain legitimacy in a new field, the state needed to centralize knowledge by collecting and legitimizing certain information as 'facts' and advice while rejecting others.[4] During the 1920s both the federal and provincial governments presented themselves as experts on mothering. Although the federal government had resisted the lobby for a national mothers' allowance policy, it established the Canadian Council on Child Welfare in 1922. This council became an expert on all child welfare issues, particularly in the area of mothers' allowance. Also, both levels of government established expectant mothers' clinics, well-baby clinics, better baby contests, and numerous advice pamphlets on home and child care.[5] In most provinces, including Ontario, there were programs in place by 1914 for nurses to visit private homes, investigate, and advise on health issues.[6] The establishment of mothers' allowance policies provided the provincial government with greater opportunities to intrude into the homes of its citizens, offering the latest advice on child and maternal development according to a bourgeois and Protestant Euro-Canadian family ideal. While the public health nurses would attempt to persuade and counsel families, the OMA workers had the power to refuse financial aid to those who would not follow the advice given.

Although OMA signalled a greater role for the state in the lives of its citizens, this policy also demonstrated some important similarities with previous welfare work. Both the administrative structure established and the procedures and routines employed were similar to welfare of an earlier era. As the provincial state undertook new welfare legislation, it established new practices, routines, and procedures; although these were often presented as neutral and natural, they tended to be based on old charity notions. In fact, Mariana Valverde argues that 'the legacy of philanthropy weighed so heavily on the "new" systems of relief that one could with some justice claim that philanthropy merely disguised itself as state-funded welfare and social work.'[7] OMA's strict eligibility and minimal payments ensured that the allowance remained a privilege rather than a right for services rendered. Even the name of the policy was carefully considered. The government chose to call the legislation an 'allowance' instead of a 'pension' because it suggested a more discretionary nature of welfare. Also, other societal leaders, not paid or accountable to the state, volunteered to counsel and supervise the OMA recipients. As such, OMA's administrative structure reflected a blurring of public and private welfare activities.

THE ONTARIO MOTHERS' ALLOWANCE INFRASTRUCTURE

No sooner was the act announced than applications and inquiries 'began to pour in at the office of the commission in great numbers'.[8] The demand was far more than anticipated. To cope with the huge number of applications, the government maintained very restrictive eligibility criteria and a miserly allowance rate during the first decade. Despite public demand to improve the policy, neither the Drury government from 1921 to 1923 nor the Conservative government of G. Howard Ferguson, which followed from 1923 to 1930, dramatically altered the OMA Act.

The eligibility criteria made the OMA Act one of the most restrictive mothers' allowance policies in North America. Initially the allowance was only available to morally upright and needy widows, although many had advocated a much broader policy. In fact, several other provinces had passed or amended more inclusive policies. For instance, the Saskatchewan and British Columbia mothers' allowance policies had expanded to include prisoners' wives.[9] Most surprisingly, British Columbia had a special assistance clause that allowed all single mothers, regardless of circumstances, to apply for assistance.[10] And all other provincial policies included mothers with one child by the end of the first decade, but Ontario would not follow suit until 1935.[11] There was considerable resentment and fear of immigrants, particularly those from central and eastern Europe, during the post-World War era, which the OMA policy reflected. Eligibility was restricted to those who were British subjects or naturalized British subjects. These criteria also included Aboriginal women, although very few became beneficiaries.[12] Applicants had to demonstrate that they had been residents of Canada for three years and of Ontario for two years.

Within the first year of administration, a lobby effort led by local OMA administrators protested the policy's restrictive eligibility. As a result, the Drury government made a number of amendments in 1921. The government extended eligibility to deserted and foster mothers, although very strict guidelines were followed in both cases. Deserted wives who could swear that they had not seen or heard from their husbands in *seven* years were eligible; this was quickly reduced to a five-year waiting period. Foster mothers (defined as a grandmother, sister, aunt, or 'suitable mother' who had the care of two orphan children and inadequate means to support them) were eligible. The amendment included wives of incarcerated husbands and wives of permanently incapacitated husbands, each with two or more children, and mothers with one child under fourteen years and one child over fourteen.

Eligibility requirements under Ferguson's Progressive Conservative government remained virtually unaltered. The government resisted calls to include mothers with one child. In 1923 an exception clause was added, granting the allowance to families in need who did not strictly meet the eligibility criteria, but this was rarely used. And in 1927 mothers' allowance was restricted by requiring recipients to submit monthly school attendance records. Also during the Ferguson era, there were charges of favouritism in the determination of eligibility. At the end of the decade patronage charges erupted in the provincial legislature when a letter from the minister of public welfare to an OMA recipient hinted that the woman's allowance might continue *if* she would support the government in the pending election.[13] Other than partisan interests, the OMA administration during the 1920s was characterized as inflexible in questions of eligibility.

On 1 October 1920, four months after the policy was enacted, the first cheques were mailed to the homes of needy mothers. Because of the overwhelming demand, the government established a flat rate and a rigid income test so 'only those that were really in need of immediate help should be recommended for an allowance'.[14] Initially the maximum flat rate was $55 monthly in the city and $45 monthly in towns, villages, and rural districts. Within a year these monthly sums were further specified as follows:

For those living in the city:

Widow with five or more children	$55 per month
Widow with four children	$50 per month
Widow with three children	$45 per month
Widow with two children	$40 per month

For those living in rural areas:

Widow with five or more children	$45 per month
Widow with four children	$40 per month
Widow with three children	$35 per month
Widow with two children	$30 per month[15]

There was no rationale given for the maximums established. The Riddell Report had suggested a rate similar to the cost of institutionalizing a child, which was estimated at $10 monthly per child.[16] The government asked each locality to draw up cost-of-living schedules for mothers with two or more children in their own communities. One county estimated a minimum of $65 monthly for a mother with four children.[17] These estimates, however, were never followed. Instead, the government rigidly adhered to its maximum flat-rate scale.

This allowance rate was minimal at best and remained unchanged during the decade. The minimum wage for women was $12.50 per week, which was based on the assumption that these women had no dependants.[18] On average a blue-collar worker in Toronto earned approximately $24 weekly, more than half of the monthly budget for an OMA mother with two children living in the same city.[19] And the average family budget for staple foods, fuel, lighting, and rent was approximately $26 per week. Clearly, by almost all acceptable standards, OMA rates fell well below subsistence (see Table 2.1).

This allowance was also significantly lower than other welfare measures of the era. For instance, it was lower than most of the other provincial mothers' allowance rates (see Table 2.2). The Canadian Patriotic Fund provided a soldier's widow and two children a minimum of $65 per month, and a widow with seven children might receive up to $100 monthly. Unlike mothers' allowance, once a soldier's dependant established her eligibility for a widow's pension, she received it as a right, regardless of ongoing need.[20] And a comparison between Workers' Compensation and OMA rates revealed that a widow with two children whose husband had died of a work-related accident would receive a maximum of $60, whereas if this same husband had died of natural causes, the family would receive a maximum of only $40 from OMA (see Table 2.3). An administrator of mothers' allowance in Alberta was struck by the divergence in amount and attitude between mothers' allowance and Workers' Compensation:

> [With workers' compensation] . . . the widow . . . receives [money] . . .
> whether she is childless or not, regardless of whether she has any funds or

not, receives it at the very day her husband was killed, receives it until the day of her death, or her subsequent marriage, when she gets 12 months pay in advance. She may go where she pleases and is subject to no inspection. She gets additional assistance for every child she has. Had this woman's husband died at home from natural causes, she would get no allowance unless she had 2 or more children [under 14 years]. . . . She would receive no allowance if she had any funds, and not until the funds were exhausted. She would abandon her allowance as soon as she remarried. She would not get her allowance until a month or so after the death of her husband. She cannot leave the province and is subject to frequent inspection. She does not know when the allowance will be removed or cut off.[21]

Part of the reason the Canadian Patriotic Fund and Workers' Compensation rates were higher than mothers' allowance payments were the very nature of the policies themselves. The former two were premised on a notion that these payments were rights as a result of past services, either to the war effort or to the labour force respectively. Both these policies granted a payment, separate from that of the children, to the mother in exchange for her care-giving services. This notion of rights was not so clearly articulated in the case of mothers' allowance. There was some effort made to distinguish mothers' allowance from charitable relief, but this was not entirely successful. The provincial government insisted that this was a

Table 2.1 Cost of Living for Ontario, 1923

The following budget appeared in the *Toronto Mail and Empire*, 12 February 1923. It is the budget for a family consisting of the father, mother, and two children, six and eighteen years of age. The father earns $100 per month, and they live in a respectable neighbourhood just outside the city limits.

Rent (six-room house)	$35.00
Fuel with furnace	8.00
Gas	3.00
Light	1.40
Water	1.00
Total for housing	**$48.40**
Food	$30.00
Clothing	10.00
Insurance	4.50
Sundries, such as soap, cleaning, stationery, stamps, newspapers	2.75
Car fare	3.00
Total for food, clothing, etc.	**$50.25**
Total cost of living for family	**$98.65**

Source: AO, RG 7, Series VII-1, vol. 5, file: Miscellaneous, 1921–25, 'Information Requested by the Canadian Government Trade Commissioner', 3 and 6.

Table 2.2 Comparison of Provincial Mothers' Allowance Rates, 1930

Province	Maximum Rate for Three Children (two of school age)
Alberta	$60 per month in the city of Edmonton (less elsewhere)
British Columbia	$57.50 per month
Manitoba	$59.75 per month (plus $14 for fuel in a house, $10 in rooms) This amount varies to a maximum of $70, depending on needs of family
Nova Scotia	$60 per month maximum to a family of any size
Ontario	$45 per month in city $40 in town $35 in country
Saskatchewan	$30 per month maximum to a family of any size

Source: Comparative table provided by Canadian Council on Child Welfare. NA, MG 28, I-10, vol. 37, file: Mothers' Allowance in British Columbia, 1931–33, 'Report of the Administration of Mothers' Pensions in British Columbia, 1920–21 to 1930–31', Summary, 7.

payment for services rendered 'to the state in bringing up of its citizens' rather than a form of public relief or charity.[22] The mother was 'to be regarded as an employee of the Ontario Government'.[23] The government believed that the impersonal payment of the allowances by cheque through the mail would contribute to this notion of service and avoid 'any humiliating feeling of "charity"'.[24] But at the same time, mothers' allowance had

Table 2.3 Comparison of Ontario Workmen's Compensation and Ontario Mothers' Allowance Rates for a Mother with Two Children, 1914–1949

Year	Ontario Workmen's Compensation	Ontario Mothers' Allowance
1914	$30 ($5 for each additional child; not to exceed $50)	N/A
1919	$45 ($7.50 for each additional child; not to exceed $60)	N/A
1920	$60 ($10 for each additional child; no maximum)	$40 ($5 for each additional child; not to exceed $55)
1941		Fuel allowance in winter months
1943		$48 ($6 for each additional child)
1944		$10 special assistance (discretionary)
1947	$74 ($12 for each additional child; no maximum)	
1948		$60 ($10 for each additional child)
1949	$74 ($12 for each additional child; not to exceed $100)	

Notes: (i) The OMA rates are the maximum rates available to families who live in the city. (ii) The OWC rates include an amount specifically for the mother whereas OMA rates are a lump sum based on the number of children with no payment specifically geared to the mothers. (iii) OWC granted money to a mother with one child, but OMA did not do so until 1935. (iv) From 1920 to 1947, the OWC maximum rate was not to exceed 66 2/3 per cent of the deceased husband's income.

Source: OWC rates: 'Report on the Royal Commission on the Workmen's Compensation Act, 1950', cited in Nancy Forestell, 'Workers, Wives and the Welfare State: Workers' Compensation and Ontario Goldminers, 1915–1940', Table 6; and OMA rates: AO, RG 29, series 74, 137.

Table 2.4 OMA Beneficiaries in Relation to Provincial Population, 1920–1930

Year	OMA Recipients	Ontario Population	Percentage of Population
1920–1	2,660	2,933,662	.091
1921–2	3,559		
1922–3	3,870		
1923–4	4,058		
1924–5	4,185		
1925–6	4,412		
1926–7	4,729		
1927–8	5,139		
1928–9	5,357		
1929–30	5,623	3,431,683	.164

a number of attributes associated with nineteenth-century welfare. The minimal payments, the lack of a separate allowance for the mothers, and a bureaucratic structure that included paid investigators whose duty was 'to investigate carefully the fitness of the applicant for her position' was more associated with charitable relief than rights-based welfare policies.[25]

Although eligibility requirements were restrictive and payments below the subsistence level, the number of recipients increased steadily during the first decade. According to the OMA annual reports, the number of beneficiaries more than doubled during the first decade of the policy (Table 2.4).[26] As the statistics demonstrate, the number of OMA beneficiaries increased at a rate faster than that of the Ontario population with OMA recipients representing .091 per cent of the provincial population in 1921 and .164 per cent in 1930.

The government expenditures for the program also steadily increased over the decade. The provincial and municipal governments shared the costs of the allowance equally, with the former absorbing administrative costs. The total government expenses of OMA administration during the decade, including allowance payments, personnel salaries, and other costs, were as follows:[27]

1921	$774,667
1922	$1,382,138
1923	$1,612,702
1924	$1,715,205
1925	$1,790,680
1926	$1,886,095
1927	$2,017,614
1928	$2,205,877
1929	$2,324,388

These statistics demonstrate that government expenditures for OMA increased at a slightly faster rate than the number of recipients. Given that the rates did not increase during the decade, the increase must be administrative costs.

The administrative structure of OMA consisted of three components: the provincial commission, the local boards, and the investigators. American mothers' allowance policies were initially administered only at a local level. This was confusing and uncoordinated at times. To avoid these problems, the Drury government, upon Riddell's recommendations, favoured a more centralized provincial system, but given that welfare had been considered a predominantly local matter for municipal governments and charitable organizations, the Drury government had to tread carefully. As a compromise, the OMA administration was jointly funded and administered by provincial and local governments, with the former having the ultimate authority.

Like the Canadian Patriotic Fund, OMA established a central or provincial commission consisting of five paid civil servants. The Drury government chose a provincial commission rather than a government department in an effort to ensure non-partisanship.[28] This provincial commission would work closely with the local boards, each of which consisted of five volunteers who would first initiate an application and advise the provincial commission on cases, but the provincial commission had the final authority to determine eligibility and the amount paid in each case. During the fiscal year the commissioners would visit numerous local boards, promoting vigilant investigation and inquiry into the applicants' lives.[29] As well, the commission had the power to appoint three of the five members of each local board.

The provincial commission was composed of the chairman, vice-chairman, and three others. Given the maternalist politics of the era, the act stipulated that two of the five appointments of both the provincial commission and the local boards were to be women. Other than that, there were no political or religious restrictions upon appointment to the commission.[30] The first chairman of the provincial commission was Peter Bryce, a Methodist clergyman who had replaced John Kelso as head of the OMA lobby. Other members of the first commission included Lt Col T.J. Murphy, KC, of London; H.A. Reynolds of Brampton; W.F. (Minnie) Singer, Labour representative of Toronto; and Dr Elizabeth Shortt of Ottawa as vice-chair. These members were pre-eminent leaders in their respective communities or associations. Murphy, an alderman for London, had helped to establish the University of Western Ontario and was a member of the university's board of governors. He was keenly interested in Canadian militia affairs and was a member of the Fourth Fusiliers. Reynolds was a well-known lawyer. Singer was a leading spokesperson for women's issues within both unions and the Independent Labour Party. As head of the Ladies Auxiliary for the machinists union, she helped to unionize other women and, along with Rose Henderson, fought for a women's caucus within the ILP. Shortt was a medical doctor and a vigorous activist in the area of child and maternal welfare who had led the NCW Committee on Mothers' Pensions.

The administration of the provincial commission did not run smoothly during the first decade. The provincial commission was reorganized following the defeat of the United Farmers of Ontario in 1923 and the beginning of an eleven-year Conservative reign. In 1927 there were cries of patronage when the Ontario minister of health bowed to political pressure and appointed two prominent Conservatives without consulting with the provincial commission or the Civil Service Commission. These appointments symbolized the declining influence of the turn-of-the-century social reformers and the beginning of a more political and more bureaucratic OMA administration. Dr David Jamieson, a medical doctor for fifty years and former speaker of the House, replaced Bryce as chairman; Miss Belle Thompson, sister of Hon. Jos. Thompson, former speaker of the legislature, and president of the woman's branch of the Ward Two Conservative Association, had no previous welfare experience, but became assistant to the chief investigator. According to the OMA Act, appointments were to be made on recommendation from the commission. In protest, Elizabeth Shortt, vice-chair of the commission, and Miss Farncombe, chief investigator, resigned. The latter was replaced by yet another Conservative, Harry Bentley, who had been a file clerk in the field of social welfare following his service in the war. As Elizabeth Shortt explained, both women resigned 'because the work is not being carried on in the proper manner. . . . Untrained people are put into positions by the chairman. Some of them are inefficient. They do not know their work.'[31] Both women had worked for the commission since it began in 1920 and had several years' prior experience in the area of social service, unlike their replacements. In response, Dr Jamieson 'pleaded guilty to being a strong Conservative and he thought that if positions or appointments were being given they would be given to Conservatives if they were just as capable of handling them as persons who were not Conservatives.'[32] Even though a number of newspapers across the province protested these patronage charges, no inquiry was conducted and the administration of OMA continued. In fact, to make matters worse, three months after this incident, the inexperienced Miss Belle Thompson was quickly promoted to vice-chair of the commission.[33]

Given that this was a joint provincial-municipal policy, local boards were established for each city, town, county, and judicial district. These local boards were responsible for receiving applications, conducting inquiries and investigations, making recommendations, and submitting quarterly reports to the provincial commission.[34] While each case required the approval of the local board, the ultimate authority rested with the provincial commission, whose decision could not be challenged. The provincial commission issued the cheques and then billed the respective municipalities for 50 per cent of the costs. The local board members were volunteers who were reimbursed for travelling expenses to monthly board meetings and to homes of applicants.

By 1926 there were 100 local boards across the province and more than 500 volunteers serving on these boards.[35] Generally, the chair was a prominent male, whereas the vice-chair or secretary was often a prominent woman in the community. Often the male members were Christian religious leaders, medical doctors, or prominent politicians (such as mayors, reeves, councillors, clerks, and wardens). Several of the members had the title of lieutenant or colonel, a courtesy granted to élite families with ties to the militia. The religious leaders were mostly Protestant. While generally well represented on local boards, their numbers were substantially higher in the northern districts and Indian reserves; for instance, one local board on an Indian reserve included *four* reverends. According to the 1920–1 records, of those local board members who listed their title, the breakdown was as follows:[36]

Reverends	40
Doctors	11
Warden, alderman, mayor	9
Major, colonel	6
Judge	3
Indian chief	2
Canon, deaconess	2
Captain	1
Professor	1

These ratios remained virtually unchanged at the end of the decade. As would be expected, many of these local board members often shared the same social circles and general values; they socialized together following the meeting, celebrating birthdays and anniversaries. They also sent letters of sympathy to the families of former board members and to the royal family, expressing their sadness 'in the passing of King George V . . . and their allegiance to King Edward VIII.'[37] As a result of this close association there were occasional complaints that the local board was a 'social clique' that based its decisions on gossip and favouritism rather than on 'objective' evidence.[38]

There were also a number of complaints about the provincial commission, primarily from local board members. First, there were concerns that the commission was too powerful and insensitive to local board recommendations.[39] Second, local board members found the commission too inflexible. A 1923 amendment that permitted the commission to grant allowances to families who did not strictly fulfil the eligibility requirements was an attempt to alleviate this problem, but it was rarely used.[40] Third, the local board members accused the provincial commission for being 'too niggardly', rarely granting the maximum allowance.[41] Finally, the criteria for eligibility were considered too restrictive and a lobby led by several local boards, which included charity and labour leaders, was formed in 1920 and 1927. As a result of this effort, the government made minor amendments to the act in 1921, but resisted the 1927 lobby to include mothers with one child.[42]

For OMA recipients, the provincial investigators were the human face of the policy. Investigators would visit the homes of applicants and make detailed reports to both the local board and the provincial commission.

These investigators represented both a continuation of and a departure from earlier philanthropic ideals.

Most of these investigators were not trained social workers. Although several OMA lobbyists and the Riddell Report had recommended that they should be experienced, professional social workers rather than political appointments, this was not the case. Initially more than 300 people applied for these positions, and those chosen were often women with public health or educational backgrounds but no formal social work training; usually they owed their appointments to good political connections. These investigators attempted to combine early philanthropy work with the newer scientific social work practices. In one sense, the investigators' visits were an extension of the state's intervention in private homes, replacing the work of private organizations. Following the Children's Aid Society worker and the public health nurse, the OMA investigator was a new government agent who 'was figuratively parachuted into the fringes of the province to inquire into basic social problems. . . .'[43] Yet at the same time, much about these visits was familiar. The word 'investigators' connotes the type of detailed, intrusive work associated with earlier philanthropic activities. Once the local board recommended a case, the provincial commission called upon these investigators to conduct 'careful, painstaking investigation . . . over the health of the family, the proper feeding and clothing of the children, housing conditions and the moral atmosphere of the home'.[44] Similar to nineteenth-century welfare activity, moral concerns tended to dominate economic issues. As well as a verbal inquiry, there would be a number of forms to fill and certificates to peruse. Upon the investigator's detailed report and the local board's approval, the provincial commission would determine whether a needy mother would receive the allowance or not. Once it was granted, the investigators would continue frequent visits to the home to ensure that the regulations were carried out (see Table 2.5). These visits were, for the most part, unannounced and if the applicant was out, the investigator would leave a calling card to arrange a return visit (see Figure 2.1). In difficult cases, the investigator would visit 'almost daily . . . keeping the mother constantly mindful of what was expected of her'.[45] As such, these investigators had a great deal of power to influence a needy mother's future as well as her day-to-day behaviour.

At the same time that these investigators were working within a philanthropic model, they were also influenced by the rapidly developing scientific study of poverty as social work schools opened their doors in the 1920s. This decade was a period of consolidation for welfare workers; the Canadian Association of Social Workers was founded in 1928 to organize and regulate these new professionals.[46] Social workers expounded on the usefulness of casework to carefully and 'objectively' detail the lives of the less fortunate. The formal OMA application forms and quarterly investigative reports were at least partly in response to this new scientific era. This contrasted with nineteenth-century welfare, which was generally conduct-

Table 2.5 Report of Investigators' Work During Fiscal Year 1922–1923

Visits of supervision to beneficiaries	15,008
Visits of investigation to applicants	1,494
Other agencies visited	7,003
Visited applicants who were out or moved	2,555
Total number of visits by investigators	**26,060**
Number of hours spent in clerical work	8,936.5
Total number of hours worked	34,330.75

Source: 'Annual Report of the OMA Commission, 1922–23'.

ed by volunteer and/or untrained labour whose record keeping was haphazard and inconsistent. Yet despite these improvements, OMA case records
remained uneven in the amount of evidence they contained, depending
mainly on the thoroughness of the individual investigator. There was considerable room for an investigator's subjective opinions as opposed to
'objective' data.

For most of these women it was their first opportunity to participate in
the paid workforce. During the first decade there were between seventeen
and nineteen investigators, most of whom were unmarried women.[47]
Ironically, the policy provided investigators with new opportunities to live
economically independent of men while reinforcing a more conventional
lifestyle on OMA recipients. The commission assigned each of the investigators a large region of the province to cover. According to their letters,
they had exhausting schedules, travelling alone by rail, buggy, car, or foot
from one home to another. A day in the life of one investigator involved a
drive of '120 miles over bad roads on Saturday, 40 on Sunday 45 the following Thursday and 80 on Friday'.[48] Another investigator explains in her
letter on Canadian National Railways letterhead: 'If not too fagged I may

Figure 2.1 Ontario Mothers' Allowance Investigator's calling card (*City of Cambridge Archives, Cambridge, Ontario, file: Ontario Mothers' Allowance*).

be at your [local board] meeting on Saturday. The country seems drenched so suppose sideroads will be almost impassable. . . . Pardon the lack of official paper, also writing, but train is rather jiggly'.[49] OMA annual reports chronicled the particular difficulties of travelling to northern communities.

> Train crews have let her [the investigator] ride miles on a freight train, having supper in the caboose and helping to wash the dishes. . . . The hardships of winter travelling are great, with delays in train service on snow blocked lines and long drives in heavy snow and zero weather. . . . In the Spring, the bad conditions of the roads makes many districts impossible of access for many weeks and itineraries have to be arranged so as to cover these territories while the frost holds.[50]

Such a life was both exhilarating and exhausting for independent-minded single women. In 1921 each investigator was responsible for an average of 156 cases, which by the end of the decade rose to approximately 300, as the chairman of the commission explained:

> On account of the increasing number of beneficiaries and the need for more careful supervision, the investigators are having rather a strenuous task to efficiently carry on their work. . . . It will be necessary to have more assistance by increasing the number, as we find by making inquiries from other provinces and from states in the neighbouring republic that none of their investigators have nearly the numbers under their care as we have in Ontario.[51]

The role of the investigator was not universally admired. Labour representatives and local board members complained about the intrusive role and the 'holier-than-thou' attitude of these provincially appointed investigators.[52] As one former member of the Simcoe County local board explained:

> As a former secretary on our local board, I had a good chance to observe the workings of this authority. I heard complaints about the domineering attitude of the investigators and was myself the victim of it, if reports were true. Why any fur-coated investigator should be allowed to go into a widow's home and demand that she give an account to her of every cent of her allowance is more than I could ever swallow for justice or sympathy. . . . Why is all this interference with widows tolerated, and not applied to the rest of us?[53]

Similarly, Toronto labour representatives also charged that these OMA investigators were class-biased and insensitive when one needy mother who worked part time as a waitress had her allowance cut off. The investigator had stated publicly that 'Waitresses were the lowest types of girls that walked.' The mother was told her allowance was cut because 'a letter had been received by the board stating she was running around with men and had been brought home intoxicated in a taxicab. . . . The story of her being brought home in a taxi was started when she was carried home [from work] suffering from burns . . . [caused] by scalding coffee knocked from her tray.' The commission refused to say who wrote the letter and did not grant the mother an opportunity to deny the allegations. In outrage, local labour officials declared that this was an 'attack upon the character of the best types of women—those who worked for a living to maintain their families—[and] would not go unchallenged'.[54] Labour officials met with the provincial government over this incident, but the intrusive, class-biased investigation of OMA applicants continued.

While OMA recipients generally viewed the investigators as intrusive, occasionally a supportive relationship developed between them. Some lonely mothers would write to the investigator, encouraging a friendly correspondence. Because the investigators travelled widely and knew many people, some mothers used them as a source of contacts to find summer jobs or boarding places for their daughters. Such 'constructive and rehabilitative work' was encouraged, although investigators were cautioned not to weaken the beneficiary's feeling of independence or erode the family's own initiative through this intensive guidance.[55] This supportive relationship, however, was an exception to the general rule. As a result of her busy schedule and heavy case-load, the investigator was rarely able to develop such a role, even if she was so inclined.

Given that the case-load averaged between 150 and 300 clients, it was impossible for investigators to provide close surveillance of all applicants. Often they relied upon members of various social agencies to pursue this work. Charities such as the Red Cross Society, Masonic Lodge, Children's Aid Society, Salvation Army, Catholic Women's League, St Vincent de Paul, Federation of Catholic Charities, Patriotic Fund, Imperial Order of Daughters of the Empire, Local Council of Women, Fresh Air Agencies, Pentecostal Tabernacle, Kiwanis Club, Rotary Club, Canadian Club, Canadian Legion of the British Empire Service League, and the Canadian League for the Advancement of Colored People were all involved in the cause of single mothers. Local politicians, bureaucrats (reeves, mayors, building inspectors, relief officers, board of education officers, police, fire marshall, and clerks), and members of the legal community (magistrates, juvenile court judges, and lawyers) all played a role. Similarly, a number of small-business people also became involved. Cattle buyers, automobile dealers, grocery store owners, dentists, and grain dealers all wrote to praise or condemn a mothers' allowance applicant. Finally, individual citizens became involved as neighbours, ratepayers, and friends. Some of these people volunteered to help supervise and 'rehabilitate' certain clients. Others advocated on behalf of needy mothers. As such, these volunteers were involved in both benevolent and investigative work.

The local board and investigators often relied upon various social organizations to aid in the board's investigative activities. Where there had been concern that the introduction of OMA would diminish the need for private charities, the opposite was true. During the first decade of OMA private philanthropy was 'greatly stimulated' and the OMA reports thanked various charitable groups for their 'splendid co-operation and practical helpfulness'.

Charitable members would help the OMA officials in their deliberation over eligibility by providing background not supplied by the applicant, offering meeting space for the local board, and overseeing certain 'questionable' mothers. Any mother who was refused OMA would be referred to a social organization for aid.[56]

The administrators of OMA and the Children's Aid Society had particularly close relations. Not only would the former refer all questionable cases to the CAS but the CAS representatives often made home visits on behalf of the OMA. In fact, the CAS often acted as the coercive arm of the OMA administration. CAS workers would go into the homes of OMA recipients and threaten to remove the children unless the living conditions improved. The OMA officials found that this rather coercive CAS visit was quite effective in shaping questionable recipients into morally deserving families.[57]

Other professionals also worked closely with the OMA administration. Doctors and public health officials appealed to the OMA administration for help with certain mothers who refused to take their children to the doctor or admit them to hospital. Teachers complained about truancy and school behaviour. The OMA administrators would threaten to withdraw the OMA cheque if the mother and children did not comply with the doctor's or teacher's wishes. Consequently, various arms of the state worked together, sharing information and helping to coerce mothers into what was considered appropriate behaviour.

Other members of the community also regulated the applicants. For example, a London city fireman told the local board that he had the following people watch Emma Ledley's house:

A man known as Tex, who lives at Red Cross Soldiers Club
A neighbour
A railway employee who says he himself caught a Chinaman
        leaving the house
A man who lives at the corner of the street
And two others who are willing to give information.[58]

In cases where the husband had deserted the applicant, a police officer would be invited to appear before the local board to outline the details of investigation into the husband's whereabouts. Business merchants often wrote or appeared before the board to demand that the money mothers' allowance recipients owed to them be paid. Neighbours and landlords frequently wrote to complain about recipients' behaviour. Because of their standing in the community, these people were often given access to what should have been confidential information about the mother.

Occasionally these people of local status abused their authority over needy single mothers and their vulnerable families. In the town of Cochrane an Anglican minister was found to have sexually assaulted a number of local girls in the church basement. Some of these young girls were daughters of OMA recipients, and the minister had bribed them to remain silent. During the court trial it was revealed that the bishop of Moosonee, who was involved in OMA administration for the district, had intervened and threatened two daughters of OMA recipients to drop their charges or their families would lose their OMA cheques.[59] In another similar case, a local doctor was the father of one OMA recipient's two children. The doctor desperately tried to keep this information quiet and persuaded the mother, Regina Wise, to sign a sworn declaration stating that he was not the father. She later regretted this decision; her OMA cheque was cancelled nevertheless. Consequently, she wrote to the local board pleading her case:

> Was it not enough that I had suffered through nine long months previous to my baby's birth, as well as constantly undergoing the humiliation for my baby's sake since her coming? What good purpose can possibly be served by further depriving my children of the very necessary assistance . . . by withholding the Mothers' Allowance . . . and so greatly adding to the anxiety and lack of peace of mind which I now feel for my children's welfare.

Despite this letter, the provincial commission denied Regina's reinstatement.[60]

At other times those of social status used their authority to help a needy mother. There are a few cases of people volunteering to recommend a needy mother's case before the board, to plead for a mother who had been rejected, or to give mothers a little extra financial help when in desperate circumstances. On the application form the mother was asked to give names of three people who had known her for at least two years. Most frequently cited were religious leaders, lawyers, or doctors. Often a religious leader would act on behalf of the mother, presenting her case before the board or the investigator. The Salvation Army was particularly known for its work with poor single mothers. Dr Jamieson, head of the provincial commission on mothers' allowance, explained that:

> . . . in some cases, the women had been given a kick down hill and perhaps made worse than she was. He mentioned a case where the local board had recommended reinstatement and the woman had been taken out of her surroundings and partial employment secured and they thought she would turn out to be a first class mother. The Salvation Army had greatly assisted in cases of this kind.[61]

As well, religious leaders were often members of local boards, blurring the line between the welfare state and civil society.

Charities would often work alongside the OMA bureaucracy, providing extended intrusive care and moral guidance to the children of needy mothers. For instance, the OMA provincial commission thanked the Kiwanis Clubs for helping the sons of OMA recipients. The Hamilton club was deemed exemplary:

> They have a medical examination board in the Club, which meets every month and the boys are examined and a record taken of any physical or

mental defects. The Kiwanis Daddy and the boy's mother are both notified of any defects and proper measures are taken to see that the defects are remedied in as far as it is possible. The boy is given a full membership in the Y.M.C.A. and equipped with a regular gymnasium outfit. The boy is also enrolled at the Public Library, without any expense, and the Kiwanis Daddy supervises the choosing of literature that would be in line with the boy's inclinations as far as possible. To promote the spirit of thrift, a bank account is opened for the boy, in the joint name of the boy and the Kiwanis Daddy, and he is started off at $1.00 at a branch where the manager is a member of the Club. The boys are supposed to visit the Kiwanis Daddy at his office and at his home at least once every two weeks, and the Kiwanis Daddy, in his turn, is also supposed to visit the boy in his home and offer suggestions as to the improvement of conditions.[62]

Clearly, this Kiwanis Club activity encouraged its members to monitor the home of a single mother under the guise of charitable work. Through these visits Kiwanis Daddies could impart middle-class values of thrift, morality, and manliness to these fatherless boys.

In a few isolated cases, businesses came to the rescue of the destitute mothers. For instance, the industrial nurse from Beatty Brothers Manufacturing Company wrote the local board to explain their aid to Sonya Tanovich:

> We visited her in London shortly ago and found her having a very hard time to get along. We purchased food and clothing for her through Beatty Brothers Welfare, but of course will not be able to keep on providing for her. We would appreciate it very much if you could let us know whether Mrs. Tanovich will be receiving the Mothers Allowance or not, also if she will be receiving it when could we expect the payments to start.[63]

In another instance, the dentist of the town of Collingwood often treated the children of mothers' allowance recipients free of charge.[64] Some local proprietors were eager to have an allowance granted to a mother if this meant that she could better afford their products. Such was the case of Mr McLaren, a storekeeper from Elgin County, who wrote in support of Maud Becker:

> I have talked to . . . [the investigator and a member of the local board] respecting Mrs. Becker's allowance which I consider she is very much in need of. But I do think it is poor policy to allow her the handling of the case. We supplied her with coal last winter and she steadily complains that she has not enough to keep her. But I think if the money was sent to some careful person in town that it would go much further and it would be much better for her than the way she is handling it now.[65]

Occasionally a neighbour would come to the aid of a single mother, and in one unique case, a group of ratepayers for the Township of Bayham, Elgin County, signed a petition requesting the local board to 'reconsider the case of

Susan Rodette who at one time received aid through the Allowance fund but was refused any more aid. This is a case that should be given some help.'[66]

From the evidence presented, it is clear that a variety of social leaders aided the administration of the Mothers' Allowance Act by policing and/or supporting the applicant. In doing so, many people were indirectly involved in the intrusive regulation of single mothers' lives.

CONCLUSION

The first decade of OMA administration reveals the complex blend of private and public welfare values. The provincial state entered new territory with the enactment of OMA. This policy showed the state's willingness to provide a fixed sum of money on a monthly basis to needy single mothers. But strict eligibility requirements and minimal payments ensured that only the most needy would receive the allowance; consequently, the policy would limit the amount of dependency on the state.

The OMA's administrative infrastructure also illustrates a combination of public and private welfare. The provincial commission, the highest decision-making body for the policy, consisted of paid state workers, most of whom had no public welfare experience or social work training but instead had long associations with charitable activities. Memberships on the local boards in each county or district were unpaid positions and tended to be held by the political, economic, and social élite, many of whom had extensive private welfare experience. The investigators were paid by the state to visit the homes of OMA applicants and report to the local boards and the provincial commission. Although they were state workers, the vast majority of these investigators also had no social work training. Finally, community members both volunteered and were requested by the state to play an active role in the administration of OMA. These people, not paid by or directly accountable to the state, both aided and scrutinized the lives of single mothers. Consequently, the OMA administrative structure established during the first decade of the policy was indeed a hybrid of public and private welfare values.

Chapter 3

'A Fit and Proper Person':
The Everyday Administration of Ontario Mothers' Allowance

The bureaucratic structure, addressed in Chapter 2, merely established the building-blocks for the everyday administration of the Ontario Mothers' Allowance policy. Once the benefit levels and eligibility criteria were established and the administrators appointed, the daily determination of worthiness could begin. Each single mother was carefully investigated to establish her deservedness for the allowance. During the first decade this investigation was thorough indeed. This chapter demonstrates that OMA administrators and others who volunteered to 'help' closely supervised at least seven distinct aspects of daily life: finances, sexuality, cleanliness, attitude, race and ethnicity, incapacitation, and behaviour of children. These investigations were not limited to financial questions. As the OMA Act stated, a recipient had to be 'a fit and proper person'.[1] This broad definition required a needy mother to prove herself continuously to be morally worthy of the allowance. This *moral regulation* of recipients' lives predominated OMA administration during this period.

FINANCIAL REGULATION

There were clear economic needs that the enactment of OMA helped to solve. Following the First World War, the concern about the growing number of unemployed soldiers led to social unrest, culminating in the Winnipeg General Strike in the spring of 1919. Women were encouraged to take on paid work during the war, but after the war government and labour representatives attempted to persuade women to leave the workforce, leaving these jobs open for the men. Public inquiries claimed that institutions to care for children were both mismanaged and expensive to operate. OMA provided a neat solution to these problems. It could persuade women to leave full-time paid work to the men, thus reducing the unemployment problem. By encouraging women to focus on domestic work, it helped to ensure the continuance of healthy male workers and healthy future workers. At the same time, it encouraged OMA recipients to do only part-time work. Consequently, OMA helped to establish a healthy, stable, and cheap labour force that was essentially male, while it simultaneously encouraged women into an economic, social, and sexually dependent relationship within the home.

Given these economic interests, it is logical that OMA administration would include a careful examination of the financial circumstances of the home. To qualify for the allowance, the investigator or local board would carefully scrutinize the father's will (if he was dead); the financial circumstances of the mother's parents; the amount of money being earned by the children; and any other potential financial aid the mother might receive. All other avenues of financial support had to be exhausted before a mother was considered eligible for OMA. In the case of Margaret Wyler, she was initially refused the allowance partly because she lived with her parents, who owned property valued at approximately $3,650. After protesting that her parents had no disposable income and were already supporting other children, she was eventually granted the allowance.[2]

A mother's personal income and assets were also carefully examined, as detailed earlier in the Introduction. How much equity and assets an applicant had was a great concern. Initially, those applicants with more than $2,500 of home equity and $350 in liquid assets were generally considered ineligible. (Liquid assets were increased to $500 by the end of the decade.) But there was a fear that these financial criteria would penalize the thrifty and reward the indolent. As a result, a financial arrangement was developed by the end of the decade to ensure that mothers with liquid assets above the acceptable limit could still be eligible. The state would confiscate these assets and have this money paid regularly in small amounts to the family. This payment would be similar to a small but steady income, making the family financially eligible for the allowance.[3] A scheme established from the beginning for those with extra cash was for recipients to buy a home if they were living in a rented house.[4] For the most part, OMA administrators discouraged other living arrangements as less morally satisfactory than a mother and children alone in a home.

Once the mother qualified on these financial grounds, an investigation of the home was conducted. Often these visitors would record that the dwelling had 'no car, no radio, no liquor permit', thus assuring OMA that the family did not spend money on luxury items or engage in immoral activities. In some cases, the applicant's bank book would be carefully scrutinized for every deposit and withdrawal along with every bill sent to the home. Investigators would advise mothers on how they should spend their money. In Ann Ruller's case, her allowance was revoked because 'it was felt that her money should have been spent on repairs for her own home and not for a married daughter.'[5] Many mothers who were not considered financially responsible had their OMA cheques paid to another person who endorsed every cheque and had complete control over everything the family spent. This financial overseer was often an OMA administrator or a leader in the community.

This financial regulation increased during the first decade. Initially the average monthly OMA payments were more than $43, but they dropped steadily to $35 by the end of the 1920s. The administration's increasing experience in financial investigation at least partially accounts for this 18 per cent drop in the average size of monthly allowances.[6] There are several examples of mothers going further in debt because the OMA was so minimal. For example, Rita Annie owed approximately $188.50 when she was granted the allowance in 1922. During this decade she struggled to reduce the debt, but fell further and further behind in her rent payments, and by 1935 when her allowance was cancelled (because there were no children under sixteen) she owed nearly $500.[7]

Since the payment was well below subsistence, it was essential that these mothers supplement their allowance with paid work. There was an inherent contradiction in this policy regarding mothers and work. The majority of OMA lobbyists, steeped in maternalist values, had favoured a policy that would not require mothers to work outside the home. In contrast, the OMA annual reports during this decade clearly stated that the allowance was insufficient on its own and would require mothers to conduct some part-time paid work:

> ... with careful management on her [the mother's] part and by doing a little work to supplement the allowance, she is able to keep herself and family comfortable in every respect. Were the allowance made to cover the full maintenance it would create wastefulness and probably laziness.[8]

Full-time work was vehemently discouraged by the commission; part-time work was advised but carefully monitored. In some cases, the investigator would go with the mother to the prospective employer's office to ensure that the type and hours of work were suitable for a single mother. As a result, OMA recipients tended to be involved in low-paying, female-ghetto jobs. It was clear that their first job was to be in the home and that financial security would come only with remarriage. As a result, this policy encouraged a

Table 3.1 Occupations of Ontario Mothers' Allowance Beneficiaries

Type of Work	1920–1 Number of Beneficiaries	1922–3 Number of Beneficiaries
No employment	1,576	1,730
Charwork	932	924
Keeping boarders or roomers (no other employment)	306	450
Sewing, knitting, etc.	248	249
Factory work	184	182
Farm work, fruit picking, etc.	107	135
Clerk	104	102
Business	60	65
Nursing	33	26
Profession	9	7
Total	**3,559**	**3,870**

Note: This occupational breakdown is not available for any other year during the first decade.
Source: 'Annual Reports of the OMA Commission, 1920–21 and 1922–23'.

maternal ideal that met Anglo–Saxon middle–class standards rather than the long–term interests of its recipients. Women were persuaded to undertake part–time paid work and unpaid domestic work, neither of which would lead to economic security. Investigators advised mothers on just what type of work they could do to earn money and still receive their allowance. Part–time work in the home that utilized the mother's 'natural' domestic skills was the preferred option. During this decade approximately 60 per cent of OMA recipients were involved in some type of part–time work. In one district, the OMA recipients did the following part–time work within the home:

> Plasticine work; women's wool hats; Christmas tree decorations; carding buttons; making artificial flowers; reed work; hair dressing; clipping wool for factory; brush making; plain sewing; ice cream and home-baking; sewing slipper soles; sewing canvas shoes; dressmaking; millinery; keeping roomers and boarders; shirt finishing and making flower buttonholes[9] (see Table 3.1).

In another case, a mother was advised to give up her professional job outside the home and instead:

> . . . take an infant to board so as to supplement her allowance. Her steady income, and small earnings without leaving her home, so encouraged the beneficiary that she became ambitious and an arrangement was made for her to handle a line of children's wear. One of her upstairs rooms was fitted up, cards were sent out and the little business launched.[10]

Rural mothers with few employment options were encouraged to be self-sufficient. These women were persuaded to live off the produce of their gardens, cows, and hens. In one case a mother with four children received $25 as a monthly allowance and another $25 per month from the sale of butter and eggs. The annual report stated: 'She raises just enough crop to feed her cattle, keeps forty hens and four cows and does everything on the farm alone, with only occasional hired help on the land during the summer season.'[11] Another rural mother helped cut hay and wood at the farm that she and her brother lived on. Yet another planted 500 strawberry plants and another sold $40 worth of bulbs and perennial roots.[12]

Annual reports boasted about how transitions from paid work outside the home to domestic work in the family dwelling turned shabby houses into comfortable, loving homes.

> All because the mothers have at their disposal time and strength formerly spent in the struggle to keep the family warmed and fed. They have time to buy economically; to sew where before they had to buy ready-to-wear articles; time to cook wholesome dishes instead of using canned goods. One mother said, 'I can save almost as much as I used to earn because while I was at work the children wasted good food and burned more gas than I did.'[13]

Many 'success' stories were recounted in the annual reports of homes that were repapered; that had fresh curtains, new cherry trees, and happy, neat, and well-cared-for children—all as a result of the mother working at home. In short, OMA administrators promoted domestic skills to the recipients, work that would not provide economic independence in the long term. While the annual reports speak of 'success' stories, the case files give a different view of events. Often mothers were further impoverished as a result of leaving full-time work. These employment choices prescribed by the OMA administration were almost always the most exploitative and the least remunerative. For example, Elizabeth Walsh, who had an incapacitated husband and several children, was advised by the commission to quit her $30-a-month job outside the home and instead send her 'mildly retarded' daughter Lulu out to work. Lulu was only able to earn $10 a month as a domestic, most of which paid her transportation and clothing expenses. As a result, the family was further impoverished by the OMA advice.[14]

The paid work of children was also considered when determining the appropriate allowance. This policy, along with other child welfare policies of the era, symbolized a new relationship between the state and children. In contrast to the nineteenth century, young children were no longer considered productive members of society. Instead, young children were recognized for their productive potential, a potential that required 'proper' nurturance and guidance in order to create industrious, moral adults. Through OMA administration, the state guided a young child's education, both at school and in the home, but encouraged a working-age child to accept his or her workforce responsibilities. Legally, children were not allowed to leave school until the age of sixteen and OMA administrators actively discouraged young children from participation in paid work. Older children, on the other hand, were encouraged to find extra work to supplement the allowance. There was a concern that OMA would encourage pauperism or dependency and 'weaken the family's own energy and self-reliance'. In an effort to curtail this potential problem, OMA recipients with older children were deducted money not on the basis of the actual earnings of these older children but what was expected of them.[15] This anticipated income from older children was deducted from a mother's OMA cheque regardless of whether or not the mother received this money. Once a child was sixteen, the OMA investigator would advise him or her on what types of jobs or apprenticeship training would be appropriate. Those older children who found suitable work were praised in the annual reports: 'This boy has earned every cent that has been spent on his education and also his clothes since he was twelve years of age, by raising rabbits, white mice, pigeons, which he sells to different laboratories for research work, and during holidays works at anything at which he can earn.'[16] These regulations made it virtually impossible for a child over sixteen to continue his or her education.

This evidence demonstrates that OMA administration encouraged needy mothers and their older children to become part of the exploited, low-paid workforce. Children with little advanced education had few opportunities to find good-paying jobs in a skilled trade or a clerical position. Mothers were encouraged to take jobs that enhanced their domestic skills; these jobs were in keeping with maternalist ideology, but did not promote long-term economic independence. Through the financial regulation of OMA recipients, the state helped to reinforce the male breadwinner model. With the male breadwinner absent, the state encouraged long-term economic dependence for his wife and children. Options for economic independence were actively discouraged.

Sexual and Social Regulation

Although certain financial criteria had to be met, the OMA administrators spent most of their time on moral issues. Sometimes financial and moral concerns overlapped, as in the case of male boarders, but there were many other aspects of OMA administration that more clearly focused on moral considerations. According to the OMA Act, a mother had to demonstrate that she was 'a fit and proper person' to receive the benefit. This broad criterion consumed the days and nights of OMA administrators and permitted the *moral regulation* of recipients. The administrators guided, 'rehabilitated', and scrutinized the moral behaviour of OMA recipients. They were encouraged to conduct extremely thorough investigations to ascertain the recipient's continued worthiness. In some questionable cases, investigators visited daily to advise on everything from bedding to school attendance. The number of cases rejected because the mother did not meet the criteria of being

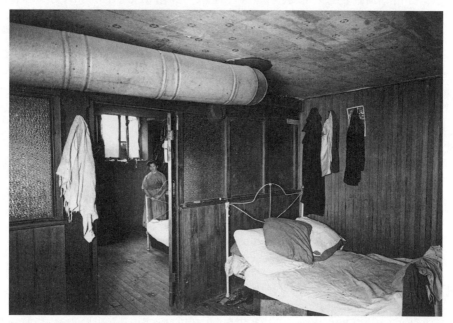

Mothers' allowance administrators were particularly concerned about the sleeping arrangements of the poor (*City of Toronto Archives DPW 32–325*).

'a fit and proper person' or because she 'refused to cooperate' were carefully noted annually.

Widows were the first eligible group and the predominant recipients, accounting for more than 75 per cent of OMA cases for this decade (see Table 3.2).[17] The administrators generally viewed these women quite favourably, provided the women did not socialize frequently, or have male callers or a male boarder. In short, these women were supposed to devote all their time and attention to their children and to never show another interest in a man as long as they received the OMA cheque. Just as their husbands had financially supported them in return for sexual monogamy, the state struck a similar bargain.

The investigators and public officials were extremely concerned about living husbands. Women deserted by their husbands were the second group made eligible by the act, but were carefully regulated. Desertion was often considered the 'poor man's divorce'. Divorce was middle class by its very nature, a costly and time-consuming means to settle questions of property and inheritance. Men without financial means or assets often deserted an unsatisfactory marriage.[18] Administrators were quite disconcerted about the growing number of desertion applications. Because of the stringent regulations, very few of the deserted applicants actually received the allowance. During the first decade less than 7 per cent of all OMA recipients were deserted mothers (see Table 3.2). Originally the mother had to swear that she had not seen or heard from her husband in seven years. The officials were very rigid about this length of separation, as in the case of Fanny Burlack. Fanny had been deserted for five years by 1921 and was in the hospital, extremely ill. She was concerned about how she would look

Table 3.2 Reasons for Granting Ontario Mothers' Allowance, 1922–1930

	Number of Families (Percentage of total OMA cases)				
Year	Death of Father	Incapacitation	Desertion	Foster	Total
1922–3	3,255 (84%)	398 (10%)	125 (3%)	92 (2%)	3,870
1923–4	3,339 (82%)	475 (12%)	138 (3.4%)	106 (2.6%)	4,058
1924–5	3,389 (81%)	513 (12%)	170 (4%)	113 (2.7%)	4,185
1925–6	4,082 (78.3%)	723 (13.9%)	256 (5%)	154 (3%)	5,215
1926–7	4,209 (76%)	843 (15%)	307 (5.5%)	181 (3.3%)	5,540
1927–8	4,340 (72.6%)	1,044 (17.5%)	351 (5.9%)	241 (4%)	5,976
1928–9	4,503 (70%)	1,243 (19.4%)	407 (6.3%)	258 (4%)	6,411
1929–30	4,507 (67%)	1,485 (22%)	452 (6.7%)	268 (4%)	6,712

Source: 'Annual Reports of the OMA Commissions, 1922–29'.

after her two little girls. If she received OMA, she could pay someone else to look after them until she got well. As the chairman of the local board explained, 'This woman is in great need as she has recently been in the hospital and has great difficulty in getting along as she is unable to work steadily even if she could get work.'[19] But the OMA commission refused her because at that time, a seven-year desertion period was required. One local board was moved by the plight of these deserted women and wrote to the provincial commission stating 'that the period of 7 years for deserted wives be reduced, as this period is too long to neglect the children'.[20] By the end of 1921 the government further amended the act to include women who had been deserted for five years. Despite this amendment, this time restriction was one of the most common reasons for the commission's rejection of applicants (see Table 3.3).

If the time restriction was not a barrier, other stipulations made it difficult for deserted mothers to be eligible. The legal procedure for declaring oneself a deserted mother was difficult and costly. Once the husband left, a warrant had to be sworn out for his arrest. For Mothers' Allowance Act purposes, the mother was asked to sign a declaration stating that she had not seen or heard from her husband since his departure. Any neighbours, friends, or employers who had spoken to the husband just prior to his departure and who might have valuable information also signed a declaration regarding any knowledge they had. The police would then attempt to search for the missing husband. If found, he was taken into custody and the legal system would attempt to make him pay child support. The majority of these deserting men went to the United States, but if located, there were no public funds available to help return them to the province: 'If the deserted wife asks to have her husband returned to Ontario where he can be brought to court, all expenses in connection therewith must be borne by her, who is in need herself, and has no money to spare for this purpose.'[21] And even if these men were found and returned home with a court order secured to grant the mother a weekly or monthly payment of the man's earnings, these payments were seldom made and the man often disappeared before another legal procedure could begin. Consequently, most mothers did not persist in this search. They would give up as a result of the public humiliation they had to face, or because they could not afford the legal fees to prosecute the husband, or because the husband, if found, may resist paying child support.

These restrictions made it extremely difficult for a deserted mother to be eligible for the allowance. As well as the administrative restrictions, there is strong evidence to suggest that the sexual and moral behaviour of deserted mothers was more carefully scrutinized than that of widowed mothers. There is an underlying assumption that the mother was somehow to blame for her husband's disappearance, regardless of the circumstances.

While deserted mothers received closer scrutiny than widowed recipients, OMA administrators kept a keen eye on all needy mothers. Beyond sexual status, these administrators were concerned about all social behaviour, which in

Table 3.3 Reasons for Ineligibility, 1920–1930

Reasons	1920–1	1921–2	1922–3	1923–4	1924–5	1925–6	1926–7	1927–8	1928–9	1929–30
Assets	242	110	94	—	78	105	89	134	103	59
One child under sixteen	101	153	38	51	28	36	45	43	33	9
Not incapacitated	75	82	71	66	59	69	70	52	40	54
Not deserted	41	58	34	35	44	54	42	48	38	26
Residence	37	29	33	23	36	26	28	40	22	12
Immoral mother	25	25	13	32	24	33	21	22	22	6
Sufficient income	100	57	67	153	65	33	41	22	34	23
Other children's earnings	78	63	28	10	—	—	—	—	—	—
Not British subject	9	7	6	5	6	10	9	8	4	5
Divorced or separated	11	3	8	4	6	4	4	8	1	1
Prison	9	8	3	2	3	1	5	4	5	2
Unwed	6	—	—	—	—	—	—	3	1	1
No proof of marriage	3	15	10	—	4	4	1	2	—	1
Remarried	—	13	1	4	2	2	2	2	—	—
Workmen's compensation	70	17	4	7	5	3	2	—	—	—
Other	121	161	91	67	40	32	35	193	72	40
Total	**928**	**801**	**501**	**459**	**400**	**412**	**394**	**581**	**375**	**239**

Notes: Residence = disqualified by residence
Not incapacitated = husband or children not totally incapacitated
Not deserted = presumption of death not established
Immoral mother = not fit and proper person; unsatisfactory home conditions
Source: 'Annual Reports of the OMA Commission, 1920–21 to 1929–30'.

their minds might lead to sex. Investigators and local board members were always on the look-out for potential boyfriends of OMA recipients. They would make surprise visits to the home, especially in the evenings, to catch the visitor. They interrogated the mother, her parents, her friends, her neighbours, and public officials, asking them to comment on the number and type of visitors to the home, the number of times the mother socialized outside the home and with whom, and the type of clothing the mother bought and wore. They wrote to the suspected visitor, advising him to keep away from the home. This scrutiny of social behaviour illustrates the contradictory position that both the policy and the administrators held regarding marriage. Marriage was one of the prescribed ideal goals of the policy, and the administrators wrote glowingly of many cases in which the mother remarried, thus taking the responsibility for her out of the hands of the state:

> The number of beneficiaries who have remarried is gratifying; this return to the normal home where the man is the wage-earner and the mother the home-maker constituting the best solution of the problem of the support and care of these dependent children.[22]

At the same time, these administrators prevented much of the social interaction with men that might have led these women towards the chapel.

Male boarders were also carefully scrutinized. The policy on taking boarders was contradictory at best. Administrators encouraged boarders insofar as boarding brought money into the home and did not require the mother to leave the children, but having a male boarder was positively disallowed and one's allowance was quickly cancelled in such cases. Melva Turmin, who ran away with a boarder, convinced the regulators that they had every reason to fear male boarders. No one would have denied that Melva Turmin had a difficult life in caring for her two children and an ailing husband, who was almost twenty years her senior and in a sanatorium. However, as her neighbour explained to the local board:

> ... Mrs. Turmin had no possible excuse for taking in a boarder, let alone running away with him, knowing him to be a married man who had deserted his wife and two small children in the Old Country, and I consider it a direct slap in the face to those friends who provided so liberally for her and family, and to the citizens in general, by her misconduct. . . . Personally, I don't think this class of people ought to be a burden on the citizens, but should be deported.[23]

Regardless of the presence or absence of boarders in the home, bedding and sleeping arrangements were of particular concern to investigators. Often the investigators commented with horror on sleeping accommodations that were no more 'than an old mattress in the corner of the room'

Opposite: Mothers' allowance administrators often described living conditions in the home before and after the allowance was granted (*City of Toronto Archives DPW 32–247*).

or bedding that 'was simply a bundle of rags'.[24] These OMA administrators took great pains to instruct a recipient on better sleeping arrangements and bedding. Clearly, the lack of bedroom furniture and the use of second-hand bedding were associated with disease and immorality.

It was clear to the regulators that boarders and male visitors could lead to several major social problems: venereal disease, illegitimate children, and prostitution. Each of these social problems was carefully scrutinized by the investigators, the local board members, and the neighbours. For instance, Velma Austin was a constant concern for her investigator. Velma not only had a man hanging around but she had also contracted venereal disease (VD). Normally, having a male caller was grounds in itself for cancellation of OMA, but it is interesting in this case that the cheques continued for the purpose of controlling Velma's VD. According to the city clerk, '[The Investigator] says she [Velma] is saucy and impudent: doubtful whether she should be getting the allowance at all, but it is the only way they can insist on her taking the treatments.'[25] In an effort to check Velma's VD, the investigator received the monthly cheques on Velma's behalf. In this way, the investigator could grant Velma the money only after she had visited the clinic. Thus, the mothers' allowance cheque served as a bribe for mandatory VD treatment.

The case files and annual reports reveal that OMA administrators scrupulously observed the sexual and social habits of applicants. Careful monitoring of everything from bedding to VD tests suggests that these administrators, much like their philanthropic sisters before them, believed that sexual desire should be contained within heterosexual marriage.

CLEANLINESS

In her book, *The Age of Light, Soap, and Water*, Mariana Valverde mentions that the Canadian social purity movement associated morality with cleanliness. Valverde suggests that maternal feminists used house-cleaning metaphors to legitimize their entry into the public, so-called 'political' sphere. During the first decade of the policy cleanliness was one of the most important attributes for OMA recipients. According to one administrator, new-found cleanliness was the first sign that a family was receiving the allowance.[26] The administrators generally mentioned that a deserving mother tried to keep a house tidy and the children clean, even though she had difficulty in making ends meet. And likewise, they almost never failed to note the dirty condition of the house in a case they refused.

Investigators were often insensitive to a mother's difficulties when they regulated cleanliness. For example, the investigator chastised Elizabeth McIntyre about her untidy house. This mother was attempting to raise six children in a four-room shack with no indoor plumbing. In order to make ends meet, she 'worked out' whenever possible, yet the investigator complained:

> Place was fearfully untidy when I called and Benef. said she was away working. I told her that there was no excuse and made her sweep while I was

there and in 15 minutes she had it looking different. She . . . [is] slack and will always be.[27]

Uncleanness was often associated with laziness. For instance, the Relief Department inspector wrote a full-page report to the local board solely on the question of cleanliness.

> I visited this home and found it in a most unsanitary condition. . . . I went into the shack, and the odour was such that the place was not healthful. . . . The place was most untidy, and looked as though the woman was a very poor manager, and certainly required some lessons on cleanliness. . . . On the table was some bread and unwashed dishes. The house consists of one living room and one bedroom. There were two beds in the room which were not made up, and the clothing was in need of attention. I consider that there was no excuse for the place being in the condition it was. I called the woman's attention to the odour, and asked her to put the place in as decent a shape as possible. She stated that she was not strong and had a young baby, and did the best she could under the circumstances.[28]

Although the mother was quite sick, the investigator showed little sympathy and assumed that the home was untidy because the mother was too lazy rather than too ill.

Occasionally a person's cleaning ability could work in her favour. A juvenile court judge recommended one woman who was raising an illegitimate child by stating that 'She quite sincerely intends to lead a clean and decent life.'[29] Another woman whose house 'was not very cleanly kept' was improving and 'promised further improvement still'.[30] And an OMA administrator was thrilled to see the progress in one home:

> It was 5:30 p.m. when I called and when met at the door by the mother I had to look closely to recognize her. She was dressed in a *clean*, neatly worn dress, her hair nicely arranged and, best of all, a look of hope and contentment on her face. She asked me to come into the kitchen which was used as a living room, and here the evening meal was ready, with a *clean white* cloth, a warm bright fire and the children sitting around a simple but wholesome meal [my emphasis].[31]

Clean, neat, white, and wholesome were all values associated with innocence and redemption in Protestantism, the dominant religion of the era. The final line of a letter from the city clerk to the Relief Department inspector sums up the values of the era: 'Yours for a better and cleaner city.'[32]

A THRIFTY, HUMBLE ATTITUDE

Moral regulation during this era included the examination and comment on the mother's attitude. Similar to nineteenth-century philosophy of welfare, an OMA recipient was to demonstrate both a thrifty and a humble attitude to be considered worthy. Mothers who did not seem thankful were commented upon, as in Elizabeth Carpenter's case. Her file stated:

> Mrs. C immediately greet[ed] the worker with a long list of her needs and felt the assistance from the Welfare Dept. was very inadequate and complained at length. . . . John [her son] talked a good deal about the family need and was rather demanding in his attitude. Albert [another son] is still at school but already shows evidence of the begging tendency his mother and older brother have. . . .

As a result, the local board decided to approve her case, but have the cheques administered through the Salvation Army. The provincial commission also agreed, but decided to grant the cheque only on a three-month trial basis to establish whether Elizabeth Carpenter 'has proven herself to be a fit and proper person' during that time.[33]

Any resistance on the mother's part to divulge all the details of her life was not tolerated by the investigators. If a woman refused to tell her age, the details of her husband's disappearance, the amount of debt she owed, or the number of visitors she had to her home, this could be grounds for rejecting the mother as an 'unworthy' character. In Mary McLean's case, the investigator said:

> I have found her very abusive in her manner when questioned in regard to any of her affairs and she has been reported to me as living under rather doubtful conditions. She was at one time helped by the Catholic people and now claims that she is a Protestant. I would not think that this woman would be a right person for the Mothers' Allowance.

After much deliberation, the local board decided to grant the allowance despite 'her temperament' because it might 'help the woman to live straight'.[34]

Another mother was initially rejected because of her son-in-law's attitude and actions. As the city clerk explained:

> [The mother's] son-in-law bought the liquor permit and gave it to her. She had some trouble with her daughter-in-law who told her that if the Board knew about the permit the allowance would be cut off, and she immediately destroyed the permit. She had done this before she got the letter from Toronto advising her of the cancellation of the allowance. . . . [Now] there is no liquor permit in the house.[35]

On the local board's strong recommendation, the mother was reinstated because she had quickly gained control of a potentially immoral situation in her home.

The regulators were sympathetic if a mother demonstrated that she had been economically self-sufficient in the past and had proudly refused any external help. In fact, the investigator would write on several application forms: 'This family has no money and has never received assistance from the public.'

If a mother was neither thrifty nor humble, the best possible option would be to repent before the investigator. Repentance could take the form of the mother attending the local church, refusing to associate with 'questionable' friends, or proclaiming that she was a 'reformed woman'. In Maud Reinhart's case, the mother 'has been in [to see the investigator] and states that she is reforming; she wants Mothers' Allowance. [A local board member] is satisfied and [the City Relief Department officer] is trying to get work for her.'[36] In this case, because the mother repented, the local board agreed to reconsider her case and attempt to find employment for her. Upon repentance of a previously bad attitude, a mother might be given another chance, but with conditions. All of these mothers would be subjected to increased surveillance of their activities to ensure that their lives had indeed changed. And those who met the attitude tests might be granted an allowance on a one- to three-month trial basis, and the mother would continually have to prove that her previous attitude had been transformed.

The importance of a grateful, humble attitude is in keeping with traditional philanthropic notions of the deserving poor. At the turn of the century, it was essential for the impoverished to prove their gratitude, humility, and desire to reform in order to receive the discretionary local charity.

RACE AND ETHNICITY

Ethnocentrism and racism flourished in the postwar era and the OMA policy reflected this. During the 1920s there was a great concern that ethnic-minority immigrants were destroying Canada's Anglo-Saxon character. The

Table 3.4 National Origins of Ontario Mothers' Allowance Recipients, 1920–1930

Year	Canadian	British	Foreign-Born
1920–1	70%	25%	5%
1921–2	41%	23%	6%
1922–3	69%	24%	7%
1923–4	69%	24%	7%
1924–5	67%	25%	8%
1925–6	66%	26%	8%
1926–7	65%	26%	9%
1927–8	64.5%	27%	8.5%
1928–9	64.5%	27%	8.5%
1929–30	63.5%	27.5%	9%

Notes: British (highest percentage to lowest) = English, Scotch, Irish, and Welsh. Foreign–Born (highest percentage to lowest) = American, Russian, Italian, Polish, Finnish, German, Swedish, Austrian, Galician, Norwegian, Roumanian, Hungarian, Armenian, French, Ukrainian, Czecho–Slovakian, Jugo–Slavian, Syrian, Danish, Serbian, Dutch, Greek, Spanish, Bulgarian, Lithuanian, Swiss, Turkish, Belgian, and Serbian.
Source: 'Annual Reports of the OMA Commission, 1920–21 to 1929–30'.

Canadian immigration policy during the early 1920s discouraged the entry of Europeans and restricted those who were admitted to dangerous and low-paid jobs. The immigration law also allowed for the deportation of recent immigrants who were unemployed and dependent upon hand-outs during their first three years in the country. Yet despite these government policy restrictions, ethnic-minority immigration climbed during the 1920s and British immigration dropped dramatically, altering the racial mix of both the country and the province.[37]

The policy and the everyday administration of OMA reflected these racial concerns. During the 1920s only British subjects and naturalized citizens were eligible to receive the benefit. The OMA policy kept a close tabulation of both naturalized citizens and the racial origin of recipients. During the decade ethnic-minority recipients never exceeded more than 9 per cent of the entire OMA case-load (see Table 3.4).[38] All mothers' allowance applicants were required to submit birth, marriage, and death certificates, which were often difficult (if not impossible) for those born outside of the country to obtain. These regulations were not relaxed until 1953, thereby guaranteeing, through a bureaucratic mechanism, the financial support of Anglo-Saxon children while excluding other racial groups.

Aboriginal women were eligible to apply for an allowance regardless of where they lived in the province, provided they had the necessary birth, marriage, and death certificates. On the reserves the Indian agent, accompanied by a local board, administered the policy. Generally, these local boards included the chief of the particular band, but were dominated by White religious leaders. Both status and non-status Indians were eligible for the allowance. Because status Indians were wards of the federal government, the cost of their allowances was jointly shared by the federal and provincial governments.

For a variety of reasons there were very few status or non-status Indian women who received the allowance.[39] Some of these difficulties are illustrated in the case of Ena Melaney. A Chippewa Indian from the Muncey Indian reserve outside the City of London, she applied for an allowance for herself and her two children following the death of her husband. First, she was denied the allowance because she lacked the necessary documentation. A second reason for refusing Ena Melaney her allowance was because she moved from the reserve to the City of London so that her son could continue to live with her while he attended the local technical school and she could receive hospital treatment. But the local board refused her on the grounds that she was 'an indigent coming to the City. . . . [She] is not entitled to residence, [and] in any event, she could live cheaper in Muncey and should be forthwith sent back to Muncey.' Considerable correspondence between the local board and the provincial commission followed, with the latter insisting that the local board could not refuse anyone on the basis of the place of residence if the person came from elsewhere *within* the province.[40]

There was also little sensitivity to the absolute destitution faced by many immigrant families who had no relations and few charity organizations willing to financially support them. Ethnic-minority women could be disqualified because they could not read or write English.[41] There was also very little tolerance for the customs to which many of these families adhered. Investigators complained of 'wine parties', of certain families not following Protestant Euro-Canadian working standards, of the mobility of Aboriginal families when they worked in town during the summer and returned to the reserve in winter. The case files also clearly suggest that families from ethnic-minority backgrounds underwent more intense investigation than did their Protestant Euro-Canadian counterparts. Also, neighbours were more likely to spy on and complain about minority families. For instance, Maria Morello lost her allowance because of her dead husband's former employee. The investigator explained:

> This gentleman, if such he may be called, was displeased at losing his job and this appears to be his motive for causing the widow to lose her allowance. I interviewed him and he persisted in saying that she was rich, but could not give me any evidence to corroborate his statement.[42]

The level of distrust for immigrants and ethnic minorities is perhaps not entirely surprising, given that this policy emerged following the First World War when there was a strong nationalist, eugenics ideology and a concern for the need to increase the Anglo-Saxon population.

Although many minority families experienced ethnocentrism and racism in the policy's implementation, it appears that Black, Aboriginal, and eastern European families suffered the most. Almost every Black mother who applied had the experience of neighbours attempting to besmirch her reputation. The investigators themselves used negative adjectives to describe Black families' behaviour—behaviour that was commended when noted in White families. For instance, Eliza Jones was considered suspicious because the Relief Department inspector had noted that her husband was a community activist 'in favor of uplifting the colored people'. The inspector concluded, 'I have known these people for a long time and they are quite aggressive and able to look after their own affairs.'[43] One wonders if the Joneses were considered 'aggressive', a term never applied to Protestant Euro-Canadian families, because they believed in supporting other Blacks. One mother, Mary Boxley, at least was reconsidered when the Canadian League for the Advancement of Colored People defended her reputation.[44]

Both Black and Aboriginal mothers often lacked the necessary certificates to qualify for the allowance. There were rare exceptions when the OMA administrators overlooked this regulation and granted an allowance. Such was the case for Mary Star, whose husband had died of cancer and left her with no income to raise her two children. She was granted the minimum allowance after much concern about the lack of records: 'The marriage certificate has not been seen but the church record at Muncey parsonage was seen . . . [and] there were not any records kept of Native Births until a few years ago.'[45]

White applicants who associated with ethnic minorities were also under suspicion. For instance, Edna rented half of her house to two boarders, an eighty-year-old man and his son. While this was completely acceptable according to the OMA regulations, Edna's boarders were carefully investigated because they were Black. The local OMA board asked the city alderman to report on the elder boarder (his character, if he was a respectable citizen, if he kept a disorderly house, if he could be considered a person that an OMA recipient could reside with). This alderman was surprised to find that he was impressed with this boarder. In fact, the alderman reported that this boarder was 'above the average colored man' and even seemed to be 'a white man in character'. As well, the Canadian Legion of the British Empire Service League wrote to the local board swearing that this man's character was beyond reproach. Despite these glowing references, Edna was advised to abandon her boarders in order to receive the allowance.[46]

Finally, there is one ethnic group that was singled out for praise. According to the local board, Annie McLaren's family warranted the allowance because:

> They are very worthy, reticent, Scotch people and I know Mrs. McLaren often goes without a meal in order that the children may have something. If there is any possibility of hurrying this allowance through, we would be most grateful to have it so done. . . .[47]

According to the case files, no one ever mentioned how worthy, reticent, or self-sacrificing the ethnic-minority families were.

The administration of OMA during the first decade clearly illustrates that this was, for the most part, an allowance for Protestant Euro-Canadian needy mothers. As a rule, ethnic-minority women were not recipients of the allowance and those who were received intense scrutiny. No statistics are available to determine the number of ethnic-minority women whose applications were refused or the number who were discouraged from applying. The low number of needy ethnic-minority women who received the allowance suggests that the majority had to look elsewhere for help. It is assumed that some of them received aid from their extended families or ethnic community organizations.[48] Others were forced to work at dead-end exploitative jobs to raise their children, and still others had to give up their children for adoption. Suffice it to say that most ethnic-minority women could not expect the state to help them when they were in need.

INCAPACITATION

Not only were mothers' lives under considerable scrutiny, so were those of other family members. For instance, a mother with two children could receive OMA if a reputable doctor signed an administrative form stating that her husband was 'totally and permanently incapacitated'. In 1921 two amendments to the incapacitation clause were made to grant an allowance to mothers who had one child under sixteen and an incapacitated husband,

and mothers with a child over sixteen who was permanently incapacitated.[49] The allowance was not given to women whose husbands were incapacitated prior to their marriage or whose husbands had any partial disability. Often men who had severe bouts of arthritis; who were crippled; who were unable to stand, walk, or exert any effort; or who were psychologically traumatized from the war were considered only partially disabled, which meant that their wives were ineligible for assistance. This is in contrast to the more generous Alberta mothers' allowance policy, which approved those who had an incapacitation that would likely continue for one year. Ontario, like Manitoba and Saskatchewan, required permanent incapacitation and believed that charities could look after those who were temporarily incapacitated.

Cases of tuberculosis were of particular concern to the OMA administration. It was one of the most common causes of death among OMA applicants.[50] Initially there was some discussion of whether TB could be considered a permanent disability since some patients did manage to recover, but the OMA administration decided to cover wives of tubercular fathers who were in a sanatorium for two reasons: (i) it would prevent their children from contracting the contagious disease, and (ii) if a death was averted, it would prevent long-term costs to the state if a woman was widowed.[51] As a result, the number of TB cases covered by OMA increased substantially during the 1920s, accounting for more than 13 per cent of the total budget for OMA during the decade.[52] Still, a number of TB patients died while awaiting OMA approval.

In some cases the mothers' allowance cheque allowed the father to regain his health after a bout of tuberculosis and return to full-time work. Annual reports would proudly recount these stories, complete with thank-you letters from the grateful wife:

> It has been possible in many cases to persuade men to enter a sanatorium because we can assure them that their family will be looked after. What a relief this is to a tubercular man, he can, having been relieved of the worry of his family's maintenance, co-operate with the sanatorium authorities and the result in scores of cases has been that he has recovered and is now again supporting his family.[53]

Despite this glowing account, there were other tubercular husbands who left the sanatorium prematurely because the allowance was never enough to live on, thereby cancelling the allowance and putting themselves and their families at risk.[54]

During the decade incapacitation cases tripled in number, climbing from 10 to 22 per cent of the total OMA case-load (see Table 3.2). As the number of incapacitation cases increased, so did the strict regulation of these applicants. For the second half of the decade, incapacitation cases were the second most common type that was refused, suggesting that these cases were vigilantly scrutinized (see Table 3.3).[55]

It is fascinating to note the distinction in the regulation of this policy depending on the gender of the recipient. The incapacitated father was subject to a medical investigation, but otherwise remained free from intervention. His moral behaviour, attitude, and cleanliness were not scrutinized by OMA administrators or community leaders. Once deemed worthy due to medical reasons, he was forever worthy. His wife, on the other hand, had to prove continuously that she was a 'fit and proper person'; one month she could be declared worthy, only to be found undeserving the next.

CHILDREN

Not only were mothers and fathers held under the prying eyes of the investigator, so were the children. The behaviour of these offspring—the very reason for the allowance in the first place—could be cause for discontinuance of the monthly cheque:

> The mother . . . is told her children must not keep bad company, must not be out late at night, in addition the children as they grow older know the income into their home depends largely on how they conduct themselves. . . . they are under this steadying influence all the time, and especially at that critical age of 14 to 16 when so many . . . make a wrong turn.[56]

It is clear from the case files that a mother was responsible for her children's behaviour as well as her own.

The children's schooling was a preoccupation of OMA administrators from the very beginning of the policy. Maternalist feminists at the turn of

Living conditions in rural Ontario were often difficult to monitor. These children lived in Uxbridge Township, 1922 (*National Archives PA181934, John J. Kelso Collection*).

the century had been quite concerned about child labour, illiteracy, and delinquency, and believed that the introduction of OMA would solve this problem. Both the OMA Act and the Adolescent School Attendance Act stated that all children under sixteen had to attend school. Truant officers were to ensure that children of OMA recipients were attending school. Exemptions to this rule could be secured if the family's financial circumstances were desperate, but these exemptions were strictly controlled. In the past, many local communities had not enforced the Adolescent School Attendance Act, but the annual OMA reports boasted that the allowance had greatly improved school attendance throughout the province:

> This aid gives the mothers an opportunity to educate their children, and make them fit members of society, with a fair chance of earning their own living, rather than having them run the streets and become later on a burden on the community. . . . [These children are now] being morally trained and cared for and will be a benefit to the community.

They hoped this moral training would encourage children to become 'loyal, patriotic citizens' and obedient future workers.[57] As a result, the allowance created a new method of regulating school attendance that complemented the work of truancy officers and teachers, and promoted literacy, industry, morality, loyalty, and patriotism.[58]

The role that OMA administration played in educating children in isolated northern communities was particularly noted:

> [There is a] decided improvement in the school attendance of not only the children of our beneficiaries but among other families since the passing of the Act. . . . The Mothers' Allowances Act has stimulated many of these [truant] officers by reminding them of what is expected of them. Many of the teachers in this district have marked the improvement in the work of our beneficiaries' children and that, through a spirit of emulation, this has had a beneficial effect throughout the school.[59]

As well, OMA administrators believed that school attendance prevented juvenile delinquency in these northern communities.[60]

Because the allowance was below subsistence level, there were attempts to escape this education requirement. Some mothers who received OMA falsified the ages of their children so the children could work full time rather than attend school. One mother who allowed her son to skip school stated that 'she did not believe in education' and subsequently had her allowance cancelled.[61] But as a rule, the provincial commission believed that the allowance persuaded children to remain in school.[62]

In 1927–8 school attendance records were submitted monthly before the mother received her allowance cheque.[63] These records would often include the student's marks, absences, number of times late, his or her attitude, and comments about the student's academic prospects for the future. The commission found this new system to be extremely effective. Betsy

Bowes's allowance was cancelled because one of her sons would not obey her and attend school regularly.[64] She was not the only mother whose allowance was cancelled because the school attendance card had not been sent to the commission office. The OMA administrators and even the police found this new card system very effective:

> School principals do not hesitate to express appreciation of the improved attendance of the children at school. The restraining influence of the monthly report on the children is quite marked. A chief of police of one city, for example, says he has little or no trouble with children of beneficiaries, if he meets with a tendency to misbehaviour, he has only to threaten to report to the Investigator, it has the desired effect.[65]

These cases suggest that the lives and behaviour of the children were closely scrutinized and affected their mother's eligibility for an allowance.

THE UNREGULATED AND THE INELIGIBLE

Finally, it is also important to examine what this policy did *not* regulate. Family violence was not an aspect of family life that was deemed to require regulation. Not only did the investigators ignore violence in the home, they were also prone to blame the mother for such problems, and indirectly contributed to this violence by refusing to grant an allowance to those mothers in desperate need. For fourteen years Vera Jackson had lived with a husband who had fits of uncontrollable rage in which he lashed out, both verbally and physically, at her and the children. Vera detailed her own experience in a letter to the local OMA board:

> My children have seen scenes since babyhood of absolute terror for them, and many times have been in real fear of my being killed by him [her husband] and his insane rages, which arose on the slightest provocation. . . . I have lived a life of misery and fear and suffering, and stayed with him when I thought I could not go on any longer and yet made myself continue for one reason and one alone—for the sake of my children. I have witnesses to what I am saying, people who have seen terrible bruises on all parts of my body, and known the condition I was in most of the time, when I was suffering the worst ill treatment. . . . I have been so near death at his hands and know to what lengths he will go in his tempers. Years ago he strangled me till I lost consciousness and told me then he would kill me some day and he has kicked me all the way as I crawled across the floor on my hands and knees while carrying his babies. . . . I am terrified to remain where he can come near me, the children have begged me repeatedly in the past to do something so that he can't come near us anymore. That was one reason for my change. . . .[66]

The change Vera alluded to was her decision to leave her violent husband and find a new home for her family, but she was ineligible for the allowance because she owed back rent on her new home.

In some cases, as Emma Buckley's, the administrators of this policy directly increased the level of violence in the home by their actions. Her son George, who was known to be violent and never financially helped his family, had left home and the mother applied for an allowance. The investigator reported that George 'used to beat his sisters and his mother had to order him out of the house'. Despite this, the investigator asked the chairman of the local board to visit George and persuade this violent son to return home. The investigator, local board, and provincial commission all agreed that 'George should not be relieved of his responsibility'.[67]

The Buckleys and Jacksons were not alone. There were many more cases of family violence, usually perpetrated by the husband, that were not deemed acceptable cases for financial support. There was Lena Trotter, whose husband had 'just recently threatened to cut . . . [her] throat'. Lena was declared ineligible because her husband's condition could not 'be considered a total and permanent disability'.[68] Or Constance Lawrence, who, according to the investigator's report, had:

> . . . valvular heart trouble and a peculiar nervous condition due to injuries she received from her husband when he beat her against bath tub and she was pregnant with Barbara. She [the child] talks backward yet, if upset the least bit, and was a serious mental case for months. . . .[69]

Constance was ineligible because she knew the whereabouts of her violent husband.

OMA administrators also did not take a mother's health into account. If anything, a mother's sickness did not provoke sympathy but stronger confirmation that her children should be taken from her and given to others, namely, the Children's Aid Society. Clara Long's husband died of tuberculosis, and both she and her daughter were infected. As the medical report explains:

> The daughter Alvina, is definitely infected, febrile, and will require at least six months further treatment in Preventorium. The mother is anxious to take her home in order that the [allowance] may be continued but we feel that this would be decidedly against the child's best interests. During Alvina's stay in the Preventorium, the mother will be responsible for the expense of the child's clothing. . . . Mrs. Long is herself an ex-patient. . . .

Unfortunately, the local board denied the case, stating: 'We have many cases that are much more serious than [Mrs Long's] when the allowance is cut off, and we feel that in the case of this one it would prejudice the whole scheme if . . . the allowance were granted.'[70] Whereas the father could be incapacitated and the family would be eligible for the allowance, the reverse was not true for the mother. This policy suggests that a mother was not allowed to be sick because she was to be the care-giver within the family.

There were other mothers who were ineligible for the allowance through no fault of their own. A few mothers discovered that their husbands were already married to other women. Such bigamy cases created a great stir in the local board meetings and were clearly not the type of families OMA administrators wished to support. A mother who was born and raised in Ontario, and who had moved with her family and was not residing in her home province during the time of her husband's disability, desertion, or death was ineligible. Often these mothers would return home to their extended families, friends, and community for support, only to find that their application for mothers' allowance was refused. For those who remained outside the eligibility guidelines, the last resort was to have the provincial commission declare them a special case, but the commission was reluctant to encourage this exception.

A FINAL WORD ON THE RECIPIENTS

This intrusive regulation of cleanliness, attitudes, and social activities clearly had a profound impact on the everyday lives of OMA recipients. Investigation and eligibility criteria illustrate that OMA was focused on the needs and interests of children rather than those of the adult recipients. OMA did not grant a sum specifically for the mother. It cut off mothers as soon as their children reached the age of sixteen. The policy encouraged mothers to undertake low-paid, domestic-related work rather than jobs that led to long-term financial security. Finally, investigation into all aspects of a mother's life was also conducted to ensure that the children had a 'proper' home. There was little attempt to focus on the needs of these needy mothers themselves.

Despite the difficulties of this policy, some, perhaps many, needy mothers did attempt to get their own needs met. Using the 'powers of the weak', as described in Linda Gordon's book about family violence, these women did everything in their power to obtain the allowance.[71] What they lacked in resources they replaced with creativity and determination. They would falsify the ages of their children, present illegitimate children as legitimate, hide information from the administrators, and enlist the help of community leaders in their struggle. Wherever possible, they would attempt to negotiate with the investigator, promising to rehabilitate if the allowance were continued. These recipients were not mere victims of an intrusive, oppressive policy.

CONCLUSION

The OMA case files reveal both traditional and 'new' scientific notions of welfare. The policy did routinize some aspects of nineteenth-century welfare for the poor with standardized application forms and regular reports and updates, but, as the case files reveal, the investigation of OMA applicants and recipients was far from 'objective'. The policy permitted much discretionary decision-making in the determination of who was or was not worthy, and this worthiness depended not simply on financial need but on a number of expansive moral criteria. Administrators of the policy, societal leaders, and community members all participated in this intrusive regulation of OMA recipients' lives, and this close supervision was ongoing as a recipient was continuously forced to prove her deservedness. This provided a greater role for the state as moral guardian of the poor, intruding into the homes of the needy in a new and more direct manner, but the intrusive and moral nature of these investigations was reminiscent of nineteenth-century philanthropic work.

Although OMA regulations and everyday administration were characterized by many nineteenth-century welfare values, this is not to underestimate their importance. For the first time, some needy mothers would receive a measure of financial assistance and security from the state. As a result, they would not have to rely on the 'whims' of charitable or municipal aid or be forced to give up their children to orphanages or foster homes. At the very least, OMA provided some with a fixed sum of money, however minimal, paid on a monthly basis.

The foundations of OMA administration were established during this decade, but would persist for many years to come. With a combination of early philanthropic values and the 'new' scientific public welfare philosophy, Ontario Mothers' Allowance illustrates that there is no clear division between private and public welfare. The values of one type of welfare did not fade with the emergence of another. Rather, both private and public welfare activities and values persisted alongside one another during this first decade of OMA administration and long into the future.

Chapter 4

Moral Vigilance During the 'Dirty' Thirties

The 1930s experienced not only an economic catastrophe but increased anxiety about masculinity, femininity, and morality. Notions of masculinity during this era associated manliness with providing for oneself and one's family. In contrast, femininity was defined by emotional and economic dependency on a man and by full-time care-giving to the breadwinner and his offspring. Because of distressing times and the shortage of jobs, there was considerable slippage in the practice of masculine and feminine behaviours as men wandered the rails aimlessly looking for work, and women, previously dependent, began providing for their families wherever possible. As well, this was a time of moral turmoil. Social reformers of the era were distraught about the fact that men often left their family hearth, away from the civilizing influence of women. Or, equally worrying, men gathered together at bars to drown their sorrows about the lack of work. Simultaneously, social workers were troubled by the increasing number of wives and mothers left on their own and considered these women both socially and sexually available to any number of transient men. Through the Ontario Mothers' Allowance policy, administrators attempted to mould or morally regulate the recipients back into their proper societal roles.

ESCALATING ANXIETIES

The economic collapse of 1929 plunged Ontario, along with the rest of the country, into an unexpected and unprecedented depression. The overproduction and overconsumption of the 1920s gave way to a severe economic crisis. The cost of living fell, income fell, unemployment rose dramatically, and there was a general decline in industrial production, profits, and investment. As labour historians have argued, the labour movement was effectively stripped of political clout in the decade prior to the Depression. As a result, workers and the unemployed had little leverage to struggle collectively against the ensuing economic crisis.[1] A larger number of Canadians were out of work for a longer period of time than during any economic crisis before or since the 1930s. At the peak of the Depression, more than 32 per cent of all wage-earners were out of work.[2] Men were leaving their families in an effort to seek employment anywhere they could. Mothers were left alone with children, attempting to keep the family together.

Wherever possible, the discouraged and disillusioned poor turned to others for help. In keeping with nineteenth-century values, poverty was still associated with idleness and unworthiness. Fearful of public condemnation, the poor would first turn to relatives or friends rather than ask for public help. After they had pawned or sold any valuables and exhausted their credit with grocers, after they could borrow or beg no more from relatives and friends, after they had their utilities cut off and faced eviction from their homes, the poor would be forced to apply for welfare. The few welfare programs available (emergency relief, charitable aid, mothers' allowances, or Old Age Pensions) were humiliating and difficult to obtain. Despite the social stigma, by 1935 it is estimated that 20 per cent of the entire population depended on some form of public assistance.[3] These welfare programs at the federal, provincial, and municipal levels were not prepared to handle the devastating economic effects of the Depression. These programs were typically haphazard, restrictive, and uncoordinated. Residence and eligibility requirements for relief varied from town to town; few cities provided any services for assisting unemployed single men and none aided single women.[4] Relief, for the most part, took the form of 'relief in kind' (rations of food and used clothing) and vouchers rather than cash. This relief was neither regular nor adequate to meet even the most basic needs of the poor. Schools of social work had only just opened their doors during the 1920s and were not prepared to train the number of state employees needed. Private charities, equally unprepared, simply could no longer support the most needy who fell through the cracks of the very limited state programs. Within two years of the Depression, private agencies were overwhelmed by the demand for help.[5]

This is not to suggest that economic disaster and government ineptitude went uncontested. Rather, poor and hungry citizens became radicalized by the decade and participated in a number of protest parties, organizations, marches, strikes, and militant gatherings. Sixty-eight University of Toronto professors formed the League for Social Reconstruction (LSR) in 1931, protesting the persecution of communists.[6] The following year, spearheaded by the LSR, an amalgamation of farm organizations and non-communist labour parties initiated the Co-operative Commonwealth Federation.[7] Similarly, strikes and lockouts erupted at company doors, and the On to Ottawa Trek in 1935 galvanized hundreds of unemployed men into active protest as never before.

This economic crisis and ensuing protest profoundly affected the lives of men and women and the relationships between them. As historians Linda Gordon, Margaret Hobbs, and Ruth Pierson have argued, the Depression was a period of 'gender crisis'. Both masculine and feminine prescribed roles were challenged by the economic difficulties of the era. Gender boundaries were under enormous stress during the 1930s as men's jobs disappeared and the female labour force expanded. Hobbs argues that these gender identities underwent 'possibly the greatest test to their strength ever experienced in the modern industrial period' during the Depression.[8]

The model of a male breadwinner with dependent wife and children underwent tremendous stress during this period. This was an ideal supported by bourgeois reformers, which few working-class families could afford to live by but many desired. The working class had fought since the latter half of the nineteenth century for a male 'family wage' that would be sufficient to support all other family members. Hobbs argues that this fight for a family wage was both a class and a gender weapon to preserve male privileges in both the workforce and the home. For half a century, this family wage demand promoted a connection between masculine identity and work. The pay cheque increasingly became a 'symbol of machismo', freedom, and independence from the domestic sphere organized and dominated by women.[9]

This dream of masculine prowess became more unrealistic during the 1930s. Since the very essence of masculinity was strongly tied to this notion of male as breadwinner and head of household, it is no wonder that many men were deeply troubled by events beyond their control. A number of unemployed husbands and fathers believed they were personally at fault for their inability to support their families, which led many of them to psychological depression, violent behaviour, or even suicide. Accepting relief was a public and humiliating admission to all of personal failure. And those who were fortunate to work often had to accept cuts in their wages, promissory notes for delayed pay cheques, and deteriorating working conditions as the Depression dragged on. Finally, there were the unemployed transient men who travelled from one town to another, making futile attempts to find work that was at best menial, infrequent, and ill-paid. There was public concern that these men would eventually give up and become part of the growing numbers of chronically unemployed, never to find work again during their lives.[10] For most of them—the unemployed husband, the working man, and the transient—the male breadwinner dream remained beyond their grasp during the Depression era, provoking considerable personal stress.

This economic and gender crisis did not affect every man equally. As working Protestant Euro-Canadian men lost jobs that they had considered their birthright, some looked for scapegoats to blame. Ethnic minorities, particularly immigrants, were popular targets for resentment. Many municipalities denied relief to certain ethnic groups. Immigration was restricted, and the federal government deported unemployed immigrants, all in an effort to save the few jobs available for Protestant Euro-Canadian men and reduce welfare costs.[11]

What has received less attention is the simultaneous concern about femininity during this era.[12] With their husbands jobless, more women were forced to seek any work they could find in order to support the family. According to census figures, the number of working women climbed from 15.45 per cent of the working population in 1921 to almost 20 per cent in 1941. Similarly, married women entered the workforce in increasing numbers, from 7.18 per cent in 1921 to 10.03 per cent in 1931, and continued to rise during the rest of the decade.[13] These figures do not include all the women who would have worked part-time during this decade. These women found work because the jobs reserved for women in the sex-segregated labour force (such as clerical, trade, and service jobs) were not as severely affected by the economic downturn. In many cases, because of the absence of a male breadwinner, these women became the main (if not the sole) wage-earners in their families. At the same time, they were expected to continue their subservient role as full-time care-giver for the family. Where there was considerable sympathy for the man who was unable to perform his 'normal' masculine role in society as breadwinner, there was less concern for the woman's conflicting responsibilities. Whereas society assumed that man's roles as worker and husband/father were compatible responsibilities, it was generally assumed that woman's roles as worker and wife/mother were not. Working women were believed to have lost their femininity and blamed for rising desertion rates and lowering fertility rates.[14]

While the 1930s is characterized as a period of tremendous social unrest, this too was gendered. Unemployed and poor men took to the streets and demanded jobs and government aid. The women's movement, in contrast, did not share the same degree of militancy. Whereas the women's movement of the 1920s had been vocal and visible with national and international alliances, women's struggles during the Depression were more scattered and locally based.[15] Consequently, there was little opposition to the conservative and antifeminist attacks on working women, and advocates for poor women did not promote gender equity or economic independence for women. Rather, they accepted the traditional gender roles of male breadwinner and dependent wife and children, regardless of economic feasibility.

Since popular opinion believed that women's first duty was in the home, there was little attention granted to women who lost their jobs during the Depression, and in fact there were several attempts to replace them, especially married women, with male workers. Many companies, labour unions, women's groups, and governments advocated the 'purging' of female workers from the workplace, replacing them with male workers wherever possible.[16] A broadly based antifeminist campaign emerged in the 1930s, which viciously attacked and blamed women, particularly working women, for these economic and social problems.[17] Women were faced with a tumultuous contradiction between what they had to do to survive and what was expected of them as women. Single mothers especially faced role conflict as they worked at low-paying part-time jobs to provide for their children while being chastised for not caring full-time for their children.

Anxieties about gender roles also provoked concern about the slippage from the moral codes prescribed for each gender. Leaders in the community were concerned about the fracture of many families and the moral dangers that could occur as a result of footloose men and the potentially sexually available mother who was working outside the home to feed her young family. As mentioned in Chapter 3, state and social agency administrators exerted considerable energy and care to guide the moral behaviour of the poor, but this concern about moral behaviour was heightened during the 1930s when traditional gender roles were particularly challenged by economic circumstances. Women, especially single mothers, had a rigid moral code prescribed for them. Whereas men on their own were considered dangerous but tolerated, the same cannot be said for women. Women without male companions were considered morally dubious at best and in need of constant guidance or surveillance by the community.

GOVERNMENT RESPONSES TO ESCALATING ANXIETIES

Various levels of the state attempted to respond to the ensuing anxieties of the 1930s. Ironically, as economic realities demanded that men and women question conventional gender roles, state administrators and social agencies did their best to reinforce traditional responsibilities through policies and practices. An examination of federal, provincial, and municipal governments' role in social welfare generally and in OMA in particular reveals that each state administration attempted to reinforce both traditional gender roles and moral codes of behaviour.

Federal Government

Generally, state involvement during the longest and most devastating depression in the country's history could be characterized as reluctant and minimal. Relief had been a local responsibility, and under enormous public pressure, the federal government reluctantly acknowledged that unemployment was a national rather than a local problem. As a result, the federal government gave emergency relief aid annually to the provinces during the Depression, but kept threatening that each year would be the last.[18] The federal government also spent money on work projects in an attempt to provide jobs for the unemployed, but both these programs reinforced the male breadwinner model. It was assumed that women's poverty was due to the lack of a man (as a result of a death, desertion, or illegitimacy) rather than their unemployment, and as a result they were not eligible for federal relief.[19] Work projects, as well, focused on providing jobs for the male breadwinner rather than women.

The Canadian government, unlike its neighbour to the south, refused to embark on a national social security system during the 1930s. The two federal income security programs that were enacted during the decade (war veterans' allowances and pensions for the blind) were meagre and means-tested like other early welfare programs. Any attempts for a more expansive welfare program subsidized by the federal government (such as a housing policy or a national insurance system) failed and the federal government refused to become significantly involved in the health and welfare of its citizens. As Dennis Guest argues, the Depression laid the foundations for a national social security plan, but only the seeds.[20]

Child and maternal welfare was a grave concern during the 1930s. During the Depression, seventy-two out of every 1,000 babies born annually in Canada died. Maternal deaths did not drop below the 1921 figure of 4.7 per 1,000 live births until the end of the 1930s; moreover, they rose during the first half of the Depression decade. These rates were higher than in many countries of western Europe.[21] There was also a concern about rising malnutrition and disease rates among children during this era.

The Canadian Council on Child Welfare (CCCW), a federal government agency, attempted to deal with these escalating health problems in two important ways. With the cooperation of the emerging medical and social work professions, the CCCW's executive director, Charlotte Whitton, spearheaded a number of educational campaigns. The CCCW widely distributed a series of letters on prenatal and child care directly to mothers and also indirectly through popular family magazines, visiting nurses, private practitioners, women's clubs, and other social organizations.[22] These educational programs promoted the belief that an enhancement of a mother's domestic skills would solve the problems of poverty and simultaneously promote the male breadwinner model. Such educational campaigns assumed that the poor did not lack resources but merely knowledge about how to provide the best care for their families; the CCCW clearly placed the blame for poverty at the door of the individual. A second method employed to improve child and maternal welfare was to scrutinize and restrict all existing welfare programs. Provincial mothers' allowance programs in particular were singled out for close supervision and comment. Whitton was afraid that this decade would encourage people to be dependent, lazy, and immoral:

> There are a great number of people who do not hesitate to apply for a Mothers' Allowance, which unfortunately is regarded as a pension. . . . I think there is a real problem of an increasing tendency to look upon a public grant as a right just by virtue of widowhood.[23]

The solution was intensified policing of the applicants to ensure that mothers' allowance cases did not climb during the difficult Depression decade.

> In order to keep MA estimates from rising steadily year by year . . . I can see no solution except by careful and assiduous case work. . . . [In Manitoba] we have been able to keep considerably within the estimated budget [for mothers' allowance] so that in the last 3 years we have been able to save approximately $100,000.00.[24]

Whitton's notion of fiscal responsibility made her violently opposed to OMA amendments that would expand eligibility. She argued forcefully against the inclusion of deserted and unwed mothers. She was appalled that more than 8,000 babies were born to unwed mothers each year in Canada and believed that these babies should not remain with their obviously immoral mothers. Like the turn-of-the-century social reformers, Whitton believed unsupervised single mothers led to delinquent children. She was particularly opposed to including mothers with one child in the OMA Act. She wrote confidentially to other provincial governments, encouraging them to write protest letters to the Ontario government. 'My own judgement is that the mother with one child is rarely in the same position of need . . . as the mother with more than one child', she argued. She even wrote a private and confidential letter to Canadian Life Insurance asking them to determine the cost of this amendment:

> I understand that the Bill is to be rushed through to third reading at once. I would prefer not to have my name brought into this matter, but I think that you might be interested in going into it from the point of view of the ultimate interests in the situation.[25]

There was an inherent contradiction in the federal government's response to single mothers' poverty. The CCCW educational programs emphasized distinct gender roles and particularly encouraged traditional domestic duties for women at a time when they could least afford to abide by these prescriptive roles. The federal government's attempts to restrict women's access to welfare forced increasing numbers of women to abandon these gender roles and work outside the home. As mentioned earlier, women were denied federal relief because it was assumed that their poverty was due to the lack of a man rather than their unemployment.[26] At the same time, the CCCW attempted to block any amendments to provincial welfare programs, such as OMA, that would have expanded eligibility and increased the monthly payments. Consequently, many poor mothers were forced to find paid work that contradicted the traditional male breadwinner model the educational programs attempted to promote.

Ontario Government

The Ontario government also attempted to resist welfare reform. During this decade the provincial government gave the illusion of reform through 'professional' administrative changes but little in the way of real material benefits to poor single mothers. During the Conservative governments of Howard Ferguson and George Henry and the Liberal government of 'Mitch' Hepburn, Ontario political representatives worried about encouraging pauperism through increased welfare provisions. Very few eligibility changes were made during the decade despite the economic devastation that many were experiencing. At the same time, these governments made significant administrative alterations to curb rising welfare costs. As one government official remembers, 'There was much talk of inflated costs due to welfare abuse, administrative laxity, client sloth and fraud, and kindred allegations.'[27] With few eligibility changes and continued vigilance in administration, the OMA case-load did not dramatically increase during this period despite evidence of unprecedented poverty.

During the 1929 electoral campaign Conservative Premier Howard Ferguson promised an inquiry in response to criticism of his government's welfare record. Following the election, the Royal Commission on Public Welfare (Ross Commission) examined the fifty-six provincial statutes on welfare and recommended dramatic administrative reform. The commissioners believed there was a great need for more professional social work and for coordination of government welfare activities. One solution was to establish a cooperative project between the government and the University of Toronto to increase both the quantity and quality of professional social workers available for government welfare administration. The vigilant casework of these professionals would reduce the admissions to orphanages, which were already overcrowded, and also ensure that recipients made full use of every welfare dollar.[28] Thus, moral regulation of welfare clients continued, albeit in the name of professionalism.

In the fall of 1930 the Ferguson government, at the inquiry's recommendation, centralized and coordinated the government's welfare activities under the Department of Public Welfare. The department's objective was to centralize existing public welfare institutions rather than alleviate growing poverty and unemployment. Consequently, the OMA commission, child welfare, Old Age Pensions, mental health, adult and juvenile corrections, juvenile courts, handicapped children, houses of refuge, and soldier's aid were all coordinated under one administrative structure. W.G. Martin, a forty-four-year-old clergyman from Brantford, undertook this new cabinet post, and Milton A. Sorsoleil, an administrator in vocational education and a prominent elder of the United Church who had a strong commitment to religious and moral social development, became the deputy minister. Thus, the new era of professionalization was not to be completely divorced from the earlier charity notions of morality.[29]

During the first harsh winds of the Depression, Ferguson's successor, George S. Henry, premier from 1930 to 1934, tinkered with the administrative details of the welfare department, but resisted any expansion in policies or expenditures. Known as 'the highway man', Henry's first goal as premier was to improve economic development—a big challenge given the realities of the early Depression years. Although he was a strong supporter of state projects such as highways to improve economic development, Henry's 'rugged individualist' philosophy rejected state social welfare projects. Henry and his contemporaries continued to believe that the depressed economy would soon improve and promoted a few 'work-fare' projects rather than new welfare programs as the temporary solution to the obvious signs of despair.[30] In Ontario industrial production fell month by month, down 25 per cent in the first year of the Depression and almost by half in 1932. Similarly, the value of farm production sank to 64 per cent of its former value. By the end of 1933, the worst year of the Depression, Ontario had 600,000 unemployed workers. Those Ontarians who had jobs had little money to spend. Income per capita in the province fell from $649 to $310 in three years.[31]

The Henry government did its best to ignore the clear evidence of increasing need. In this effort, the government centralized and reduced OMA administration. The local board members' powers were reduced because they were considered too generous to applicants; they were merely to recommend applicants and leave the decision-making in the hands of the provincial commission. Second, the government then fired the previous provincial OMA commission of five people and replaced them with three full-time civil servants from the welfare department: Dr Jamieson as chairman, joined by deputy minister M.A. Sorsoleil and chief investigator H. Bentley. Henry believed that this would ensure a more professional, less patronage-fashioned commission, but labour protested this administrative change. In 1920 the government had appointed Mrs Singer as labour's representative to the provincial commission, but with the bureaucratic overhaul Mrs Singer was demoted to the role of a special investigator. The Toronto Labour Council opposed this administrative move, arguing that it signalled the loss of labour's authoritative voice in the highest level of OMA administration.[32]

In 1934, after three Conservative terms of office, the Elgin County gentleman farmer 'Mitch' Hepburn and his Liberals won the provincial election with the promise to reduce and 'overhaul the machinery of government'.[33] Hepburn's eight-year term of office as premier left an indelible impression upon welfare politics. Initially, his new government fired all twenty OMA investigators, believing their work could be done by the field crew of provincial relief investigators. These relief investigators would be responsible for the investigation of both needy single mothers and all other relief recipients. Applications would be taken by the municipal clerk. Whereas Henry had reduced the provincial commission from five to three people, a 1935 amendment under Hepburn allowed the lieutenant-governor-in-council to further reduce the commission from three administrators to one.[34]

There were numerous complaints about this further centralization of the OMA administration. Relief investigators were too busy with their own work to scrutinize the homes of single mothers as well. The local boards and the provincial commission questioned the relief investigators' observations and recommendations. At the same time, debt-ridden municipalities were not able to pay their half of the OMA administration bill each Depression year. Given that the provincial government was already refunding from 75 to 100 per cent of local relief expenditures and bailing out defaulting municipalities with special grants, it seemed ludicrous to expect the local governments to keep paying 50 per cent of the OMA costs. Following municipal pressure, on 31 March 1937 the provincial government assumed 100 per cent of the cost of OMA. The welfare department excused the municipal clerks from accepting applications. The government reassigned staff to investigative fieldwork, and in line with an increased case-load and a policy of closer inspection, the staff was increased to fifty-six, four of whom were special investigators who supervised the work of the other investigators.[35] New administrative forms for investigation, verification of all facts, and annual visits were all part of the new intensive investigation process undertaken solely by the provincial government. The results were both intrusive and time-consuming. As the commission admitted:

> [The] . . . first visit often involves several calls to different sources before the Record is complete, as all information must be accurate and verified in every phase. One problem with which the investigator frequently contends is the applicant's reaction to the apparent delay from the time the application was taken to the time of visit.[36]

But this new provincial formalized process did not mean that the municipal governments were relieved of all welfare for single mothers.

> Local organizations, both public and private, should realize that occasions may arise when these families will be in need, and should be given additional assistance through the same channels as any other family which may require help. For local organizations to discriminate to the detriment of the family simply because such a family is in receipt of an allowance is quite unjustified.[37]

Thus, the provincial government gained control of all aspects of the allowance, formalized administration, intensified investigations, yet encouraged the municipalities to 'help make ends meet'.

Along with administrative changes, the government introduced a few amendments to the OMA Act as the Depression continued and public pressure mounted. In 1934 the commission included children between sixteen and eighteen who were attending school, provided there was another child under sixteen. This amendment was partly in response to the Depression when older children could not find work to support their mother-led families. A year later, the government made two important amendments to the OMA Act. One reduced the period of desertion from five to three years, acknowledging the rise of deserted mothers and children in desperate straits. Another amendment included needy mothers with one child for the first time, despite virulent opposition orchestrated by Charlotte Whitton. While the federal officials and other premiers opposed this legislative amendment, there was little opposition within the province.[38] Hepburn had promised this change if elected during the 1934 electoral campaign.[39] Following electoral victory, the Hepburn government was quite tentative in fulfilling the promise. Concerned about the expense of this proposed amendment, the commission soon requested all local boards to determine the additional number of eligible families if such an amendment were passed.[40] Once passed, the amendment resulted in an enormous increase in applicants, as the next annual report explained: 'The number of applications increased from 2,000 to 7,704 in the first year, 3,862 were found to be eligible, 2,688 of the eligible cases were from applicants under the amended act.'[41] According to these statistics, the commission and its administrators were refusing allowances to half of the applicants. Wherever possible, they encouraged young widows with one child to seek employment and have relatives care for the child. Other one-child applications 'were refused because the circumstances did not reveal the need for an allowance'.[42] So despite the progressive potential of this amendment, there were administrative attempts to limit its ability to provide for needy one-child families.

All of these amendments reveal that the provincial government and the welfare department in particular were stringent in their policing of all single mothers during the 1930s. To enforce OMA regulations, Chairman H. Bentley made frequent visits to the local boards during this decade. He encouraged the local administrators to be vigilant in their work, as recorded in one minute book:

> Mr. Bentley discussed with the members of the Board the various phases of the Mothers Allowance work outlining the viewpoint of the officials in Toronto and what they are endeavouring to accomplish, their purpose being to discourage as far as possible the tendency to lean upon the Mothers' Allowance and the main aim being to tide mothers and children over a difficult period and to endeavour to get them on a self-sustaining basis and to keep in mind the taxpayer who is footing the bill. . . .[43]

As a result of this heightened policing in the worst years of the Depression, the number of OMA beneficiaries remained unchanged and even started to decline slightly by the end of the decade, but the vigilant and restrictive nature of provincial OMA administration during the Depression era did not go unchallenged.

Municipal Government

The most organized opposition to OMA administration was orchestrated by municipal governments. As never before or since, the Depression decade was characterized by local politicians challenging the restricted eligibility requirements of OMA and pressuring the provincial government for more inclusive amendments. While organizations and individuals occasionally became involved in these campaigns, it was primarily local councils that spearheaded OMA legislative reform during the 1930s. As a rule, individuals would write the premier or even the prime minister to complain about a particular case rather than urge a broad policy reform for all mothers in similar circumstances. It was the local politicians and local OMA board members who saw the human face of the Depression. They personally knew many of the needy single mothers in their locale who were ineligible for OMA for one administrative reason or another. This is not to suggest that local politicians were magnanimous in their efforts to ease the struggle of needy single mothers. Rather, they were concerned about their debt-ridden local coffers and protests from taxpayers about tax increases. If OMA expanded to include new types of needy single mothers, that would mean fewer mothers for the municipality to feed and house, and so they organized political campaigns to broaden OMA eligibility. During the early 1930s, these local politicians urged the inclusion of one-child families, children between sixteen and eighteen, divorced wives, and families deserted for less than the obligatory five-year period. They cried out about the discriminatory nature of the act for rural and northern Ontario women, and they exposed examples of political patronage and fraud in OMA administration.

Some of these municipal campaigns were more successful than others. The two strongest campaigns were for one-child family inclusion and an increase in eligible children's age from sixteen to eighteen. Local politicians promoted the one-child inclusion long before the provincial government began to consider this amendment. As early as 1931 local county councils were petitioning the provincial government to make this amendment.[44] Soon county councillors sent petitions to the provincial legislature to demand this one-child amendment. Similarly, county councils sent resolutions about raising the age limit of eligible children from sixteen to eighteen to both the provincial government and fellow county councils, thus creating an effective campaign in early 1933.[45] Rural and urban tensions emerged as local politicians complained about the differentiating rates according to the population size of the community.[46] Between 1935 and 1937 municipal politicians and the Ontario Mayors' Association urged the provincial government to increase its contribution to OMA and simultaneously reduce the local rate.[47] Two years later, as the campaign continued and more municipalities declared bankruptcy, the provincial government took over the entire costs of OMA.[48]

Other local campaigns were not as successful. Local councils also petitioned to include families whose breadwinner was sentenced to jail for six months or more.[49] The provincial government refused this request, and prisoners' families were not eligible until 1957, more than two decades following the organized local protest. Once municipalities were relieved of their financial responsibilities for OMA, they began to demand an increase in the allowance.[50] Local boards would also attempt to lobby for single mothers in their district who for one reason or another were considered ineligible by the OMA Act. The board would urge the provincial commission to consider such cases as 'exceptional' and, through an order-in-council, provide an allowance for the mother in need, but these were rarely successful campaigns.

Local politicians also organized protests, exposing patronage and fraud within the OMA administration. These complaints were partly in response to the centralization of authority and administration and the result of several patronage indiscretions. Patronage issues were rampant in the 1930s as jobs were scarce and people depended on political allegiances for economic security. The Henry government received a number of letters requesting political preference. As one mother wrote, 'I feel I must appeal to you, and being a good conservative I know you will do all in your power to aid me. I am trying my best to raise five more good conservatives.'[51] Patronage escalated during Hepburn's term as many loyal Liberals wrote their dear friend 'Mitch' to request help or a job. One man, asking for a job as an investigator of either bakeries or mothers' allowance recipients, explained, 'surely you can help me with [a job]. . . . so I may have something in return for my work towards the Liberal party'.[52] But Mrs Eva Birss's story was particularly illustrative of the degree to which party preference mattered. She wrote requesting investigative OMA work:

> You see my husband has been physically and mentally ill, since three years ago last February—the night of the Banquet here for you, at the Winter Gardens. He was in a motor accident that night and . . . has done nothing since. . . . My political activities are well known—They began in 1921 when I spoke in every centre in Peel—my home county. . . . In 1925 I spoke at the City Hall at Niagara Falls the night before Election, and although I was President of the Liberal Women in Brampton—just managed to get home at 4:30 p.m. Election day to vote. I love the work. I am Liberal through and through—and Elizabeth [my daughter] is too. . . .'[53]

Who could refuse a woman whose husband had almost died in the line of Liberal Party duty and was raising her daughter to be a good Liberal like herself? Needless to say, such political appointments to OMA administrative positions created a perception of partiality. Several recipients were afraid that their political preference would deny them an allowance. One incapacitated man whose family received OMA wrote about this concern:

> The main point is I was at a conservate [sic] meeting the other night with some of my friends. We listened to all the promises which Mr. R.B. Bennett would do if returned to cabinet. We said nothing. But when they came to the King Government we cheered for our old leader Hon. Makenzie [sic] King. . . . I have ben [sic] told since the meeting that some of the conservates [sic] are going to send in some kind of reports to the Mothers' Allowance Board against me and are going to try to get my wifes [sic] Pension stopped. . . . Could it be possible for them dirty sneaks of conservates [sic] be the cause of us loosing [sic] our pensions.[54]

There were also charges of fraud during this decade. One administrator's fraudulent activities became widely publicized in 1937. A Mr Teall promised applicants that he would advocate on their behalf for a certain amount of money. The wife and six children of Wakely, a farmer who lost his entire arm in a corn shredder, applied for OMA under the incapacitation clause. The commission refused on the grounds that the farmer could not be considered totally and permanently incapacitated. Mr Teall arrived on the scene and promised to help the family obtain OMA in return for a percentage of the cheque. The family agreed, and shortly thereafter the commission overturned their previous decision and granted the family the allowance. Eventually the family complained and the commission discovered that Mr Teall had demanded similar bribes from other families. This administrator was arrested, accused of 'contracting for a percentage of any pension he was successful in securing from the government', and sentenced to six months in jail.[55] Such was the seamier side of Depression welfare administration.

Municipal politicians were particularly frustrated by the diminishing powers of the local boards during the 1930s. If the local board became obstinate, the provincial commission would replace its three provincial appointees on these boards with people who would more vehemently defend provincial interests. Such a manoeuvre incensed local communities, which charged the provincial government with political interference in OMA administration. Such was the case with the Toronto local board in 1931. The provincial commission replaced provincial appointees to the Toronto board, arguing that the local board was granting too many applications and should be curbed. The city was home to one-quarter of all OMA recipients in the province. The provincial commission stopped providing the provincial investigator's reports to the local board, and consequently made it impossible for the board to make informed decisions on who should be granted the allowance. Incensed, the local board demanded 'an investigation into the whole system of administering mothers' allowances in Toronto', claiming that the number of OMA recipients was high because needy mothers flocked to the urban centre in search of work. There were charges and countercharges. The press charged that the provincial commission delayed cheques to Toronto's needy mothers, and in return, Toronto refused to pay its share of OMA administration costs. 'What good is a local board if the Provincial board is supreme', asked one local politician. Even the Toronto Ratepayers Association and local citizens became involved.[56] The episode left a sour mood between local boards and the provincial commission that continued for the remainder of the decade.

THE MORAL REGULATION OF SINGLE MOTHERS

The everyday administration of OMA reflects both the social and economic anxieties of this period and governmental attempts to alleviate these fears. An examination of OMA case files reveals that there are four aspects of OMA regulation that intensified during this period: family finances, a husband's physical condition, desertion, and cleanliness. This section will explore each of these in turn and demonstrate that these regulations attempted to meet *moral* as well as economic needs of this era. During this period the policy attempted both to shore up the traditional male breadwinner family and to create 'respectable mothers'. In doing so OMA administrators did more than alleviate economic distress; they also promoted traditional notions of masculinity, femininity, and morality at a time of great social flux, and it was the moral objectives that dominated OMA administration during this period.

Financial Matters

The administration of OMA reflected the government's general reluctance to improve the financial circumstances of the poor and working class during this difficult period. For the OMA commission generally, as with other welfare administration, there was a great concern about encouraging state dependency as more and more citizens turned to them for help. Since the early pioneering days, there was an assumption that if welfare was readily available, it would promote a lazy and immoral citizenry that would become too dependent on hand-outs. These fears, which were never too far from the surface of popular opinion, emerged once again during the Depression. Also, there was a concern that private social agencies would retreat from their previous responsibilities, leaving the state to meet all economic need in society. As the OMA commission experienced a sharp rise in applications during the 1930s, they expressed concern about these possible trends in their annual reports:

> These conditions . . . indicate a definite loss of morale. To administer relief and welfare so as to foster the characteristically Canadian spirit of independence, to retain the desire to be self-sustaining in those forced to accept relief, and to maintain a constant cooperation between private benevolence and government responsibility has . . . been a dominant motive in the administration of this Department.[57]

In keeping with this goal, the OMA administrators increased their scrutiny of many aspects of the legislation. The number of applicants denied the allowance nearly tripled during this decade (see Table 4.1). The annual reports documented the number of accepted, rejected, and discontinued cases (mothers who had previously received the allowance and then were disqualified for one reason or another). The OMA commission was so scrupulous in regulating these mothers that the overall budget and number of recipients did not rapidly expand during the 1930s. In fact, during the first five years of the Depression, the amount spent on OMA remained unchanged one year and decreased by $40,000 the next.[58] OMA annual reports boasted that 'while larger sums are required to meet the demands of other types of social relief, the requirements for Mothers' Allowances have not risen above the normal.'[59] In 1932 the commission stated that '47 per cent of [the] allowances were discontinued' that year as a result of the 'faithful efforts of the Supervisory Staff', resulting in a calculated saving of $279,720 to the taxpayers of Ontario.[60] There were few changes in eligibility during this decade and consequently no dramatic increase in the number of beneficiaries with the exception of 1935 (see Table 4.2). During that year the number of beneficiaries increased by one-third as a result of the one-child amendment, but the number of refusals doubled during this year. From 1929–30 to 1939–40 the average increase was approximately 325 new recipients—not a generous figure given the devastating economic conditions experienced by most families. Thus, it was an era of economic restraint and state resistance to its role as welfare provider.

Concerned about fiscal responsibility, the OMA commission closely monitored the financial circumstances of recipients during the 1930s. Similar to the previous decade, administrators examined all aspects of a needy mother's finances, including wills, insurance policies, income, and the economic conditions of her parents. Sufficient financial means was one of the most common reasons why an applicant was denied the allowance during the 1930s (see Table 4.1).

There were many destitute mothers who applied for the allowance during this decade. Widowed Noriana de Trula's financial situation was not atypical. She and her five children owed $4,994—a sum they could not begin to repay during the Depression.[61] Other applicants were unable to meet their mortgage payments, as in the case of Elsie Moran. When she applied for the allowance she had 'lost her home and her furniture [and] was set out on the road'.[62] Another applicant lived without water or hydro.[63] One charity organization, the Visiting Housekeepers' Association, declared it 'absolutely impossible to stretch the allowance to meet the essentials' and presented the case of Mrs A:

> [She] has no private income and by reason of health and family cares is unable to supplement the allowance by earnings, is trying to feed and clothe herself and 5 children, buy household essentials and pay the odd doctor's bill on $7.86 a week. Can she do it? Long-due bills are part of the answer. The

Table 4.1 Reasons for Ineligibility, 1930–1937

Years	1930–1	1931–2	1932–3	1933–4	1934–5	1935–6	1936–7
Assets	79	72	64	54	32	135	80
Not incapacitated	128	133	155	190	116	275	308
Not deserted	72	82	122	102	64	238	222
One child under sixteen	51	53	63	67	44	138	73
Residence	33	66	41	45	18	88	45
Unsatisfactory home	15	17	39	24	10	56	54
Sufficient income	48	55	65	56	28	224	240
Not British	18	20	22	7	8	10	11
Divorced or separated	2	5	—	2	1	30	28
Prison	1	6	2	—	—	10	13
Unwed	7	11	—	—	—	6	3
No proof of marriage	3	6	9	10	5	39	36
Remarried	1	1	3	1	—	10	1
Total	**458**	**527**	**585**	**558**	**326**	**1,259**	**1,114**

Notes: 1934–5 fiscal year is only from November to March. There were a large number who were ineligible, especially from 1935 onwards, even with the act's amendments. There were no statistics kept after 1936–7.
Source: 'Annual Reports of the OMA Commission, 1930–31 to 1936–37'.

fact that her church has to provide most of the children's clothing gives further reason to believe that she cannot. The present grocer won't carry her any further and she says that the butcher is also through. She says she is finding it increasingly difficult to find any place where she can get credit. . . .[64]

In another desperate case, an OMA recipient in Lincoln County paid the local school board $200 so she and her two children could live in the skaters' shelter.[65] And a neighbour described Edna Lockland's financial circumstances at the time of her application as follows:

. . . I neither saw nor heard of her before the day she came to my door asking for a room. . . . She has absolutely nothing in the way of clothes except what has been given her. She has one towel. . . . When she washes her pillow cases she sleeps in the tick till the cases dry and you can imagine the rest. . . . She says she cannot see to sew. She had her eyes tested some months ago but cannot get the glasses till she pays for them.[66]

Although the allowance provided some relief for these needy women, it did not solve their financial woes. The OMA rates did not alter from the previous decade and remained well below subsistence. By the mid-1930s a

Table 4.2 Mothers' Allowances, Province of Ontario
(number of beneficiaries at the end of each fiscal year)

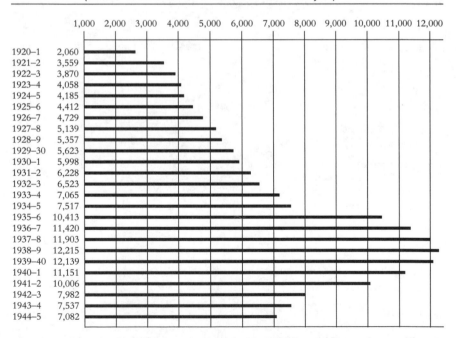

		1,000	2,000	3,000	4,000	5,000	6,000	7,000	8,000	9,000	10,000	11,000	12,000
1920–1	2,060												
1921–2	3,559												
1922–3	3,870												
1923–4	4,058												
1924–5	4,185												
1925–6	4,412												
1926–7	4,729												
1927–8	5,139												
1928–9	5,357												
1929–30	5,623												
1930–1	5,998												
1931–2	6,228												
1932–3	6,523												
1933–4	7,065												
1934–5	7,517												
1935–6	10,413												
1936–7	11,420												
1937–8	11,903												
1938–9	12,215												
1939–40	12,139												
1940–1	11,151												
1941–2	10,006												
1942–3	7,982												
1943–4	7,537												
1944–5	7,082												

Note: Large increase in 1935–6 was due to allowances granted to mothers with one child.
Source: 'Annual Report of Public Welfare, 1944–45', *Ontario Sessional Papers,* LXXVIII, Part III (1946):17.

Single mother and children during the Depression (*Archives of Ontario ACC 6520 515591*).

mother with one child living in a city received a maximum OMA of $35 and lesser amounts in rural areas. In comparison to other provincial mothers' allowance schemes, the same mother and child received $12.50 more if living in Alberta, $7.50 more if residing in British Columbia, and approximately the same in Manitoba. Mothers in Nova Scotia and Saskatchewan received lesser amounts (see Table 4.3). These OMA rates also continued to be substantially lower than Ontario Workers' Compensation (OWC) payments. A mother with one child received $50 from OWC, approximately one-third more than the same mother would receive from OMA (see Table 2.3). The OMA rates were approximately 33 per cent below the minimal acceptable standard of living, according to a study conducted in 1939.[67] In fact, the OMA rates dropped below relief rates in Toronto by the late 1930s.[68] According to these comparisons, it was virtually impossible to survive on just OMA.

To survive on OMA, a mother would attempt any number of creative financial projects. Where possible, she would attempt to find paid work for herself during the desperate 1930s, but this was a more difficult task than during the previous decade. Administrators strongly encouraged recipients to find work close to home that emphasized their domestic skills; consequently, many mothers took piece-work or char work. For example, Gertrude Willis made $2 a week for two days' housework, and Millie Tales tried to earn a little from her chickens.[69] Others, particularly in the rural

Table 4.3 National Comparison of Mothers' Allowance Rates in 1936

	Alberta	British Columbia	Manitoba	Nova Scotia	Ontario	Sakatchewan
Dependent children	Two or more (except special cases)	One or more	Two or more (except special cases)	Two or more	One or more	One or more
Age limit	Boys under fifteen Girls under sixteen	Under sixteen	Under sixteen	Under sixteen	Under sixteen	Under sixteen
Monthly allowances	$37.50 for mother $10.00 for first child ($7.50 if under ten) $7.50 to second child, $5.00 to each additional child, rent computed at $12.00. Scale allowed would vary with rent.	$35.00 for mother $7.50 for each child ($7.50 may be allowed for disabled husband living at home)	Budget system used, varied for type of locality. 90% of city rate allowed in towns, 80% in rural districts. Each allowance established by Child Welfare Board after study of circumstances.	Average monthly payments are $29.02	For mother and one child, maximum is $35.00 in larger cities. ($30.00 in towns and smaller cities, $25.00 in rural areas. $5.00 for each additional child.)	No allowances for mother and home. $8.00 for one child, $4.00 for one each additional child up to a maximum of $44.00
Maximum monthly allowances	$60.00	$42.50 maximum for mother and one child. $60.00 would be maximum for typical family.	(City scale) Two children $50.00, three children $60.00, etc. Up to seven or more, $89.00. The maximum may be increased if incapacitated father is living at home.	No standard allowance. Amount determined by family's needs and assets.	No maximum set except for above maximum rates.	$44.00
Standard maximum monthly allowance for typical family (mother and three children)	$64.20	$60.00	(See above)	$45.00 (larger cities) $40.00 (smaller cities) $35.00 (towns and rural)	$16.00	

Source: NA, MG 28, I-10, vol. 62, file: Mothers' Allowance, 1935–40.

areas, sought part-time seasonal work conducted away from the family hearth, but administrators often criticized such mothers for spending too much time away from their children.[70] Another solution was to take in boarders in order to make ends meet, even though that work was considered morally dubious. One single mother, Caroline Mullen, explained her decision to board people in her home:

> All I ever got was the Mothers' Allowance of which in 1923 was only $40.00 a month. Do you honestly believe I could pay taxes and debts out of that allowance? I naturally got deeper in debt, through sickness of my own, I am still unable to go out working. I did not neglect my children, but strugled [sic] along. My home being small I took in a roomer who was a family friend in 1927, and he helped me a great deal then the Mothers' Allowance condemed [sic] me and said get two roomers, I did do what they told me but being in the country as you know it was hard to get roomers. . . .[71]

All of this work promoted a gender identity that few could afford to live by. These jobs promoted domesticity and feminine dependence. Consequently, the OMA administrators reinforced traditional gender roles over the economic needs of the family. The welfare department, along with most branches of government, was not terribly concerned about the lack of jobs for women during the decade.[72]

When a mother could not find work for herself during the 1930s, she might send her children to work, but there was very little work available for children during the Depression decade. It was illegal for children under fourteen to work, and those between fourteen and sixteen required work permits from school attendance officers and were still required to attend part-time classes if they were available.[73] The older children were often less reliable in bringing money home. Many young girls sixteen and over could not earn enough to help finance the family.[74] Other young girls married and moved away from home. Young men often left home, travelling the rails in search of work. It was particularly difficult for children to find work in rural areas.[75]

Jobs were also scarce for the older children in female-led families who had previously been able to support the family. A public outcry from taxpayers, county councils, and labour organizations encouraged the provincial government to amend the act in 1934 to permit families with children between sixteen and eighteen to continue to receive the allowance, provided the children were in school and another child was under sixteen. According to the OMA report, it was hoped that 'the oldest child can take advantage of continuing at school and be better prepared to secure employment'.[76] Thus, the amendment would reduce short-term competition for scarce jobs and provide more self-sufficient workers in the future.

The paid work of needy mothers and their older children was quite controversial during the 1930s when most jobs were scarce. Many were concerned about OMA recipients taking jobs away from others who could not rely on public assistance. One single woman who was a union member wrote to Premier Henry complaining of this:

> I was employed with MacDonald Furriers . . . and there were two women retained in their positions with this firm and both of them were receiving the Mothers' Allowance. . . . The business hours were from 8:30 a.m. to 9:30 p.m. and during this period these two women did not see their children. . . . I belong to The Fur Makers' Union and was receiving the union wage, and at Christmas, the two recipients of the Mothers' Allowance, cut the union wage and thereby I was discharged. Now, if the Mothers' Allowance is going to prove a menace to single women earning a living wage, and as we have to pay in our Taxes for the up keep of this allowance and they are going to get the work and cut the wage too, what is going to become of the single woman.[77]

Other citizens complained that single mothers were coddled by the state and granted allowances to stay home while others had to go out and search for work.

Very little was done to alleviate the destitution experienced by single mothers and their families during the 1930s. Administrators carefully monitored the financial circumstances of OMA recipients. OMA rates remained well below subsistence and also below other welfare payments in the country. The age amendment made to the OMA Act during this era reduced job competition, but did little to improve the financial circumstances of the recipients. Consequently the increasing economic needs of these recipients were virtually ignored.

Incapacitated Male Breadwinners

A second aspect of the policy that received special attention during the 1930s was the physical condition of the male breadwinner. As in the previous decade, a husband had to be 'totally and permanently incapacitated' to qualify for OMA. The number of applicants in this category rapidly increased during the 1930s. Many men who were only partially disabled found it increasingly difficult to obtain employment and their families appealed to social welfare for help. During the first year of the decade the OMA commission experienced an increase of 16 per cent more incapacitated beneficiaries than the previous year.[78] The next year, the proportion of incapacitated cases increased more than that of widowed recipients (see Table 4.4).[79] Despite this increase, incapacitated cases remained below one-third of the total recipients throughout the decade. This was achieved by increasing the regulation of these cases. The lack of incapacitation was the most common reason an administrator refused an applicant (see Table 4.1). During the early 1930s, approximately 70 per cent of all incapacitation applicants were granted an allowance, yet this dropped to 62 per cent by the mid-decade.[80]

The OMA administration expanded its bureaucratic measures to scrutinize incapacitated cases during this decade. Perhaps most pivotal was the appointment of J.A. Faulkner, a medical doctor, as the new chairman of the

OMA commission in 1936.[81] Before this appointment there were a number of other measures implemented to intensify the examination of incapacitated applicants. During the 1920s a local doctor or specialist would write a note detailing the type of illness and the commission would determine whether the case was eligible or not. In 1931 the commission hired a full-time medical officer to review all local doctors' recommendations and hospital reports, and conduct a personal examination in many cases. Where possible, the medical officer would travel to a local community and hold a clinic, examining all incapacitated OMA applicants for the area. A three-page detailed medical history and assessment would be completed for each applicant. The most important questions on the form were the following:

15. Is this man unemployable now by reason of a mental or physical disability? If 'yes' approximately when was he last mentally or physically able to undertake some type of gainful work? Does any known type of treatment offer any likelihood of rendering him employable? Explain nature of treatment.

16. With or without treatment would you expect sufficient recovery to take place in the mental or physical condition of this man at any time in the future to render him employable?[82]

Table 4.4 Reasons for Granting Ontario Mothers' Allowance, 1930–1940

| | Number of Families (percentage of total OMA cases) | | | |
Year	Death of the Father	Incapacitation	Desertion	Total
1930–1	4,614 (64%)	1,761 (25%)	521 (7.2%)	6,896
1931–2	4,654 (63%)	1,982 (27%)	542 (7.3%)	7,178
1932–3	4,722 (62%)	2,149 (27%)	577 (7.5%)	7,448
1933–4	4,999 (61.4%)	2,341 (29%)	587 (7.2%)	7,927
Nov.–March 1934–5	4,732 (60%)	2,379 (30%)	550 (6.9%)	7,661
1935–6	7,030 (63%)	3,031 (27%)	818 (7.3%)	10,879
1936–7	8,142 (63%)	3,415 (27%)	910 (7%)	12,467
1937–8	Missing			
1938–9	7,668 (55%)	3,480 (25%)	718 (5.2%)	11,866
1939–40	7,580 (62.4%)	3,536 (29%)	670 (5.5%)	11,786

Notes: For 1935–6, the large increase in total allowances was due to the inclusion of mothers with one child and the fact that the previous fiscal year was only five months. The total number of foster parents granted the allowance is not included in this table.
Source: 'Annual Reports of the OMA Commission, 1930–31 to 1939–40'.

If the medical examiner wrote that the man might be employable to a degree in the future and was therefore not 'totally and permanently unemployable', the family would be ineligible for the mothers' allowance.

As the provincial medical officer himself admitted, the classification of 'total and permanent incapacitation' was a fuzzy one. The act did not cover any partial disability, and any disability associated with morality was also firmly denied. For instance, one annual report clearly stated that any man admitted to hospital for alcohol addiction was ineligible.[83] The war veterans' allowance was more lenient than OMA's classification as it was based on whether someone was 'permanently unemployable' rather than on a condition of 'permanent and total incapacitation'.[84]

This administrative process from medical officer to commission and back was a lengthy one.[85] In more than one case, the incapacitated husband died while awaiting the provincial commission's decision. Others died shortly after having been pronounced ineligible. This was even more common for ethnic-minority applicants. For instance, Mary Bruce and her husband were Aboriginal. Mary's husband suffered cancer of the rectum, and the local city hospital claimed he was incurable. Still, OMA administrators refused the application, claiming that Mary's husband could not be considered totally incapacitated. Five months later her husband died.[86]

Incapacitation cases were carefully streamed so that only the most helpless were granted the allowance. And since the allowance was never enough to live on, if the husband attempted to work, administrators would quickly cut off the allowance. During the 1930s there were an increasing number of cases that were rejected because the incapacitated husband had attempted to work, as in the case of Mrs Jennie Busca:

> From a physical standpoint the Board is of the opinion that Mr. Busca is permanently unemployable. The man however insists upon doing some type of remunerative occupation and although the earnings therefrom may be small, if the man persists in doing this type of work, he cannot be considered a total disability within the meaning of the Act.[87]

Mrs Pierre Lamoureux had a similar problem. According to a local minister's report, Mrs Lamoureux's husband had left the family in London and went to Montreal where he:

> . . . was a patient for some time at an insane asylum and, although [he] has been discharged, he is not normal. . . . He lives in a little shack by himself . . . as a hermit and rises about three or four o'clock in the morning and goes out through alley-ways and back lanes to collect tin cans, bottles, etc., which he sells later in the day for a few cents with which he buys his daily fare.[88]

Mrs Lamoureux's application was declared ineligible because her husband, though considered permanently incapacitated,

> . . . is employed as a junk collector. He is not making a big success of it apparently. Nevertheless, in view of the fact that he is capable of participating in

some kind of employment it debars his wife from benefiting under the provision of the Mothers' Allowance Act.[89]

Therefore, if a totally incapacitated husband attempted, against all odds, to
do some type of menial work, the OMA administrators would disqualify
the family.

Regulators of incapacitation were not sensitive to urban and rural distinctions in work. For example, Francis Neely's husband broke his back at a
barn raising, was in the hospital for six months, and was diagnosed as having a fractured lumbar vertebrae, arthritis, and hernia. He could walk
unsteadily with a cane for very brief periods. After five separate applications
by Mrs Neely, each complete with provincial medical examinations stating
that there was 'no improvement [over a period of] . . . 18 months', and a
request by the local board to approve the case, the family was nevertheless
considered ineligible. The provincial commission believed that the husband
should be able to do some type of work that did not require standing or
physical motion.[90] But it remains unclear what type of work a disabled
farmer living in a rural area during the late 1930s would be expected to find.

Likewise, there was little sympathy given to mothers whose husbands
were frequently inmates at the local 'insane asylum' or sanatorium for
tubercular patients. TB cases escalated during the Depression. A provincial
study estimated that 'the mortality from TB in 1936 in Ontario alone
resulted in a total collective loss of life amounting to 40,000 years, taking
into consideration the life expectancy at the time of death of those dying
from TB.'[91] At the beginning of the Depression, more than 13 per cent of
all OMA recipients had TB and the percentage increased to more than 25
per cent by mid-decade.[92] A mother with young children could be granted the allowance while the father was in the asylum or sanatorium, but
once the father returned to the family, the allowance was cut off. In Mrs
Pearl Gray's case, her husband was considered 'a mental case. Mrs. Gray is
in constant terror of him and as a result her Dr. reports that the nerves and
muscles of her heart have been affected. She is recommending reinstatement.'[93] It was decided that the unstable man should go to his brother's
home rather than his family home. Despite this arrangement, the administrators cut off Mrs Gray's allowance once her husband left the asylum.
Similarly, the administrators disqualified Mrs Beulah Torent when her husband, diagnosed with tuberculosis, returned home. When the local board
asked the provincial commission to reconsider its decision, the commission
wrote that the woman was disqualified because 'tuberculosis is not considered by the Commission to be a total disability'.[94] Mrs Helen Spratt, whose
husband was tubercular and refused to return to the sanatorium despite the
doctor's and wife's wishes, was also disqualified.[95] These cases suggest that
the allowance was not flexible for patients who may frequently be in and
out of the local asylum or sanatorium during their treatments.

Finally, the allowance did not cover husbands who were incapacitated
before their marriage. Violet Marsden, whose husband was diagnosed by

the medical examiner as 'totally and permanently incapacitated . . . with chronic asthmatic bronchitis and chronic myocardial degeneration', was ineligible because the 'disability antedated marriage'.[96] The mother was perceived as somehow to blame for marrying a man who was already incapacitated and could not support a family.

The regulation of incapacitated applicants shored up traditional values of masculinity and femininity. The OMA administrators assumed that the man of the house was the main (if not sole) breadwinner, and if he was incapacitated, the family would require compensation for this loss of income. There were no medical examinations or compensation for a similarly disabled mother. Whereas a man's work was financially rewarded with either a pay cheque or, in its absence, an OMA cheque, a woman's work was not. The caring work associated with femininity was not given a monetary value.

Desertion

Through desertion cases OMA administration dealt not only with questions of finance and gender roles but also with issues of morality. Deserted women and children left to fend for themselves led to increased destitution and the breakdown of traditional gender roles. But as well, desertion was believed to promote the moral decay of society. Consequently, OMA administrators were alarmed by the growing number of desertion applicants in the 1930s and urged that there be more checks on 'this type of social evil'.[97] As a result of their vigilance, deserted applicants had greater difficulty receiving the allowance than incapacitated or widowed applicants. Generally, more than two-thirds of widowed and incapacitated applicants received the allowance during this decade, whereas approximately one-third of deserted applicants were granted the OMA.[98]

There were a number of methods used to screen out deserted applicants. Investigators were always on the look-out for potential boyfriends of OMA recipients. One local investigator was very concerned about Gladys Walker and made several surprise visits to better assess the 'boyfriends'. The investigator wrote:

> I was mystified by a 'boy friend' who was in the house when I called and stayed right through the time I was there and had many suggestions as to *why* the allowance should be granted. I didn't like his manner at all—he was decidedly too much at home. I asked Mrs. Walker if he boarded there—'No, just a *close friend.*' Mrs. Walker seemed most anxious to secure the allowance at once as she needed some new clothes for a *special occasion*. I thought the *close friend* would likely be there for life when the *occasion* occurred. . . .[99]

The occasion the investigator had in mind was probably marriage. Investigators would also chastise or discontinue an allowance because the mother bought new clothes, socialized frequently, had male visitors, or any association with alcohol or tobacco.[100] They believed these activities might lead directly to sexual permissiveness and that such activities should only be permitted within the bounds of heterosexual marriage.

During the Depression it was extremely difficult for a deserted mother to qualify for OMA. At the beginning of this decade a mother had to be deserted for five years to qualify for the monthly allowance. In 1935, following enormous public pressure, the government reluctantly amended the act to include mothers who had been deserted for three years.[101] This time restriction was particularly difficult for mothers during the Depression era as more and more men left their families in a vain attempt to seek employment elsewhere. Husbands hitchhiked to the west, went south to the United States, went back to their homelands, or even moved to a town nearby in search of work. Even when the period of desertion was reduced from five to three years, many families continued to be ineligible because someone knew of the man's whereabouts. Despite the rising number of desertions in Ontario and the 1935 amendment, the percentage of deserted women who were granted the OMA never reached more than 7.5 per cent of all OMA cases and actually declined during the latter half of the decade (see Tables 4.1 and 4.4).

OMA administrators increased their scrutiny of deserted mothers during one of the most desperate periods for many such women. A careful exploration of the man's whereabouts ensured that many deserted mothers were ineligible for the allowance. If anyone knew the whereabouts of the husband, the case was dismissed. This was the plight of Nellie Todd, whose husband had deserted her and her family of five daughters under sixteen and three daughters over sixteen, the latter three all married and unemployed. According to the declaration of a man travelling by boat to England, Mr Todd had said on the boat 'that he wished to go to . . . England to see his Mother'. Because it was known that Mr Todd was alive and well in England, Nellie and her family were ineligible for the allowance.[102] Even the OMA chairman acknowledged the insensitivity of this regulation:

> . . . [there] are a number of children and mothers who have been deserted, yet cannot receive help from the Mothers' Allowance Commission because the whereabouts of their fathers or husbands is known. This is a cruel situation and very difficult to handle.[103]

If the time and location restriction was not a barrier, other stipulations made it difficult for deserted mothers to be eligible. For instance, in several cases, the mother had been deserted for the required time, but unfortunately she had lived in another province when her husband deserted her. These women often returned to their families in Ontario following their husband's extended absence. These mothers were refused OMA. The regulations stated that a woman had to be in the province where the husband deserted, died, or became incapacitated.

As desertion cases rose during the 1930s, the Ontario government became more concerned and attempted to reunite families. By 1935 the provincial government's responsibilities for desertion cases included contributing half of the transportation costs associated with returning the deserting husbands to the authorities when their wives took court action. As well, the government staff were to consult with law officers on this issue, to inform municipalities of the procedures associated with desertion, and to discuss with husbands their responsibilities to support their families.[104] To what extent the provincial government actually carried out these responsibilities is difficult to determine. Despite a desire to reduce government dependency and reunite families with their male breadwinner, many a deserted mother never received support from her husband or qualified for OMA because she knew of his whereabouts, which often forced a desperate mother to give up her children to the Children's Aid Society.

Cleanliness

The regulation of cleanliness had deep moral implications. Although cleanliness had been monitored to some extent during the previous decade, the Depression years held a particular challenge. Tuberculosis was rampant in some poor neighbourhoods, and the medical profession was deeply troubled by the contagious nature of the disease, thereby linking uncleanness with illness. In 1937 the TB mortality rate was 35 per 100,000 Ontarians. Many more were in and out of sanatoriums, slowly dying of the debilitating disease. More than 50 per cent of those who entered a sanatorium were never able to resume work, and many who returned to work suffered a relapse.[105] While families with permanently incapacitated fathers became eligible for mothers' allowance, administrators rarely accepted tubercular cases because this disease was considered a temporary rather than a permanent disability. Interestingly, the case files demonstrate how OMA administrators associated cleanliness with morality rather than illness or disease. This is particularly surprising given the prevalence of TB during this period.

In the regulators' minds, cleanliness and morality were firmly related. One investigator clearly associated lack of cleanliness with a variety of immoral behaviour: 'They are so shiftless and lazy. . . . It is reported that every cent Mr. Deter gets is spent in liquor. The house is very untidy— practically no furniture and we are always having complaints about the filthy condition of the yard.'[106] Often OMA administrators made a strong association between cleanliness and sleeping arrangements, again connoting immoral activities: 'The home was poorly furnished and most untidy and the bedding very dirty with no sheets or pillow slips and every indication of poverty and lack of industry. . . . Sleeping accommodation was inadequate. . . .'[107] Cleanliness was also linked to delinquency, especially when there were boarders involved:

> The home and the woman herself were unspeakably filthy. It is difficult to imagine any employed man remaining in such squalor, and incredible that anyone could pay for meals or lodging. . . . The woman seems to have no sense of responsibility with respect to cleanliness or morality. . . . To grant Mothers' Allowance into this home would only furnish means for further methods of delinquency.[108]

Boarding men was already a dubious moral practice, and a lack of cleanliness ensured that delinquency would be the result, according to this investigator.

Finally, administrators continued to associate uncleanness with ethnic-minority applicants. OMA administrators were quick to comment on the unclean and immoral habits of eastern European and Aboriginal families. During this decade 'foreign-born' OMA recipients never accounted for more than 12 per cent of the total case-load (see Table 4.5). This figure does not include ethnic-minority recipients who were born in the province. At least 26 per cent of the Ontario population were non-British during this period.[109] While it is difficult to discern how racially representative OMA was, the case files suggest that only a small minority of non-British applicants received the allowance and that they experienced more careful scrutiny and criticism than their Anglo-Saxon counterparts.

Cleanliness had long been associated with morality, but this connection was strengthened during the 1930s. At the turn of the century a number of social reformers conflated cleanliness with moral and racial purity—a connection that OMA administrators encouraged during the Depression. The case files demonstrate that administrators linked lack of cleanliness with alcohol abuse, lack of industry, delinquency, and permissive sexual habits. All of these traits were of particular concern during the Depression. Turn-of-the-century temperance values revived during this period as unemployed men were found drinking away their sorrows. Many blamed individuals for their unemployment problems, calling them delinquent or lazy. As mentioned earlier, there was also a great fear about the numbers of aim-

Table 4.5 National Origins of Ontario Mothers' Allowance Recipients, 1930–1940

Year	Canadian	Other British	Foreign-Born
1930–1	63%	27%	9.8%
1931–2	64%	26%	10%
1932–3	64%	25%	11%
1933–4	64%	25%	11%
1934–5	64%	25%	11%
1935–6	64%	26%	11%
1936–7	64%	25%	11%
1937–8	Missing		
1938–9	64%	24%	12%
1939–40	65%	23%	11%

Source: 'Annual Reports of the OMA Commission, 1930–31 to 1939–40'.

less men searching for work and the many deserted women and children; many believed this situation might encourage sex outside of marriage. As a result, there was a heightened concern about the moral fabric of society during the decade. OMA administrators, in turn, carefully scrutinized many aspects of moral behaviour. Utilizing the language of earlier social reformers, these OMA administrators often conflated morality with questions of cleanliness, not to mention sexuality.

Faces of the Depression (*Archives of Ontario ACC 6520 515584*)

CONCLUSION

In many ways the Depression era was a desperate time. In addition to the economic catastrophe, Ontario citizens experienced increasing anxiety about masculinity, femininity, and morality. The loss of jobs challenged the traditional notion of manliness, which was associated with providing for wife and children. Therefore, the notion of femininity, which was defined by a woman's emotional and economic dependence on a man and her role as care-giver of the family, was also challenged. This created moral concerns for social workers, charity leaders, and government agents as they observed the social effects of many aimless unemployed men and abandoned families. Their anxieties were reflected in the administration of the OMA policy during the decade. The regulation of incapacitation and family finances had moral ramifications, but primarily shored up the traditional male bread-winner model, which encouraged a woman's economic dependence on either her husband or, in his absence, the state. On the other hand, the exhaustive and intrusive scrutiny concerning desertion and cleanliness reveals that there was more at stake than the fragile ideology of masculinity and femininity. Clearly, OMA investigators and administrators were deeply troubled about the moral character of needy single mothers and endeavoured to ensure that the recipients led proper lives. This detailed regulation of single mothers' lives reveals a less-than-benevolent state in the face of challenging social and economic times.

This is not to suggest that the state was all powerful during the Depression decade. This era was also the scene for both organized and individual action to change welfare state policies, such as OMA. Local politicians were especially active towards this end with their organized protests against restrictive OMA eligibility requirements. Occasionally, local neighbours or taxpayers would also organize to support an individual applicant or a group of women excluded from the policy. Very occasionally, recipients themselves would be agents of social change, arguing that they were unjustly treated by the OMA administration. For example, Mrs Caroline Truro was refused the allowance because she had a male visitor. She wrote the premier, arguing that she 'could have any visitor as long as my charactor [*sic*] was upheld. . . . He is my friend the same as you was to your good wife before you got married, why should I be condemned by the Mothers' Allowance. . . .'[110] Mrs Caroline Truro, however, was a rare example of a needy mother speaking back. The few times they did so, they complained to the premier rather than directly confront the investigator or the OMA administration. The latter action would likely result in the termination of the allowance, given the tremendous power and discretion that OMA administrators had over the lives of the poor recipients. Even a protest letter to the premier was dangerous, for the premier's office often referred these letters to the provincial commission for further investigation. More often a mother would appeal to a local lawyer, businessman, or politician to take on her case rather than attempt to remedy the situation herself. And where possible a mother would attempt to hide her indiscretions from the OMA investigators. More than one mother claimed she was deserted, although she knew the whereabouts of her husband. Another mother would have male visitors frequently to her house. Yet another would claim she was married when no marriage certificate could be found. It must be remembered that while the allowance was miserly, it was an act of courage simply to apply for the OMA and attempt to keep one's family together despite the economic difficulties of the decade. Despite many obstacles, mothers applied for the allowance, subjected their families to intense public scrutiny, and, where possible, hid their transgressions from the public eye. As a result of their limited resources, the protest of single mothers during this decade was individual and rarely recorded.

Chapter 5

A Turbulent Time:
War and the Postwar Era, 1940–1965

FEDERAL WELFARE STATE EXPANSION

The war and postwar era was a time of dramatic changes in both public and private life. Anxieties that often accompany periods of rapid economic, political, and social change were also characteristic of this time. To date, examinations of this period have tended to emphasize the political and economic transformations with little regard to the equally turbulent social realm. Only recently have there been attempts, primarily by social historians, to rectify this omission.[1] This chapter will explore how the political and economic changes of the war and postwar period affected social relations, particularly the lives of poor single mothers.

The tremendous expansion of the federal state was among the most significant alterations in the public sphere. During the war the federal government 'became the largest and most important employer of labour; it used its fiscal and monetary power to effect maximum war production, borrowing billions [and] raising billions by taxation.'[2] Through these war efforts the federal government increased its responsibility for the welfare of its citizens. More than 10 per cent of the Canadian population were in the armed forces during the war. Consequently, thousands of families received federal allowances and assigned pay because they had relatives in the navy, army, and air force. These payments and their attendant social services represented a new level of federal involvement in the field of welfare. Following the war the federal government, under Prime Minister Mackenzie King, desired to maintain its political authority in the field. Despite some provincial opposition, postwar concerns with maintaining high employment and promoting familial security permitted unprecedented federal involvement in the everyday welfare of its citizens.

Prompted by the Royal Commission on Dominion-Provincial Relations Report of 1940, an enormous debate about welfare developed in the immediate postwar era. Haunted by memories of economic devastation during the 1930s, Canadian citizens encouraged the federal government to enter the field of welfare and promote economic stability. Nine other studies or inquiries were initiated as a result of this public demand for change in welfare. Although these reports contained, for the most part, very different proposals, they all agreed on two fundamental principles: that existing welfare programs such as OMA were woefully inadequate, and that the solution involved some form of consolidated welfare state.[3]

Three of these government reports directly affected the future of the OMA policy. The Marsh Report was prepared by Leonard Marsh, McGill sociologist and founding member of a group of left-wing intellectuals and social reformers called the League for Social Reconstruction. His report was the most generous of the three, calling for an income security program, including children's allowances, a national health policy, and postwar employment and training for men, youths, and younger widows. As such, the Marsh Report proposed a greatly expanded social insurance plan that was largely federally administered and provided all Canadians with a better-than-subsistence standard of living by establishing a nationwide universal minimum. This was also the first time it was suggested that younger widows on mothers' allowance should be retrained rather than continue as permanent welfare dependants, a proposal that was not to be seriously addressed for another four decades.

The Cassidy Report focused specifically on the Ontario welfare bureaucracy and recommended the immediate expansion of all existing welfare programs, including mothers' allowance. Harry Cassidy, director of the University of Toronto's School of Social Work, found Ontario's welfare bureaucracy complicated, irrational, and riddled with patronage. As a professional social worker well versed in the emerging science of public administration, he proposed a more coherent, efficient, and professional structure. He recommended that the provincial government consolidate the delivery of all provincial and local welfare programs, including OMA, into regional welfare agencies. He advocated that the federal government should provide partial funding and supervision for Ontario welfare programs to curb incompetence and patronage. In addition, Cassidy called for a federal family allowance program and a comprehensive social security system financed by the employer, worker, and the federal government.[4]

Charlotte Whitton, former director of the Canadian Welfare Council, produced a report calling for welfare reform tempered by conservatism. Like Cassidy, she also found the Ontario welfare structure uncoordinated and recommended a similar solution: to consolidate all provincial and local welfare services under one program with regional welfare offices, but unlike Marsh and Cassidy, she vehemently resisted a national welfare structure. Her report opposed automatic and universal programs that she believed would encourage idleness and dependency. Instead, she recommended a national health service and the expansion of community services (such as schools, hospitals, and housing) that would reinforce the work ethic by providing emergency rather than continual care for the needy.[5] Consequently, her solution was primarily an extension of the existing welfare system, requiring additional federal contributions to provincial and local programs already in operation.

While the federal government resisted the calls for a comprehensive social security system, it did initiate a number of new federally funded welfare programs. The two major social security programs introduced during the 1940s were unemployment insurance (UI) and family allowance. UI became the largest social security program to date. This federal program, which was introduced in 1940, established unemployment insurance as a right covering 75 per cent of all wage-earners, provided they had made contributions to the scheme. Technically, the policy was not universal since workers in agriculture, forestry, fishing, government, hospitals, charities, domestic service, and schools were excluded. Yet it was the most comprehensive welfare program introduced at that time, protecting 4.6 million workers and their dependants during its first year of operation.[6] And in 1944 family allowances, the first universal welfare program, was initiated. This federal program ensured that all mothers would receive a monthly cheque for each child until the child turned sixteen. Initially, the payments were between $5 and $8 per month, depending on the age of the child.[7] While this cheque would not in itself provide for the child, it would help to supplement the inadequacies of several provincial and local welfare programs, including mothers' allowance. Old Age Pensions, previously a provincial policy, became a universal federal program during this period, and in 1954 the federal government agreed to share the costs of allowances paid to the severely disabled.[8] This policy would include incapacitated breadwinners who were previously eligible for mothers' allowance. While these programs did not provide a comprehensive social security system, they promoted federal responsibility in welfare matters as rarely seen before and supplemented the inadequacies of several provincial welfare policies, such as mothers' allowance.[9]

These new programs departed from previous welfare practice in a number of ways. Welfare became more centralized with the introduction of federal policies. These programs, for the most part, were universal, based on a notion of welfare as a right rather than the charity-style welfare based on privilege. As a result, the administrative style of welfare administration also transformed during this period. The universal nature of these programs made them non-interventionist.[10] Instead of a *mélange* of paid and volunteer welfare administrators, these federal programs were administered solely by trained social workers and other professionals. These federal initiatives set the stage for changes in provincial welfare programs.

ONTARIO MOTHERS' ALLOWANCE AND THE WAR YEARS

Unprecedented employment opportunities characterized the war years and had a dramatic impact on all Ontario welfare programs. Those considered employable but who were unable to find work during the Depression were quickly absorbed into the expanding war economy. Even marginal workers (the partially disabled, single mothers, and even seniors) were also attractive to employers during this economic boom. Consequently, provincial welfare rolls were greatly reduced during this period and did not rise again until long after the war. OMA cases declined from almost 12,000 in 1939 to less than 7,000 in 1945 as single mothers took advantage of the new opportunities for paid work (see Table 5.1). During this period of full employment, OMA administrators encouraged increasing numbers of their clients to find paid work. While many administrators had been ambivalent about single mothers working in the past, this was not the case during the war, as demonstrated by one annual report:

> The fact that the mother is allowed, and in fact encouraged to work, gives her better satisfaction and tends to raise the morale of the family and creates a hope that she will eventually become independent of any public assistance. The fact that children in these homes have to assume some responsibility fairly early in life is undoubtedly one reason why juvenile delinquency is a negligent quantity in the families of our beneficiaries.[11]

This assertion is in direct contrast to popular opinion at the turn of the century. During discussions regarding the introduction of OMA in 1920, it was generally believed that most juvenile delinquent cases were a result of single mothers working outside the home (see Chapter 1).

Increased employment opportunities also led to increased surveillance. The OMA commission became suspicious of the possibility of mothers and children secretly doing paid work while collecting the OMA cheques. Consequently, the commission almost doubled the number of its investigators to ninety-five by 1943. The average investigator's workload 'increased in order that a competent check of the earning powers of a family might be afforded'.[12] Often the OMA administration was insensitive to the difficulties involved in the transition from receiving the allowance to starting employment, as in the case of Dorothy Gray, who had her allowance of $35 a month cancelled when she got a job at the knitting company where she had worked before her marriage:

> [She] was called back to help with some War orders they had received and has only had 1/2 day last week as the order has been fulfilled and they are just on their own work at the present time. She pays a woman $20 to take care of her child and her home. . . . Since she started to work she has purchased clothing for the winter for herself and her boy, as she [did] . . . not receive sufficient from Mothers' Allowance to do this. . . . [Her doctor] stated that this Woman was in poor health [with tuberculosis] and it was doubtful if she would be able to continue the work.

It was the opinion of Helen Lordan, the OMA administrator, that this woman should never have had her allowance cancelled. Lordan had seen many other single mothers who were caught between the cancelled allowance cheque and the promise of a better life from paid work:

> Those women are wrecks over the cancellation of their checks . . . they would be better off to remain at home. . . . When the War is over they will have no work and they may as well quit now and preserve their health and energy. As it is no easy work to go to work all night and have shifts changed every two weeks.[13]

The dramatic improvement in employment opportunities, combined with the popular belief that all energies and tax dollars should be utilized for the war effort, permitted the provincial government to neglect the field of welfare. Welfare initiatives under Premier Mitchell Hepburn, who governed Ontario from 1934 to 1943, were few and far between. The Depression and the war certainly hindered the introduction and expansion of welfare legislation at the provincial level. The war in particular reduced

Table 5.1 Survey of OMA Costs, 1938–1965

Year	Total Cost	Number of OMA Families
1938–9	$5 million	12,215
1939–40	$5 million	12,138
1940–1	—	11,151
1941–2	$4.4 million	10,086
1942–3	$3.7 million	7,892
1943–4	$4 million	7,527
1944–5	$3.9 million	7,082
1945–6	$3.7 million	6,687
1946–7	$3.7 million	6,587
1947–8	—	6,300
1948–9	$4.9 million	6,815
1949–50	$5.7 million	7,304
1950–1	$5.9 million	7,382
1951–2	$6.5 million	7,748
1952–3	$6.8 million	7,621
1953–4	$6.6 million	7,059
1954–5	$6.9 million	7,294
1955–6	$7.2 million	7,266
1956–7	$7.4 million	7,418
1957–8	$9.4 million	8,580
1958–9	$11 million	9,433
1959–60	$12 million	9,722
1960–1	$12.8 million	10,149
1961–2	$13.6 million	10,359
1962–3	$12.9 million	10,171
1963–4	$11.1 million★	7,550
1964–5	$12.2 million	8,134

Notes: Total cost includes administrative work (salaries, equipment) as well as the allowances granted. As of 1953–4, the total cost included free medical services for the recipients' families.

The number of OMA families is the number of families receiving OMA on the last day of the fiscal year. Therefore, this does not include those who benefited for part of the year and whose allowance was subsequently cancelled.

★ As of 1963–4, this does not include incapacitated fathers.

Source: Ontario Department of Public Welfare, 'Annual Report, Fiscal Year 1950–51', 8.

the provincial legislature's importance as more and more power devolved to the central federal authority. This, combined with Hepburn's rural conservative leanings, helps to explain the lack of provincial social legislation during this period. Hepburn's political biographers assert that he believed his greatest contribution was legislation requiring the pasteurization of milk. As one biographer suggests, 'it was no doubt an important piece of legislation, at a time when tuberculosis was rife, but hardly a substantial monument to nine years in office'.[14]

The provincial election of 1943 upset Hepburn's reign and introduced Ontario to George Drew, the first of six consecutive Tory premiers. During the campaign Drew had promised a twenty-two point program of reform. The election resulted in a minority government with thirty-eight seats for the Progressive Conservatives and thirty-four to the Co-operative Commonwealth Federation (CCF) as the official opposition.[15] Partly to stave off the growing popularity of the CCF, Drew quickly implemented a number of his electoral promises, including several social welfare improvements: the provision of universal medical and dental health care, a complete revision of the educational system, an improvement in Old Age Pension rates, and an immediate increase in OMA rates.[16] There had been mounting public pressure to improve the conditions of poor single mothers. OMA rates had never been altered since the policy's introduction in 1920, despite a gruelling Depression decade followed by wartime inflation. The war years, despite the revival of employment generally, were particularly difficult for OMA recipients who had not found work. A 15 per cent rise in the wartime cost of living between 1939 and 1942 exacerbated the perpetual inadequacy of OMA cheques.[17] During this period OMA rates dropped to only 44 per cent of what was required for an average family (see Table 5.2). A number of single mothers lived in deplorable conditions. For example, Beulah Lord lived with her nine-year-old daughter 'in a garage with cement floor [and] has always had delicate health so much so that she is beyond being able to work at all'.[18]

Many protested these impoverished conditions. In 1941 the municipal city councils of London and St Thomas wrote the following petition to the premier:

> WHEREAS since the outbreak of war there has been a marked increase in the cost of living, and such increases bear most heavily upon those in receipt of fixed incomes, and particularly upon those in lower income class;
>
> AND WHEREAS no provision has been made in the case of those receiving Mothers' Allowance or those depending upon relief for meeting increased costs of the necessities of life;
>
> BE IT RESOLVED that the Provincial Government be asked to give consideration to the matter of an adjustment in the amounts provided for Mothers' Allowance and the maximum fixed for relief allowances, to permit of the absorption of the increased costs of necessities of life.[19]

That same year, social agencies from Ottawa, Hamilton, Toronto, and Cornwall formed a delegation to protest the inadequate OMA rates:

> Coming so closely into contact with those mothers who have to make do on a meager allowance—so much the more meager against increased wartime prices—these delegates to the provincial minister are in a position to point out the difficulties with which many mothers must contend.[20]

This delegation specifically recommended that the allowance be increased in the case of very young children and during sickness when a mother could not go out to work. The National Council of Women also participated in the campaign.[21] As one editorial insisted, 'Penny-pinching by government authority at the expense of the mothers and children is unworthy of a great Dominion. It is unworthy of the fight for freedom and democracy in which Canada is engaged.'[22]

Table 5.2 Changes in the Purchasing Power and Adequacy of Mothers' Allowance, 1921–1986

| | Purchasing Power | | | Adequacy | |
Year	Allowance Current $	Family Budget Guide 1971 $	Family Budget Guide % Change	Family Budget Guide Current $	Ratio OMA/FBG
1921	480	1,004		1,152	.42
1926	480	1,090	+9	1,056	.45
1931	480	1,218	+12	948	.51
1936	480	1,352	+11	852	.56
1941	480	1,188	−12	1,080	.44
1946	804	1,787	+50	1,260	.64
1951	948	1,436	−20	1,632	.58
1956	948	1,384	−4	1,812	.52
1961	2,052	2,736	+98	2,760	.74
1966	2,556	3,061	+12	3,660	.70
1971	3,324	3,324	+9	4,908	.68
1976	5,784	3,884	+17	8,640	.67
1981	7,926	3,345	−14	13,644	.58
1986	10,459	3,333	−0.4	19,484	.54

Notes: This table is the work of Lorna Hurl, 'The Nature of Policy Dynamics: Patterns of Change and Stability in a Social Assistance Program', unpublished paper presented to the National Conference on Social Welfare Policy, Toronto, October 1989, Table 4, 17–18.

'Allowances' refers to all financial benefits available to OMA recipients, including the OMA basic allowance, health benefits, federal family allowances, and child tax credits.

The Family Budget Guide is a shopping basket approach of pricing essential foods and services developed by the Social Planning Council of Metropolitan Toronto. This standard was described as 'sufficiently above subsistence level to ensure good health and a sense of self respect, but below any level that could be called luxurious' (Social Planning Council, 1976, as cited in Lorna Hurl, 'The Nature of Policy Dynamics', 19).

A year later, local politicians recommended an increase in OMA rates at the Ontario Municipalities Association Conference. One conference participant wrote the premier:

> I have written you time and again putting a case before you of a Mother with four children who is receiving the Mothers' Allowance of $50 per month. . . . I cannot for the life of me see how a Mother can raise four children, pay rent, light, heat, feed and clothe them, with the price of goods are today on $50 per month, you couldn't do it and your wife couldn't do, and nobody else could. . . . Take $50 as follows:

For rent—say 3 rooms	$25.00 per month
Milk (7 quarts per week)	$3.92 per month
Bread (2 loaves per day, 14 per week)	$5.60 per month
Groceries per week $3.	$12.00 per month
Electric, light	$.80 per month
Gas	$2.00 per month
	$49.32
Repairing Shoes	$1.75 per month
Total	**$51.07 per month**

> That is a very conservative estimate, could not pay a Doctor out of that, or a Hospital bill, or buy Clothes. . . .[23]

Labour also joined this campaign in 1942. The Toronto Municipal Employees' Association, Local 79, wrote the provincial government:

> [This issue] should receive your immediate attention and we strongly urge that you at least follow the lead given by the Provinces of Alberta and British Columbia and . . . that you increase the OMA amounts by at least 25 per cent. In as much as the cost of living has not taken time to select its victims, we feel that no time should be lost in investigating those now receiving benefits under the [OMA and OAP] Acts mentioned. At no time have these amounts been considered adequate and an additional 25 per cent increase now will not make them so, but such amounts will go a long way to make an equitable effort to that end.[24]

In response to this mounting pressure from social agencies, labour unions, and municipal politicians, Premier Hepburn conducted a survey regarding the financial conditions of OMA recipients. The government sent a questionnaire to each beneficiary requesting information on their earnings and that of their children. Upon reviewing the findings, government statisticians determined that:

... children over 16 years and all adults could be clothed and fed for $15.16 per month; children 11 to 12 [years] for $13.50 per month and graduated accordingly for younger children. The Commission had decided that children earning and living at home would be expected to pay $8.00 per week ... for their board if earning $60 per month or more. . . .[25]

The survey concluded that the solution to the problem was not to increase OMA rates but to increase the financial contributions of older children.

Following the 1943 election, George Drew kept his election promise and increased OMA rates by 20 per cent.[26] This was the first rate increase in the history of OMA and boosted the maximum monthly benefit for a mother with three children to $54. Still, most welfare experts considered the new rate inadequate. The Visiting Homemakers' Association of the Red Cross argued that a minimum monthly budget for a mother with three children in Toronto was $113.32; the Toronto Welfare Council estimated $86.60; and a report by the Ontario Department of Welfare estimated $117.57.[27] In 1944, to resist mounting pressure to increase further the OMA rate, the government established a $10 monthly emergency allowance for those in desperate need. This extra allowance was granted only in the most extreme emergencies and was not widely advertised.[28] In addition, allowable cash assets climbed from a maximum of $500 to $1,000. These improvements had a significant impact on the lives of poor single mothers. The rate increase, along with the introduction of federal family allowances, doubled the purchasing power of OMA recipients. According to the Family Budget Guide, a shopping basket method of pricing essential foods and services, the OMA rates climbed from 44 to 64 per cent of what was required for an average family from 1941 to 1946 (see Table 5.2). While this new rate placed OMA above the national average, it was still below the rates granted in Manitoba and British Columbia.[29] And, most importantly, the rate still remained well below subsistence.

Other than these financial improvements for poor single mothers, there were no other changes to the OMA policy during the war years. Eligibility requirements and administrative procedures did not alter. It was only during the postwar boom and the subsequent explosion in the field of welfare that significant changes to OMA were considered.

OMA IN THE POSTWAR ERA

The postwar era marked an explosion in welfare activities generally and the OMA policy was no exception to this trend. As one Ontario civil servant recalls:

This was an era of good feeling. . . . The prosperity of the period . . . created a mood of uncritical generosity towards social services, in sharp contrast to the attitudes in the legislature during the Depression days when the . . . Welfare Minister promised grudging and suspicious MPPs more rigid restrictions and a crackdown on the undeserving poor. [Instead, this was a period when almost] no Session of the Ontario Legislature went by without the announcement of at least one new project in the Department of Public Welfare, a new Act, an Act amended significantly beyond its former level, or a set of regulations enhancing available benefits.[30]

During this reform period there were four significant changes to OMA: bureaucratic reorganization, eligibility expansion, overhaul of the determination of rates, and the addition of new services. These important changes were the result of several socio-economic factors. This period was characterized by an increasingly organized labour movement, high employment, mass production, and mass consumption. Ontario's postwar boom was buoyed 'on a sea of billions of dollars of U.S. investment'.[31] This economic growth was accompanied by dramatic technological and social change. The railway and the radio gave way to airplanes and television. An influx of hundreds of thousands of immigrants also accounted for much of the labour force growth and helped to transform the province from a largely Protestant Euro-Canadian rural community to an urban, multiracial society.[32] All of these economic and social changes paved the way for a significantly reconstructed and expanded provincial welfare state.

Bureaucratic Reorganization

The federal government's trend towards a centralized, universal, and professional welfare state that began during the war years deeply affected the nature and administration of provincial welfare policies such as OMA in the postwar era. First, OMA administration was centralized during this period. The role of municipal governments in OMA dissolved in 1948. Local administration of this policy had diminished during the Depression decade, and by the early 1940s they no longer helped to finance the policy. The OMA and Old Age Pension (OAP) local boards had amalgamated during the previous decade, and by the early 1940s the majority of the local boards' energy and time was consumed by OAP applications. With the dissolution of local boards in 1948, local politicians and societal leaders no longer had direct access to the workings of the OMA. Many local newspapers, such as the *Stratford Beacon-Herald*, marked the passing of an era:

> We agree with The Windsor Daily Star that it is fitting that those who have served so faithfully on these boards, without remuneration and often at a cost to themselves, should be extended the grateful thanks of the community. Too often too many take for granted such service, without considering the time, effort and trouble it causes those who undertake it. Members of these Boards have been sincere in their efforts to do good work, and to contribute to the welfare of those in need. In Stratford this has been so obvious that no one can have missed seeing it. . . .[33]

From this time onward, municipal participation in OMA administration was generally from the outside looking in.

At least one local board was unhappy with this erosion of municipal power. Tension between the Toronto mothers' allowance local board and the provincial OMA office that had surfaced in previous decades continued to erupt. In 1941 the provincial government informed the Toronto local board that copies of the provincial investigators' reports would no longer be sent to the local board. When this privilege came to an end, two members of the local board resigned in protest.[34] In previous conflicts between the Toronto local board and the provincial commission, the municipality had refused to pay its portion of OMA administration costs. This financial weapon was no longer possible given that municipalities no longer financially contributed to the policy. As a result, the Toronto protest was ineffective and possibly provided the provincial government with further reason to take over the entire administration of OMA.

Along with the centralization of OMA administration, William Goodfellow, the newly appointed minister of public welfare, promised that the new OMA bureaucracy would be streamlined and efficient. Under the old system, a mother would first visit the county office where the clerk would help her fill out an application. This application was sent to the local board, the local board sent it on to the local provincial investigator, who would visit the applicant's home and report to the local board. The local board would then make a recommendation to the provincial commission in Toronto. The provincial commission made the final judgement and informed the applicant, the local board, and the investigator. Naturally, this process involved a lot of paper and time. On average, this application process took three months, but could take up to seven months.[35] Under the new system the mother could mail, visit, or telephone a district office and the provincial investigator (called a fieldworker) would visit the home, write the application on the spot, and send it to Toronto for judgement.

The provincial commission was also overhauled during this period. In 1944 the government appointed the first civil servant as chairman of the three-person commission, and in 1952 the government disbanded the commission and replaced it with a director. Because procedures were standardized and the discretionary powers had supposedly been written into the act, it was believed that one person alone could make the necessary decisions. Concerned that this might become 'too mechanical or impersonal', the government established an appeal panel in 1954 that consisted of three senior officials of the branch who were appointed by the director. This panel met on a weekly basis to discuss contentious cases.[36] Through these bureaucratic changes OMA became administered solely by civil servants, similar to all other branches within the department of public welfare. Previously these administrative positions were held by prominent societal leaders, usually with connections to the political party in power.

Below the director and appeal panel were seventeen district offices.[37] Fieldworkers at each office would be involved in the 'impartial' task of taking down the applicant's particulars. These fieldworkers would visit each beneficiary at least four times a year and complete quarterly reports. Unlike the local boards, these professionally trained fieldworkers would not know the applicant personally and so would be able to make a more objective judgement of the case. Other staff, such as psychologists, doctors, etc., would provide counselling, investigating, or special services, but this would be done in a professional rather than a personal manner. In each area, a supervisor would oversee the activities of fieldworkers.[38] There was no explanation given for the name change from investigator to fieldworker, but in this era of professionalization it was perhaps thought that the word 'investigator' was easily associated with punitive, intrusive charity-style administration, whereas the word 'fieldworker' was a more neutral, scientific term.

Office procedures became increasingly mechanized in the name of modernization. Electrical accounting machines replaced a great deal of manual labour. Time studies were conducted to determine the optimal size of case-loads and the most efficient processing method. One time study revealed that it took seventy-two days to render a decision as to eligibility for OMA.[39] As a result of these studies, the department advocated an administrative process that reduced paper work, consolidated forms, and introduced a new accounting procedure.[40] In 1955 a combination application and investigation form was introduced, and in the same year the alphabetical file system was replaced by a numerical one.[41] The result was believed to 'save many thousands of hours' of administrative work. One of the crowning glories of the remodelled department was the destruction of virtually all previous files. The 1953–4 annual report triumphantly recorded this event:

> Action was long overdue in the destruction of a huge volume of files and papers. Some 300,000 files, with approximately 8,000,000 dust-laden and dog-eared papers have served all useful purpose and have now been destroyed. It is probably as well that these records of human adversity be forgotten. The tragedies and despair recounted in all these files include stores of broken lives—every phase of ill-luck, ill-health, and emotional distress.[42]

Only a very few of these papers were microfilmed for posterity.

This new professional and mechanized administration required improved training of provincial welfare workers. Annual reports emphasized the need to train workers, simplify procedures, and eliminate paper work to reduce the workload and promote fair and uniform treatment for all. By 1950 a new training system was in place. New staff were initially trained at the Parliament buildings and then sent out to the area supervisors for further hands-on education. A series of training institutes for welfare workers offered workshops throughout the province. Refresher courses were also available at the Parliament buildings on a continuing basis. Bulletins, training pamphlets, and other related literature were circulated to each district office, and, finally, conferences for all provincial welfare administrators and supervisors were established—all in an effort to standardize the treatment of welfare recipients.[43]

The provincial government also worked closely with the two provincial schools of social work to ensure a ready supply of professionally trained administrators. There was a concern about the high turnover rate among social workers:

> The majority of graduate social workers are, of course, women and, frequently, within approximately two years after graduation (like nurses) they marry. The rate of attrition in social work is very high and causes an abnormal turnover in the staff of organizations that rely upon these graduates.

In 1951 the provincial government granted $10,000 to the University of Toronto for welfare student bursaries. 'We are anxious to encourage students who might decide to join the welfare staff of the Ontario Department', said the minister of public welfare. A decade later an advisory council on public welfare training was established with Professor Charles Hendry, director of the University of Toronto School of Social Work, as chair. This council created a pamphlet entitled 'Social Work—a Rewarding Career', which was distributed to 5,000 Ontario university students.[44]

This professionalization and reorganization of the OMA bureaucracy resulted in a clearer division between public and private welfare than what existed in earlier welfare administration. Although the activities of charities and social agencies became distinct from those of the state, they continued to play a significant function alongside professionally trained government staff. Often these organizations filled in the cracks by providing additional relief to supplement inadequate OMA payments. As the provincial government acknowledged:

> Some of the most effective private welfare services are made available [by a] . . . multitude of small voluntary groups, whether as part of a local church— such as women's societies or institutes, men's clubs and church boards and sessions—or as part of an ethnic society, the Canadian Legion, lodge or local service club. [These groups] often furnish emergency or temporary material aid or provide special or supplementary assistance to individuals or families where illness, debts, or other misfortune have caused distress.[45]

In most annual reports, the work of religious and secular charities was gratefully acknowledged and the provincial government expressed no desire to alter this arrangement. As late as 1961 the OMA administration stated:

> Some private interests would apparently prefer to have the total welfare responsibility assumed by governments. . . . There can be no question that there is an important and essential place for neighbourly and informal endeavours of the smaller voluntary groups within the social welfare program of this Province.[46]

Besides supplementing OMA payments, these agencies continued to promote moral values to the community and OMA recipients.

Expanded Eligibility

Expanded eligibility requirements were a key feature of OMA reform. Before 1940 only widows, mothers who had been deserted for at least three years, families with permanently incapacitated husbands, and foster parents could apply for the monthly allowance. Following the war, however, OMA opened its doors to five new groups: divorced and unwed mothers, non-citizens, families with imprisoned husbands, and sole-support fathers who were permanently unemployable. The administration also relaxed many of its previous requirements, thus permitting far greater numbers of needy single mothers to apply. One annual report called these amendments a 'revolution in our thinking. . . . This change of attitude and the acceptance of public responsibility for the Biblical concept, "We are our brother's keeper".'[47]

This 'revolution' was also a result of tremendous pressure from a number of areas. With rapid immigration following the war, a number of agencies attempted to be more inclusive than in the past, which had both positive and negative effects. Although these agencies opened their doors to new groups and attempted to respect some of the cultural traditions of immigrants, their primary goal was to Canadianize them. This Canadianization of immigrants was part of a cold war project that 'associated the willingness of newcomers to adapt to a Canadian lifestyle and adopt Canadian citizenship as a victory in the struggle against the Soviet Union and as proof of the moral superiority of Western democracies like Canada'.[48] The OMA bureaucracy participated in this process; the policy eliminated citizenship requirements in 1948 and five years later relaxed the requirements for birth, death, and marriage certificates.

A number of other groups were also included in the OMA policy following the war. Several local boards had protested the exclusion of divorced women during the previous two decades; in 1951 this group became eligible. A mother had to secure a divorce decree and the custody of her children before she could apply. These divorce decrees were often difficult to obtain, as Judge Kenneth M. Langdon, Ontario provincial magistrate, explained:

> A woman can be deserted by her husband, or be beaten, or he may be living with another woman—but unless both parties agree to a divorce, or unless adequate funds are available, the wife is unable to proceed with a divorce action.[49]

Four years later the government also granted the allowance to sole-support fathers who were permanently unemployable. This was closely followed by fathers who were imprisoned for six months or more. The latter amendment was a result of more than three decades of debate. At the turn of the century OMA lobbyists and the provincial government had considered including families with imprisoned fathers, and in 1949 the Northwestern Ontario Municipal Association advocated this amendment.[50]

The inclusion of unwed mothers, the most controversial amendment in the entire history of OMA, was introduced in 1956 following a lengthy lobby campaign. Concern about this group of needy mothers escalated during the war years when illegitimacy in Ontario climbed from 4.2 per cent of all live births in 1935 to 5.2 per cent by 1945.[51] Women's groups, such as the National Council of Women and charity organizations, worried that the war allowed for more sexual freedom. Charlotte Whitton wrote,

> In the aura of war, restlessness seizes the boy, 'uniformphobia' (induced by the male species), the romantic girl, and as guidance is unavailable or lacking, so we can prove in England and Canada, delinquency has increased especially in homes from which one parent is absent and the other at work.[52]

During the war there was one particular unwed mother's case that gained considerable public sympathy and provoked a massive campaign. Marjery Pearson and John Dunn had two illegitimate children. Each of them had been deserted by their former spouses and had no money to secure a divorce, so they did not remarry. Instead they lived together and John supported the family until he died. In 1943 Marjery applied for OMA and was refused because she was unmarried. This was the start of a provincial campaign on behalf of unwed mothers. John Flett, a well-known local judge, led the protest. He contacted labour, charity, and women's groups, threatened to print a booklet of articles supporting his position, and wrote letters to the premier, attorney-general, and other provincial notables. Local and provincial media also took up the cause. Stories and editorials appeared in a number of newspapers and magazines, including the *Globe and Mail*. Some were more cautious in their support:

> Defenders of the Commission's decision will doubtless accuse us, and the other advocates of a more generous policy, of desiring to bonus immorality. We have no such desire. Our belief is that the living together of two persons who could not get married is not always and necessarily immorality, except in a purely technical sense.

Others took a more progressive stance, calling for the inclusion of all unwed mothers. Despite the campaign, the OMA commission refused because the mother was neither a British subject nor a widow.[53]

Although this campaign failed the Pearson family, it did provoke ongoing debate on the topic. During the same year as the Pearson lobby, the Toronto Welfare Council conducted a thoughtful study of ninety unwed mothers and the 'adjustment' of the children, and called for individual assessment of each case. 'No one solution will suit all unmarried mothers', the study admonished. The report argued that forcing an unwed mother and child back to the folds of the extended family, as previously encouraged, would cause more cases of illegitimacy. Instead, the council promoted long-term counselling for both the mother and the father. The mother needed psychological guidance to make the best possible choice for the future—to keep her child, to have her child adopted, to live with her family, to live alone, or to unite with the father. The father also required help rather than the punitive legal method usually employed to ensure that he paid child support. Counselling could encourage the father to provide a role model for the child and increase the possibility of reuniting the family.[54]

This study signalled a departure from previous notions of how to treat unwed mothers and their children. From the turn of the century onwards, social reformers and welfare administrators had perpetuated biological explanations for unwed motherhood. They believed these women were 'feeble-minded' and argued that state aid would only exacerbate the problem by reproducing more 'feeble-minded' offspring. In the postwar era, unwed motherhood was redefined. No longer considered a hereditary weakness, social workers familiar with the newly popular psychiatric and psychoanalytic literature considered the unwed mother a treatable neurotic. With psychological rather than biological frailties, an unwed mother could escape being permanently defined by her error; she could be 'cured' provided she received professional help. Popular magazines were entranced with the subject and ran story after story about an unwed mother's neuroses and treatment, seeking advice from psychiatrists, social workers, and administrators at homes for unwed mothers. They recounted stories of unwed mothers who came from broken or violent homes, and who had since married and become 'well-adjusted rehabilitated women'. Other unwed mothers were shown to be exceptionally intelligent but 'unstable and quick tempered [who] . . . defiantly tried to be bad'. Elaborate statistics on these women were carefully detailed.[55]

In 1956, following more than a decade of heated discussion, the first unwed mothers were granted the allowance. That year unwed mothers who had cared for their children for a period of at least two years became eligible for the allowance. The annual report explained the reasoning behind this change:

> For some years past, it has been the policy of the Department to extend benefits to foster mothers on behalf of children born out of wedlock. However, as a condition of grant, it was necessary to assure that the natural parents' whereabouts were unknown. . . . In dealing with Mothers' Allowances legislation, the welfare of the child is our chief concern. Therefore, there seemed no logical reason why one group of children should benefit as a result of the mother's desertion and the other group be deprived of benefits simply because their mother tried to provide a home for them. It also followed that since we are interested primarily in the child's welfare, the emphasis should not be placed on the marital status of the child's parents.[56]

In addition to newly eligible groups, the OMA administration relaxed a number of existing regulations. During the previous two decades there were many complaints from local boards and community organizations regarding the lengthy desertion period required before eligibility. This period was reduced from three years to one in 1946 and further reduced to six months during the mid-1950s. Families with incapacitated fathers had suf-

fered tremendously during the Depression decade. In an attempt to alleviate their need, the government included incapacitated fathers as dependants
during the 1940s, therefore increasing the monthly rate to these homes.
Also, the OMA Act extended the maximum age of eligible children from
sixteen to eighteen years in 1950 and in 1963 extended this beyond eighteen years, provided the child was making satisfactory progress in school. In
individual cases a number of local boards had protested the strict residence
requirements. The Trades and Labour Congress requested that:

> ... provision be made to permit payment of benefits to dependents who have
> resided temporarily outside the Province in order to be near the husband or
> father who has, on the orders of the doctor, undergone treatment outside
> Ontario.[57]

In 1951 the government relaxed these restrictions, thus permitting mothers whose husbands had died, deserted, or become incapacitated outside the
province to remain eligible for the allowance.[58]

Minor administrative shuffling during the early 1960s also relieved the
OMA administration of some previous clients. In 1963 widows and single
women's allowances were introduced, providing a monthly allowance to
widows aged sixty or older. This addressed the problem of middle-aged single mothers who had been recipients of OMA for many years but no longer
qualified once their last child reached the age of eighteen. These women
tended to be untrained, inexperienced in the workforce, and generally
impoverished. In the same year the general welfare policy expanded to
include incapacitated fathers. In the first year of operation 2,805 families
with incapacitated fathers, representing approximately 25 per cent of OMA
cases, were transferred to this program.[59]

Despite this expansion in eligibility, the act continued to exclude three
categories of single mothers during this period. Separated mothers represented the largest group who remained ineligible. A number of women separated when their husbands returned home from the war.[60] Even though
the agreement was mutual, as in divorce, these cases were ineligible. This
was the case of Stella Marsden, who separated from her husband because
he 'would not work to support her. Would steal only. . . . She has managed
through working herself to pay her way until about three years ago when
her son took ill and died.' Six years after the separation, Stella applied for
OMA, but she was rejected because she was separated and because the
whereabouts of her husband was known.[61]

Common-law cases were also refused. By the early 1960s the OMA staff
discovered a number of these families.

> We are finding an increasing number of these cases, especially where the man
> living in a common-law union is the father of the children within the
> household. Many of these men have left their original families to their own
> devices. The common-law arrangement is an evasion of the laws of marriage
> and certainly not in keeping with legal responsibility.[62]

The OMA administrators conducted investigations in the evening to weed out such common-law situations.[63] Closely associated with common-law mothers were mothers who had 'unwittingly married bigamists'. In 1948 the Ontario Association of Rural Municipalities attempted to have this second group included. One Ancastor councillor claimed:

> There is a case in our township of a woman who had four children by a man she married in good faith and later found out he was a bigamist. . . . He was sentenced and our township was made responsible for the relief of these children while this man was in jail for two years. He said . . . the mother and children have been a charge on the township since that time.[64]

The provincial government denied this proposed amendment.

Rate Changes

Premier Drew opened the door for a restructuring of OMA rates when he increased the monthly payments by 20 per cent in 1943. The same year the Canadian Welfare Council (CWC) launched a campaign to convince the government that the OMA rates, despite the increase, were very inadequate.[65] The provincial CWC conducted a survey and compared OMA with other policies in the country. In 1951, with their findings in tow, the Ontario Welfare Council 'approached [the] Ontario Department of Public Welfare regarding inadequacy of mothers' allowances and other unsatisfactory features of the Act'.[66] Finally, in 1957 the government replaced the flat rate with a rate based on individual family need. This involved the establishment of a family budget for each applicant, taking into account the family's specific needs for food, clothing, shelter, utilities and fuel, sundries, life insurance premiums, and household maintenance.[67]

In actual fact, the budgetary calculation was not entirely needs based. As one civil servant explains:

> . . . the method of calculation matters little in welfare allowances. What matters is the sum the government is prepared to spend. The allowance affordable determines both the components of 'need' and the calculation's outcome, not as some fondly imagine, the reverse. . . . The needs calculated cannot be the personal decisions of applicant or assessor; equity and practicality require that each item be based on some average need for some average person, in other words on a flat rate sum. . . .[68]

Although the 1957 rate amendment was not entirely needs based, it did represent a significant improvement in the financial circumstances of needy single mothers. This amelioration had more to do with the department's decision to assign a value to the items approximating market costs rather than the method of calculation.[69] As a result, the average OMA allowance climbed from $79 to $117 per month, resulting in a dramatic increase in purchasing power for recipients. This 1957 rate represented 74 per cent of that recommended by the Family Budget Guide, an unprecedented high that has yet to be surpassed (see Table 5.2).

Additional Services

Along with expanded eligibility and increased allowance payments, the OMA administration also extended a number of services to its clients. In 1937, when the provincial government became the sole financier of the program, fuel allowances and emergency medical and dental care were provided on the investigator's recommendation and at the discretion of the commission. This provision granted many mothers a fuel allowance, but medical and dental care were granted only in the most extreme cases. All provincial welfare recipients received free medical services as of 1942 and free hospital care from 1959 onwards. Also in 1959 the government granted free dental care to OMA recipients' children who were younger than sixteen.[70] Alongside these medical services, the provincial government provided free legal assistance to all provincial welfare recipients in 1950.[71] Consequently, with the cooperation of the Ontario Medical Association, the Royal College of Dental Surgeons of Ontario, and the Legal Society of Upper Canada, the provincial government was able to standardize certain additional services for its clients rather than rely upon the generosity of individual professionals.

Despite these improvements in administration, eligibility, rates, and services, the allowance remained below subsistence and the number of recipients actually diminished from the previous era. During the war and the postwar era, women's participation in the Canadian labour force rose approximately 10 per cent as the economy shifted from resource extraction and manufacturing towards the public service sector.[72] As a result, the number of OMA recipients during this period never reached the heights of the Depression era. By the end of the Depression, more than 12,000 received the monthly allowance. During the war years, when there was an increasing demand for women workers, the number of OMA recipients dropped as low as 7,000. In 1947–8 OMA cheques were issued to approximately 6,300 families, the smallest figure since 1931, and this case-load never increased much beyond 10,000 during the entire postwar period (see Table 5.1).

MORAL REGULATION REDEFINED IN THE POSTWAR ERA

Accompanying changes in eligibility, rates, and regulations, the OMA's everyday administration also altered over the postwar period. OMA applicants continued to prove themselves both *financially* and *morally* worthy for the monthly allowance, but these definitions took on new meanings and consequently new types of regulation in the postwar era. As new categories of single mothers were included within the policy, new regulations were implemented. Consequently, as the OMA policy became more generous and inclusive, the everyday administration of the policy became more careful to distinguish between various types of recipients, creating a 'hierarchy of deservedness'. While widows were considered the most worthy and continued to receive the most favourable treatment, deserted, unwed, and ethnic-minority applicants still often experienced considerable difficulties from OMA administrators and society generally.

Financial Issues

Following the war, the financial regulation of OMA recipients was transformed. Many single mothers and their children had sought paid employment during the fluid wartime labour market. As a result, surveillance of OMA applicants had escalated to ferret out any who were secretly doing paid work. This increased scrutiny of women's and children's work continued during the postwar period. The fact that OMA payments remained below subsistence led many mothers to take some type of paid work, but employment for women in the postwar era was more narrowly defined than it had been during the war years. Fieldworkers assessed the employment possibilities for each single mother in their region, keeping in mind both the size of the family and the type of local work available.[73] Some women were able to enter the low-paid, part-time, flexible labour force. Others supplemented their allowance through insurance policies or by taking boarders, and still others were forced to take farm work or other poorly paid seasonal work. As the 1950s ended the OMA administrators assumed more and more that most single mothers did not rely upon the allowance alone but found some additional income, mainly through part-time employment. By the mid-1950s approximately 15 per cent of all refusals were a result of income and assets (see Table 5.3).

The regulation of children's labour also fluctuated with labour market needs. During the war years children had been encouraged to seek paid work to support their families, although school attendance and performance were still vital for OMA eligibility. As one annual report explains:

> The investigator, however, is on the alert to see that the boys and girls do not work to the point where they are too tired to attend to their school work. Two such brothers worked long hours, and on enquiry at the school it was found that they were not too alert in the morning. One boy was encouraged to give up his job, and an arrangement was made with his brother's employer to divide the work between the two brothers so that the boys each work three evenings a week.[74]

Following the war, OMA amendments encouraged children to prolong their stay in school. During the 1948 session of the Ontario legislature, when 'many thousands of persons were unemployed', the OMA was amended to continue the allowance until the end of the school term in the child's sixteenth year. In 1950 this was further amended to continue until the end of the school term in the child's eighteenth year. And in 1963 the allowance could continue after the child turned eighteen if he or she continued in

Table 5.3 Reasons for Refusals of OMA Cases, 1954–1964

	1954–5	1955–6	1956–7	1957–8	1958–9	1959–60	1960–1	1961–2	1962–3	1963–4
Full-time employment	48	37	23	61	84	100	74	65	58	94
Income	10	4	12	77	108	97	103	92	86	122
Assets	77	89	207	195	190	164	136	141	123	136
No need	124	111	62	95	65	73	40	—	—	—
Children of age	21	15	6	5	3	12	2	7	9	14
Children not at school	12	10	3	9	7	—	—	—	—	—
Not incapacitated	251	227	106	59	152	157	195	216	179	198
Man's whereabouts known	120	126	66	192	195	202	171	151	121	142
No proof of birth/death/ marriage	74	55	103	78	60	—	—	—	—	—
Unsatisfactory	31	23	63	282	328	243	248	191	159	163
Application withdrawn	131	142	75	81	87	61	—	—	—	—
Other	293	359	266	303	477	389	415	409	393	460
Total	**1,192**	**1,198**	**992**	**1,567**	**1,756**	**1,498**	**1,310**	**1,272**	**1,128**	**1,329**

Note: Statistics not available for 1964–5.

school and was 'making satisfactory progress with his studies'.[75] These amendments simultaneously discouraged child labour and reduced the competition for jobs.

The nuclear family unit was remodelled through financial regulation of women and children in the postwar era. During this period of rapid social and economic change, the family model was used to reduce anxieties and achieve both political and personal goals. On the political front, this model was to exemplify the success of capitalism and Western democracy. And on the personal front, a home filled with children would create a feeling of warmth and security—a haven from the threatening social, economic, and political forces outside the door.[76] OMA regulation reflected this desire to preserve and bolster the nuclear family model. Although the policy extended eligibility to new groups of single mothers, the regulations continued to favour the nuclear family. While OMA administrators sent mothers outside the home in search of paid work, it did not threaten the male-breadwinner family model as the ideal familial unit. Mothers were not encouraged to take jobs that would lead to long-term financial security. Rather, they were urged to reinforce their domestic skills through paid work. The OMA policy assumed that these single mothers were only temporarily in the labour force and would return to their domestic subservient role if and when the right male breadwinner came along. Simultaneously, OMA amendments concerning children encouraged the youth to extend their time as familial dependants and consequently prolonged a mother's duties within the home. Also in support of this male-breadwinner familial ideal, the OMA administration offered rehabilitation services for incapacitated husbands by the mid-1950s so that they could once again resume their responsibilities as male breadwinners.[77] Consequently, the postwar definition of financial worthiness was a variation on the traditional male-breadwinner family form.

Newly Eligible and Newly Scrutinized

While financial worthiness was important, the majority of the OMA administrator's time was spent discerning whether the applicant was morally suitable or not. Throughout this war and postwar period, the OMA Act continued to state that the applicant must prove herself to be 'a suitable person to receive an allowance'.[78] This definition of moral worthiness was based on the heterosexual nuclear family model as the norm. OMA administrators were very concerned about the fragility of this family unit and every effort was made to reduce all factors that threatened its security. As more than one annual report attests, 'Investigation on Mothers' Allowances cases is carried out with emphasis on the value of keeping families intact.'[79] Considerable money and expertise were spent on this goal.

The moral regulation of OMA recipients changed in several significant ways during this period. In the 1930s when every attempt was made to discourage the number of applicants, administrators were urged to weed out the unworthy ones. During this period when the number of applicants declined, emphasis was placed on moulding the applicants into proper citizens through the provision of the appropriate services:

> In visiting Mothers' Allowances beneficiaries, the investigator is expected to have an understanding and sympathetic attitude toward her client. . . . She must be prepared to advise the . . . beneficiary in all matters pertaining to the home and to suggest to her the resources available which would be of benefit to the children.[80]

This does not mean that all applicants received the allowance, but evidence suggests that there was an increase in successful applicants during this period. In the 1940s an average of 53 per cent of all applicants received the allowance, whereas during the next decade an average of 58 per cent were granted OMA.[81]

The influence of psychology also transformed the nature of everyday OMA administration. Whereas Christian notions of morality pervaded OMA administration of previous decades, they were now replaced by a psychological discourse during the postwar era. Administrators used the new psychological language to describe the poor single mother and children as the 'multi-problem family' and prescribe methods for 'coping' and 'adjusting' to this irregular family form:

> *Maladjustment* of society is being recognized in Ontario as elsewhere on the continent. A solution has largely been found to *cope* with the problems of dependency. This is in contrast to the humiliation which frequently coloured the noble principles of charity-giving in the past. Legislation with privileges and rights often gives advantage to *social casualties* on a more orderly basis [my emphasis].[82]

Dependency was considered a psychological condition that needed to be cured through studies, surveys, and counselling.[83] Annual reports concerned themselves with the *treatment* of OMA recipients.[84]

Psychological study and treatment were considered part of the solution to family discord. A joint study conducted by the province and the City of Toronto examined families who had received direct relief for more than twelve consecutive months. The description of the study reveals the emphasis on psychological rather than economic concerns:

> Two hundred cases fitting this description were selected, at random; one hundred were retained as a control group, while the other hundred cases came under the active treatment. . . . The purpose was largely that of endeavouring to bring about a replacement of dependent attitudes, on the part of the individuals served, by the adoption of more constructive approaches, self help and a restoration of belief in themselves.[85]

Through such studies, counselling, and the provision of services, it was believed that the monthly allowance could guarantee family stability. This goal of family stability was in contrast to the focus of previous OMA administration. In the 1920s and 1930s the goal of OMA administration was primarily to avert poverty. During this postwar era it was believed that poverty was being eradicated and attention could now be focused on psychological measures that would ensure long-term family happiness.[86]

Finally, the terrain for moral regulation also altered. Previously, moral regulation had included a broad range of activities and behaviour, including an applicant's cleanliness, use of alcohol, living arrangements, and visitors. During this era questions of morality were more clearly confined to issues of sexual exploration and containment. The limits of social behaviour were continually discussed in local newspapers and popular magazines. The proper development of adolescent heterosexuality was of grave social concern, and all types of sexual deviance—from unwed motherhood to homosexuality—were explored.[87] Generally it was believed that women were to enjoy sex, but within the confines of a monogamous heterosexual marriage. According to this logic, single mothers were not to participate in sexual activities. As in previous decades, sex was seen as detracting from the welfare of their children.

This discussion of sexual mores had a direct impact on OMA administration. While the OMA policy expanded to include new types of single mothers during the postwar period, this created new anxiety. The OMA administration created a 'hierarchy of deservedness' through a series of regulations. Widows had the least restrictions and were considered the most worthy, whereas *deserted* and *unwed mothers* experienced a number of eligibility barriers and were considered the least deserving. The debates surrounding the latter two categories of OMA recipients will be examined later.

It is not surprising, given the concern about adolescent and female sexuality, that deserted and unwed mothers were particular targets for anxiety during this era. It was generally believed that both desertion and illegitimacy were escalating at an alarming rate, shattering the very foundations of the heterosexual nuclear family model. Popular magazines, local newspaper accounts, the Children's Aid Society, and OMA annual reports argued that these two types of family breakdown had reached crisis proportions during the postwar era. However, there is little evidence to support this claim, although it is true that public awareness of these social issues had grown dramatically. The publicity of these issues might be partially a result of the increasing numbers of deserted and unwed mothers who became eligible for OMA. From 1940 to 1965, the number of deserted and unwed OMA recipients increased while the number of widows declined, with deserted beneficiaries increasing from 5 to 14 per cent of the entire OMA case-load. Once unwed mothers were included in the OMA Act, their numbers climbed to also represent 14 per cent of the total cases (see Table 5.4).

Immediately following the war, desertion rose among the general public, and OMA administrators worried about the long-term impact of the war on families:

One of the most serious social situations facing society today is that of the mother with young children who has been deserted by her husband. This problem was particularly alarming in the immediate post-war years when many fathers discharged from the Services found it difficult to adjust to a normal home life.[88]

Many of these women were excluded from OMA because deserted applicants who knew the whereabouts of their husbands were ineligible. In response to this immediate postwar problem, the OMA commission reduced the desertion period from three years to one year in 1946. During the first year of this new amendment the number of deserted OMA beneficiaries increased from 4 to 9.3 per cent of the total case-load. This increase distressed the administration. One annual report clearly stated that an increase in OMA desertion cases did not imply an increase in desertions in the general population. 'At the same time', the report argued, 'these figures do point to a form of family break-down which constitutes a serious social problem.'[89] In 1954 the government further reduced this desertion period to six months. These amendments more than doubled the percentage of successful desertion applicants (see Table 5.4).

By the end of the 1940s, many believed desertion had reached crisis proportions, although there was no strong evidence to prove this. Mr Goodfellow, minister of public welfare, 'was concerned over the increasing number of desertions in Ontario and the lack of parental responsibility'.[90] Journalists fuelled this panic by writing articles in newspapers and popular magazines entitled 'Deserted Families: Our Secret Shame', the 'Spouse-Hunt', and 'Runaway Husbands'.[91] Charlotte Whitton, of the Canadian Council on Child Welfare, blamed men for their naturally evil ways:

> Spring is in the air, sap in the trees, ice melting in the rivers and an itch in the soles of the feet of men. And, like as not, there's another baby on the way; so, the wanderlust and the high road call! It's 'follow the Romany pattern,' and away until the child of autumn goes the man, loose of foot and of conscience.[92]

Children's Aid Societies and family court judges throughout the country reported an increase in deserted mothers at their doors and concluded that desertion was on the rise as a result.[93] Instead, it could be argued that desertion was no longer a taboo topic and that deserted women were more inclined to seek help from social and legal agencies than they did in the past.

The most publicized desertion case occurred in Timmins on the night of 12 December 1949. Thirty married men mysteriously deserted their wives and ninety children. The newspapers across the province gave dramatic details about this event:

> Alarmed police and welfare officials announced today that warrants have been issued for the arrest of 30 married men. . . . Chief Leple insisted police were bending every effort to locate the 30 wanted men but it was 'a very dif-

ficult task' as most of the men are miners. Police circularize their descriptions among other mining communities in Ontario and Quebec in the hope they will undertake their usual line of work after they disappear. . . .[94]

There was enormous speculation about why these men deserted. Chief Leple believed it was 'more than coincidence' that almost half of the deserters had abandoned their families when their wives were expecting additional children. 'That seems like the one time a man would stick by his

Table 5.4 Reasons for Granting Ontario Mothers' Allowance, 1939–1965

	Number of Families						
Year	Widow	Incapacitation	Desertion	Foster Parents	Divorce	Prison	Unwed
1939–40	61.4%	29%	5.5%	—	—	—	—
1941–2	68%	24%	%	—	—	—	—
1942–3	69%	23%	4.3%	2.3%	—	—	—
1943–4	70%	23%	3.6%	3%	—	—	—
1944–5	84%	22%	3.3%	3%	—	—	—
1945–6	71%	21%	4%	4%	—	—	—
1946–7	71%	21%	4%	2.7%	—	—	—
1948–9	69%	22.7%	9.3%	3.2%	—	—	—
1949–50	66%	25%	5.5%	3.4%	—	—	—
1950–1	62.7%	21%	12.5%	3.5%	—	—	—
1951–2	61%	21.6%	12%	3.6%	.3%	—	—
1952–3	58.7%	24.4%	12%	3.8%	1.4%	—	—
1953–4	60%	22.5%	10.5%	4%	.8	—	—
1954–5	61%	22.5%	10.3%	3.7%	1%	1%	—
1955–6	61%	22.3%	10%	3.6%	.8%	1.5%	—
1956–7	57.6%	23%	10%	4.5%	.8%	1.4%	1.8%
1957–8	50%	24%	10%	4.7%	.9%	1.4%	7.6%
1958–9	44.9%	26.7%	—	5.5%	—	—	8.4%
1959–60	47%	25%	9%	5.6%	1.5%	2%	7.8%
1960–1	46.7%	25%	9%	5.6%	1.6%	2%	8%
1961–2	46%	25.5%	8.9%	5.8%	1.7%	2%	8.6%
1962–3	63%	—	11%	7.8%	2.5%	2.7%	11.8%
1963–4	62%	—	11%	7.9%	2.9%	2.9%	12.4%
1964–5	56%	—	14%	8%	3.2%	3.8%	14.6%

Notes: This table explains the percentage of each category in relation to the total number of families on OMA during the fiscal year.

No data available for 1940–1 and 1947–8.

As of 1962–3, incapacitated cases were no longer eligible for OMA but received a separate provincial allowance.

wife, but with these men it hasn't been the case. . . . They saw ahead of them a doctor's bill and a hospital bill for the new child and they packed up and left someone else to pay the bills.'[95] While Chief Leple blamed the men for deserting, others blamed the women. One editorial stated: 'Some women, of course, are almost impossible to live with. Their personal characteristics make them almost unbearable. Occasionally their moral conduct forfeits any sympathy for them.'[96]

One of the most striking features of the media accounts of this incident was the regional exchange it provoked. The Timmins story was carried in the local newspapers throughout the province and reinforced notions of a 'rough', unrefined masculine culture in northern Ontario. The provincial police reported that this event was an indication that northern Ontario experienced a desertion rate ten times higher than that of southern Ontario. Timmins journalists pointed fingers at the desertion rates in Toronto and Windsor. William Goodfellow, minister of public welfare, denied that desertion rates differed by region. Toronto officials claimed their record of desertion was 'by no means spotless but . . . not proportionately as serious as that of Timmins.'[97] While all agreed that desertion was a societal problem, officials quarrelled over which site was the desertion capital of the province.

The Timmins case only escalated the desire to stamp out desertion. There was a great concern about the many deserting men who refused to pay family support. Kenneth Bryden, a member of the New Democratic Party and MPP for Woodbine, argued forcefully on behalf of the deserted mother in 1964:

> There are cases of women who spend endless time going down to Family Court, trying to collect on an order made by the Court. Unfortunately we have situations where a mother with 2 or 3 small children is deserted by her husband, his whereabouts is known, he is earning an income, there is a court order against him for the maintenance of his children . . . but who is fundamentally responsible for making sure that he pays up to the mother? If he does not pay she has to go down to Family Court and they have to chase after him. He may pay or he may not. If he does not, she can get some general welfare assistance. . . .[98]

Many protested the hardships that deserted mothers endured. The West Algoma Council of Women tried in 1951 to get the deserting man's wages garnisheed.[99] Other women's groups advocated the criminalization of desertion as late as 1961.[100]

James S. Band, deputy minister of public welfare from 1953 to 1970, was particularly concerned about the 'desertion crisis'.[101] He wrote many long exposés in his departmental annual reports, ruminating about the associated moral problems; the following was written at the beginning of the 1960s:

> I wonder in cases of abandonment—and that is what desertion is, particularly where children are involved—whether we should not consider that a crimi-

nal offence has been committed. . . . Desertion and abandonment of children are cowardly and thoughtless offences. . . . The major effects of desertion and abandonment are related to the financial hardships which cause children to suffer. More than that, the deserter foists his own responsibilities on neighbours and other taxpayers of the community at large. We are aware of the handicaps and risks for children who are deprived of one parent—in most instances, the father. Broken homes do create many difficulties in living which do not apply to the *normal family setting.* . . . I have dwelt at some length on this subject since it presents complications to beggar the wisdom of Solomon when we are called upon to treat such cases [my emphasis].[102]

In keeping with the rise of psychology and a concern for desertion, the OMA administration discussed various types of 'treatment' for deserted cases. The primary goal was to reunite the family if at all possible. Many of the new administrative methods used to achieve this end were benevolent in appearance, but intrusive in practice. Counselling became an integral part of desertion cases. In cooperation with the General Welfare Assistance Branch, the OMA offered guidance to mothers who had been deserted. As one annual report stated: 'The problems of deserted families are often complex and require specialized treatment. Further efforts to strengthen this aspect of the services are being made especially in the large urban areas.'[103] In another attempt to reunite deserting families, the OMA administration granted a three-month bonus to all families where the husband had been found and returned home. This could require a great number of visits or interview sessions to ensure that the family was living together. Special investigation was also required at the home of the deserted mother and dependent children. There was always a suspicion that deserted applicants were not honest. To determine an applicant's integrity, 'special investigations [were] . . . made in the evening hours' to determine if the woman was in fact deserted.[104]

More coercive methods were also applied to reunite the family or at least capture the deserting father. In 1960 the province, in cooperation with the City of Toronto, established the Special Investigation Unit (SIU) to devote more attention to desertion cases. This unit of eight full-time provincial staff and three municipal staff was hired primarily to locate the deserting men. As well, the unit helped women to lay charges at the family court, detected fraudulent desertion cases, attempted to reconcile the family wherever possible, and studied the causes and effects of desertion. In the latter case, the SIU staff conducted meticulous investigations and provided detailed accounts of the personal habits and lifestyles of these families.[105]

Despite all the hysteria about rising desertion rates and the costly initiatives to deter this, there is no evidence to suggest that desertion was an increasing social problem. One annual report acknowledged that 'desertion does not appear to be increasing but more cases are being brought to light'.[106] In 1962 the Canadian Welfare Council declared that this 'lack of statistics on separations and desertions results in a serious lack of information on Canadian family life.'[107] Following the two amendments to the OMA Act, the number of deserted beneficiaries increased from 4 to 12 per cent in the late 1940s but remained relatively stable for the rest of the postwar period (see Table 5.4).

Unwed mothers faced even more public attention and controversy than deserted women. This group became eligible for OMA in 1956, but the OMA annual report was careful to insist that the 'putative father [is not to be relieved] . . . of his legal and financial responsibility'.[108] Rather, the mother was to visit the local Children's Aid Society, which would attempt to procure payment from the father before the mother became eligible for the allowance. As well, the two-year waiting period was to ensure that the mother was 'fit' to care for the child and that she did not continue her 'improper' sexual practices. The six-month waiting period for deserted mothers suggested that mothers who were unmarried were more morally questionable than those who were deserted.

The 1956 inclusion of unwed mothers provoked heated debate in the provincial legislature. Politicians such as Ross Mackenzie Whicher, Liberal MPP for Bruce County, worried that the introduction of such an amendment would encourage extramarital sex. He believed it was all right to pay for an unwed mother of one child, but any more children 'might encourage this sort of thing'.[109] In 1958 the government waived the waiting period for unwed mothers, but the allowance was restricted to unwed mothers with only one child. A year later this was further amended to establish a six-month waiting period and require the mother to be at least eighteen years old. These restrictions ensured that many unwed mothers did not qualify for the allowance. Those who were ineligible had to give up their offspring to private or public adoption agencies, to depend on their extended families, or to rely on general welfare.

The debate inside Queen's Park was only part of a larger controversy that continued concerning morality and premarital sex. Unwed mothers became the scapegoats for much of this societal turmoil about moral standards. Dr Marion Hilliard, chief of obstetrics and gynecology at the Women's College Hospital, believed that an unwed mother should be punished by having her child adopted: 'When she renounces her child for its own good, the unwed mother has learned a lot. She has learned to pay the price of her misdemeanor and this alone, if punishment is needed, is punishment enough.'[110] Other social workers and officials representing homes for unwed mothers echoed Dr Hilliard's philosophy.

Others blamed unwed mothers for many of society's evils. For example, one newspaper account believed unwed mothers were partially responsible for higher taxes:

> The $41,920,231 spent on Public Welfare caught our eye because of many stories we have been hearing of how high area indigents are living off the hog. . . . We have heard of [one] . . . family drawing down almost $250 per month in

Mothers' Allowance, in addition to its sizeable baby bonus cheque. That sounds like soft living, but it could be even softer if an unmarried daughter got into trouble. Then an extra $75 might be added . . ., not counting the extra baby bonus. Sounds almost like an invitation to illegitimacy, does it not? . . .[111]

This argument ignores the fact that full-time institutional care for these illegitimate children was far more expensive.

Like desertion, this anxiety about unwed mothers and rising illegitimacy rates was unfounded. The highest rate of illegitimacy in the province (at 5.2 per cent of all live births) was immediately following the war when many found family life difficult. But from 1945 the rate steadily decreased. In 1951 Ontario had the second lowest illegitimacy rate in the country at 3.3 per cent.[112] By 1960 Ontario had one of the lowest illegitimate birth rates in the English-speaking world at 3.2 per cent; in comparison, the illegitimacy rate in London, England, was 9.9 per cent.[113] But the inclusion of unwed motherhood in the OMA Act meant that the issue became more apparent to provincial government officials. By the end of this period unwed mothers accounted for 14 per cent of the total OMA case-load (see Table 5.4).

THE EBB AND FLOW OF NATIONALISM

The regulation of ethnic-minority single mothers changed dramatically between the war and the postwar era. During the war years the OMA administrators justified their nationalist bias, as one annual report illustrates:

> The success in life of very large numbers of young men and young women who were children in the homes of beneficiaries is evidence of wise administration. . . . Many hundreds of sons and daughters are in the Armed Forces, and not a few have paid the supreme sacrifice.[114]

War widows and single mothers whose children were soldiers were highly praised during these years. Whereas most applicants demonstrated a humble attitude towards OMA administrators, there is evidence to suggest that this group of mothers expected to receive the allowance as a right for their familial sacrifice. For example, widowed Mrs Isabelle J. Watson wrote to the OMA administration:

> I have a son 11 years old, my other boys' [sic] are men. Neil is a Pilot Officer . . . John is an A/C2. in the R.C.A.F. at Trenton, he is married his wife receives his allowance. My eldest son is married, he helps me all he can. Bob is unimploved [sic], he plays in Don Hopkins Orchestra when they have jobs, he has signed up with the Air Force at London and is hoping to be called soon as a pilot. Doug, my eldest son has also signed up with the Air Force. . . . I would like to keep the home together till my sons come home. I am not asking for charity, just what my sons are fighting for—British fair play.[115]

Antagonism towards immigrant or non-British subjects escalated during the war. Some municipalities argued that welfare programs should only be available to British subjects or citizens of allied countries.[116] During the war years ethnic-minority OMA applicants received more scrutiny and criticism than their White Anglo-Saxon counterparts, such as Russian-born Helene Gosner. Widowed, she was ill and attempting to raise her son by 'trying to make a little [money] out of chickens. . . .'[117] A neighbour wrote a letter complaining about Mrs Gosner:

> [Mrs Gosner said] that the boy is sick and she cannot work but that is not so as she works steady and the boy could work if he wanted to but he is too lazy. . . . I believe she is quite well off but only puts in a poor mouth like all foreigners do. . . . There is something going on right now as I see Germanys [sic] going there all the time. Something is up but its [sic] hard to say she is so sneaky.[118]

A month later the neighbour wrote another letter to the OMA administration. 'I have just found out a man by the name of . . . he is a German. He is trying to get Mrs. Gosner in the secret service as an interpreter.'[119] For a year the provincial commission suspended Mrs Gosner's OMA cheques while they conducted a thorough investigation into the case. And then in 1941 she was granted the allowance with a notice stating that the 'Commission is satisfied this applicant is not disloyal to Canada and the British Empire.'[120] In another case, a Galician-born family was disqualified simply because of suspicions. In this case the local OMA board stated: 'If [the provincial commission has] . . . *the least* suspicion as to the loyalty of the . . . family we feel that during war time the *suspicion* alone is quite sufficient reason for having this family "cut off" [the] allowance.'[121]

With the influx of immigrants following the war, increased attention was focused on these 'New Canadians'. Previously, biological explanations were given for why immigrants were morally inferior and should not be encouraged to reproduce. Therefore, state aid such as OMA was extremely difficult for immigrants to obtain, but following the war, immigrants were considered in a new light. Biological explanations of inferiority were discarded. Instead, the immigrant was considered redeemable if given proper instruction on how to be Canadian. Consequently, OMA regulations relaxed to permit more immigrants to be properly socialized through the helping hands of the state. In 1953–4 regulations concerning the type of evidence accepted for birth, marriage, and death records were relaxed:

> This is of particular help to New Canadians, who, for the most part, were unable to bring proper records with them from their European homelands. All in all, the effect has been to include many applicants who may otherwise have been denied the benefits of Mothers' Allowances assistance on technical grounds.[122]

During the early 1960s attention was given to the inclusion of immigrants among the provincial welfare staff, as one annual report stated: 'It is interesting to note, too, that our staff has been augmented by some New

Canadians who are maintaining their duties and the services of the Department in a most acceptable and helpful way. . . .'[123]

Also during the 1950s, the OMA administration expressed a growing concern about the plight of Aboriginal peoples. Unlike most provincial welfare policies, the OMA policy had always included Aboriginal single mothers, although very few qualified. An Indian Advisory Committee, which was established in the early 1950s, regularly toured the reservations and examined the living conditions of the Aboriginal population. Among other issues, the committee discussed the relationship between various Children's Aid Societies and the reservations.[124] In 1955 the government introduced the Indian Welfare Services Act, which granted Aboriginal residents of Ontario the same welfare benefits as other residents (this included general welfare, blind persons' allowances, disabled persons' allowances, old age assistance, as well as the previous arrangement for OMA).[125] The elected council of each Indian band would participate in the administration of this assistance.[126] This meant that Aboriginal single mothers would be eligible to receive general welfare while they awaited a decision from OMA about their application.

CONCLUSION

The war years prompted a national debate on the state's obligations regarding the welfare of its citizens; this debate would have a dramatic impact on postwar life. During the war the federal government introduced new universal welfare programs, such as unemployment insurance and family allowances. Following the war, provincial welfare policies, such as OMA, expanded. While the OMA policy did expand in a number of important ways, there were also new regulations that exemplified the fears associated with the postwar period. In many ways, the single mothers who applied for OMA were the antithesis of the postwar ideal and therefore provoked enormous anxiety. The postwar era's repressive domestic ethos and heightened concern about the containment of female sexuality ensured that these single mothers outside the heterosexual nuclear family unit would be carefully regulated. While OMA applicants were financially and morally regulated as in previous decades, there were also new administrative means established during this era to promote the heterosexual nuclear family ideal. Single mothers with living male partners (be they divorced, deserted, or unwed) were considered to be particularly suspicious, requiring careful scrutiny and counselling. The OMA administration made many benevolent and coercive attempts to reunite these 'broken' families. The hysteria surrounding deserted and unwed mothers, despite evidence that both these social phenomena were declining, was part of a general concern about the fragility of the family unit. The regulation of poor single mothers in Ontario typified a historical period characterized by tremendous social and economic transformation and the anxieties that often accompany rapid change.

Chapter 6

The Struggle Over the Meaning of Deserving, 1965–1995

In April 1965 Prime Minister Lester Pearson declared 'war on poverty' and promised $25 million a year to needy mothers and their children through the introduction of the Canada Assistance Plan (CAP), thus providing guaranteed unlimited funding for provincial and municipal welfare programs. This marked the beginning of a new era of federal and provincial welfare state expansion.[1] This expansion in the field of welfare was partly a result of the continuation of the postwar economic boom, as well as an active and vocal antipoverty movement. The decade 1965–75 marked the tail end of the Fordist postwar compromise, which was characterized by mass production, mass consumption, and a consistent pattern of bargaining between labour and capital. Corporations acknowledged the legitimacy of unions and implicitly recognized some obligation to workers and citizens. Simultaneously, labour accepted corporate control over production and investment and agreed to work within the limitations of a capitalist economy. This compromise resulted in a stable economy that enabled politicians to promise new and improved welfare programs to ensure that those who fell through the cracks of this economic boom would be provided for. An increasingly active antipoverty movement helped to ensure that the welfare programs promised were indeed implemented and expanded.

By the mid-1970s the postwar compromise was severely challenged by new economic realities. Stagflation, the economic phenomenon of high unemployment and high inflation, precipitated the end of this postwar era. Labour and capital relations became increasingly strained from the late 1970s to the early 1990s. Corporations looked increasingly beyond the national border to increase their profits, while the real wages of Canadian workers were rolled back. As well-paying, full-time jobs diminished, part-time, temporary, and low-paid employment expanded, creating an increasingly marginalized and flexible workforce. Simultaneously, more and more citizens became unemployed. This period of increasing disparity and impoverishment placed growing and conflicting demands upon the state and its welfare programs.

As the global economy dramatically restructured, causing severe unemployment and disparity, there were enormous pressures upon governments to restrain their social welfare expenditures. The general acceptance that the state should intervene in the economy was increasingly challenged. Where 'the Keynesian state asserted the primacy of the public over the "invisible hand" of the market and engendered expectations that the state was responsible for meeting the basic needs of its citizens', the post-Keynesian or post-Fordist state is a very different one.[2] The new nation-state is increasingly seen as subject to the unpredictable forces of the global economy. Where once social programs were considered a tool to sustain consumption patterns, minimize social conflict, and protect citizens from the extremes of the business cycle, the same policies are increasingly viewed as a fetter on global capitalist accumulation, hampering worker flexibility. The post-Fordist welfare state model is one with a much trimmer bureaucracy, which lightens the tax burden and lowers social benefits, abandoning universality and targeting benefits and services to a needy population.[3]

These changes deeply affected single mothers on welfare in Ontario. During the first decade of this period (1965–75), stable economic growth permitted both the federal and provincial governments to expand their definitions of the deserving poor. The introduction of the CAP permitted the Ontario government to rewrite many social policies, such as Ontario Mothers' Allowance, and simultaneously to expand eligibility and services to the needy. As part of the new, more generous welfare state, OMA accepted new types of single mothers for the allowance. These eligibility amendments were significant, providing new possibilities for some women and encouraging a rights-based discourse for the antipoverty movement. Despite certain amendments, this did not mark the end of a deeply stigmatizing policy. As more single mothers became eligible, there were new hierarchies of deservedness established and new methods introduced to distinguish between the worthy and the unworthy. As such, this social welfare legislation remained true to its roots as a charity-style program based on a notion that welfare is a privilege rather than a right that must be earned through careful scrutiny.

The Ontario government promoted a new type of welfare for poor single mothers, welfare that would include retraining and the possibility of employment. Whereas single mothers had been previously considered 'unemployable', they became increasingly redefined as potentially employable, given the right types of retraining and employment incentives. Such reforms provided some women with helpful counselling and their first opportunity to leave welfare and find secure jobs, but these women were the minority. Other OMA recipients participated in retraining programs that were ineffectual and did not lead to full-time jobs. This emphasis on retraining and employment foreshadowed a new era when welfare recipients would be forced to work for welfare.

By the early 1990s there were a number of signposts demonstrating that even a social democratic government would consider adapting welfare programs to capital's desire for a more flexible, low-wage workforce. Single mothers, experiencing escalating hostility from both federal and provincial governments and the public, increasingly became the scapegoats of the era—the victims of increased surveillance, welfare cuts, and escalating pressure to get off welfare and find work when there are few jobs available.

These policy changes over a thirty-year period are the result of tremendous political struggle to determine who is or is not a deserving mother. The notion that welfare is a privilege rather than a right opened the door to the possibility of a return to a more restrictive and punitive policy. By the early 1990s new battle lines between the deserving and undeserving were being drawn with the lives of single mothers and their children at stake.

WELFARE REFORM AND ANTIPOVERTY ACTIVISM, 1965–1975

Under the CAP agreement, the federal government promised to finance 50 per cent of any provincial or municipal aid 'for the purpose of providing . . . food, shelter, clothing, fuel, utilities, household supplies and personal requirements'.[4] As such, this plan was a significant departure from previous welfare programs in a number of ways. First, it illustrated the federal government's increasing role in social welfare as the CAP consolidated a number of federal and provincial programs into a single agreement. Through the CAP agreement the federal government expanded its responsibilities to include aid to needy mothers and children. Whereas unemployment assistance, old age assistance, blind persons' allowances, and disabled persons' allowances were previously cost shared, mothers' allowance had received no federal funding until the CAP. Second, the plan promised to eradicate many of the punitive features of earlier welfare policies. In order to receive this federal grant, welfare programs had to meet three conditions: benefits must be based solely on financial need; all provincial residence requirements must be eradicated; an appeal board must be established in each province to protect recipients' rights. Finally, the CAP promised not only to help the poor but to provide for those 'about to become in need' in the hopes of *preventing* poverty.[5]

The introduction of the CAP in the 1960s dramatically transformed the provincial welfare scene. During this decade the Ontario Progressive Conservative Party continued to enjoy majority governments under premiers John Robarts and William Davis.[6] Their popularity and their political philosophy did not make them natural leaders in the field of welfare reform, but even they were influenced by the times. As one senior civil servant recalls, the CAP 'launched the Ontario Department of Public Welfare into the greatest writing and rewriting of legislation in its history'.[7] Programs were expanded, expenditures soared, and the provincial welfare bureaucracy was reconstructed. To reflect this period of welfare expansion, the department of public welfare was renamed the Department of Social and Family Services in 1967 and the Ministry of Community and Social Services in 1972.

One of the most significant changes in the Ontario welfare field was the establishment of a two-tiered welfare structure. In 1966 the OMA policy for needy single mothers was replaced by the Family Benefits Act (FBA). All welfare payments issued directly by the province, including mothers' allowance, were incorporated under this one piece of legislation.[8] This established two tiers of the provincial welfare system: (1) the Family Benefits Act with joint federal-provincial funding on a 50/50 basis for long-term or 'unemployable' recipients and (2) general welfare assistance (GWA) with federal, provincial, and municipal funding on a 50/30/20 basis for short-term or 'employable' recipients. The creation of these two tiers affected single mothers in a number of ways. First, single mothers were no longer targeted as a distinct group with specific needs and regulations. Instead, the specific rules and regulations for single mothers under the OMA Act were replaced by a policy that provided financial assistance not just to single mothers but also to the blind, disabled, and elderly. Second, the FBA further clarified what had long been assumed—that single mothers were unemployable and that their first priority should be the full-time care of their children. Third, recipients' rights were enhanced through the establishment of an appeal board as stipulated under the CAP agreement. Fourth, the moral criteria clearly stated in all previous mothers' allowance acts were deleted. Welfare was to be provided as a result of financial need with no discretion or moral criteria attached, suggesting a new era of rights-based welfare legislation.[9]

The impact of CAP's cost-sharing agreement on the new FBA policy was twofold: a dramatic and unprecedented increase in the number and types of recipients and the creation of additional services. Within the first three years of the CAP the number of FBA recipients increased from 10,056 to 20,428, and the costs associated with this group also escalated, from $17 million to $58.9 million during this period.[10]

The number and type of recipients increased as a result of several factors. The FBA policy minimally altered eligibility requirements. The age of dependent children was extended from eighteen to under twenty-one, provided the child was attending school and 'making satisfactory progress with his studies'.[11] The waiting period for deserted mothers was reduced from six to three months as had already happened for unwed mothers in 1964, but eligibility qualifications for the majority of single mothers remained unchanged from the previous era, as illustrated below:

Widows—no stipulations

Mothers whose husbands were patients in a sanatorium, hospital or similar institution

Mothers whose husbands were imprisoned provided their husbands had at least 6 months more to serve

Divorced mothers provided they had not remarried

Unwed mothers provided the mother was 16 years or more and the dependent child was three months old or more[12]

What did change, however, were the *types* of single mothers who received the benefit. With the introduction of the CAP funding, a number of deserted and divorced women were transferred from general welfare assistance to FBA in order to cut provincial expenditures and obtain the maximum federal financing. As a result, widows, who represented half of all FBA recipients in 1965, fell to 10 per cent in 1975. In contrast, deserted and unwed mothers began at approximately 12 per cent each and doubled ten years later. The percentage of divorced mothers also climbed, from 2.7 to 10.3 per cent, during the same period. Generally, this dramatic change in the percentage of FBA recipients reflected the changing family form in the provincial population at large.[13]

Services also expanded following the CAP agreement. In 1966 universal medical and hospital insurance was established for low-income people in Ontario through a special arrangement with the Ontario Medical Association.[14] In addition, the province increased its commitment to child care. The provincial subsidy to municipalities to establish child care centres increased from 50 to 80 per cent of the total costs, although this new arrangement did not begin to meet the demand.[15]

The improvements the CAP agreement made to welfare had not solved many of the long-standing concerns of the poor, least of all needy single mothers. The three conditions established for CAP funding were weak and virtually unenforced. One condition stipulated that benefits must be based solely on financial need, but did not establish a minimum benefits level. The provincial government was under no obligation to increase the monthly payments. Despite the expectation that CAP's injection of federal funds

Table 6.1 Marital Status of Female FBA Recipients, 1965–1984

Year	Widow	Desertion	Divorce	Single/Unwed	Separated	Married	Other
1965–6	51%	15.4%	3.6%	17%	—	—	12.6%
1966–7	44.6%	18.6%	4%	19.5%	—	—	13.4%
1967–8	24%	31%	3.6%	21%	5.3%	15.1%	—
1968–9	23%	29%	3.5%	23.6%	5%	15.9%	—
1977–8	9.3%	44%	13%	32%	—	—	1.7%
1978–9	8.7%	43%	14%	32.6%	—	—	1.7%
1979–80	7.9%	42%	14.6%	33.4%	.8%	—	1.5%
1980–1	7.3%	40%	15%	34%	2.3%	—	1.4%
1981–2	6.6%	38%	15.6%	35.7%	3.6%	—	1.4%
1982–3	5%	35.5%	16.6%	35.4%	5%	—	1.6%
1983–4	5.3%	34%	16.8%	36.3%	6%	—	1.7%

Note: These figures do not include single-parent fathers who received FBA.
Source: 'Annual Reports of the Community and Social Services Ministry, 1965–66 to 1983–84'.

would encourage provincial and municipal governments to do likewise, this did not occur. During this decade provincial and municipal expenditures on social assistance remained virtually constant as a proportion of their total expenditures.[16] Consequently, the financial circumstances of poor single mothers did not significantly improve. With spiralling inflation, the FBA rates did not keep pace with rising costs, and the purchasing power of FBA recipients actually declined during this period (see Table 6.2). The disparity between FBA recipients and other citizens also widened. In 1961 the FBA family received approximately 35.5 per cent of the average family income in Ontario; by 1971 they received approximately 29 per cent, which continued to decline in 1981 to approximately 25 per cent (see Table 6.2).

Another condition of the CAP created the appeal procedure but did not give it any teeth. Provincial governments were generally slow to introduce appeal boards and, once established, limited the types of cases that could be appealed. The CAP did not require applicants to be informed of their rights and benefits. To this day, most provinces (including Ontario) do not adequately inform recipients of their basic rights to privacy, information, or the appeal procedure. Decisions are not based on precedence, so each case must be appealed on its own merits, and recipients are not informed of previous important decisions. This lax appeal procedure with virtually no federal enforcement allowed provincial and local officials to continue to provide services as they saw fit.

These CAP conditions marked neither the establishment of rights-based welfare nor the end of punitive social programs. Poverty was neither eradicated nor effectively prevented by these CAP conditions, but the appeals board, while imperfect, did reinforce the notion that welfare recipients had rights and thereby legitimized further antipoverty organizing. The rights-based discourse that emerged during the 'war on poverty' continued to persist, partly as a result of these CAP conditions. This does not mean that welfare programs were no longer moralistic or stigmatizing, but certain administrative practices could be questioned.

A close examination of the FBA policy, including annual reports, administrative records, and media accounts, suggests that moral concerns continued to persist. This was especially the case concerning the administration of

Table 6.2 A Comparison of FBA in Relation to the Average Family Income

Year	FBA Rates	As a Percentage of Average Family Income	Average Family Income
1961	$2,052	35.5%	$5,773
1971	$3,324	28.9%	$11,483
1981	$7,926	24.6%	$32,170

Source: Table 5.32 in *Canada Year Book*, cited in Lorna Hurl, 'The Nature of Policy Dynamics: Patterns of Change and Stability in a Social Assistance Program', unpublished paper presented at the Fourth National Conference on Social Welfare Policy, Toronto, 24–7 October 1989, 20.

deserted and unwed FBA applicants. An amendment in 1966 reduced the waiting period for deserted applicants from six to three months. The waiting period had been similarly reduced for unwed mothers two years earlier. This desertion amendment provoked considerable controversy within the provincial legislature. Stephen Lewis, Ontario New Democratic Party MPP for Scarborough West, argued that no waiting period should be required given that 'the needs of mother and children after the three-month period [were no different] . . . than the needs during that original three-month period'.[17] But the government argued that a limited waiting period was necessary to ensure that needy single mothers did not make false claims. As Minister of Public Welfare Louis Cecile explained, without a time limit people would take advantage of the benefit and 'it might be[come] a game'.[18]

Following this 1966 amendment, deserted mothers became the largest category of female FBA recipients. Within a year the number of deserted recipients almost doubled from 18.6 per cent to 31 per cent, representing one-third of all female FBA recipients. For the remainder of this period deserted recipients continued to represent approximately one-third of the total cases. As of 1967–8, deserted mothers became the largest category of female FBA recipients, only to be eclipsed by unwed mothers in 1983–4 (see Table 6.1).

In order to ensure that deserted mothers did not take advantage of this amendment, the Special Investigation Unit (SIU) continued to search the country for deserting husbands. The SIU often worked closely with other agencies to obtain information about a particular case. In Susan Billing's case the superintendent of the public housing project where she lived told the SIU:

> . . . that she was still living with a negro fellow . . . that this man leaves for work at 6:20 a.m. daily, returning at 6:30 p.m. . . . At Christmas, when a local church visited to make a Christmas donation, the donor reported that a negro answered the door. . . . When both the Children's Aid Society worker and the welfare visitor confronted the woman with this information, Mrs. Billings stated she was not living common-law nor did she have her boyfriend stay overnight on any occasion.[19]

Evidence suggests that deserted recipients like Susan experienced more intense scrutiny from social workers, landlords, and neighbours than other single mothers.

There was also considerable anxiety about the supposed increase in unwed motherhood throughout the province. Unwed mothers continued to increase as a percentage of female FBA recipients and became the largest category of recipients in 1983-4. Since unwed mothers had to wait three months before they could apply for FBA, they would first apply for general welfare assistance. Since GWA was municipally administered, many unwed mothers were refused, especially if the mother refused to name the father of the child.[20] In one celebrated case, a 'pretty blonde Polish girl of 16 . . . became a prostitute to feed her 8-month-old daughter after the [local] welfare department refused her aid.'[21] Teenage pregnancies such as this case were of particular concern to the media in the 1960s. Newspapers reported that more and more of these young unwed mothers were keeping their babies. Headlines such as 'Miniskirts Blamed for Illegitimate Births', 'The Unwed Mothers' Dilemma', and 'Problems of Illegitimacy Frightening' were splashed across the pages of numerous newspapers.[22]

Even though the federal and provincial commitment to welfare reform in the mid-1960s did not significantly improve the lives of many needy single mothers, the FBA did provide increasing numbers of women and children with benefits as well as much-needed medical and dental services. The variety of recipients diversified as the FBA permitted increasing numbers of deserted and unwed mothers. However, benefits remained well below subsistence throughout this period and did not begin to meet the needs of recipients. Also, the FBA administration continued to distinguish between the worthy and unworthy through a number of intrusive measures, such as the SIU activities. Despite the CAP provision, the FBA policy continued to determine eligibility on the basis of both financial and moral criteria, particularly in the case of deserted and unwed mothers.

The Poor Get Organized

The CAP agreement did not end poverty. Indeed, it was introduced just as the battle lines for the war against poverty were beginning to be drawn. Collection of statistical data on poverty began in the early 1960s and increased public awareness of the problem. In 1962 the publication of Michael Harrington's *The Other America: Poverty in the United States* provided clear proof that not all were prospering in the postwar boom. In 1964 the Ontario Federation of Labour published a study that showed that more than 1 million Ontarians were living in poverty. A year later the Canadian Welfare Council conducted a study of rural poverty and found the 'extent . . . staggering'.[23] Another report concluded that more than a million Canadians were illiterate and almost 4 million lived below the poverty line.[24] The Economic Council of Canada claimed that one in five Canadians lived in poverty in 1968.[25] The most ambitious study on the subject began in 1968 with the federal government's establishment of the Special Senate Committee on Poverty. With Senator David Croll as chair, a $1 million budget, and a mandate to 'inquire into the causes of poverty . . . and to make recommendations for its elimination', the committee embarked on a cross-country tour.[26] A number of organizations provided statistical data documenting the growing disparity. This committee provided a forum for the mobilization of a grassroots antipoverty movement.

The poor had already begun to organize in the mid-1960s, but the Senate committee provided a needed focus for this activism. This type of grassroots, antipoverty organizing had only occurred in Canada during one other period, the Depression. Both the Depression and the mid-1960s provided an opportunity for the voices of the poor to be heard. During the economic crisis of the Depression newly unemployed men were outraged that they had lost their jobs and were forced to rely on the punitive relief system. The mid-1960s, in contrast, was not a period of economic instability, but it was a time of rising expectations and a concern about 'poverty in the midst of plenty'. Federal funding through the Senate committee provided a new avenue for political action, and, for the first time, a large number of low-income Ontario women, particularly single mothers, raised their voices in protest.

According to the OMA records, there was no collective protest by single mothers prior to 1966. Previously individual single mothers would often write the premier or a local official regarding their mothers' allowance cheque, but in 1966 fifty single mothers from Sarnia collectively wrote Prime Minister Lester Pearson:

> We have had a great deal of difficulty with the Mothers' Allowance lately. It is totally inadequate in face of the rising cost of living. Sarnia has the highest wage scale in Canada and food, clothing, rent and services are fantastically high. Some of our Mothers have not purchased milke [sic] for 3 months. It is 32 cents a quart here. The children in many cases, are going to bed hungry and if their stomachs are full often it is with macaroni and 3 day-old bread. . . . We understand that the Canada Assistance Act may help us, especially in the way of rehabilitation so that we may become independant [sic].
> . . . Could you please try to 'hurry up' the CA Act? . . .[27]

The fact that these women directed their protest to the prime minister rather than to the premier or a local official also demonstrated the growing awareness of the central importance of the federal government in welfare. This collective action in the form of non-confrontational lobbying heralded a new era of antipoverty organizing.

Other antipoverty groups practised more disruptive strategies; one of the most effective was the Toronto-based Just Society Movement (JSM). This group 'organized by the poor, for the poor' began in 1968 as a result of a discussion between several poor women on welfare, mainly single mothers.[28] They took Prime Minister Pierre Trudeau's term 'just society' and pushed the limits of this liberal philosophy.[29] JSM restricted its membership to welfare recipients and developed 'a flamboyant style of action which attracted a good deal of press coverage'.[30] The organization's political actions included setting up help booths inside the welfare offices, sit-ins, and other demonstrations.[31] JSM was highly critical of professional agencies, such as United Appeal, Metro Toronto Social Planning Council, and the Ontario Welfare Council, which documented poverty and provided financial aid but did not involve poor people in their decision-making structures. JSM members stormed the boardrooms of these organizations, demanding that poor people be fairly represented on their boards.[32]

This organization developed a close association with Praxis, a more professional group committed to social change and critical research. Praxis's members included radical-thinking academics, social workers, and students. Praxis members joined many of the JSM protests, but also contributed analysis and statistical information to the cause. The relationship was not always an easy one between radically minded professionals and welfare recipients, and eventually the alliance dissolved.[33]

Two government initiatives helped to provide antipoverty groups with the resources to organize. In 1966 the federal government established the Company of Young Canadians (CYC). This arm's-length government agency provided youth with a stipend of $135 a month and a mandate 'to give power to people who were powerless, to reach out to the victims of society and transform them into agents of their own lives and communities.'[34] Government officials hoped that this relatively autonomous organization would help quell student protest and concurrently demonstrate the government's commitment to poverty issues. CYC members travelled throughout the country, helped to organize communities, and were instrumental in a number of antipoverty protests. While the majority of CYC members were middle class, some low-income people used the CYC to get off welfare, develop their political skills, and organize their communities.[35]

The Senate committee of 1968 provided a second avenue of funding and a federal forum for a number of antipoverty groups to emerge and register their complaints. According to the historical record, this was the first time federal funding was available to the poor in order to organize and present briefs. Media reports of the Senate hearings provided free publicity for these groups. A number of antipoverty groups formed throughout the country and took advantage of these opportunities to demonstrate that the federal 'war on poverty' was ineffective. The cross-country committee hearings had an ominous beginning. At the very first stop in Halifax, a group of local antipoverty activists jeered the committee members as they toured the slum areas.[36] In order to avoid such conflicts, the committee abruptly ended scheduled tours of Canada's ghettos, but this led to renewed queries about the committee's sincerity.[37] A number of antipoverty groups across the country protested the fact that these public hearings were held in ornate ballrooms.[38] The JSM called the Senate committee 'a farce', and read the following statement to the hearings:

> We demand that if this committee wishes to study anything, it should study wealth, not poverty. We demand that this committee study the nature of oppression in this country—not the oppressed; there are answers to poverty. You refuse to ask the right questions and until you do there will be no right answers—only more deceit.[39]

In April 1971, following the cross-country tour, four Senate committee staff members resigned and joined the antipoverty voices, charging that the committee 'was not going to live up to its mandate'.[40] This staff produced a 255-page report that explored the depths of poverty in the country and condemned the welfare policies of the day:

Welfare systems treat people like animals. They encourage dependency. They do not provide enough money to ensure a decent living for the people trapped within them. They reinforce, they do not break, the cycle of poverty. They are corrupt and ugly embodiments of prejudice and brutality, and they cannot be reformed; they must be replaced.[41]

This further fuelled the antipoverty movement for it was widely distributed among activists and extensively used in university social science courses.

Given that the Senate committee provided both funding and exposure for antipoverty groups, it is not surprising that the movement peaked at the culmination of the inquiry. In January 1971, just prior to the Senate committee's report, the first National Conference of Poor People's Organizations met in Toronto. More than 500 activists from across the country attended. Howard Buchbinder, a Praxis member and one of the organizers of the conference, describes this event as the highlight of antipoverty organizing during this period. 'It was the first time anything like that had ever happened', he recalled. During the conference the participants called for a radical redistribution of profit and formed the National Anti-Poverty Organization (NAPO).[42]

Once the federal funding dried up, the strength of the antipoverty movement rapidly deteriorated.[43] With the publication of the Senate report in 1971, this funding base disappeared. Two years earlier the CYC lost its autonomy from the federal government, and in 1976 the agency was disbanded. Following these federal decisions, the poor continued to protest against their conditions, on both an individual and collective basis when possible, but, for the most part, this activity was sporadic and locally based. Although a few antipoverty groups, including the JSM, had refused federal grants, the majority of the poor organizations depended upon this funding source. Without federal government support, the poor could not maintain a cohesive, national protest movement. NAPO continued to organize in the 1980s and early 1990s, but some antipoverty activists criticized it for focusing on lobbying and producing statistical reports as opposed to grassroots mobilizing.[44] This is a common characteristic of antipoverty organizing. Because of the lack of resources and infrastructure, it is always difficult for antipoverty groups to sustain long-term membership and protracted political lobbying.[45] Antipoverty organizing was never to be as popular again as it had been during the 1960s and early 1970s. The protests did not stop, but media and popular attention began to waiver during the economic crisis in the latter years of this period.

ECONOMIC CRISIS AND ONTARIO SINGLE MOTHERS, 1975–1995

By the mid-1970s Canadians began to experience an economic crisis that would severely shake the confidence of the postwar era. As unemployment and inflation rose to double digits by 1982, the postwar era compromise of high wages and high levels of production and consumption, alongside a social welfare net, began to lose popularity. Stagflation prompted dramatic economic restructuring. As profits fell, corporations embarked on two significant economic strategies. On the international scene businesses searched for new sources of cheap labour and resources, mainly in the 'underdeveloped' world. Domestically, companies reorganized their labour processes by introducing new technologies and hiring more part-time labour. These two economic strategies helped to undermine the strength of the Canadian labour movement as workers faced lay-offs, reduced wages, and replacement by part-time, non-unionized workers. At the same time, business leaders began an aggressive campaign against state intervention, which has had a tremendous impact on the nature of the Canadian welfare state.

This era signalled the end of the once-popular Fordist compromise. Forty years of seemingly inexhaustible economic growth and government policies promoting employment and domestic consumption came to a halt. No longer was the state considered the proper tool to manage the economy, to redistribute income, and to promote some modicum of economic and social equality. Instead, neoconservative faith in the 'invisible hand' of the global market returned and dominated the political universe in most industrialized countries, including Canada. Globalization was viewed as an external constraint upon all nation-states. Politicians became convinced that they could do little but 'follow the dictates of footloose capital in a downward spiral of deregulation, lower social spending and lower taxes. . . .'[46]

The dismantling of the postwar Keynesian compromise occurred in most industrialized nations, but with distinct variations. In 1984 the federal Progressive Conservative Party swept into power in a landslide victory that marked the beginning of Canada's post-Fordist era. Two features of the Mulroney government era from 1984 to 1993 demonstrate the Canadian style of post-Fordism. First, the Mulroney government resituated Canada within the global economy through a flurry of international trade negotiations. The Free Trade Agreement with the United States was established and negotiations began for the North American Free Trade Agreement with the US and Mexico, which would be ratified under Mulroney's successor, the Chrétien Liberal government.

Relying upon global trade rather than domestic consumer demand provided the foundations for the rapid dismantling of the postwar welfare state. During this period the federal government did not dismantle the welfare state; rather, in a process known as 'social policy by stealth', it slowly but steadily eroded the foundation upon which several of the programs were built. This was achieved in a number of ways. First, the government cut unpopular minority programs, such as the low-income housing program. Second, the government made an appeal to the private sector to take up the slack. But most importantly the federal government preferred to develop a gradualist strategy of underfunding mainstream welfare programs.[47]

These social policy initiatives have generally been undertaken without democratic consent. The Mulroney government promised to protect social programs as a 'sacred trust' while whittling away the very principles upon which these programs were founded through a series of budget cuts and regulatory changes. Without advance notice or wide public consultation, the Mulroney government reduced or altered almost every single federal government social program.

The erosion of two particular welfare policies had a profound impact on Ontario single mothers. In 1985 the universal family allowance program was partially de-indexed, signalling the beginning of the end for this universal program. Family allowance payments only increased when inflation exceeded 3 per cent, thus diminishing the value of the benefits over time. Four years later the allowance was further eroded so that some families had their entire benefit taxed back. These clawbacks meant that the universal quality of the program had become an illusion. While family allowance payments had greatly supplemented the income of single mothers on welfare in the 1960s, their financial significance steadily declined after that. Although all families continued to receive an allowance cheque, the payments became so minimal as to be virtually meaningless to middle- and upper-class Canadians. Consequently, their support for this universal program waned. Gosta Esping-Andersen argues that the health of a welfare state depends on broad support for its activities, which is generally achieved through universal programs that benefit all citizens as opposed to targeted policies that benefit and often stigmatize only the needy.[48] Certainly this was the case with family allowance. In 1993, an election year, the government announced its elimination with little public opposition. Family allowances were replaced by the child tax benefit, a targeted program for both the working and unemployed poor. Not only was the universal program gone but in its place was established a work-incentive program, tying welfare benefits to employability. The child tax benefit provided a monthly cheque to those who earned below $20,921 annually. The working poor received a larger cheque than the previous family allowance cheque, whereas unemployed single mothers remained at the same level as previously. Consequently, the demise of universal family allowances further impoverished unemployed single mothers in relation to the working poor. Through the child tax benefit single mothers were financially penalized if they were not involved in paid work.

The second and most devastating welfare cut for single mothers was the federal government's unilateral decision to limit its contributions to the CAP. In 1990 the federal budget placed limits on welfare payments to the three wealthiest provinces (Alberta, British Columbia, and Ontario) where almost half of Canada's poor reside. This broke the CAP agreement of unlimited cost-sharing to all provincial and municipal welfare programs, provided certain minimal conditions were met. In 1991 the federal government announced that this 'cap on CAP' would be extended for another three years to the end of 1994–5. This five-year cap resulted in more than $2.1 billion savings for the federal government and drastic reductions in provincial and municipal welfare programs.[49]

These federal initiatives have had three major effects on provincial welfare programs. First, this policy direction demonstrates that the federal government was relinquishing some of its previous welfare responsibilities and assuming that the provincial or municipal governments would fill the gap. Second, as the federal government eroded certain welfare policies and transformed others into work-incentive programs, the provincial government was increasingly restricted in its ability to fill those resulting gaps in need. And third, this erosion of universality began to diminish the widespread popularity of social programs generally.

The End of the Ontario Tory Regime, 1975–1985

In 1975, following thirty-two years of Progressive Conservative rule in Ontario, the Tory dynasty was beginning to show a number of frailties. While the economy faltered, antipoverty groups emerged to create conflicting pressures for the provincial government. The recession of the early 1980s resulted in a new group of unemployed workers and jobless youth. Some of these newly unemployed formed the Union of Unemployed Workers in London, Hamilton, Toronto, and other urban centres and organized sit-ins in welfare offices and protest marches in which they shouted the 1930s slogan, 'We refuse to starve in silence!' Simultaneously, a number of feisty single mothers organized groups and stood up against charity leaders and social workers 'where it had been assumed that they should bow their heads and accept whatever was offered'.[50]

As they continued to mobilize, these antipoverty groups had some notable victories in welfare reform. During the 1975 election campaign poverty issues began to emerge on the political agenda. Stephen Lewis, leader of the NDP, demanded a higher minimum wage and led the attack on the Tories' lack of rent controls. As one political observer maintains, 'Who could withstand the ... tragedy of single moms unable to clothe their children because some unfeeling lout had jacked the rent up 75 per cent? [Despite Tory resistance] rent controls soon became the only issue of the campaign.'[51] As a result, the Progressive Conservatives lost twenty-seven seats during the election while the NDP doubled their seats and the Liberals also increased their numbers.[52] This marked the first minority Tory government in thirty years and signalled the crumbling of a dynasty.

During the final decade of Tory rule (1975 to 1985) when their popularity was waning, the Ontario government made two welfare amendments that affected needy single mothers. First, separated mothers became eligible for the FBA policy in 1979. There was very little fanfare regarding this amendment, partly because it was a result of legal changes rather than an antipoverty lobby. The Progressive Conservatives had been reluctant to introduce such an amendment. They deliberated about exactly when a family should, in situations where 'the parents had *voluntarily* separated, become a permanent public charge'.[53] Finally, the government was forced to act. 'The Family Law Reform Act of 1978 dropped the distinction between deserted and separated mothers and so we did the same', recalls John

Stapleton, senior Ministry of Community and Social Services bureaucrat. 'I was 26 years old at the time and I actually made the change-over of separated mothers from GWA to FBA—I did the cost analysis, etc.'[54] Following this amendment, separated mothers were eligible for the FBA after a three-month waiting period, similar to deserted and unwed mothers.

The second newly eligible group was healthy sole-support fathers. Unlike that for separated mothers, this amendment in 1983 was a result of two distinct lobby efforts. Elie Martel, New Democratic Party MPP for Sudbury, made several attempts to include sole-support fathers in a series of private member's bills during the late 1970s and early 1980s. Simultaneously, Len Walker, a sole-support father, constructed a one-man campaign to attempt to get child support from his wife. His wife had deserted him and the children for another man and had publicly stated that she did not want the children. 'Len gained a lot of public sympathy for his cause. He was studying law at Osgoode Hall and he used everything he learned there to pursue his case', recalls Stapleton. 'The government took note that Len had considerable public support.'[55] But the government was still hesitant to 'break the taboo against supporting an able-bodied man on social assistance'. In early 1982 the government permitted a disabled woman on social assistance to include her male able-bodied partner. The tide broke: 'changing FBA to include sole support fathers would not be making a precedent', said Stapleton.[56] And so the amendment was made a year later.

Neither of these amendments produced a significant increase in the number of FBA recipients. Separated mothers have never accounted for more than 6 per cent of all female FBA recipients during this period (see Table 6.1). Also, few healthy sole-support fathers have applied for FBA since the 1983 amendment.[57] Evidence from FBA recipients across the province suggests that these fathers do not experience the same degree of moral or financial scrutiny that single mothers encounter.[58]

Opening the Door to Welfare Reform:
The Liberal-NDP Accord, 1985–1987

In 1985 the Progressive Conservatives lost their forty-two-year reign of power when the Liberals and the New Democratic Party signed an accord and formed the first coalition government since 1919.[59] The accord specified that the NDP would not call an election for two years. In return the Liberals promised a number of long-overdue reforms, including freedom of information legislation, environmental action, a ban on extra billing by doctors, an equal-pay-for-work-of-equal-value policy, extended rent review, protection for workers, better child care, and more affordable housing.

This two-year accord and the mood of reform enabled antipoverty activists to make a number of gains. The Liberal government made three important changes: the announcement of an in-depth study of social welfare reform, a 25 per cent increase in welfare rates, and an amendment to permit cohabiting mothers to be eligible for the FBA policy.

To demonstrate the Liberal government's commitment to welfare reform, Premier David Peterson announced the creation of the Social Assistance Review Committee (SARC) in July 1986. George Ehring and Wayne Roberts, two prominent NDP analysts, believed SARC to be 'the most thorough and far-sighted approach to social assistance reform anywhere in North America in decades.'[60] This committee involved social workers, academics, recipients, antipoverty activists, business representatives, and community leaders in a detailed examination of a wide range of welfare issues. The review committee heard from people in fourteen cities and received over 1,500 submissions:

> When the report was handed down in September 1988, it contained 274 recommendations for sweeping changes to virtually every aspect of social assistance. The report lifted the veil of secrecy that shrouded the extent of poverty in the province. . . .[61]

After two years of work, the first report, *Transitions*, was released with 274 recommendations. The report recommended $2 billion worth of reforms, yet there was 'scarcely a whisper of dissent'.[62] These recommendations included the following:

> i) to replace the two-tiered welfare system of FBA and GWA with an integrated, uniform welfare rate based solely on need. The report stated that the existing two-tiered system and 22 categories of eligibility were confusing, stigmatizing and encouraged social workers to conduct intrusive investigations and to make decisions based on discretion rather than standards. Ontario is only one of three provinces which has not unified its welfare system.[63]
>
> ii) to improve benefits by using the market basket approach and index benefits annually to increases in the Consumer Price Index. The report provided considerable evidence to prove that existing welfare rates were woefully inadequate by any standards.[64]
>
> iii) to establish a Council of Consumers which would allow clients to have an on-going voice in the administration of welfare.[65]
>
> iv) to provide on-going counselling or opportunity planning as well as financial supplements to help recipients make the 'transition' from welfare to full-time employment.[66]

These first three recommendations suggest an attempt to provide an adequate allowance as a right for all in need and at the same time establish non-punitive, high-quality employment and counselling services. Yet the final recommendation calls for a closer association between the welfare cheque and the pay cheque. The latter recommendation opened the door to possible coercive measures and spawned the business community's enthusiasm for this report.

Antipoverty activists used this SARC platform to press for their own demands. In 1986, following the announcement of SARC, antipoverty groups organized a successful campaign to increase welfare rates by 25 per cent. Public forums to discuss local poverty issues occurred in several communities across the province. These forums launched a number of antipoverty groups, including the March Against Poverty Committee, which organized a march from London to Queen's Park in 1987 and a march from Hamilton to Queen's Park in the spring of 1988. In 1989 activist groups came together for 'the largest anti-poverty rally in Ontario since the 1930s'—a three-pronged March Against Poverty that began in Windsor, Sudbury, and Ottawa and ended at Queen's Park.[67] Modelled after the 1935 On to Ottawa Trek, this march brought together the poor, women's groups, religious organizations, members of the labour movement, and a number of NDP politicians. The NDP met with march organizers prior to the event and financially contributed to the cause.[68] The march endorsed the first stage of the SARC recommendations, which called for rate increases and the end of penalties for welfare recipients who work. It culminated with a massive rally of thousands of supporters at Queen's Park on 8 April, at which NDP leader Bob Rae spoke. There were two important results of this march. It created the momentum to establish the Ontario Coalition Against Poverty (OCAP), an ongoing provincial antipoverty organization, in 1990. Just one month following the march, the Liberal government announced that the first stage of *Transitions* would be implemented.[69]

The final important change for single mothers during the accord period was the FBA amendment to include cohabiting mothers. This was the most controversial amendment ever made to the seventy-three-year-old policy and the result of persistent lobbying by recipients, community legal clinics, the Canadian Civil Liberties Association (CLA), and the Legal Education and Action Fund (LEAF). With the introduction of the FBA policy in 1967, the regulations stipulated that a woman could be ineligible if she were 'not living as a single person'. According to senior Ministry of Community and Social Services bureaucrat John Stapleton, this regulation replaced the earlier 'fit and proper person' clause. 'Historically we got rid of the fit mother rule and we didn't have anything in its place to reflect societal values. "Not living as a single person" took care of the problem.'[70] But this regulation created as many problems as it solved. 'The definition was vague and did not say anything about sex or having brothers, fathers or other visitors', recalls Nancy Vander Plaats, a community legal worker who was active in the cohabitation campaign. During the late 1970s and early 1980s legal clinics criticized the procedures for determining a live-in relationship. 'Single mothers were not believed and denied benefits on mere suspicion and hearsay from landlords, employers, relatives and neighbours', says Vander Plaats.[71] Legal clinics took these cases to the Social Assistance Review Board (SARB) and appealed several to the divisional court. By the mid-1980s the legal clinics began winning a number of these cases and throwing the regulation into question. Simultaneously, LEAF organized a legal challenge, using section 15 of the Charter of Rights. Alan Borovoy of the CLA also widely criticized this regulation, gaining media attention on the issue.[72]

The Liberals came to power in the midst of this controversy, giving new momentum to the lobby effort. 'With the Liberals in power there was a tremendous explosion of activity on gender issues, a climate of change', recalls senior bureaucrat Judy Wolfe.[73] The media approached Attorney-General Ian Scott on the cohabitation issue, and Scott publicly stated that the regulation made no sense. 'This put the policy in complete jeopardy', recalls Stapleton. 'I had bureaucrats from other provinces coming to me scared that they would have the same problems—the same publicity.'[74] The individual cases brought forward by community legal workers, the LEAF challenge, the public condemnation by the CLA, and the attorney-general's public denunciation of the regulation all culminated in the government's decision to amend the legislation. In 1987 the provincial government granted the benefit to cohabiting mothers on the following conditions:

• the cohabiter was not the father of any of the children;
• the cohabiter was not legally married to the client;
• the benefit would be reduced since 'two people can live cheaper than one';
• this benefit would be immediately cut off after three years of cohabitation.[75]

This amendment created the most progressive cohabitation regulation in Canada. For the first time the policy recognized single mothers as sexual beings. Some mothers took advantage of this legislative amendment and invited male partners to live with them. 'Given that many single mothers come from abusive relationships this change allowed women to try out new relationships—to try them out without any financial penalty', explained Ian Morrison, executive director of the Clinic Resource Office.[76] Yet according to FBA recipients and legal workers, this achievement had little impact upon many single mothers' lives. Often the cohabiter was the father of the children and the mother was therefore disqualified. The reduced cheque and the three-year time limit also discouraged a number of FBA recipients from living with their partners. There was evidence to suggest this amendment resulted in new types of intrusive investigation of a recipient's life. An applicant had to sign a questionnaire stating the nature of the relationship in order to receive the benefit. This questionnaire asked whether the cohabiter disciplined the children, gave them birthday presents, spent Christmas with them, etc.[77] 'The very fact of having to answer these questions scares people', said Vander Plaats. 'The cheque [was] ... delayed until the questionnaire [was] ... signed. There [were] ... cases where a client [was] ... intimidated, desperately needing the cheque and signed the questionnaire against her better judgement.'[78]

With the expiry of the Liberal-NDP accord in 1987, an election was called and the Liberals swept into power with the largest majority government in Ontario's history.[79] Such a majority provided little necessity for promises or compromises. Despite antipoverty organizing, there were no significant welfare reforms from 1987 to 1990. Antipoverty activists waited impatiently for a chance to express their frustration with this three-year interlude, and in the fall of 1990 their voices were heard.

Promises Not Kept: The NDP in Power, 1990–1995

The announcement of an election for September 1990 provided a new opportunity for antipoverty activists to promote their interests. Whereas the 1985 campaign involved the NDP speaking on behalf of the poor, the 1990 election campaign included the voices of antipoverty activists and welfare recipients speaking for themselves. In 1990 an economic recession gripped the province. The welfare rolls and the lines at the food banks were increasing at an alarming rate. 'But the Liberals . . . would not free up special funding, even in the name of political expediency at election time.'[80] Antipoverty activists took the opportunity to ridicule the Liberal government. During David Peterson's nomination meeting in London, an antipoverty protest erupted, which had a dramatic impact on the entire campaign:

> [When Peterson tried to speak, John Clarke, of OCAP] leaped to his feet to berate him. An angry exchange raged. . . .
>
> 'You don't care about justice for those living in poverty; you're the poverty premier!' . . . [Clarke] screeched.
>
> 'If you went out and got a job you could make a decent contribution to this country,' Peterson shot back. . . .
>
> Edited down to a few tight seconds, the image of Peterson sneering at an 'unemployed' person to 'Get a job!' was riveting, revealing T.V. The clip became one of the most widely repeated of the campaign, showing up on the news in summaries, weekly reports and campaign features until election day.[81]

Highlighting the concerns of the poor, OCAP's slogan of 'Down with the poverty premier' became a popular campaign expression that was shouted by a number of protest groups. This helped to provide even more public support for the NDP. Hastily, the NDP adopted a twenty-point 'Agenda for the People', which included promises to raise the minimum wage, to increase welfare rates, and to initiate a corporate tax.[82] While not solely responsible, the antipoverty campaign played a role in the defeat of the Liberal government and the election of the first New Democratic Party government in Ontario's history.[83]

As during the early 1960s, women continued to be well represented in antipoverty organizing in the early 1990s. Their voices spoke to the long-time invisibility of single motherhood and the need to recognize the gendered nature of poverty. These voices of poor women were particularly audible in Kitchener, North Bay, Belleville, and Toronto. From 1988 well into the early 1990s, approximately twenty-five members of Mothers and Others Making Change met at their office in Kitchener. These members, predominantly single mothers, organized protest events and shared food, furniture, and advice with those in need. In total, the group boasted more than 200 members. 'We see ourselves as a watchdog of COMSOC, Children's Aid Society, the Foodbanks—the whole lot', explained Past President Carole Silliker.[84] In North Bay, Low Income People Involvement (LIPI) had a Main Street office from which its staff, the vast majority of whom were single mothers, helped individuals to find work, retraining courses, affordable housing, and a number of other services. In 1991 alone LIPI served more than 2,500 people.[85] In Belleville, Citizens for Action was based in the home of one single mother who kept her basement supplied with clothing and second-hand furniture for someone in need.[86] And in Toronto, Low Income Families Together's (LIFT) staff (all single mothers) were always busy advising clients of their rights and advocating on their behalf. Individual members of LIPI and LIFT were particularly active in the SARC process and, following SARC, continued to organize province-wide conferences for recipients and advise the government on welfare reform.

Yet despite the growth in Ontario's antipoverty movement, activists began to feel that their influence was waning during the 1990s. 'During the 1980s if we had eight people stand outside [Premier] Peterson's constituency office we could change policy', explained John Clarke. 'Now a busload of angry [welfare] recipients can't even get noticed.'[87] Activists attribute this loss of political clout to a number of factors. Clearly, the political climate had changed dramatically with the economic recession. Middle-class citizens began to view themselves as taxpayers and the poor as a drain on the public purse. The poor themselves, to some extent, accepted this ideology and they, too, began to differentiate between the worthy and unworthy recipients. The NDP government created another stumbling-block for antipoverty activists. Those who had previously been active in the women's and antipoverty movement were now part of the governing party or the government bureaucracy. To criticize the government was to throw stones at one's political allies. As the NDP government began to consider neoconservative welfare measures, the tensions between antipoverty activists and their political allies grew.

During the NDP government's reign there was only one minor expansion to FBA policy. In 1991 the government eliminated the three-month waiting period for deserted, unwed, and separated mothers. 'Historically, we believed the three months was important to assess whether the marriage or relationship had really broken down or not', explained senior Ministry of Community and Social Services bureaucrat Chandra Pala.[88] Municipal welfare rolls were growing in the late 1980s and municipal politicians were in favour of this amendment as a way to reduce their welfare clients. The SARC report also recommended this change.[89] While there was little attention given to this amendment, this marked the end of all policy distinctions between needy single mothers except cohabiting recipients.

Despite these improvements, antipoverty activists and the poor were quite concerned about the number of cost-cutting welfare reforms that the NDP government implemented. These welfare reforms, often begun by previous governments but adopted by the NDP, took three forms: reducing welfare rates, introducing new coercive measures to combat fraud, and tightening the association between welfare and employment.

The NDP government, like the Liberals and Tories before them, resisted calls to improve welfare rates. The NDP refused to alter the trend significantly even though FBA rates fell further and further below the level of subsistence. In 1966 the monthly benefit represented 70 per cent of that required according to the Family Budget Guide, a shopping basket measure of the basic needs, but two decades later the benefit had deteriorated to only 54 per cent of the Family Budget Guide (see Table 5.2).[90] Even the supplementary aid and special assistance introduced in 1978–9 to augment the monthly benefits remained inadequate and unavailable to the majority of recipients.[91] Additional benefits fell under municipal jurisdictions and many municipalities have either refused or severely limited their provision. A 1981 study revealed that only 32.3 per cent of FBA recipients received either of these additional benefits even though all of them lived below the poverty line.[92] The demise of family allowances in 1993 further impoverished single mothers who were not involved in paid work, and for those who were separated or divorced, the vast majority were unable to obtain support payments.[93]

The NDP government continued the trend to reduce the real value of FBA cheques. Although *Transitions* called for a substantial improvement in benefits, this never happened. Instead, in 1993 the provincial government announced a 1 per cent increase in welfare rates. Given that inflation rose approximately 2.5 per cent in 1993, this was actually a welfare rate reduction and the first rate cut in almost twenty years.[94] This decision was partly a result of the curb on CAP funding, which is believed to have cost Ontario a $1.1 billion loss for the 1991–2 fiscal year alone.[95] In a further betrayal of his social democratic roots, Premier Rae announced in December 1993 that he would consider further cuts to welfare rates if federal transfer payments were frozen.[96] The 1 per cent increase and the threat of further cuts changed the course of welfare reform. There was no more discussion of welfare rates meeting subsistence needs. Instead, these welfare cuts of the early 1990s opened the door to deeper and more devastating welfare cuts that the Harris government era would bring.

As well as introducing welfare cuts, the NDP government moved away from the provision of services and towards an enforcement-oriented welfare administration. During the early 1990s there was increasing public and media concern about the extent of 'welfare cheating'. The first notorious media event to spark hysteria regarding welfare fraud attacked both the poor and the immigrant population. In October 1993 Liberal Opposition Leader Lynn McLeod stated that a Somali organization was 'importing refugees to systematically pillage our vulnerable and exposed social welfare systems', costing the Ontario taxpayers 'tens of millions of dollars'. Further examination revealed that there were only nine refugees guilty of fraudulent behaviour.[97] But the damage had already been done. Welfare recipients, particularly immigrant welfare recipients, were increasingly considered criminals defrauding 'worthy' taxpayers of their hard-earned dollars.

The NDP government legitimized this concern through its development of enforcement-oriented welfare administration. In 1992 the NDP government established 'enhanced verification' to ensure that recipients did not cheat the system. While social work positions in the Ministry of Community and Social Services were frozen, the ministry announced that it would hire 250 new investigators to review every single provincially administered welfare case file. The cost was estimated at $20 million for the fiscal year 1994–5 and an additional $10 million a year for municipalities to carry out similar initiatives.[98] This investigation also required school officials to fill out attendance and progress records for children of welfare recipients, thus denying welfare recipients and their children confidentiality.[99] This announcement signalled the most intrusive and intensive welfare fraud investigation in the country. Quebec welfare administrators, known for their extensive policing techniques, only examined every *third* welfare file. This coercive mechanism was created even though *Transitions* clearly stated that approximately 3 per cent of all general welfare and FBA payments were fraudulent.[100] While *Transitions* had strongly recommended a less intrusive style of welfare administration that de-emphasized suspicion and fraud detection, the NDP government did just the opposite.

A year later the government announced that all welfare recipients who remained on welfare beyond the average period would be reviewed.[101] This latter administrative procedure was implemented despite *Transitions*'s discovery that there was a high turnover rate within the welfare system. According to the report, single mothers generally remained on family benefits between 3.5 to four years. This period of dependency was greatly reduced if the mother received child support payments.[102]

The establishment of new welfare policing mechanisms only convinced the public that welfare fraud was indeed a growing problem. The NDP government and Tony Silipo, the Minister of Community and Social Services, in particular, added fuel to the welfare fraud flames. In February 1994 Silipo proposed fingerprinting all welfare recipients as a 'way to crack down on welfare fraud'.[103] Just seven months later, Silipo said that welfare fraud was as high as 20 per cent. As part of 'enhanced verification', the government had investigated 40,000 welfare cases in which they suspected a high risk of administrative error or abuse. Of these 40,000 cases, the government claimed approximately 20 per cent involved either fraud or error, totalling $21.3 million. The reaction from politicians and the public was dramatic. The Progressive Conservative finance critic, Dave Johnston, falsely assumed that there was 20 per cent fraud in the *entire* provincial welfare case-load and charged that this was costing the province $1 billion a year. The *Toronto Sun* went even further, claiming in a headline, '$1.3B down the toilet.' But a close examination of the government report revealed that 1,029 of these high-risk cases were suspected of fraud and reported to the local police, representing a mere .15 per cent of the provincial case-load.[104] The welfare fraud study and its publicity were indicative of this period in welfare history. Although the study reported that welfare fraud had not increased during the economic recession of the early 1990s, the media and the politicians, including the NDP, encouraged welfare fraud hysteria and consequently incited hostility against the poor.

Perhaps the most important development in the FBA during these three decades was the promotion of full-time employment for single mothers. This was a significant departure from previous policy, which only advocated part-time work that did not interfere with parenting responsibilities. This trend began in 1960 when the regulations accompanying the policy included provisions permitting the director to deny benefits to any applicant or recipient for whom suitable employment was available.[105] With the introduction of CAP, counselling and retraining programs were implemented to encourage single mothers to become economically self-sufficient.[106] During the early 1970s a variety of programs that provided monetary rewards for work were attempted, the most notable being the Work Incentive Program (WIN), established in 1979.[107] WIN provided an initial back-to-work grant, plus additional financial support for two years following a recipient's entry into the full-time labour force.[108] But the financial incentives were low, and no more than 3 per cent of single mothers on welfare entered the program. Eventually the government froze supplements at 1981 levels, allowing its value to erode over time.[109]

In 1982 the government shifted from monetary rewards to a service strategy through the introduction of the Employment Supports Initiatives (ESI).[110] ESI provided recipients with a number of employment-related services, such as job assessments, educational upgrading, child care, and work placements. It was believed that these services would remove the barriers to unemployment. Studies suggest that only 10 per cent of all eligible welfare recipients participated in these service programs.[111]

Supports to Employment Program (STEP) was established in 1989. This program included both monetary rewards and service provisions. STEP increased earning exemptions, provided special exemptions for training allowances, provided for the first month's cost of child care, and offered start-up benefits for people starting new jobs. With STEP the government also eliminated the '120-hour rule' that made single mothers ineligible for family benefits if they worked full-time for four consecutive months.

Under the NDP government, single mothers were increasingly seen as employable. In 1992 the government released *Time for Action,* a follow-up report to *Transitions,* which recommended increased powers for the employment counsellor or opportunity planner. The agreement between worker and recipient was more clearly spelled out in this latter report: 'The [opportunity] plan should set out concrete actions and achievable goals and it should be a document that is signed by a worker and the recipient.'[112] If the recipient did not live up to this agreement, sanctions would be implemented that would 'be great enough that it is clearly perceived to be a sanction, and not so substantial as to cut off assistance completely'.[113] This opportunity plan or resulting sanctions could be appealed by the recipient.

Following the release of *Time for Action*, the government began to consider further penalties for welfare recipients who were not working. A government document leaked to the media in January 1993 proposed dramatic changes to welfare, including a form of partial work-fare and mandatory 'volunteer' work as conditions for receiving benefits. If implemented, recipients' welfare cheques would be reduced by $100 to $200, and monthly penalties of $46 would be applied to those not involved in retraining or employment programs. According to the document, single mothers with children under twelve years would be exempted from the employment sanction.[114] Premier Bob Rae said, 'My own view about welfare . . . is that simply paying people to sit at home is not smart.'[115] Antipoverty activists and welfare recipients were outraged. Ruth Mott, a Toronto NDP member and community activist, was 'shocked and devastated' by the leaked document. 'The fact these ideas were even down on paper is a complete betrayal of everything we've ever worked for', said Mott.[116] Some cabinet ministers, namely Community and Social Services Minister Marion Boyd and Treasurer Floyd Laughren, attempted to distance themselves from this proposal, but the damage had already been done.[117] According to one civil servant, the government received an unprecedented number of phone calls protesting this proposal.[118]

In April 1993 the Ontario government announced its expenditure control plan or mini-budget with a $313 million cut to the Ministry of Community and Social Services. Along with a reduction in a number of welfare benefits and services, the mini-budget clearly stated that the ministry would 'work with parents whose children are over 12 to help them prepare to enter the workforce'.[119] Following the mini-budget, single mothers received a notice along with their July FBA cheques restating this employment commitment.[120]

Three months later the NDP government released *Turning Point*, the White Paper on social reform. With this paper Tony Silipo, Minister of Community and Social Services, announced that the government was 'about to dismantle welfare as we know it'. This paper, while more carefully written than the previously leaked document, contained many of the same recommendations. It called for the end of the two-tiered system and the dissolution of a distinction between 'employables' and 'unemployables'. As well, *Turning Point* proposed benefit rates below minimum wage, employment counselling and training, and financial rewards (as opposed to penalties) for those who retrained or found paid work.[121] While this latter paper was extremely vague, it did not mention any exemption for single mothers with young children. The government planned to overhaul welfare by late 1993 with a start-up date in 1995, but by the end of 1994, the writing was on the wall. Public support for an expensive revamping of welfare had waned. The NDP government quietly scrapped the recommendations of *Turning Point* and turned its attention to its rapidly declining popularity.

The scrapping of *Turning Point* represented the end of the NDP government's initiatives in the field of welfare and employment. There was a noticeable shift in the government's attitude towards single mothers and employment during its tenure. Initially, it actively encouraged single mothers to pursue work, but rejected any mandatory schemes. However, later reports suggested that even the NDP were willing to consider tying welfare to employment. While the NDP government did not endorse work-for-welfare programs *per se*, it considered a number of options that, if implemented, would have pressured individuals to participate in a variety of employment-related activities.

By the end of this era, the NDP government had proven that they were not substantially different from previous provincial governments when it came to welfare reform. Despite their promises to advocate on behalf of the poor, the NDP government developed a number of proposals that directly attacked the poor. It was the NDP government that initiated the first welfare cut in two decades. It was the NDP government that introduced new coercive measures to combat welfare fraud, and it was also the NDP government, through several reports, which proposed that welfare be more closely tied to employment. As such, the NDP government abandoned its commitment to represent the poor and opened the door for further and more vicious assaults on the poor.

CONCLUSION

This thirty-year period of Ontario history was one of tremendous economic flux and political struggle. This period began in 1965 with the promise of eliminating poverty and discrimination against the poor. An antipoverty movement flourished and demanded that the interests of the poor be addressed. Initially the introduction of the CAP heralded a period of welfare reform that greatly influenced a number of provincial welfare programs such as the FBA. During this period the FBA's eligibility expanded to include cohabiting and separated mothers along with healthy sole-support fathers. Distinctions between eligibility categories were, for the most part, discarded. Policy amendments reduced and eventually eliminated all waiting periods for most FBA applicants, and services such as counselling and retraining were expanded.

But the promise of this period was not fulfilled. During this era needy single mothers and their children experienced increasing poverty. Simultaneously, there were attempts to improve these recipients' financial circumstances through retraining and work-incentive programs. These programs did not significantly alter the recipients' financial means, but they represented a significant shift in policy. Whereas previously single mothers were only expected to do part-time work that did not interfere with their first priority of caring for their children, by 1995 they were expected to embrace full-time work outside the home. There was little acknowledgement of the contradictory responsibilities placed upon single mothers who must both provide for and care for their children at the same time. This placed increasing pressure upon single mothers during a period of double-digit unemployment.

Chapter 7

'Manhunts' and 'Bingo Blabs':
Single Mothers Speak Out

It is time to realize that the poor are neither 'worthy' or 'unworthy', they are simply poor.[1]

This is a common plea made over and over again by poor single mothers across the province. Every day they come face to face with a welfare system that creates a 'hierarchy of deservedness'. Every day they try to convince their neighbours, their children's teachers, and social workers that they are worthy of the monthly family benefits cheque. This suggests that there is a large discrepancy between the printed regulations and the administration of this policy. This chapter will examine the daily concerns, frustrations, and rebellions of poor single mothers throughout Ontario.

Although the notion of the deserving mother has changed over time, single mothers have had to establish their worthiness throughout the history of this policy. Interviews with single mothers illustrate that the determination of deservedness includes both financial as well as moral regulation of applicants' lives. This worthiness is not simply determined by social workers, hired and paid by the state. Instead, as other scholars of moral regulation have suggested, there are many different agents and sites of moral regulation.[2] Interviews disclose that neighbours, teachers, store owners, and other recipients continue to scrutinize the daily lives of single mothers. As Josephine Grey, a single mother and leading antipoverty activist, explained, 'when you live on social assistance, you live in Stalinist Russia—your neighbour, your [social] worker, even your friend might report you. You live with all kinds of terrorist fears.'[3]

By the mid-1990s mothers' allowance had expanded to include widows, deserted, divorced, separated, unwed, and cohabiting mothers. This suggests a more generous and inclusive policy than that of previous decades, but along with these progressive changes, new regulations and new definitions of worthiness had also emerged. These new regulations and new definitions involved both financial and moral criteria.

As Chapter 6 suggested and the interviews confirmed, financial regulation of single mothers' lives has significantly altered since the 1960s. Until recently, single mothers were generally encouraged to consider part-time work, but their first priority was to care for their children. This was in keeping with the heterosexual nuclear family model (male breadwinner, dependent wife and children) with the state as the substitute for the missing father. But from the mid-1970s onwards, there has been increasing pressure upon recipients to retrain and seek *full*-time employment. This represents a significant break from the previous familial model.

Moral considerations have also changed noticeably. Generally, welfare scholars have assumed that moral scrutiny of recipients ended with the emergence of the post–Second World War welfare state.[4] But evidence presented in this chapter illustrates that questions of morality continued to permeate the everyday administration of this policy, albeit in new as well as long-established forms. In the early 1990s the moral terrain had shifted from a broad range of moral questions to focus more exclusively on issues of sexuality and cohabitation. But by the mid-1990s, the moral discourse had altered once again to reintroduce concerns about cheating and laziness. While moral criteria have changed over time, what is perhaps more significant is the fact that they continue to exist at all. Although the post-1960 period is associated with welfare state expansion and the establishment of more generous programs, a moral definition of the worthy single mother still persisted. And at the end of this century there is every indication that morality has increasingly become a tool used to define welfare deservedness.

Although financial and moral regulation continues, it is also clear that single mothers attempt to use the limited resources they have to resist and alter these oppressive structures and relationships. Power is not static, nor is it an attribute or possession; instead, it is relational, an ongoing process of human interaction. Feminist scholar Elizabeth Janeway explains: '[W]e must expect to find participants with different and separate interests, and differing amounts of authority, but each capable of influencing the other to some degree.'[5] As the interviews demonstrate, single mothers creatively manipulate, stubbornly refuse, and strategically argue with social workers in an attempt to get the help they require. While they may receive some of the financial support and services they need, they are generally not in control of the degree of intervention such 'help' includes. Yet this is not to say that they accept the intrusive aspects of state assistance. The interviews clearly demonstrate a number of ways that single mothers individually and collectively resist and renegotiate this regulatory process.

METHODOLOGICAL QUERIES

This chapter is based on a series of interviews with sixty-one single mothers, three community legal workers, five antipoverty activists, two Family Benefits Act workers, and six Ministry of Community and Social Services officials. These interviews were conducted in six different areas of the province and dealt with both urban and rural concerns: (1) Belleville (representing recipients in Hastings County), (2) Kitchener, (3) London (representing recipients in Middlesex County), (4) St Thomas (representing recipients in Elgin County), (5) Toronto, and (6) North Bay (representing recipients in Nipissing District). Although these interviews occurred from 1991 to 1995, prior to the election of the Harris government, they represent the general issues facing single mothers on welfare today. As Chapter 6 illustrated, the early 1990s was the beginning of welfare restraint. The issues these women spoke about are similar to those raised by single mothers under the Harris government; the only difference is that the problems have now intensified. The majority of these interviews were conducted with single mothers. My journalism training, antipoverty activism, and feminist education helped to inform my interview techniques. As a former newspaper journalist, I was familiar with the reporter's basic interview style. As an antipoverty activist, many of the interviewees were familiar with my face and/or my political activities. I had also conducted a number of participatory workshops on the subject of welfare and wanted to employ some of these popular education techniques.[6] As a feminist, I had considered the particular difficulties in interviewing women (especially low-income women) for their voices are rarely heard or adequately appreciated in society. Also, I was aware of feminist methodological discussions about the complex and often unacknowledged power relations between the interviewer and interviewee.[7]

Despite what I considered a rather informed position on the difficulties and responsibilities of conducting oral interviews, I learned a great deal from those I interviewed on how to adapt and improve my interview style. My first interview for this project was with Mothers and Others Making Change (MOMC) in Kitchener. I walked into MOMC's office with a list of prepared questions. The office was full of single mothers who were absorbed in their weekly meeting. I sat down inconspicuously in the corner of the room. I recognized a number of women from several antipoverty demonstrations and they, in turn, nodded at me. I listened to the meeting for more than one hour. Then when the meeting was over, I suggested that we have a tape-recorded group discussion. No go. Everyone wanted to participate in this project, so they told me how the interview should be conducted. They asked me to stand up and shout out a question. While MOMC members were putting up the Christmas tree in the far corner, clearing the tables, answering the phone, and chatting with each other, they would join in the discussion if a question interested them. So I yelled out a question, a group of women would come forward and tell me their personal experiences in relation to the question, and then I would yell out another question. When asked a question, occasionally one of the women would respond, 'That's not very interesting. We don't care about that—ask another question.' And so it went. Every now and then they would stop and ask me a question about the history of the policy. I never felt that *I* was in charge of the interview. We were jointly engaged in the process. They answered some of my questions, devised other questions, and refused to answer others. In turn, I gave them some information about the history of the policy and we cooperatively discussed patterns that emerged. This experience set the tone for other interviews with single mothers. I had previously determined that the majority of my interviews would be conducted with already established groups of single mothers. Also, I decided that the location and time slot should be when and where the group usually met. All of this provided a certain degree of comfort for the interviewees because they were already familiar with each other and the setting. I felt it was important that the interviewees not feel overwhelmed by my power as the interviewer and ultimate editor. While I made my purpose clear and provided them with some historical information, I generally allowed them to determine the direction and the length of the session. Usually these group interviews were between two and three hours long. While the group setting does not enable the interviewer to follow one story line, it does offer other benefits. Through these participatory workshop-style interviews, the women stimulated each other to produce an answer to a particular question. We were able to assess both how the policy had changed and how it had not through their collective experiences of the policy.

There were two types of groups interviewed: active antipoverty organizations and community drop-ins for single mothers. While the first group was more consciously a political group, I would argue that all of the single mothers interviewed were, to an extent, political activists. They had all actively chosen to define themselves as low-income single mothers. They met with other similarly defined people to socialize and politically strategize around their common interests. From learning about each other's experiences, they were able to examine the policy that so deeply affected their daily lives.

While the majority of single mothers were interviewed in this group setting, there were three single mothers who were interviewed separately, partly because they had a long involvement in antipoverty organizing and I wanted to explore their personal experience in greater detail than a group setting would allow. Also, because of their hectic schedules as mothers and activists, it was simply easier for me to interview them in their homes. While these interviews allowed for more detailed questions about a specific mother's life, they were also distinct from the systematic and formal interview style practised by journalists. A single mother's daily life can rarely be broken down into neat compartments of time. She is always at the beck and call of her children. This naturally affects the style and direction of the interview. In the midst of our discussions, the interviewee and I would make peanut butter sandwiches for the children's lunch, answer the phone, and help put the children to bed.

I had hoped to tape-record these interviews to document the lives of low-income single mothers. Not one group wanted to have a session tape-recorded and I did not press the issue. Their decision made abundantly clear their anxiety that a social worker, a neighbour, or a friend may repeat something that they have shared with a group they trust. Those who requested anonymity chose their own pseudonyms. Finally, I sent a draft of this chapter to the groups interviewed to request their opinions. All but one group responded with suggestions, criticisms, and enthusiasm.[8]

Unlike the case files that document the lives of single mothers in the previous decades from the administrator's viewpoint, face-to-face interviews provide an opportunity for welfare recipients to talk about their own lives. This is not intended to be a representative sample of all those involved in FBA as workers, recipients, and activists. Rather, this chapter focuses on the experiences recounted by poor single mothers, who are seldom heard. Interviews with legal workers, social workers, Ministry of Community and Social Services officials, and activists are merely supplementary evidence to provide a broader understanding of everyday FBA administration.

EVERYDAY EXPERIENCES OF SINGLE MOTHERS IN THE 1990S

Financial Regulation

The boundaries between financial and moral worthiness for poor single mothers have often been blurred. Throughout the history of this policy, single mothers were forced to meet the contradictory expectations of both raising and providing for their children. The allowance has always been below subsistence, forcing these mothers to work at least part-time, but paid work always interfered with their other prescribed role as mothers dedicated to domestic duties. Thus, poor mothers have had to juggle two incompatible responsibilities and have often been criticized when they were not up to the task.

In the 1990s financial concerns dominate many poor single mothers' lives. As government budgets are slashed, single mothers experience increased financial scrutiny of their lives. One single mother in Kitchener said her bank book is constantly examined. 'Every time they [the social workers] come, they see your bank book. They have a release form, so [they] have access to your bank account at any time.'[9] Others recalled 'interrogations' because they had received a gift of furniture, groceries, or clothing from a friend or relative. For single mothers, gifts were considered income and were deducted from FBA cheques. Suzanne remembered when her parents gave her a car because she lived outside of town. 'It was new and they [the social workers] questioned me like crazy. It was a gift, but they considered it an overpayment and started to take it off my cheques.'[10] Still others have their cheques withheld if they are not home when the social worker makes a surprise visit.[11]

Because the monthly benefit remains woefully inadequate, many single mothers spoke about the many ways they survive. Food is one of the few non-fixed items in a single mother's monthly budget and therefore the one sacrificed to meet rent, hydro, and phone payments. Given the inadequacy of the family benefits cheque most mothers have not had enough money to meet Canada's Basic Food Guide requirements (see Tables 7.1 and 7.2). Everyone agreed that the last ten days of the month are the toughest. 'That's when I hear the rumble in my stomach. That's when there's no milk in the fridge and I have to give my kids dry cereal to eat', said one Kitchener mother.[12] 'Those last ten days are really bad for groceries', remembered another mother from North Bay. 'I would be counting the slices in a loaf of bread to make sure my son had at least two slices a day, but I just could- n't make it.'[13] Many women said they had to use their food money to pay the rent and then visited the local food bank to make up the difference. Many food banks, however, have put conditions on the use of their services. In North Bay single mothers are only permitted to visit twice a month, and even then they receive only enough food for three days. In Belleville 'you have to show your stub of assistance and [explain] where the money went and if your reasons don't meet with their satisfaction, they say no', explained Laurie Hannah, president of Citizens for Action.[14] At least one Salvation Army food bank in downtown Toronto has told FBA recipients that they should visit only once every three months. 'They've told us that their food is *really* for those who are newly unemployed—not for us', said one single mother.[15] Food banks have begun to install sophisticated com- puter systems to keep track of who uses the service. In at least one com- munity the single mothers have found a collective solution. 'In order to get around this ridiculous policy, we all go to get food for the families who need it', explained one single mother who has a job.[16] But many other mothers who are isolated in their homes refuse to go to the food banks because of the humiliation.

Table 7.1 Monthly Budget of an FBA Recipient with Two Children

Monthly FBA cheque	$856.40
Rent	441.00
Phone	20.00
Hydro	22.00
Total	**$483.00 (56.4 per cent)**

After paying $483.00 out of the monthly cheque of $856.40, $373.40 (44.6 per cent) is left to cover all other needs.

Other essentials, including clothing, extra medication, personal care, and transportation	$198.02
Subtract $198.02 from $373.40	$175.38
Add baby bonus	64.82
Total	**$240.20**

With $240.20 left for groceries (based on a thirty-day month), the mother can only spend $2.67 per meal, or 89¢ per meal per person.

Source: Consumer Focus Group Project, Advisory Group on New Social Assistance Legislation, Ontario Government, Toronto, 1992.

Other single mothers find alternative ways to make ends meet between FBA cheques. For some, bingo provides a way to make a little extra money and socialize at the same time.[17] During a study of leisure activities for low-income women in Kingston, one single mother said that 'Bingo was the only time I got to drink a whole Coke by myself without having to share it with my kids.'[18] Bingo participation is often heavily scrutinized. Single mothers in North Bay have to beware of the 'bingo police' or social work-

Table 7.2 Meal Budget for FBA Recipient

Breakfast	
Milk	$1.19
Hot cereal	0.50 (including sugar)
Toast	0.17
Juice	0.37
Total	**$2.23**
Lunch	
Soup	$0.54
Sandwich	
Bread	0.17
Peanut butter	0.12
Honey	0.24
Vegetables (Carrots)	0.42
Milk	1.19
Total	**$2.68**
Supper	
1 box of Kraft Macaroni & Cheese	$0.79
1 lb ground beef	2.70
1 can of peas	0.69
1 can of corn	0.79
Milk	1.19
3 apples	0.42
Total	**$6.58**

These meals follow Canada's Basic Food Guide.
The cost of all three meals is $11.49.

Multiply this by thirty days equals	$344.70
Barbara's grocery money for the month	$240.12
Cost of the above groceries	344.70
Balance	**$(104.58)**

If a mother has only $240.12 for groceries and Canada's Food Guide's least expensive meals cost $344.70, how is she supposed to feed herself and her children when she receives only about 69.5 per cent of the money she needs to feed her family?

Source: Consumer Focus Group Project, Advisory Group on New Social Assistance Legislation, Ontario Government, Toronto, 1992.

ers who attend bingo, take note of the winners, and then automatically subtract the amount from the family benefits cheque.[19] In Elgin County, neighbours referred to as 'bingo blabs' have been encouraged to tell the family benefits office who attended the game.[20] According to both federal and provincial taxation laws, winnings from legal lotteries are not considered taxable income, and yet single mothers are forced to live by different rules.[21]

Some single mothers work 'under the table' in the underground economy. They babysit, sell items from mail-order catalogues, collect empty beer bottles, and do whatever they can to survive. Some set up extra bank accounts or give money to a relative or friend for safe keeping. 'That's called abuse, but we call it survival', explains Jennifer Myers, vice-president of Mothers and Others Making Change.[22] A few single mothers said that their social workers had helped them hide money. 'My worker said don't tell us what you're getting from the father of the youngest child', said one single mother. 'And mine told me not to report any gifts from my parents', added another.[23]

Retraining and employment are other areas for financial scrutiny. The recent employment initiatives have raised a number of concerns for single mothers. Many women said they were unable to participate in such training programs because they could not find subsidized child care, and those who had day care considered themselves exceptionally lucky.[24] Carole Silliker, a long-time antipoverty activist from Kitchener, is a strong opponent of retraining programs:

> Retraining is a farce. It is Band-Aid solutions. . . . You learn to be things that the market is saturated with—it makes no sense at all. And they think they're doing us a favour—and it's our fault when there is no job out there at the end. It's a big scam to make them look good.[25]

There are many other single mothers from rural areas or one-industry towns who are discouraged by the lack of available jobs. As one single mother in North Bay explained, 'We lost industries before the recession. Now the only one major employer is the [military] base and they're not exactly interested in hiring single moms.'[26]

Many single mothers who have returned to paid work found their social workers unsupportive. They said their social workers did not inform them of retraining programs, of start-up grants and other support systems that would help them make the transition. One mother recalled, 'My worker didn't encourage me to go back to school and then when I got my full-time job and was very excited, my worker said, "Oh you'll be back on FBA soon enough".'[27] Sally remembered her first job interview, 'I had a dress from the Salvation Army, no nylons, high-heeled shoes with the heels cut off.' Also Sally had a tooth missing and FBA does not cover dental plates or tooth replacements. 'I burnt off crazy glue and then put new stuff on to make it look O.K. . . . Needless to say, I didn't get the job. I couldn't compete with people who had jobs already and were looking for better ones.'[28] Other single mothers have been discouraged from taking long-term training. One mother interviewed wanted to complete her high school training and go on to study chemistry at university, but she was told this was not possible.[29]

Those single mothers who have found jobs have noticed a tremendous improvement in their treatment when they were no longer on FBA. As one single mother who now works as a community legal aid worker explained:

> Now I'm working—I've been told by the [FBA] workers—say your name, that you are from the ... Legal Clinic and that you're *not* a client and I'll be put right through [on the phone]. All of a sudden I'm important enough to talk to, but a week ago when I was just a client, not one worker wanted to talk to me.[30]

Given the increasing emphasis on employment, it is expected that single mothers will experience more differentiated treatment depending on their employment status in the future.

Despite this improved status, many single mothers have found that their new jobs do not make them more financially secure. Because they are working, they lose their drug benefits, housing subsidy, and child care subsidy. Most of the single mothers who have jobs work for minimum wage with few or any fringe benefits to offset the FBA services they have lost.[31] Since 1975, the purchasing power of minimum wage has declined by 22 per cent, leaving a single mother less able to make ends meet.[32] One mother explained her frustration during the SARC hearings: 'Even though I'm working I'm making less than if I'd be on Mothers' Allowance, which is very discouraging to me. I'm trying to raise four teenagers on a very small budget and I feel I'm sinking lower and lower all the time.'[33] Single mothers who have found jobs have moved from the unemployed poor to the working poor. They are no longer scrutinized by their social workers, but they continue to live below the poverty line.

Poor single mothers have always experienced intrusive financial scrutiny of many aspects of their lives. They have always had to juggle the incompatible responsibilities of caring and providing for their children and this contradiction will, in all likelihood, become more profound in the near future. With double-digit unemployment and limited child care spaces and other support services, it is unlikely that most single mothers on welfare will find jobs. But this emphasis on employment may encourage the public to blame single mothers who do not find full-time work. This may also result in reduced welfare payments to those who, for whatever reasons, remain on family benefits.

The Persistence of Moral Regulation

Although the Canada Assistance Plan, established in 1965, required all welfare programs receiving federal funds to base eligibility solely on economic need, single mothers continued to experience moral regulation. According to those interviewed, questions of morality permeated the everyday administration of this policy in both new and long-established forms. It is the visits by the workers and the whispers from the neighbours about how they talk, dress, and manage their homes and their children that most irritate and humiliate the single mothers on welfare. Even those who now have full-time paid work will never forget the moral scrutiny they experienced during their years of poverty. At the end of the interview with Sally, she said, 'This has left such a scar. It's ten years later and just talking to you—I want to go and cry. It's brought up such terrible memories.'[34]

To a great extent, the moral terrain has shifted from a broad spectrum of questions to more narrowly defined issues of sexuality. There can be both financial and moral elements to these inquiries. Whereas the discourse of, and justification for, intrusive investigations is largely financial, this scrutiny can also have moral implications. In keeping with the male-breadwinner ideology, the state is reluctant to financially support single mothers when fathers could do so. Consequently, there are a number of administrative procedures to track down or identify the male breadwinner, which involve intrusive investigation into a mother's intimate life. Single mothers often refer to these investigative procedures as 'manhunts'. These intrusive questionnaires and the time-consuming investigations conducted by state workers to identify and locate a male breadwinner are not cost efficient, especially given the low incidence of fraud. This suggests that there is more at stake than merely balancing the government's books.

At the same time, there are a number of others who volunteer to scrutinize a mother's behaviour. Again, this is often justified on financial grounds. Teachers, judges, landlords, and a number of taxpayers have made it their personal mission to ensure that single mothers do not 'cheat'. The implication in much of this scrutiny is that those who pay the bills also have the right to define moral codes of behaviour for society. Similar to charity work, these workers and volunteers feel justified in imposing their moral values upon others they are 'helping'.

This blurring of financial and moral activities is particularly evident in the case of deserted, unwed, and cohabiting mothers. Deserted mothers complained about social workers pressuring them to pursue the father of their children through the court system. 'There's nothing in this battle for me. When I charge him, he gets mad and comes after me. And even if he agrees to pay me support, I have to claim it as income, so I'm no further ahead', explained one mother.[35] Another recipient remembered the court procedure as both lengthy and emotionally exhausting: 'It was really embarrassing to go through the personal stuff before the lawyer and then the court. And then the judge said, "If you had two children by him, he can't be all that bad."'[36] Still another mother who had been abused by her husband summed up her experience on assistance: 'I felt like I was being bashed around all over again—only this time it was a welfare worker rather than my man.'[37]

Single mothers attempt to avoid or diminish this intrusion by welfare workers. Some try to arrange under-the-table support payments from their ex-partners, but these agreements are also fraught with anxiety, as one mother described: 'My ex pays $100 a month under the table and says he'll stop paying this if I tell mothers' allowance—and if I tell mothers' allowance, they'll go after *me* for fraud. He gets off. I get the blame.'[38] In order to avoid all this examination of their intimate lives, the women in one single mothers' group agreed it was best to tell the social worker you did not know the former partner's whereabouts. 'You're better off saying you got drunk and got raped by several guys than to say there was one', claimed one recipient.[39]

One unwed single mother, Dorothy, recounted her story of the social worker's attempt to discover the name of the father:

> The social worker asked, 'Well did you *actually* go out with him [the father]? I said, 'No, I screwed him on the bar stool—what the hell do you think?' Then the worker asks, 'Do you know his name?' I said I only have his first name: Frank. So she writes that down on her form: F-R-A-N-K. Then she says, 'Well, have you gone looking for him?' Well yeah, like I'm going to run across the country yelling, 'Frank, Frank!'[40]

Even when the cohabitation amendment of 1987 was in place, which permitted a woman to cohabit for three years with a man who was not the father of her children, mothers were still carefully watched by social workers.[41] According to the FBA manual, workers were expected to investigate *every* complaint. 'This is an open warrant to investigate a recipient's home at any time, over and over again if they wish', said John Clarke of Ontario Coalition Against Poverty.[42] In order to be eligible for benefits, the applicant had to fill out a questionnaire in front of the social worker that determined whether the respondent's circumstances fit the definition of cohabitation. In 1992 a revised questionnaire was implemented, which asked approximately fifty questions. 'This questionnaire is designed like a cross-examination; it tries to trip you up. It asks the same question in several different ways', explains legal advocate Nancy Vander Plaats.[43] While the Ministry of Community and Social Services is not permitted to ask questions about sex *per se*, the questionnaire includes a broad array of questions about a respondent's intimate life. For the most part, the questionnaire deals with social, economic, and familial ties within the household: whether household members eat meals together, wash dishes together, spend holidays together, and socialize together.[44]

The regulations concerning cohabitation are confusing at best, and the lengthy questionnaire encourages social workers to observe the most minute details of a single mother's life. Consequently, many women live in fear and confusion. 'I was frightened to have my brothers to stay over [for] the night', explained one mother. 'No one told me I could.'[45]

Most of the women interviewed had their own experience of the 'manhunt'. The bathroom investigation was the most common:

> One worker looked behind the shower of a friend of mine. He [the worker] was looking at absolutely everything. They ask to use your washroom, they go through your shaving cream, razors, three toothbrushes. Those are the things they looked for.[46]

Another mother recalled a boot investigation at her home: 'I had to try on my boots in front of them [social workers] because I took size 11. I had Cougar winter boots, which could be unisex. It was so humiliating.'[47]

Social workers have also been known to check for tire tracks in the snow, examine fridge notes, search for hunting equipment and evidence of dogs, stake out parking lots at night, throw sand on the doorstep in order to trace footprints—all in an effort to confirm that a man is living in the home.[48] While many women feel powerless to challenge these intrusive investigations, one mother attempted to establish boundaries by simply asserting *where* the interview would be conducted: 'I tell the worker to sit in the kitchen. That was a major victory for me.'[49]

As well as direct supervision of a woman's intimate relationships, there are also indirect forms of scrutiny. The cohabitation amendment, when it was in place, had suggested that a mother could be sexually active in her own residence, provided her partner is not the father of her children. Yet at the same time, the drug plan does not allow for the purchase of a variety of contraceptive products. The birth control pill is the only reproductive device permitted by the drug plan. In the era of the AIDS epidemic, condoms are not covered by the drug plan. Binkie, an FBA recipient, is exasperated by this regulation: 'I'm thirty-six years and they would give me the pill, but I had to pay for my own diaphragm and gel. Even though I had a doctor's certificate saying I need a diaphragm, they still won't pay for it.'[50]

Although questions regarding sexuality dominate the moral regulation of needy single mothers in the 1990s, other moral concerns emerge from time to time. Occasionally, single mothers are scrutinized regarding cleanliness and gratitude, suggesting that there is some continuation of previous moral issues. As one mother stated, 'Children's Aid Society, cops, society—everyone judges you on cleanliness. The teachers in the school system. How they see them [the children] dressed. . . .'[51] Another single mother believes social workers expect your house to be especially spotless if you do not have paid work.[52] As Ruth Mott, one antipoverty activist, explained, 'Nowadays a worker knows they can't make negative comments on cleanliness, so they talk about how clean [everything is] when you wouldn't say that to your mother or your sister; it's very patronizing.'[53]

Attitude is also periodically scrutinized. Several mothers interviewed agreed that a humble, grateful attitude was essential when dealing with the social workers. As one mother explained, 'I'm not human to them, and I have to be subservient, or they just won't even talk to me.'[54]

Race and Ethnicity

Whereas all single mothers on welfare receive a certain degree of financial and moral scrutiny, women from ethnic-minority backgrounds tend to experience a disproportionate amount. Ethnic-minority women complained about their workers being negative and insensitive. 'Social workers' attitudes are very demeaning. They do not take the time to see you. They treat you as if you are wasting their time', explained one woman.[55]

These problems are often compounded by language difficulties. During recent public hearings to review the Ontario welfare system, many ethnic-minority women whose first language is Cantonese, Tamil, Spanish, Portugese, Vietnamese, Farsi, and Somali spoke about their confusion and fear because they could not understand the welfare regulations.[56] Franco-Ontarians also experience difficulties. In the District of Nipissing, 28 per cent of the population is Franco-Ontarian, and yet there are some social workers who do not speak French and cannot understand their clients' questions.[57] Aboriginal applicants experience difficulties qualifying for and maintaining their benefits. Aboriginal single mothers have found welfare administrators to be insensitive to Aboriginal cultural values and often fear that their children will be apprehended by the Children's Aid Society.[58]

Women of colour also experience racism from social workers. Carolann Wright has encountered racism both as a low-income, Black single mother and as an advocate for others:

> I've seen their [the workers'] racist attitudes. Women of colour say that they're treated poorly. The workers automatically assume you're not Canadian. You are not given enough information. They make disparaging comments. The women of colour have more trouble than White women getting the money and any additional benefits.[59]

Former FBA worker Nick di Salle remembered racist comments made by his colleagues around the lunch table. 'Black women get blamed more than White women. They get blamed when their men leave—as if it is their fault.'[60]

This racism can also be camouflaged in bureaucratic regulation. When FBA worker Kathleen Lawrence was reassigned to a new work area, she noticed that there was a great deal of discrepancy in child support deductions taken from the monthly FBA cheque of single mothers. These deductions are made when an FBA worker determines that a client did not make adequate attempts to obtain child support from the father. When Lawrence explored the cases of 311 single mothers, she discovered that racial-minority mothers were *six* times more likely than White recipients to experience these deductions, regardless of the similarity in their situations. Also, she found the deductions charged to racial-minority recipients to be considerably higher than those charged to White women.[61] These bureaucratic decisions discriminated against Black single mothers and also reinforced the racist stereotype of the absent and irresponsible Black father.

'Policing the Police': The Workers' Environment

Welfare scholars and social workers claim that welfare workers are also victims of a punitive policy and oppressive bureaucracy. Many well-intentioned social workers told the SARC hearings that they were frustrated and disillusioned in their jobs.[62] This is a result of several factors. First, the system is adversarial in structure. According to welfare state theorist Allan Moscovitch, 'the whole welfare system is based on a 19th century notion of recipients going to rip off the system and this assumption is reflected in the rules and routines of everyday administration.'[63] Many welfare workers do not agree with the regulations they must enforce, and yet this is how they spend the majority of their time.

Another problem is the limited training a worker receives. Nick di Salle, a former FBA worker and union activist, recalled his training:

> The first day we came in and the supervisor gave us the Act and some hypothetical cases, a stack of forms and we were to figure out on our own how it all worked. . . . This three-day training included home visits with a worker. . . . I remember the one client I saw. . . . I'd never been into a recipient's home before. She was an alcoholic, the home was filthy. I was shocked out of my mind—there was peanut butter and marmalade spread on the walls, the kitchen cupboards, everywhere. The woman was a Native Canadian in her twenties with three or four kids. . . . The worker was a White middle-class woman, very well dressed, and she takes out this yellow form and starts checking off this form, asks the woman to sign it and says to the woman: 'Do you need anything?' 'No', said the woman—but you could see that absolutely *everything* was needed. It was overwhelming, where to begin to help. . . . First I thought the worker was cruel and callous, but it was so beyond their capacity to suggest how to change that. . . .[64]

Soon di Salle learned what was expected of him. 'You were judged on the number of phone calls you made, the number of home visits—but not on whether you really helped someone or not.'[65] Workers who got involved with their clients and therefore did not keep up with their paperwork were more carefully supervised. This policing of social workers to ensure economic efficiency does little to promote understanding between worker and recipient.

The complexity of the rules is another factor. This encourages both confusion and tremendous opportunity for decisions based on discretion rather than entitlements, as di Salle explained:

> You could never get a grasp of what was legitimately allowed to clients. . . . When you're at a loss as to what you can do, you learn to routinize—what is easy to do, you do. What is not usual (i.e., send the child to camp, etc.) then you say you can't get that and do the easiest stuff. . . . Workers abide by the rule that the more the recipients know, the more they'll ask for, so don't tell them anything . . . otherwise your case-load becomes too overloaded and you get in trouble. . . .[66]

Given these circumstances, it is no wonder that workers, who are overwhelmed by the clients' problems and feel powerless to help, become disillusioned and insensitive. Antipoverty activists and community legal workers are concerned that social workers will become increasingly frustrated and unhelpful as they continue to be overworked with ever-rising case-loads and cut-backs. In the London area social workers are already saying to the clients, 'Listen, I have more important things than this to take care of.'[67]

Welfare workers also have to work within an oppressive hierarchical bureaucracy. Although they have the best intentions of helping clients, workers are forced to obey regulations and procedures that limit their ability to do this. One study showed that on average, FBA workers carried a case-load of approximately 330 cases in the 1990s.[68] Consequently, they could not begin to meet the real needs of the clients or prevent further impoverishment. The rigidities of this bureaucratic structure discourage many welfare workers.[69]

There is also a gendered component to this bureaucratic hierarchy. The majority of FBA fieldworkers tend to be women, whereas the majority of managers are men. Welfare state theorists Jennifer Dale and Peggy Foster argue that these women social workers 'have never exercised control over their profession nor over those organizations in which social work takes place.'[70] As women, they remain vulnerable in a male-dominated management, which, in keeping with societal values, does not adequately appreciate the caring functions that they attempt to perform.

Finally, workers tend to be the human face on a punitive welfare system. Clients tend to 'shoot the messenger' when they are outraged by the regulations. All of these difficulties have resulted in low morale and a high turnover of welfare staff, particularly among those who conduct fieldwork.[71] In the face of escalating welfare cuts, social workers must deal with increasingly hostile clients. These cuts will only lead to heavier case-loads, which will further prevent the worker from meeting the clients' everyday needs.

Other Agents of Moral Regulation

Social workers are not the only people to scrutinize single mothers on welfare. Given the heavy case-load of welfare workers, it is not surprising that they rarely see the majority of their clients. Others, however, are willing to volunteer to oversee a single mother's activities. Over and over again, the mothers interviewed emphasized that there are very few people they can trust. As one mother explained, 'You try not to tell anyone you're on FBA. You feel very threatened.'[72] There are many instances of social workers bribing welfare recipients to inform on other recipients.[73] Moral scrutiny is particularly rampant in small communities or low-income housing projects. As Patsy Turcotte from North Bay explained, 'Small-town politics makes it really hard on single moms—there's an awful lot of social stigma. People know what side of the tracks you are from and they never forget it.'[74] Low-income housing projects in urban centres have many similar traits to small-town life. One welfare recipient interviewed called them 'holding pens of the poor'.[75] Another single mother in Toronto moved out of a housing project and spends almost twice as much money to rent a townhouse in Scarborough. She saw this as the only way to give her children a fighting chance against stigmatization. As she reasoned, 'In Metro Housing,

there's lots of spying. . . . The neighbours go to the worker. If you're dress-
ing up too much, they think you're doing drugs or selling them.'[76] Another
single mother said she distrusts co-ops. 'Some co-ops keep track of how
much make-up you wear, or give you a hard time because you can't attend
the [general members'] meetings. I've seen those Attila the Hun board of
directors who discuss your sex life at their board meetings.'[77]

Single mothers in rural communities face intense scrutiny from others.
Residents in farming communities often have a strong belief in individual
initiative and self-reliance; consequently, they tend to blame the victim of
poverty. Poor single mothers feel they are under constant scrutiny in these
communities. 'They are afraid to get together, to meet at someone's house
because everybody knows what everybody is doing', explained Josephine
Grey, who has attempted to interview rural antipoverty groups.[78]

There are some communities of single mothers, however, who struggle
together against the rest of the world. Sally found her low-income neighbourhood in North Bay very supportive. 'There was no spying—instead,
we pooled everything—cigarettes, kids [child care], groceries. We would
make a big deal of birthday parties and Christmas and stuff. I could never
have done that on my own.'[79] And Jennifer Myers of MOMC agreed:

> In Ontario Housing we start comparing notes with each other—all the sin-
> gle moms on FBA. My previous worker didn't make adjustments for two
> years—I got over $1,000 afterwards, but I never would have pressed it, I never
> would have even known about it if I hadn't talked to other single moms.[80]

There are many others involved in the moral regulation of single mothers' lives. According to Carole Silliker, single mothers are 'shunned and
treated with contempt by society in general, but the main culprits are cops,
lawyers, judges, school officials, professed Christians . . . charitable organizations, and the general public.'[81] Landlords also act as spies on single mothers. Landlords for low-income housing complexes in Toronto have been
known to let welfare workers into recipients' apartments without the latter's permission.[82]

According to the single mothers interviewed, schoolteachers are considered one of the most powerful agents of moral scrutiny. A single mother can
still have her welfare cheques cancelled if her dependent child is not in
school; this grants schoolteachers considerable power over a single mother's
life.[83] When asked at one Toronto single-mothers' group 'what bugs you
most about family benefits', the first response was 'the attitudes of teachers'.
These women had numerous stories about their interactions with teachers.
'Teachers watch you and your children like a hawk. They see what is for
lunch, if [the children have] new snowsuits, the teachers say you are scam-
ming the system. But if they are threadbare, they say you are not a responsible mother. You can't win.'[84] Bambi, another single mother, explained how
the teachers changed their attitudes once she started to work:

> If your kids do anything and you're on mothers' allowance, they phone you up and tell you to come right here—your son is acting up. As if I didn't have enough to do. . . . [But after I started working] when my son acts up, they say to him, 'Now we don't want to have to tell your mother about this.' Just because there is change in my pocket she [the teacher] starts to treat me differently.[85]

Given these accounts, the school is clearly a site of moral scrutiny for poor single mothers.

It is evident that moral judgement comes from a variety of sources. Whether it be the teacher at school, the store owners at the corner or the neighbour next door, single mothers live with a great deal of moral scrutiny. It is no wonder that single mothers live in fear and censor their own activities. This self-censorship allows moral scrutiny to continue long after a punitive aspect of the policy is amended. For example, several of the single mothers interviewed said they were careful not to socialize in public, to accept a drink from an unknown man at a bar, or to permit a man to stay in their home even though they knew this was condoned by the welfare policy.[86] Because of the high level of distrust for others and the discretionary nature of welfare administration, single mothers devise additional rules and regulations in order to guarantee their monthly cheque.

CONCLUSION

These interviews demonstrated that current single mothers on welfare encounter both financial and moral regulation of their lives. Although the definition of worthiness has changed over time, perhaps what is most remarkable is the fact that social workers continue to expend considerable energy in this determination. While legislation and regulations have altered, the current administrative procedures continue to determine worthiness on the basis of intrusive and discretionary criteria. As welfare rolls continue to grow and governments attempt to restrain their budgets to appease taxpayers, there will be increased differentiation between the worthy and unworthy poor. This will lead to new definitions and new regulations to justify who will or will not receive assistance.

It is also important to note the many agents and sites of moral regulation. Social workers, hired and paid by the state, have the written authority to scrutinize welfare recipients' lives. But the interviews revealed that there are many others, not hired or paid by the state, who *voluntarily* investigate and report on the activities of poor single mothers. The combined efforts of state workers and volunteer citizens help to create a climate of fear and suspicion for single mothers. With increasing demands upon the state to curb social welfare expenditures, single mothers will only experience rising levels of public scrutiny.

This is not to suggest that single mothers simply accept the oppressive and intrusive aspects of state assistance. The interviews demonstrate the multitude of ways single mothers have used their very limited resources to protect and nurture both themselves and their children. They have applied for state benefits, aware of the oppressive regulations. They have argued with state workers that they deserve more money and services. Poor single mothers have individually and collectively resisted the most intrusive aspects of the welfare state and, in all likelihood, they will continue to do so in the future.

Conclusion

C. Wright Mills warned his students never to divorce their life from their work and instead use that life experience to influence and shape their intellectual projects.[1] Feminists have also echoed this thought in their maxim 'the personal is political'. For those of us who attempt to be both academics and activists simultaneously, the world is often a challenging place. While pouring over the yellowed papers of case files in the quiet archives, I also conducted workshop-style interviews with single mothers who told me how this policy had dramatically altered every aspect of their daily life. While writing this book, politicians of every partisan stripe began leaping to the platform, promising new and innovative ways to reduce the deficit through dramatic cuts to single mothers and other welfare recipients. During the final editing of this book, Mike Harris and the Progressive Conservative government rolled back the clock on welfare reform and began the most aggressive campaign to slash welfare rates and services ever seen in the history of Ontario welfare. On 28 November 1997 the Harris government passed Bill 142. This new legislation incorporates the disabled, elderly, single adults, and single parents under one welfare policy that links all welfare benefits to employment. Consequently, single mothers are no longer a distinct welfare recipient category and their special needs and responsibilities are no longer recognized.[2] This marks the end of seventy-seven years of mothers' allowance policy in Ontario.

As we face the rapid erosion of a wide spectrum of welfare programs, I believe that it is more important than ever to explore the nature of the Canadian welfare state, its evolution, and its limitations. To date there have been few studies of early welfare policies. There has also been little examination of women's role as initiators, administrators, and recipients of many of these formative programs. These omissions severely limit our understanding of the very foundations of the Canadian welfare state. An examination of Ontario Mothers' Allowance from its enactment in 1920 to its conclusion in 1997 helps to remedy these previous omissions. This study of mothers' allowance has provided an opportunity to rethink our understanding of the welfare state generally and explore the distinctive traits of this policy in particular. In doing so, it helps to prepare us as social scientists and as activists for the challenges ahead.

A NEW UNDERSTANDING OF THE WELFARE STATE

This examination of OMA challenges traditional conceptions of both political actors and political arenas. Bourgeois women, often working outside the traditional spheres of political and economic power, helped to establish a number of early welfare reforms. For the most part, their efforts have not been duly recognized. In the case of OMA, bourgeois women led the campaign for the enactment of this policy. They began this campaign not in the legislature but through their charity and women's organizations. Through their previous and personal involvement in helping the poor, they became aware of the growing numbers of fatherless children, which led them to discuss and later lobby for social reform. When the politicians were slow to enact such legislation, these women took it into their own hands to demonstrate how such a policy could be implemented. Outside the corridors of political power they developed a three-year pilot project in Toronto, dispensing small sums of money to six needy families. Through this project they gained considerable 'expertise' on just what type of policy should be established and precisely how it should be administered. Their opinions were highly regarded by those politicians and bureaucrats formulating the initial legislation. Undoubtedly their vision of OMA reflected their class, race, and gender position. They showed disdain for non-Protestant Euro-Canadian cultures and arrogance towards the poor generally, but on balance, their lobby efforts benefited poor single mothers; without the allowance, many of them would have been forced to give up their children to the orphanage for adoption.

This lobby effort clearly demonstrates that political actors are not always those with great political power. Women had not yet achieved the vote when they began this mothers' allowance lobby and therefore were not full political citizens. Despite barriers to their political participation, these women developed local projects and created national and international alliances with like-minded women who also called for social reform.

Because these women were not full political citizens, their arena for political activity was also restricted. Not able to vote or be members of the legislatures, they chose other forums to achieve their political aspirations. For the most part, they promoted welfare reform through private women's and charitable organizations. In the case of OMA, lobbyists were appointed to the state as public welfare administrators. Others volunteered to scrutinize the behaviour of various recipients, although they were not paid by or directly accountable to the state. This suggests that the welfare arena can be a complex relationship of private or charity-run welfare and public or state welfare, and that one does not necessarily function autonomously from the other. Given the state-centred nature of much welfare scholarship, this connection between public and private welfare has not been adequately explored. An exploration of OMA recipients' lives illustrates the importance of this intersection of public and private welfare.[3]

THE NATURE OF ONTARIO MOTHERS' ALLOWANCE

An examination of the particulars of this policy has also helped to elucidate further the complex relationship between women, children, and social policy. The treatment of single mothers affects all women. If the state policy to help single mothers is moralistic, stigmatizing, and well below subsistence, this impinges upon all women's 'choice' to leave a difficult or abusive relationship. Consequently, the details of the policy help us to understand how society values women and mothers generally.

While noting considerable changes in eligibility and administration, I have argued that there were two important features that persisted throughout the history of OMA. First, the OMA rates always remained well below subsistence, which fulfilled two functions. It protected the work ethic and ensured that the poor would choose work over welfare, if given a choice. These low OMA rates always encouraged recipients to seek at least part-time work. Simultaneously, this made the policy less than attractive to ensure that women would not easily leave their marriages or relationships.

Low rates, however, were not unique to OMA. Other welfare programs, especially those designed for the long-term unemployed, are known for their below-subsistence rates. I have argued that what was most distinctive about this policy is how it morally regulated single mothers' lives. The central argument of this book is that moral regulation is an important analytical tool to highlight the many processes, methods, and procedures implemented to inform a citizen's moral character. This analysis highlights certain processes and regulations that are otherwise obscured. In the case of OMA, this moral regulation took several forms. Moral criteria articulated in the early policy for the act stipulated that a recipient had to be 'a fit and proper person'. Eligibility distinctions between various types of single mothers created a 'hierarchy of deservedness' in which certain mothers were considered more morally worthy than others. Along with these regulations came intrusive investigations of recipients' daily lives in an attempt to determine whether the mother was indeed beyond reproof or not. Economically speaking, it was not efficient to expend a great deal of time and money on this type of intrusive investigation. These investigations were carried out not simply by state-paid officials but also by charity women, neighbours, and friends.

Through this chronological examination of OMA, I have argued that moral regulation changes with time. Initially, widows who were impoverished as a result of the unfortunate death of their husbands were the majority of OMA recipients, but over time unwed and deserted mothers who would have been considered ineligible in the 1920s became the predominant types of OMA recipients. The regulations of the policy also altered with time. Whereas cleanliness and the absence of alcohol were crucial factors in determining worthiness in the early periods, the moral terrain shifted to questions of sexuality, fraud, and employment.

This moral regulation of single mothers is not to suggest that OMA recipients were powerless beings. In their own way, these applicants and recipients challenged the very regulations meant to humble them. On an individual basis they withheld information about their finances and their living arrangements. They acted grateful and obedient when necessary to achieve their goals. They argued, bargained, and pleaded with OMA officials in an effort to get what they wanted or needed. Collectively they shared, in an informal way, information about the policy's complex regulations and about the difficulties of particular OMA workers. More formally, they organized antipoverty groups, protest rallies, and fund-raising events. Through this individual and collective protest they demonstrated themselves to be survivors and heroes of their own lives.[4]

NEW CHALLENGES TO THE DEFINITION OF DESERVING

An examination of the historical development of Ontario Mothers' Allowance has provoked questions about the origins and nature of the welfare state. This exploration is not conclusive but illustrative of the need to study neglected aspects of our welfare system. As social scientists and community activists, we need to understand the underpinnings of welfare policies such as OMA and their influence in society before we can effectively create progressive change. With this in mind, this section will briefly explore both the contemporary challenges to single mothers, the family, and the welfare state and the limited possibilities for transformative change.

Today there are dramatic challenges to the definition of a deserving single mother. By the mid-1990s, the category of deserving began to shrink and continues to do so at an alarming rate. Federal, provincial, and municipal governments are all restricting eligibility for social programs and social services. With each day, a growing number of poor single mothers are cast aside as a result.

By the late 1990s, the federal government renounced its responsibility to the poor in two important ways: by reducing funding and by obliterating almost all national standards. The cap on the Canada Assistance Plan in 1990 heralded the end of federal commitment to improving or even sustaining the lives of low-income Canadians. During the two economic recessions and the jobless economic recovery of the 1990s, Ontario was devastated by this cap on federal funding. But on 1 April 1996, the federal government withdrew even further from its commitment to the poor, announcing billions of dollars in cuts to welfare transfers and the end of the CAP. The CAP was replaced by the Canada Health and Social Transfer (CHST), a program that provides limited block funding to the provinces for education, health, and welfare. The impact of this change has yet to be fully realized. The CHST has no federal funding specifically designated for welfare programs. Instead, each province receives a lump sum to spend on education, health, and welfare; each province can choose just how much to spend in each of these three areas. Given the popularity of health and education, it is likely that provincial governments will concentrate spending in these areas at the expense of welfare programs.

Under the CHST the federal government has erased almost all national standards for welfare. Poor Canadians no longer have a right to welfare based on economic need. Now provinces can establish their own eligibility requirements. This change permits not only work-fare but any other eligibility criteria that the provincial and municipal governments wish to implement. It also allows provincial and municipal governments to refuse a person welfare for any reason they deem appropriate. A second change is that the CHST, unlike the CAP, does not provide welfare recipients with the right to appeal welfare decisions. Consequently, welfare applicants may have no recourse if they are unfairly treated or denied welfare.[5] The only condition the CHST put on the funding was to prohibit a provincial government from denying a person welfare because he or she is from another province. This is a very weak condition given that a provincial government can deny a person welfare for any reason other than residency. While the rights of the poor have always been weak, they are virtually non-existent with the introduction of the CHST.

This federal withdrawal of funds and rights for the poor has permitted provincial governments to transform their welfare programs. This transformation has been particularly dramatic in Ontario. On 8 June 1995, Mike Harris led the Progressive Conservatives to a landslide victory in Ontario, taking eighty-two of 130 seats. Harris ran a populist-style campaign called 'The Common Sense Revolution', which promised a 30 per cent tax cut for the taxpayers, a 20 per cent cut in non-priority government spending without touching the health care budget, and an overhaul of welfare.

In a very short period, Harris has transformed the field of welfare in five important ways. The Harris government has drastically cut welfare rates, restricted eligibility, increased welfare policing, implemented work-fare, and enacted Bill 142, thus marking the end of Ontario Mothers' Allowance. The results are devastating for all Ontario's poor, but are particularly difficult for single mothers. Single mothers' risk of poverty is five times greater than that for two-parent families, and these mothers are experiencing increased poverty in the 1990s. In 1987 approximately 84,300 single mothers comprised nearly 30 per cent of all welfare recipients in Ontario. By 1994 the number had increased to nearly 200,000.[6] Consequently, single mothers are one of the groups most affected by these welfare changes.

First, true to his election promise, Harris announced a 21.6 per cent cut in welfare rates to come into effect 1 October 1995. Whereas the NDP government allowed welfare rates to fall below inflation, the Harris government has taken one of every $5 out of a welfare recipient's pocket. The impact is seen on every street corner and in every shelter, every food bank and every welfare office. Evictions have escalated as some welfare recipients can no longer afford their housing. Shelters and food banks cannot cope with the increased demand for their services. The needs of single mothers and their children are particularly urgent. Single mothers are begging on street corners, starving themselves, or returning to abusive relationships—all in an effort to keep food in the mouths of their children. And other single mothers have given up hope; they are suicidal or are giving up their children for adoption, or both.[7]

Second, the Harris government announced a policy amendment that restricted eligibility for those living with an adult of the opposite sex. As of 1 October 1995, recipients were no longer eligible for family benefits if they were living with a spouse of the opposite sex. This replaced the 1987 regulation, which permitted family benefits recipients to live with an opposite-sex spouse for a limit of three years. The three-year rule permitted recipients to explore a new relationship without economic penalty and was in agreement with the mutual support obligation as specified in family law. The impact of this change is only beginning to be realized. This policy amendment signals a return to the 'manhunts' of a previous era. Welfare workers have heightened their scrutiny of single mothers' homes to determine who is or is not in a spousal relationship. Community members have also been encouraged to report on the social activities of single mothers. Within six months of this legislative change, more than 10,000 recipients were deemed ineligible under this new definition, 89 per cent of whom were women. Some have reapplied for assistance as a couple, but the majority have remained off assistance. When couples receive welfare, the cheque arrives, almost invariably, in the man's name. Consequently, single mothers are forced into an economically dependent relationship with their spouse in order to receive welfare. Other single mothers have been cut off assistance without a hearing that might have proven their innocence. In all cases, a single mother is considered guilty until she proves herself innocent—until she demonstrates that she is not in a spousal relationship. As many single mothers have realized, providing evidence that you are *not* in a spousal relationship is indeed a challenge.[8]

The Ontario government has also increased the investigation of welfare recipients. In 1994 the government initiated an intensive review of all social assistance files in Ontario. The first round of investigations, from April to August 1994, specifically targeted 'high-risk' cases and referred a total of 1,029 cases of 'suspected' fraud to the police. This represented .15 per cent of the total monthly case-load during this period. Despite this low rate of suspected fraud, the Harris government introduced a province-wide fraud telephone line in the summer of 1995. The government promised more than $15 million in savings from this welfare fraud hotline and encouraged people with complaints about potentially fraudulent relatives, friends, and neighbours to call in. As of March 1997, a total of ninety-two snitch line allegations were referred to the police for further action and *only nine resulted in charges.*[9]

Both the investigations and fraud lines are examples of the state providing new bureaucratic tools to encourage the community to gossip about and scrutinize welfare recipients' activities. Many of the alleged welfare cheaters who are reported to welfare snitch lines are not even on welfare.[10] According to antipoverty advocates, single mothers in particular have been the target of welfare fraud investigations. In a number of cases single mothers have been cut off the welfare benefit while undergoing this investigation.[11] This suggests once again that single mothers on welfare are considered guilty until they prove their innocence.

The introduction of work-fare is another revolutionary shift in welfare policy. On 10 June 1996, the Ontario government announced its work-fare pilot project in twenty communities, with the province-wide program to be instituted by 1998. With work-fare, welfare recipients are obligated to work for their welfare cheques. Although single mothers with young children are to be exempt, the details are still unclear. The *Common Sense Revolution* document exempted mothers with children under three years old. According to early reports, single mothers are participating in the work-fare pilot projects.

This shift to work-fare is the most dramatic change in welfare policy for single mothers. Whereas single mothers have always had to prove moral worthiness and were always forced to live on menial allowances, they were not expected to do paid work. Although the welfare rate was always minimal and many single mothers often did some type of work to augment their welfare cheques, employment was carefully monitored to ensure that it did not interfere with what was considered a mother's primary goal: caring for children. Now the majority of single mothers on welfare are expected to retrain and find full-time employment.

This emphasis on employability may further stigmatize those single mothers who, for whatever reason, are not in retraining, employment, or work-fare programs. This may also encourage governments to withdraw from their previous responsibility to provide for unemployable single mothers. Today the majority of poor single mothers are already working or retraining. A recent study of social assistance recipients in Ontario revealed that 26 per cent of single mothers were employed, 15 per cent were doing regular volunteer work, 42 per cent were looking for employment, and another 8 per cent were pursuing training or attending school full-time.[12] Those fortunate to undertake retraining find that these courses train women for gender-segregated, low-paid jobs (such as dressmaking, hairstyling, data entry, and child care work) rather than career advancement.[13] Finally, global economic restructuring has reduced the number of full-time unionized jobs available. Instead, job opportunities of the 1990s are characterized as low-paying, non-unionized, part-time employment with little chance of advancement. Thus retraining and work-fare programs generally prepare poor single mothers for exploitative part-time work that will not substantially improve their economic circumstances. For the majority of single mothers who cannot obtain adequate child care in order to participate in retraining courses or full-time work, the only option is continued dependence on a policy that remains well below subsistence. For these reasons the labour force participation of Canadian single mothers is actually declining, while it is increasing or remaining relatively stable for other groups of women in society.[14]

The final dramatic change in Ontario welfare policy is the introduction of Bill 142. In a number of ways, Bill 142 crystallizes the Harris government's approach to welfare. According to this legislation, single mothers will no longer be treated as a distinct welfare recipient group with unique needs because of their parenting responsibilities. Instead, single mothers, along with the unemployed, elderly people, and people with temporary illnesses or disabilities, will all be recipients of the same welfare policy. All will be subject to increased policing from welfare workers and the community, and all but the severely disabled and single mothers with very young children will be expected to work.

This legislation heightens the policing of welfare recipients. It authorizes the province and municipalities to set up 'fraud control units' to investigate the eligibility of recipients. Most of this investigation has nothing to do with 'fraud', but the title helps instil in the public mind that welfare fraud is indeed a growing problem and requires new measures to stamp it out. Similarly, this legislation will enhance the power of welfare workers, called eligibility review officers (EROs), who review the eligibility of recipients. EROs will be granted the power to get and act on search warrants, and will be given additional police powers by regulation at any time. These regulations to increase the policing powers of EROs can be passed without notice, consultation, or political debate. These EROs will also be able to demand information from any number of third parties, such as family members, neighbours, landlords, teachers, employers, doctors, priests, and others.[15] As demonstrated in Chapter 7, these people often have considerable power over single mothers, and Bill 142 increases their ability to harass, intimidate, and threaten these mothers—all under the guise of rooting out welfare fraud.

Bill 142 also establishes province-wide work-fare. Under this legislation, welfare will provide '*temporary* financial assistance to those most in need while they satisfy *obligations to become and stay employed*' (my emphasis).[16] Clearly, welfare will be only for temporary help. Equally important, all welfare recipients under this legislation will be expected to work. This includes single mothers who, until Bill 142, were eligible for long-term assistance and did not face mandatory employment requirements as a condition of receiving this financial aid.

This transformation of welfare under the Harris government has dire consequences for single mothers. Welfare rate cuts, eligibility restrictions, greater welfare policing, and work-fare have all increased the stigmatization of welfare recipients generally and poor single mothers in particular. All of these changes have promoted the notion that the poor are lazy, immoral, and generally undeserving of state aid. Welfare cuts have hurt all welfare recipients, but especially single mothers, who, without adequate child care, do not have the same ability to seek employment. Eligibility restrictions have clearly focused on single mothers and their relationships with men. Investigations into the bedrooms and the bathrooms of single mothers' homes has intensified during the 1990s and will likely escalate once again with the increased policing powers granted under Bill 142. Simultaneously, welfare fraud lines have ensured that the state is not the only one involved in the moral regulation of single mothers' lives. Instead, neighbours, friends, and even family are encouraged to report on the activities of poor single mothers. Finally, work-fare provides a new avenue for scrutiny and blame. Welfare recipients who are unable to find work during a jobless economic recovery are viewed as personally responsible for their failure. And work-fare will permit employers to become actively involved in the determination of eligibility for welfare benefits. All these changes demonstrate that the moral terrain has shifted dramatically for poor single mothers. This victimization of poor single mothers justifies increased moral regulation by both the state and the larger community.

The history of this policy helps us to understand better these contemporary changes. Given that the policy's benefits were never premised on recipients' real economic needs, it is not hard for the state to justify cutting these welfare rates to more miserly levels. Given that this policy always distinguished between the worthy and the unworthy, it is not difficult for the state to reinforce this distinction. Single mothers have always had to prove moral deservedness to guarantee their monthly welfare cheque. Today the state is renegotiating this moral terrain and rewriting exactly what moral criteria must be met in order for single mothers to receive government aid. This is not merely a class war; it is also a moral war—a battle about who is or is not deserving.

Chronology of Ontario Mothers' Allowance

1914	Ontario workers' compensation enacted.
1919	Provincial inquiry regarding mothers' allowance (public hearings in Hamilton, London, Ottawa, and Toronto).
1 July 1920	Ontario Mothers' Allowance bill is passed.

Eligibility requirements:
- Widows with two or more children younger than sixteen
- A British subject or naturalized (includes First Nations)
- A resident of Canada for three years and of Ontario for two years
- Birth, death, and marriage certificates as proof of eligibility
- Must be a 'fit and proper person'
- Rates set at $30 for mother with two children in a rural area and $40 in an urban area; allowance increased by $5 for each additional child with maximums of $45 and $55
- Equity assets of no more than $2,500 in a home, and liquid assets of no more than $350
- OMA amendment to include: deserted mothers with two or more children younger than sixteen whose husband has not been seen or heard from in seven years; foster mothers; mothers with one child under sixteen and a husband who is permanently incapacitated; mothers with a permanently incapacitated child who is older than sixteen

1921	OMA Act amended to include:

- Widows or the wife of an inmate of an insane asylum
- Desertion period reduced from seven to five years
- Mother with one child under fourteen and one child over fourteen
- Mother with two children whose husband is permanently disabled
- Rates for foster mothers were $20 per month for one foster child in cities and $15 in other areas, with $5 per month for additional foster children

1927–8	School attendance records sent in monthly by school officials before the OMA cheque is released to the mother.
1931	The Ontario Department of Public Welfare is created. OMA administration is included within this new department.

1934   OMA amendment to include children between sixteen and eighteen who are attending school, provided one child is under sixteen.

1935   OMA amendment to include: desertion period reduced from five to three years; mothers with one child; foster mothers with one child.

                Ontario government agrees to finance 50 per cent of the transportation costs to return the deserting husband to the authorities when a wife takes legal action.

                OMA rates revised: mother with one child, $35 in the city, $30 in villages, and $25 in rural areas, with $5 for each additional child.

March 1937   Ontario government assumes 100 per cent of the costs of OMA administration.

                Ontario government finances fuel, emergency medical and dental care following a recommendation from the provincial OMA investigator.

                Local boards jointly administer OMA and Old Age Pension applications.

Fall 1938   Ontario government agrees to pay fuel after 'a proper investigation of the need'. The municipality is responsible for 20 per cent of the fuel cost.

1940   Medical board established to review incapacitation cases. Medical Appeal Board established to hear appeals regarding incapacitation cases.

1942   Free medical service and medication granted to provincial recipients of OMA, old age pension, and blind welfare as the result of an agreement with the Ontario Medical Association.

1943   First increase in OMA rates since the 1920 enactment. The rates are increased by 20 per cent. As a result, the basic allowances are $42 per month for a mother and child in the city, $36 in a village, and $30 in rural areas, plus $6 for each additional child. Foster mothers receive $24 for one foster child and $18 for each additional child.

1944   OMA Act amended to read: allowable cash assets increased from $500 to $1,000.

                First civil servant appointed as chair of the OMA provincial commission.

                A $10 monthly special assistance established above the regular OMA payment for those in desperate need. The need is determined at the commission's discretion.

1946   OMA Act amended to include:

- Desertion period reduced from three years to one
- Residency requirements changed from two years to one year in Ontario
- Permanently unemployable husband granted an allowance similar to a dependent child
- Children in their sixteenth year up until the completion of the school year

1947   OMA rates are revised as such: all increased to city rates; foster mothers receive $24 for one child, $48 for two children, and $6 for each additional child.

1948   Local OMA boards disband.

OMA Act amended to include: non-British subjects, 'a fit and proper person' eliminated from the act.

OMA rates revised: $50 a month for a mother with one child, with $10 more for each additional child and unemployable husband; for each additional foster child above and beyond two, the rate is increased from $6 to $10 per child.

1950   Free legal assistance available to all provincial welfare recipients.

OMA Act amended to include children in their eighteenth year until the completion of the school term.

1951   OMA Act amended to include: residency in province reduced to one year; divorced mothers; 'a suitable person to receive an allowance' added to the act.

OMA special assistance increased from $10 to $20; fuel is granted to foster-mother cases.

1952   OMA provincial commission of three appointees is replaced by a director.

1953   Relaxation of requirements for birth, death, and marriage certificates.

1953–4   Ontario Department of Public Welfare destroys 3 million files. A sample of these files is microfilmed.

1954   An appeal board is established. The director appoints three senior officials to this board.

OMA Act amended to read: desertion period reduced from one year to six months.

1955   OMA Act amended to include long-time residents of Ontario who were temporarily outside the province at the time of application or death, disability, or desertion.

1956   OMA Act amended to include: unwed mothers who have cared for the child for a period of two years following the birth; mothers with children aged eighteen, provided they are attending school; permanently unemployable fathers who are caring for the children and whose wives are dead or absent.

1957   OMA Act amended to include foster parents of either sex.

OMA rates revised: flat rate replaced by a budgetary-based rate, which included the establishment of individual family budgets; the maximum allowance is $180 monthly for seven or more beneficiaries.

1958   OMA Act amended to read: two-year waiting period for unwed mothers waived; unwed mothers with more than one child are no longer eligible.

1959   OMA Act amended to read: an unwed mother must be at least eighteen; a six-month waiting period is established for unwed mother applicants.

All provincial welfare recipients receive hospital care on a premium-free basis.

OMA recipients' children who are under sixteen receive free dental care from the dentist of their choice.

1960   Special Investigation Unit established to locate deserting husbands.

1963   Widows and single women's allowance established to provide monthly allowance to widows sixty years or older.

General welfare assistance expands to include incapacitated fathers.

OMA Act amended to include children older than eighteen who are still in school and 'making satisfactory progress'.

1964   OMA Act amended to read: waiting period for unwed mothers reduced from six to three months.

1966   Canada Assistance Plan established. Through this unlimited cost-sharing plan, the federal government agreed to fund 50 per cent of any provincial or municipal aid for the purpose of providing food, shelter, clothing, fuel, utilities, household supplies, and personal requirements.

Family Benefits Act established to replace OMA, the Blind Persons' Allowances Act, the Disabled Persons' Allowances Act, and the Old Age Assistance Act.

FBA broadened eligibility in the following ways: the age of children attending school and 'making satisfactory progress' was increased from eighteen to twenty-one; universal medical and hospital insurance with premium-free coverage for all persons of low income; waiting period for deserted mothers reduced from six to three months.

1976   FBA recipients are eligible to enrol in Canada Manpower training courses, keep a portion of their benefits, and receive phase-out payments when they begin full-time work. If they could not find work following this course, these FBA recipients became eligible for unemployment insurance.

1979   Work Incentive Program established. This includes initial back-to-work grant, plus additional financial support for two years of full-time employment.

FBA amended to include separated mothers, provided they have been separated for five years.

1982   Pilot project established in seven municipalities, which transfers FBA administration to the same offices as general welfare assistance.

1983   FBA amended to include healthy sole-support fathers.

1986   Social Assistance Review Committee established to review all welfare legislation in Ontario.

1987   FBA amended to include cohabiting mothers for the first three years of cohabitation.

1989   Family allowance is de-indexed.

A three-pronged March Against Poverty leaves Windsor, Sudbury, and Ottawa and ends at Queen's Park.

Federal government announces a commitment to eliminate child poverty in Canada by the year 2000 (House of Commons, 24 Nov.).

1990   An antipoverty campaign is organized during the provincial election under the slogan 'Down with the Poverty Premier'.

The federal government announces a three-year limit on Canada Assistance Plan spending for the three wealthiest provinces (Alberta, British Columbia, and Ontario).

Ontario Coalition Against Poverty, an umbrella provincial antipoverty organization, is established.

1991   Federal government announces continued restrictions on CAP funding until 1995.

FBA amended to read: three-month waiting period for unwed mothers eliminated, three-month waiting period for deserted mothers eliminated.

1992   Family allowance abolished and replaced by children's benefit, a targeted program for the poor and working poor.

            Federal government announces another three-year limit on CAP funding to the three wealthiest provinces. This limit will extend until the end of 1995.

            Ontario welfare fraud squad is established.

1993   Ontario government announces a 1 per cent increase in welfare rates (inflation rose 2.5 per cent).

1995   Progressive Conservative government announces an overhaul of Ontario welfare, which includes: a 21.6 per cent welfare rate cut, repealing the three-year cohabitation rule, and establishing a province-wide telephone fraud line.

1996   Federal government eliminates the Canada Assistance Plan and replaces it with the Canada Health and Social Transfer. This change means: reducing federal funding to the provinces for health, education, and welfare; repealing the right to welfare based solely on economic need; and repealing welfare recipients' right to appeal welfare decisions.

            Women's March for Bread and Roses, a cross-Canada march against poverty.

            The Ontario government launches twenty work-fare pilot projects and promises to implement a province-wide program by 1998.

1997   Bill 142 is passed by the Ontario legislature. This bill means:
            • The end of the Family Benefits Act and the General Welfare Act
            • Single mothers, single adults, the elderly, and those who are minimally disabled are eligible for welfare under this bill
            • Welfare is considered temporary financial assistance
            • All welfare is tied to employment and employment-related activity
            • The policing powers of welfare workers are dramatically increased

Notes

INTRODUCTION

1 My thanks to Carole Silliker, past president of Mothers and Others Making Change, Kitchener, Ontario, and long-time antipoverty activist for permitting me to reproduce her song.

2 Allan Moscovitch and Jim Albert, Preface in *The 'Benevolent' State: The Growth of Welfare in Canada* (Toronto: Garamond Press, 1987).

3 This has previously been argued by Gosta Esping-Andersen and characterizes many neo-Marxist studies, particularly those of Gough, O'Connor, and Offe. O'Connor and Offe argue that social welfare reforms emerge in response to the needs of capitalist reproduction. Gough asserts more working-class agency and claims that wages and government expenditures increased in postwar Britain because of the strength of the labour movement *vis-à-vis* the capitalist class. More recent Canadian work in the neo-Marxist tradition, such as *Family, Economy and State* and *Private Lives, Public Policy*, offer a gender analysis to the field, but tend to set up the welfare state as a case-study regarding the contradictions between capitalism and patriarchy. Canadian liberal scholars, such as Banting, Simeon, and Ismael, have assessed the welfare state in terms of institutional factors such as federalism. See Gosta Esping-Andersen, 'The Three Political Economies of the Welfare State', *Canadian Review of Sociology and Anthropology* 26, no 1 (February 1989):18; Ian Gough, *The Political Economy of the Welfare State* (London: Macmillan, 1979); James O'Connor, *The Fiscal Crisis of the State* (New York: St Martin's Press, 1973); Claus Offe, *Contradictions of the Welfare State*, edited by John Keane (Cambridge: MIT Press, 1984). For Canadian scholarship, see James Dickinson and Bob Russell, *Family, Economy and State: The Social Reproduction Process Under Capitalism* (Toronto: Garamond Press, 1986); Jane Ursel, *Private Lives, Public Policy: 100 Years of State Intervention in the Family* (Toronto: Women's Press, 1992); Keith Banting, *The Welfare State and Canadian Federalism* (Kingston: McGill-Queen's University Press, 1982); Richard Simeon, *Federal-Provincial Diplomacy: The Making of Recent Policy in Canada* (Toronto: University of Toronto Press, 1972); Richard Simeon, ed., *Division of Powers and Public Policy* (Toronto: University of Toronto Press, 1985); and J.S. Ismael, ed., *Canadian Social Welfare Policy: Federal and Provincial Dimension* (Kingston: McGill-Queen's University Press, 1985).

4 Canadian books on the welfare state that are exceptions to this general rule have tended to be written by historians, social work theorists, and sociologists rather than political scientists, for example, Allan Moscovitch and Glenn Drover, eds, *Inequality: Essays on the Political Economy of Social Welfare* (Toronto: University of Toronto Press, 1981); Moscovitch and Albert, eds, *The 'Benevolent' State*; Dennis Guest, *The Emergence of Social Security in Canada* (Vancouver: University of British Columbia Press, 1980); and Jim Struthers,

Through No Fault of Their Own: Unemployment and the Canadian Welfare State 1914–1941 (Toronto: University of Toronto Press, 1983).

5 From 1984 to 1986 I volunteered at Bridge House in Kingston, Ontario, which is a shelter for women and children who are visiting family or friends in prison.

6 During the last eight years I have facilitated a number of workshops in Kingston and Toronto for poor single mothers on issues relating to their lives. I jointly conducted an eight-month participatory research project regarding low-income teenage women's participation in recreational activities in inner-city Toronto. This report has been widely distributed and its findings presented at a number of public forums. I have also been an active member of Ontario Coalition Against Poverty, a board member of Low Income Families Together, and a participant in a number of Toronto-based coalitions, including Fight Back Metro Coalition and the Bread Not Circuses Coalition. See Margaret Little and Janet Borowy, '"A Time and Space Just For Us": The Young Women's Recreational Research Project', Central Neighbourhood House, Toronto Association of Neighbourhood Services, 21 June 1991; and Margaret Little, 'Evaluation of Fight Back Metro Coalition', Metro Social Planning Council, Fall 1992.

7 Linda Gordon, *Heroes of Their Own Lives: The Politics and History of Family Violence, Boston, 1880–1960* (New York: Penguin Books, 1989):113.

8 Through case-studies and comparative work these authors raise important questions about the circumstances that permitted the introduction of maternalist policies, about the class, race, and gendered nature of these initiatives, and about the lasting impact on the development of the welfare state. In their detailed case-studies of mothers' pensions in the US, Joanne Goodwin and Dawn Saunders investigate the relationship between this welfare policy and labour market needs. On another front there has been considerable debate about whether American maternalist reformers had a vision that crossed class and race divisions or not. (See Kathryn Kish Sklar, Sonya Michel and Seth Koven, Theda Skocpol, and Lori Ginzberg.) See Joanne Goodwin, *Gender and the Politics of Welfare Reform: Mothers' Pensions in Chicago, 1911–1929* (Chicago: University of Chicago Press, 1997); Joanne Goodwin, 'An American Experiment in Paid Motherhood: The Implementation of Mothers' Pensions in Early Twentieth-Century Chicago', *Gender and History* 4 (1992):323–42; Dawn Saunders, 'Class, Gender and Generation: Mothers' Aid in Massachusetts, 1913–1935', unpublished paper presented to Economic History and Development Workshop, Department of Economics, University of Massachusetts, 13 September 1989; Seth Koven and Sonya Michel, eds, *Mothers of a New World: Maternalist Politics and the Origins of Welfare States* (New York: Routledge, 1993):esp. Introduction by Sonya Michel and Seth Koven and articles by Kathryn Kish Sklar and Sonya Michel; Theda Skocpol, *Protecting Soldiers and Mothers: The Politics of Social Provision in the United States, 1870s–1920s* (Cambridge: Harvard University Press, 1992):esp. Introduction and Part III; Lori Ginzberg, *Women and the Work of Benevolence: Morality, Politics, and Class in the 19th Century United States* (New Haven: Yale University Press, 1990); Gisela Bock and Pat Thane, eds, *Maternity and Gender Policies: Women and the Rise of the European Welfare States, 1880s–1950s* (London: Routledge, 1991); Valerie Fildes, Lara Marks, and Hilary Marland, eds, *Women and Children First:*

International Maternal Infant Welfare, 1870–1945 (London: Routledge, 1992); and Carol Smart, ed., *Regulating Motherhood: Historical Essays on Marriage, Motherhood and Sexuality* (London: Routledge, 1992).

9 In 1979 historian Veronica Strong-Boag was the first to rectify this omission in her examination of the national campaign for the policy at the turn of the century and the early policy's characteristics. James Struthers provides a thoughtful and detailed account of the early years of the Ontario policy. Jane Ursel situates the introduction of mothers' allowance within the context of a number of Canadian social policies that reinforced women's domestic and reproductive roles. A number of sociologists have explored the contemporary issues of the policy. See, most notably, Veronica Strong-Boag, 'Wages for Housework: Mothers' Allowances and the Beginning of Social Security in Canada', *Journal of Canadian Studies* 4, no. 2 (Spring 1979):24–34; Veronica Strong Boag, 'Canada's Early Experience with Income Supplements: The Introduction of Mothers' Allowances', *Atlantis: A Women's Studies Journal* 4, no. 2 (Spring 1979):35–43; James Struthers, *The Limits of Affluence: Welfare in Ontario, 1920–1970* (Toronto: University of Toronto Press, 1994):esp. Ch. 1; Ursel, *Private Lives, Public Policy*, esp. 125–74; Patricia M. Evans and Eilene L. McIntyre, 'Welfare, Work Incentives and the Single Mother: An Interprovincial Comparison', in *The Canadian Welfare State: Evolution and Transition*, edited by Jacqueline S. Ismael (Edmonton: University of Alberta Press, 1987):101–25; Patricia M. Evans, 'Single Mothers and Ontario's Welfare Policy: Restructuring the Debate', in *Women and Canadian Public Policy*, edited by Janine Brodie (Toronto: Harcourt Brace, 1996):151–72; Barbara Blouin, 'Women and Children Last: Single Mothers on Welfare in Nova Scotia' (Halifax: Institute for the Study of Women, Mount Saint Vincent University, February 1989); Brenda Thompson, 'The Single Mother Movement', *Resources for Feminist Research*, Feminist Perspectives on the Canadian State, Special Issue (September 1988):124; and Jane Haddad, 'Sexism and Social Welfare Policy: The Case of Family Benefits in Ontario', Occasional Papers in Social Policy Analysis, no. 8, Department of Sociology in Education, Ontario Institute for Studies in Education, Toronto, February 1985.

10 Dennis Guest and James Struthers both make this argument with regard to the Canadian welfare state literature. See Guest, *The Emergence of Social Security*, x; and Struthers, *The Limits of Affluence*, 3–4.

11 Esping-Andersen is particularly noted for his attention to the interests, struggles, and alliances of social classes in the formation and preservation of particular welfare states. Esping-Andersen, 'The Three Political Economies of the Welfare State'.

12 There has been much debate about the extent to which the family wage model was realized or, rather, remained a bourgeois ideal. It is not necessary to enter this debate in order to understand the origins of OMA. Rather, it is important to understand that regardless of its realization, bourgeois and working-class families were heavily influenced by this ideology. I wish to thank Roberta Hamilton, Jane Jenson, and Pat Armstrong for their helpful comments regarding the application of family wage theory to OMA. See Jane Humphries, 'The Working Class Family, Women's Liberation, and Class Struggle: The Case of Nineteenth Century British History', *The Review of Radical Political*

Economics 9, no. 3 (Fall 1977):25–41; Michele Barrett and Mary McIntosh, 'The "Family Wage": Some Problems for Socialists and Feminists', *Capital and Class* 11 (1980):51–72; Patricia Connelly, 'Women Workers and the Family Wage in Canada', in *Women and the World of Work*, edited by Anne Hoeberg (New York: Plenum Press, 1982):223–37; Jenson, 'Gender and Reproduction: Or, Babies and the State', *Studies in Political Economy* 20 (Summer 1986):9–46; Dorothy Smith, 'Women's Inequality and the Family', in Moscovitch and Drover, eds, *Inequality*, 156–98.

13 In sociologist Pierre Bourdieu's terms, these women used their 'cultural/symbolic capital' to assert their authority as mothers. See Pierre Bourdieu, *Distinction: A Social Critique of the Judgement of Taste* (Cambridge: Routledge and Kegan Paul, 1984):esp. Ch. 1 and p. 483; and Pierre Bourdieu, *In Other Words: Essays Towards Reflexive Sociology* (Cambridge: Polity Press, 1990):111–12 regarding a clarification of the term.

14 Among the most notable contributions to this debate are: Skocpol, *Protecting Soldiers and Mothers*; Linda Gordon, *Pitied But Not Entitled: Single Mothers and the History of Welfare* (New York: The Free Press, 1994):esp. Ch. 3; Sonya Michel and Seth Koven, 'Womanly Duties', in *Maternity and Gender Politics: Women and the Rise of the European Welfare States, 1880s–1950s*, edited by Gisela Bock and Pat Thane (London: Routledge, 1991); and esp. Linda Gordon and Theda Skocpol, 'Gender, State and Society: A Debate', *Contention* 2, no. 3 (Spring 1993):139–89.

15 For further discussion of the relationship between public and private welfare activity with regard to OMA, see Margaret Little, 'The Blurring of Boundaries: Private and Public Welfare for Single Mothers in Ontario', *Studies in Political Economy* 47 (Summer 1995):89–110.

16 Frances Fox Piven and Richard A. Cloward, *Regulating the Poor: The Functions of Public Welfare* (New York: Pantheon Books, 1971):Ch. 1.

17 For example, see Mimi Abramovitz, *Regulating the Lives of Women: Social Welfare Policy from Colonial Times to the Present* (Boston: South End Press, 1988).

18 For a more detailed discussion of the impact of the Factories, Shops and Mines Acts upon women's paid work, see Ursel, *Private Lives*, 91–6.

19 Gordon, *Pitied But Not Entitled*, 7.

20 Questions of morality and welfare have not been adequately addressed in the Canadian welfare state literature. Liberal scholars such as Guest and Splane have argued that charity-style social programs involved in moral investigation were replaced by a rights-based welfare system. The majority of Canadian welfare state scholars have focused on questions of federalism (Banting), production (Finkle, Swartz), or the relationship between production and reproduction (Dickinson and Russell, Ursel) and virtually ignored moral concerns. While several articles in *The 'Benevolent' State* and the title itself speak to the punitive nature of public and private welfare programs, they do not directly address the question of morality (i.e., Struthers, Mitchinson, Schnell, and Taylor). Guest, *The Emergence of Social Security in Canada*, 45 and 203. See Richard Splane, *Social Welfare in Ontario* (Toronto: University of Toronto Press, 1965); Banting, *The Welfare State and Canadian Federalism*; Alvin Finkel, 'Origins of the Welfare State in Canada', in *The Canadian State*, edited by Leo Panitch (Toronto: University

of Toronto Press, 1977):344–72; Donald Swartz, 'The Politics of Reform: Conflict and Accommodation in Canadian Health Policy', in *The Canadian State*, edited by Leo Panitch (Toronto: University of Toronto Press, 1977):311–43; Dickinson and Russell, eds, *Family, Economy and State*; Ursel, *Private Lives, Public Policy*; Moscovitch and Albert, *The 'Benevolent' State*.

21 Bruce Curtis applies Corrigan and Sayer's approach to the introduction of public education in Canada. See Philip Corrigan and Derek Sayer, *The Great Arch: English State Formation as Cultural Revolution* (Oxford: Basil Blackwell, 1985) and Bruce Curtis, *Building the Educational State: Canada West, 1836–1871* (London, Ontario: Althouse Press, 1988).

22 Mariana Valverde and Lorna Weir, 'The Struggles of the Immoral: Preliminary Remarks on Moral Regulation', *Resources for Feminist Research* 17, no. 3 (September 1988):31–4; Mariana Valverde, *The Age of Light, Soap, and Water: Moral Reform in English Canada, 1885–1925* (Toronto: McClelland and Stewart, 1991):esp. Ch. 6; Lorna Weir, 'Sexual Rule, Sexual Politics: Studies in the Medicalization of Sexual Danger, 1820–1920', Ph.D. thesis, York University, 1986.

23 Valverde, *The Age of Light*, 39.

24 Although Althusserian philosophy is no longer in vogue and lacks an adequate appreciation of the possibilities of agency, it does attempt to explore the relationship between regulator and regulated. Through 'hailing' or 'interpellation', Althusser believes a person becomes defined by the regulations she or he applies or adheres to. See Louis Althusser, 'Ideology and Ideological State Apparatuses', in *Lenin and Philosophy and Other Essays* (London: New Left Books, 1971).

25 Caroline Andrew was one of the first to address this issue in Canada during her presidential address to the Canadian Political Science Association in 1984. During the last fifteen years scholars in the UK, Europe, Australia, and the United States have produced a number of books documenting a gender analysis of the welfare state. A similar book-length exploration of the Canadian welfare state has yet to be conducted. Those who have written a gendered analysis of the Canadian welfare state are Caroline Andrew, 'Women and the Welfare State', *Canadian Journal of Political Science* 17 (December 1984): 667–83; Janine Brodie, *Women and Canadian Public Policy* (Toronto: Harcourt Brace and Company, 1996); and Ursel, *Private Lives, Public Policy*. The most notable international literature on the subject includes Abramovitz, *Regulating the Lives of Women*; Cora V. Baldock and Bettina Cass, *Women, Social Welfare and the State in Australia* (Sydney: Allen and Unwin, 1983); Bock and Thane, eds, *Maternity and Gender Policies*; Jennifer Dale and Peggy Foster, *Feminists and State Welfare* (London: Routledge and Kegan Paul, 1986); Linda Gordon, ed., *Women, the State, and Welfare* (Madison: University of Wisconsin Press, 1990); Jane Lewis, ed., *Women's Welfare, Women's Rights* (London: Croom Helm, 1983); Susan Pedersen, *Family, Dependence, and the Origins of the Welfare State: Britain and France, 1914–1945* (Cambridge: Cambridge University Press, 1993); and Elizabeth Wilson, *Women and the Welfare State* (London: Tavistock, 1977).

26 This would include the works of Mary McIntosh, Jane Lewis, Eli Zaretsky, Mimi Abramovitz, Jennifer Dale, and Peggy Foster. See Abramovitz, *Regulating the Lives of Women*, Ch. 1; Mary McIntosh, 'The Welfare State and the Needs

of the Dependent Family', in *Fit Work for Women*, edited by Sandra Burman (New York: St Martin's Press, 1979):153–72; Jane Lewis, 'Dealing with Dependency: State Practices and Social Realities, 1870–1945', in Lewis, ed., *Women's Welfare, Women's Rights*, 17–37; Eli Zaretsky, 'Rethinking the Welfare State: Dependence, Economic Individualism and the Family'; Dickinson and Russell, eds, *Family, Economy and State*, 85–112; and Dale and Foster, *Feminists and State Welfare*, Ch. 6.

27 These theorists have disagreed about whether this transition from private to public patriarchy has been beneficial to women or not. See Zillah Eisenstein, *The Radical Future of Liberal Feminism* (New York: Longman, 1981); Ursel, *Private Lives, Public Policy*; and Wendy Brown, 'Finding the Man in the State', *Feminist Studies* 18, no. 1 (Spring 1992):7–33.

28 American political scientist Barbara Nelson introduced this two-tiered concept. See Barbara Nelson, 'The Origins of the Two-Channel Welfare State: Workmen's Compensation and Mothers' Aid', in Gordon, ed., *Women, the State, and Welfare*, 123–51.

29 Frances Fox Piven, in particular, is one of the strongest proponents of the view that the welfare state has provided women with more economic and political avenues for self-determination. Frances Fox Piven, 'Ideology and the State: Women, Power and the Welfare State', in Gordon, ed., *Women, the State, and Welfare*.

30 Andrew Armitage, *Social Welfare in Canada: Ideals and Realities* (Toronto: McClelland and Stewart, 1975):272.

31 While case files and interviews were of primary importance to this project, other archival sources were also examined. A number of federal, provincial, and municipal documents were explored. At the federal level personal manuscripts of welfare leaders, records of the ministries of health and labour, the prime minister's correspondence files, and those of the National Council of Women and the Canadian Council on Social Development were examined. Provincial records included those from the Ministry of Labour, the premier's office, and the department responsible for the administration of OMA. With regard to the latter, most of these records were destroyed in the 1950s, which restricted my ability to analyse the provincial welfare administration. Provincial commissions of inquiry, legislative debates, and OMA annual reports were also studied. Municipal records included an examination of the available local OMA board minutes. This latter source permitted a close study of those who were appointed to the boards, the types of discussions held when considering a particular applicant, and the relationship between these boards and the provincial government. Finally, journalist accounts from more than eighteen newspapers across the province documented the plight of the poor single mother, the inconsistencies of OMA administration, and the lobby efforts for welfare reform.

CHAPTER 1

1 This old rabbinical saying was invoked by the Ontario superintendent for trades and labour in 1917 during his report on mothers' allowance to emphasize the importance of motherhood. Archives of Ontario [AO], Department of Labour, RG 7–12–0–21, 'Memo on Mothers' Pensions Prepared by the Superintendent of Trades and Labour', Ontario government, 1917, 3.

2 In the US literature there is a tendency to focus on women's contributions to the mothers' pension campaign, often at the expense of other lobbyists, particularly in: Theda Skocpol, *Protecting Soldiers and Mothers: The Political Origins of Social Policy in the United States* (Cambridge: Harvard University Press, 1992). In contrast, the approach used here is informed by the work of Gosta Esping-Andersen and feminist applications such as that of Jane Jenson. Esping-Andersen addresses the different class forces whereas Jenson provides a gender dimension to this analysis. See Gosta Esping-Andersen, 'The Three Political Economies of the Welfare State', *Canadian Review of Sociology and Anthropology* 26, no. 1 (1989):11–31; and Jane Jenson, 'Making Claims: Social Policy and Gender Relations in Postwar Sweden and France', unpublished paper, Social Science History Association Conference, November 1991.

3 Lynne Marks argues that nineteenth-century welfare administration in Ontario had rural and urban distinctions. In rural communities the local government would often provide minimal publicly funded relief whereas in urban centres organized charitable associations were often responsible. Lynne Marks, 'Indigent Committees and Ladies Benevolent Societies: Intersections of Public and Private Poor Relief in Late Nineteenth Century Small Town Ontario', *Studies in Political Economy* 47 (Summer 1995):61–88.

4 For further discussion regarding the rise of poverty and welfare during the nineteenth century, see Karl Polanyi's epic treatise and Richard Splane for an Ontario perspective. Karl Polanyi, *The Great Transformation: The Political and Economic Origins of Our Time* (New York: Rinehart and Company, 1957):esp. Chs 9 and 10; and Richard B. Splane, *Social Welfare in Ontario, 1791–1893* (Toronto: University of Toronto Press, 1965).

5 From 1881 to 1911 Ontario had the lowest fertility rate in Canada. Angus McLaren and Arlene Tigar McLaren, *The Bedroom and the State* (Toronto: University of Toronto, 1986):17. For further discussion of infant concerns during this period, see Cynthia R. Comacchio, *'Nations Are Built of Babies': Saving Ontario's Mothers and Children, 1900–1940* (Montreal: McGill-Queen's University Press, 1993).

6 Tuberculosis, the disease most feared by the working man, was the foremost killer of Canadians between the ages of fifteen and fifty during the first forty years of the nineteenth century. TB claimed at least one in ten children under ten during the early nineteenth century. According to an Ontario study in 1909, 6,932 of 52,629 children died before their first birthday. In Toronto alone, the rate was 230 deaths per 1,000 live births. Comacchio, *'Nations Are Built of Babies'*, 30–1; Dr Helen MacMurchy, 'Infant Mortality: First Special Report', Toronto, 1910, cited in Comacchio, *'Nations Are Built of Babies'*, footnote #105, 36.

7 H.E. Spencer, 'For a Healthy Canada', *Chatelaine*, August 1930, cited in Comacchio, *'Nations Are Built of Babies'*, footnote #63, 56.

8 Historian Don Avery claims that there was 'Canadian consensus . . . that Orientals and Blacks were unassimilable', and that their immigration should be restricted. Eastern and southern European immigrants, on the other hand, 'were allowed into the country because of their brawn and industry'. Don Avery, *'Dangerous Foreigners': European Immigrant Workers and Labour Radicalism in Canada, 1896–1932* (Toronto: McClelland and Stewart, 1979):7–8; and McLaren and McLaren, *The Bedroom and the State*, 17.

9 Mariana Valverde, *The Age of Light, Soap, and Water: Moral Reform in English Canada, 1885–1925* (Toronto: McClelland and Stewart, 1991):19.

10 This movement has yet to be carefully examined and theorized. For further discussion, see Carol Bacchi, *Liberation Deferred: The Ideas of the English Canadian Suffragists, 1877–1918* (Toronto: University of Toronto Press, 1983); Linda Kealey, ed., *A Not Unreasonable Claim: Women and Reform in Canada, 1880s–1920s* (Toronto: The Women's Press, 1979); Jim Naylor, *The New Democracy: Challenging the Social Order in Industrial Ontario, 1914–25* (Toronto: University of Toronto Press, 1991); Linda Kealey and Joan Sangster, *Beyond the Vote: Canadian Women and Politics* (Toronto: University of Toronto Press, 1989); Richard Allen, *The Social Passion: Religion and Social Reform in Canada, 1914–28* (Toronto: University of Toronto Press, 1973); Ramsay Cook, *The Regenerators: Social Criticism in Late Victorian English Canada* (Toronto: University of Toronto Press, 1985); and, most recently, Nancy Christie and Michael Gauvreau, *A Full-Orbed Christianity: The Protestant Churches and Social Welfare in Canada, 1900–1940* (Kingston: McGill-Queen's University Press, 1996).

11 Valverde, *The Age of Light*, 21.

12 Ibid., 29.

13 AO, 'Mothers' Allowances Investigation, 1920', 26–7, as cited in James Struthers, *The Limits of Affluence: Welfare in Ontario, 1920–1970* (Toronto: University of Toronto Press, 1994):footnote #17, 24; AO, Mothers' Allowance Investigation, Ontario, 1920, 16, cited in Struthers, *The Limits of Affluence*, footnote #31, 29; and AO, RG 7, 'Memo on Mothers' Pensions, 1917', report by Dr Bruce Smith, April 1913, cited in Struthers, *The Limits of Affluence*, footnote #17, 24.

14 AO, Commissions and Inquiries, RG 18, B-10, 'Commission Regarding Prison and Reformatory System of Ontario, 1891', 40, 45–6; and AO, RG 18, D-I-20, 'Select Committee on Child Labour, March 25, 1907', 4–12.

15 Reverend Bryce wrote a letter of support for mothers' pensions and the Trades and Labour Congress of Canada sent a resolution adopted at their convention in 1915. AO, RG 18, B-40, 'Ontario Commission on Unemployment, 1916', 64–5.

16 Ibid., 63–4.

17 AO, RG 18, B-49, 'Royal Commission: Care of the Feeble-minded and Mentally Defective and the Prevalence of Venereal Disease, October 18, 1919', 6. Helen MacMurchy, a medical doctor who was the inspector of the feeble-minded in Ontario between 1906 and 1916, was a leading proponent of this eugenics position. Other social reformers, including the National Council of Women, also adopted this view. See Lykke de la Cour, 'Dr Helen MacMurchy on "Feeble-Minded" Women and Children: Examples of an Unconstrained Campaign', unpublished paper, Department of History, University of Toronto, December 1986; and Kathleen McConnachie, 'Methodology in the Study of Women in History: A Case Study of Helen MacMurchy, MD', *Ontario History* LXXV, no. 1 (March 1983):esp. 67–9.

18 While this legislation was commonly referred to as the Children's Act, its formal title was An Act for the Prevention of Cruelty to, and Better Protection of Children. For a more detailed discussion of the importance of this legislation, see John Bullen, 'J.J. Kelso and the "New" Child-Savers: The Genesis of

the Children's Aid Movement in Ontario', *Ontario History* LXXXII, no. 2 (June 1990):107–28.

19 For a more detailed discussion of developments leading up to its enactment, see Eric Tucker, *Administering Danger in the Workplace: The Law and Politics of Occupational Health and Safety Regulation in Ontario, 1850–1914* (Toronto: University of Toronto Press, 1990):esp. Ch. 7; and Michael Piva, 'The Workmen's Compensation Movement in Ontario', *Ontario History* LXVII, no. 1 (March 1975):39–56.

20 For a detailed discussion of veterans' allowance, see Margaret McCallum, 'Assistance to Veterans and Their Dependants: Steps on the Way to the Administrative State, 1914–1929', in *Canadian Perspectives on Law and Society: Issues in Legal History*, edited by W. Wesley Pue and Barry Wright (Ottawa: Carleton University Press, 1988):157–77. Quotation cited on p. 160.

21 Valverde, *The Age of Light*, 29.

22 Bullen, 'J.J. Kelso', 117.

23 National Archives [NA], J.J. Kelso Papers, MG 30, G97, vol. 5, file: Mothers' Allowances, 1.

24 NA, Kelso Papers, file: Mothers' Allowances, 'Report of Ontario Superintendent of Neglected and Dependent Children, 1896', 1.

25 Ibid.

26 Kelso's involvement with American social reformers began as early as 1888 when he brought the American Humane Convention to Toronto. Subsequent to that, he was a guest speaker at the International Conference at Chicago's World Fair in 1893, brought the American Social Welfare Convention to Toronto in the mid-1890s, and generally played a very active role in the North American child welfare movement. Nationally, he was very involved in promoting the establishment of Children's Aid Societies across the country, lecturing to provincial legislatures and social workers in Manitoba, British Columbia, Nova Scotia, and Saskatchewan. NA, Kelso Papers, vol. 24, file: Outstanding Events in Mr Kelso's Life, 'Circulars 1888–89', 5.

27 NA, Kelso Papers, file: Mothers' Allowances.

28 This position was also advocated by Mr Axford during the provincial inquiry into mothers' allowance. NA, Kelso Papers, file: Mothers' Allowances. See also 'Reforming Delinquent Children', an address given by J.J. Kelso to the Thirtieth National Conference of Charities and Correction, Atlanta, 8 May 1903, reproduced in *Family, School & Society in Nineteenth-Century Canada*, edited by Alison Prentice and Susan Houston (Toronto: Oxford University Press, 1975):286–90. AO, RG 7–12–0–21, 'Hamilton Enquiry into Mothers' Allowance, February 29, 1919', Axford, Children's Aid Society, Brantford, 51.

29 NA, Kelso Papers, file: Mothers' Allowance, 'The Creche a Compromise'.

30 NA, Kelso Papers, vol. 5, file: Reform—Women—1921, 'No Family Ties'.

31 AO, RG 7, 'Memo on Mothers' Pensions, 1917', 3.

32 Andrew Jones and Leonard Rutman, *In the Children's Aid: J.J. Kelso and Child Welfare in Ontario* (Toronto: University of Toronto Press, 1981):157; and AO, RG 7, 'Mothers' Pension Allowance, Hamilton Enquiry, Thursday, February 20, 1919', Mr Axford, Children's Aid Society, Hamilton, 56–7.

33 Leonard Rutman, 'J.J. Kelso and the Development of Child Welfare', in *The 'Benevolent' State: The Growth of Welfare in Canada*, edited by Allan Moscovitch and Jim Albert (Toronto: Garamond Press, 1987):76; and NA, Kelso Papers, file: Mothers' Allowances, 'National Council on Children's Work: Interesting Public Meeting Held in Centenary Church Lecture Room Last Evening', *Times*, 12 October 1906.

34 Kelso prepared a book entitled *Laws Affecting Children*, which was sent to the presidents of local councils in 1904. Cited in 'The Messenger', the National Council of Women newsletter, November 1904, 57. Kelso was a guest speaker at the annual convention of the National Council of Women in Hamilton, October 1906. The content of Kelso's proposal for mothers' allowance was detailed in a newspaper article: NA, Kelso Papers, file: Mothers' Allowance, 'National Council on Children's Work: Interesting Public Meeting Held in Centenary Church Lecture Room Last Evening', *Times*, 12 October 1906.

35 Very little is known about this committee or its subsequent recommendations. National Council of Women Collection, vol. 67, file 1, 'Letter from the Corresponding Secretary, National Council of Women to Dr Elizabeth Sloan Chesser, Toronto, March 21, 1913', and Veronica Strong-Boag, 'The Parliament of Women: The National Council of Women of Canada, 1893–1929', History Division Paper no. 18 (Ottawa: National Museum of Canada, 1976):252.

36 Historian Veronica Strong-Boag documents one other initiative of this kind in Canada. In 1910 the Mother's Association of Winnipeg paid *one* woman using their day nursery to stay at home and look after her children. This subsidy ceased after one year when the woman remarried, but the Associated Charities of Manitoba joined the association in this experiment and supplemented the income of needy mothers until 1915. The closest American approximation to these Canadian experiments is the 'widows' scholarships'. American sociologist Theda Skocpol states that certain American women's groups and local charities sometimes offered financial recompense to widows to encourage their children to attend school. This money was to replace the children's factory wages. Neither Strong-Boag nor Skocpol gives an indication of the scope of these initiatives. See Veronica Strong-Boag, ' "Wages for Housework": Mothers' Allowances and the Beginnings of Social Security in Canada', *Journal of Canadian Studies* 14, no. 1 (Spring 1979):25; Strong-Boag, 'The Parliament of Women', 298; and Theda Skocpol, *Protecting Soldiers and Mothers* (Cambridge: Harvard University Press, 1992):443–4.

37 'Conditions During April Affecting Women Workers in Leading Industrial Centres—Reports of Women Correspondents to the Labour Gazette', *The Labour Gazette*, May 1914, 1286.

38 AO, RG 7, 'Memo on Mothers' Pensions, 1917', 24.

39 AO, Toronto Local Council of Women Collection, Minutes F805–1–0–1, 'Women's Council Reports Progress', *Mail and Empire*, Toronto, 22 January 1914.

40 The TLCW proposal to the Toronto Social Service Commission stated: 'Many children are constantly being taken from school before the age of 15 years to become wage earners. We feel that something should be done to prevent the handicap with which these children are starting life. We would like to have permission to create a fund which would be carefully dispensed to the mothers

of such children which would enable each child to remain in school the minimum time required by law. It is hoped that in one year we may prove to the Government the necessity of making this a law, so that these children may obtain their rightful claims to future good citizenship.' Metropolitan Toronto Records and Archives [MTRA], Policy and Planning Division of Community Services Department Records, RG 5.6, Toronto Social Service Commission, 'Annual Report, 1914'.

41 'Conditions During April Affecting Women Workers in Leading Industrial Centres—Reports of Women Correspondents to the Labour Gazette', 1286.

42 AO, RG 7, 'Memo on Mothers' Pensions', 24.

43 Ibid., 24–5.

44 Toronto Local Council of Women Collection, 'Minutes of the December 16, 1914 meeting'.

45 The Leek Players donated the benefits of their play in February 1915, and the Technical School donated a total sum of $551.63 from a concert given 'under the distinguished patronage of the Lieutenant Governor and Lady Hendrie' in December 1915. The 15 May 1917 minutes read: 'The Mothers Pensions is now closed and the Committee owe the Council $55.86'. Toronto Local Council of Women Collection, 'Minutes of the December 1915 Meeting'.

46 A resolution from Victoria Local Council of Women to be approved by the National Council of Women, vol. 68, file 3 Resolutions 1914–1915, National Council of Women. The BC local councils of women's position may help to explain why the British Columbia Mothers' Allowance, enacted the same year as the Ontario policy, was more flexible in eligibility than any other provincial allowance in Canada. For a detailed account, see Megan Davies, 'Services Rendered, Rearing Children for the State: Mothers' Pensions in British Columbia, 1919–1931', in *Not Just Pin Money: Selected Essays on the History of Women's Work in British Columbia*, edited by Barbara Latham and Roberta Pazdro (Victoria: Camosun College, 1984):249–64; Margaret Little, 'Claiming a Unique Place: The Introduction of Mothers' Pensions in B.C.', *B.C. Studies*, Special Issue entitled Women's History and Gender Studies, edited by Annalee Golz and Lynne Marks, no. 105 (Spring 1995); and National Council of Women Collection, vol. 68, file 4, 'Resolution Passed at the Annual Meeting of the National Council of Women, 1916'.

47 National Council of Women Collection, vol. 68, file 3, 'Letter from Vancouver Local Council to Mrs. Cummings, National Council of Women, Explaining the Vancouver Position, November 5, 1914'. Some local councils of women dealt directly with desertion cases. One example is the Lindsay Local Council of Women, which placed a deserted mother and children in an institution and charged the man for non-support. National Council of Women Collection, vol. 67, file 10, *The Messenger*, November 1904, 62.

48 Veronica Strong-Boag, *The New Day Recalled: Lives of Girls and Women in English Canada, 1919–1939* (Markham: Penguin Books, 1988):191–2; Bacchi, *Liberation Deferred*, 17; and National Council of Women, *Women's Century*, March 1915, 9, cited in Carol Cole, 'An Examination of the Mothers' Allowance System in Ontario, 1914–1940', MA thesis, Department of History, University of Waterloo, 1989, footnote #24, 11.

49 For further details, see Alice Klein and Wayne Roberts, 'Besieged Innocence: The "Problem" and Problems of Working Women—Toronto, 1896–1914', in *Women at Work, Ontario, 1850–1930*, edited by Janice Acton and Bonnie Shepard (Toronto: Canadian Women's Educational Press, 1974):214–16; and Strong-Boag, 'The Parliament of Women', 250–2.

50 The 1914 Social Service Council membership was composed of the Church of England in Canada, the Methodist Church in Canada, the Presbyterian Church in Canada, the Baptist Church in Canada, the Congregational Church in Canada, the Salvation Army, the Canadian Purity Education Association, the Evangelical Association of North America, the Dominion Woman's Christian Temperance Union, as well as the Trades and Labour Congress of Canada and the Dominion Grange and Farmers Association. *Social Service Congress, Ottawa, 1914: Report of Addresses and Proceedings*, iii, and National Council of Women Collection, vol. 28, 'Letter from the Social Service Council of Canada to the National Council of Canada, October 8, 1915'. Although Christie and Gauvreau overstate the case, their study provides ample evidence of the leadership role Protestant churches played in the Canadian social reform movement. Christie and Gauvreau, *A Full-Orbed Christianity*.

51 Reverend W.B. Tighe, Hamilton Ministerial Association, 'Hamilton Enquiry, 1919', 21–2.

52 Mr Dickie, minister, 'Hamilton Enquiry, 1919', 32 and 34.

53 Ibid., 33; and Tighe, 'Hamilton Enquiry, 1919', 22.

54 As well as setting the guidelines for the TLCW project, the Toronto Social Service Commission helped Mrs Struthers conduct the initial investigations that helped to select the appropriate six families to be financially and morally supported. Also, there is evidence to suggest that the TLCW consulted the commission from time to time regarding the project.

55 Spokesperson for The Girls' Home, Toronto, 'Memo on Mothers' Pensions', 12.

56 During the Hamilton inquiry, one representative of an infants' home said that they were 40 per cent beyond capacity and hoped that mothers' allowance would relieve this overflow problem. 'Hamilton Enquiry, Thursday, February 20, 1919', Mrs Evans, Infants' Home, 26.

57 AO, RG 7, 'Memo on Mothers' Pensions', 8.

58 Mrs J.H. Herring, one of the oldest visitors of the poor in Hamilton. 'Hamilton Enquiry, 1919', 62.

59 During the Hamilton inquiry the only charity that endorsed deserted women was the Canadian Patriotic Fund. Representatives of two infants' homes spoke resolutely against unwed mothers. 'Hamilton Enquiry, 1919', Mr Lovering, 5; Mrs Evans, Infants' Home, 26; Mrs Hawkins, representative of the Local Council of Women and on the board of Infants' Home, 29.

60 'Hamilton Enquiry', Mrs Hawkins, 30.

61 Guest suggests that the ambivalence of charities in Ontario had a significant impact on the timing of the OMA Act. While this may be true, Guest grants the Social Service Council of Toronto more influence than historical record would suggest it deserves. Guest believes that the Social Service Council of Toronto caused the TLCW pilot project to be dropped within a few months

of its operation. According to TLCW minutes and newspaper accounts, however, the TLCW project continued for three years until it eventually ran out of funds. Guest, *The Emergence*, 51–3.

62 AO, pamphlet, 1920, no. 85, 'The Annual Meeting of the Canadian Conference of Public Welfare', cited in Cole, 'An Examination of the Mothers' Allowance System', footnote #34, 15.

63 Although Charlotte Whitton was not a professional social worker herself, she did promote the professionalization of the field of welfare. For further discussion of the emergence of social work and Charlotte Whitton's particular role, see Struthers, ' "Lord Give Us Men": Women and Social Work in English Canada, 1918–1953', in Moscovitch and Albert, eds, *The 'Benevolent' State*, 126–43.

64 Judge Boyd, 'Memo on Mothers' Pensions, 1917', 7; Henderson, *Social Service Congress, 1914*, 113; and 'Memo on Mothers' Pensions, 1917', 7.

65 For the role of medical experts in the social reform movement, see Cynthia Comacchio Abeele, ' "The Infant Soldier": The Great War and the Medical Campaign for Child Welfare', *Canadian Bulletin of Medical History* 5, no. 2 (Winter 1988):99–119. For details of the workplace child-care arrangements in France, see Susan Pedersen, *Family, Dependence, and the Origins of the Welfare State: Britain and France, 1914–1945* (Cambridge: Cambridge University Press, 1993):Chs 2 and 3; and Jane Jenson, 'Gender and Reproduction: Or, Babies and the State', *Studies in Political Economy* 20 (Summer 1986):9–46. For medical testimony, see AO, RG 7, Department of Labour, 'Mothers' Allowances: An Investigation, Toronto, 1920', 24–6, 28–9; and Dr Mullin, 'Hamilton Enquiry, February 1919', 38.

66 Stephen Leacock, *The Social Criticism of Stephen Leacock*, edited and introduced by A. Bowker (Toronto: University of Toronto Press, 1973):60, as cited in Strong-Boag, 'Wages for Housework', footnote #3, 24.

67 Ceta Ramkhalawansingh, 'Women During the Great War', in Acton and Shepard, eds, *Women at Work, Ontario, 1850–1930*, 262–4.

68 Naylor, *The New Democracy*, 131.

69 For further discussion, see Klein and Roberts, 'Besieged Innocence: The "Problem" and the Problems of Working Women—Toronto, 1896–1914', 211–60; and Ruth Frager, 'No Proper Deal: Women Workers and the Canadian Labour Movement, 1870–1940', in *Union Sisters: Women in the Labour Movement*, edited by Linda Briskin and Lynda Yanz (Toronto: Women's Press, 1983):44–66.

70 H.A. Logan, *Trade Unions in Canada* (Toronto: Macmillan, 1948):399, cited in Frager, 'No Proper Deal', footnote #27, 51.

71 Frager, 'No Proper Deal', 51.

72 Margaret McCallum, 'Keeping Women in Their Place: The Minimum Wage in Canada, 1910–25', *Labour/Le Travail* 17 (Spring 1987):37.

73 Naylor, *The New Democracy*, 135.

74 There are numerous information sheets created by the provincial department of labour addressed to working women. AO, RG 7–12–0–11, file: Employment, General, 1918–1919, 'To Women Workers'.

75 Despite the important role Henderson played in social reform issues and the mothers' allowance debate, historians know very little about her. See Kealey and Sangster, *Beyond the Vote*, 121–2; Joan Sangster, *Dreams of Equality: Women on the Canadian Left, 1920–1950* (Toronto: McClelland and Stewart, 1989):111. Informal discussion with Linda Kealey, St John's, Newfoundland, 7 July 1993. For resolution, see Trades and Labour Congress of Canada, 'Report of the Proceedings of the Annual Convention, 1912', 102.

76 One newspaper dated 8 January 1915 stated: 'An amendment to the Industrial Disputes Act, Old Age Pensions, pensions for mothers, greater safeguards for men employed in transport work and other important concessions will be among the reforms demanded by the Trades and Labour Congress of Canada, which will wait upon Sir Robert Borden on January 15. The unemployed problem will also be dealt with and a scheme projected for its solution.' The Trades and Labour Congress of Canada passed the following resolution, September 1915: 'That the Executive of the Congress press the question of Mothers' Pensions upon the members of the Dominion Parliament, asking that a pension system be inaugurated as soon as possible.' AO, RG 18, B-40, 'Ontario Commission on Unemployment, 1916, Report', 64–5.

77 For a more detailed discussion of the religious-labour alliance known as the 'social gospel movement', see Craig Heron, 'Labourism and the Canadian Working Class', *Labour/Le Travailleur* 13 (Spring 1984):esp. 63–4; and Allen, *The Social Passion*.

78 Letter from Jessie MacIver, editor, *Woman's Century*, official organ of the Toronto Council of Women to Mrs Willoughly Cummings, corresponding secretary, NCW, 9 January 1915.

79 Naylor, *The New Democracy*, 140.

80 TLC, 'Report of the Proceedings of the Annual Convention, 1912', 44, cited in Cole, 'An Examination of the Mothers' Allowance System', footnote #42, 18.

81 Tom Moore, TLC president, 'Preface', J.L. Cohen, *Mothers' Allowance Legislation in Canada: A Legislative Review and Analysis with a Proposed 'Standard' Act* (Toronto: Macmillan, 1927):7.

82 My thanks to Jim Naylor for this evidence. *Industrial Banner*, 29 July and 7 October 1921 and 21 April 1922, cited in Naylor, *The New Democracy*, footnote #39, 228.

83 Rose Henderson, 'Pensions for Mothers', *Social Service Congress, Ottawa, 1914*, 112.

84 It was Helena Gutteridge of the Vancouver TLC who proposed a separation of mothers' allowance and Old Age Pensions in 1915. TLC Report, 1915, 65, cited in Cole, 'An Examination of the Mothers' Allowance System', footnote #54, 22.

85 Moore, 'Preface', in Cohen, *Mothers' Allowance Legislation*, 7.

86 AO, RG 7–12–0–31, Trades and Labour Congress of Canada, 1918, 'Resolution 6', [from the Street Railway Men, Toronto, Division No. 113]. Tom Moore quotation cited in Struthers, *The Limits of Affluence*, Ch. 1, footnote #31, 20; 'Hamilton Enquiry', Mr Rollo, TLC, 16–17. District 18 United Mine Workers of America proposed the following resolution at their 1919 annual convention:

... that all married women and children should be paid a monthly salary by the Dominion of Canada; . . . and that all children should have a monthly allowance paid to the mother for the keep of the child until said child is 16 years of age if a boy, and 17 years of age if a girl; . . . that the amount to be paid should be $50 for a woman, $10 for a child up to 10 years, and $12.50 per month up to 16 or 17 years (*Labour Gazette*, March 1919, 321–2).

87 'Hamilton Enquiry, 1919', Rollo, TLC, 19–20, and Griffiths, ILP, 73.

88 Ibid., Rollo, 15.

89 Ibid., Griffiths, 68–9.

90 Ibid., Rollo, 18–19.

91 Moore, 'Preface', in Cohen, *Mothers' Allowance Legislation*, 5.

92 Henderson, *Social Service Congress, Ottawa, 1914*, 112, 115.

93 Joanne Goodwin's study of the introduction of mothers' pensions in Chicago suggests that labour advocates used a maternalist rhetoric but rejected the maternalist values for a class-based analysis. This is less clear in the Ontario case. Labour lobbyists had strong alliances with the Social Service Council and other social reformers. According to the speeches of Henderson, Moore, and other ILP and TLC representatives, it appears that labour advocates did adhere to these maternalist values. Joanne Goodwin, 'An American Experiment in Paid Motherhood: The Implementation of Mothers' Pensions in Early Twentieth-Century Chicago', *Gender and History* 4, no. 3 (Autumn 1992):323–42, esp. 327.

94 AO, RG 7–12–0–21, 'Report on Mothers' Allowances, Prepared by W.A. Riddell, Superintendent Trades and Labour, 1919', 4.

95 Kelso was predominantly the author of these articles. Initially he chaired the committee, but Premier Sir William Hearst was annoyed by these outbursts from one of his civil servants and refused to allow Kelso to continue as chair while maintaining his position as superintendent of neglected and dependent children. As a result, Kelso reluctantly resigned as chair and withdrew from active participation in the mothers' allowance lobby. Jones and Rutman, *In the Children's Aid*, 152–4.

96 Linda Gordon, *Pitied But Not Entitled: Single Mothers and the History of Welfare* (New York: The Free Press, 1994):27.

97 This was not atypical of social reform lobbies. During the debate for protective legislation, working women 'were not consulted in any meaningful way as to whether the protections they were being given were the protections they wanted'. Tucker, *Administering Danger*, 215.

98 AO, RG 7–12–0–21, 'Letter from Premier W.H. Hearst to Dr Riddell, January 16, 1919, re: Inquiry Leading to Ontario Mothers' Allowance'.

99 These public hearings were held in Ottawa, Toronto, Hamilton, and London. Only the transcripts of the Hamilton inquiry have survived. Fortunately, Riddell quoted extensively from all four public hearings in his final report.

100 These investigators wanted to know the number and ages of the children; their nationality; the number of children at home, at school, and at work; whether the

family occupied the whole house or part of it; whether they kept lodgers or boarders; whether the mother worked or stayed at home with the children, and if she worked, for whom and at what wage; what other income the family received, whether from children or otherwise; what other assets were available, whether in property or insurance; how long the family had lived in Canada and in Ontario; and some estimate of the general circumstances of the home and of the mother's ability as a home maker. 'Report on Mothers' Allowance, 1919', 11.

101 Ibid., 4.

102 Ibid., 2.

103 Ibid., 25.

104 Ibid., 24–5.

105 Ibid., 32–4.

106 Cited in Struthers, *The Welfare State in Ontario*, footnote #32, 21–2.

107 'Hamilton Enquiry, 1919', 17.

108 During the Hamilton inquiry representatives of the Local Council of Women and a local infants' home strongly opposed including deserted women in the act. Mr Lovering of the Canadian Patriotic Fund gave limited acceptance, provided it could be ascertained that these women were deserted through no fault of their own. 'Hamilton Enquiry, 1919', 5, 16, and 31.

109 Those who advocated this position included representatives of women's, church, and charity organizations. 'Report on Mothers' Allowance, 1919', 16–17.

110 TLC, 'Report of the Proceedings of the Annual Convention, 1912', cited in Cole, 'An Examination of the Mothers' Allowance System', 24–5 and 35.

111 'Report on Mothers' Allowance, 1919', 27–30.

112 'Hamilton Enquiry, 1919', 24.

113 'Report on Mothers' Allowance, 1919', 23.

CHAPTER 2

1 Theda Skocpol, *Protecting Soldiers and Mothers: The Political Origins of Social Policy in the United States* (Cambridge: Harvard University Press, 1992):457.

2 The 1919 election results were as follows: UFO (forty-five seats), Liberals (twenty-nine seats), Conservatives (twenty-five seats), ILP (eleven seats), Independent (one seat). Brian D. Tennyson, 'The Political Career of Sir William Hearst', MA thesis, Department of History, University of Toronto, 1963, 247.

3 For further discussion of Drury's social welfare legislation, see Charles M. Johnston, *E.C. Drury: Agrarian Idealist* (Toronto: University of Toronto Press, 1986):150–4.

4 For a detailed discussion of how the state centralizes and legitimizes certain types of knowledge, see Phillip Corrigan and Derek Sayer, *The Great Arch: English State Formation as Cultural Revolution* (Oxford: Basil Blackwell, 1985):esp. 2–4, 103, 123–4, 141–2, 163, and 180.

5 For a discussion of the Canadian state's role in shaping child care during the early 1900s, see Katherine Arnup, *Education for Motherhood: Advice for Mothers in*

Twentieth Century Canada (Toronto: University of Toronto Press, 1994); K. Arnup, Andrée Lévesque, Ruth Roach Pierson, eds, *Delivering Motherhood: Maternal Ideologies and Practices in the 19th and 20th Centuries* (New York: Routledge, 1990); Cynthia R. Comacchio, *'Nations Are Built of Babies': Saving Ontario's Mothers and Children, 1900–1940* (Montreal: McGill-Queen's University Press, 1993); and Veronica Strong-Boag, 'Intruders in the Nursery: Childcare Professionals Reshape the Years One to Five, 1920–1940', in *Childhood and Family in Canadian History*, edited by Joy Parr (Toronto: McClelland and Stewart, 1982):160–78.

6 For further discussion of the role of public health nurses in private homes, see Comacchio, *'Nations Are Built of Babies'*, esp. Ch. 7.

7 Mariana Valverde, *The Age of Light, Soap, and Water: Moral Reform in English Canada, 1885–1925* (Toronto: McClelland and Stewart, 1991):22.

8 'First Annual Report of the OMA Commission, 1920–21', *Ontario Sessional Papers* LIII, 10.

9 'Extension of Mothers' Pensions in Canada', *Labour Gazette* (January 1920):2.

10 Margaret Little, 'Claiming a Unique Place: The Introduction of Mothers' Pensions in B.C.', *B.C. Studies*, Special Issue entitled Women's History and Gender Studies, edited by Annalee Golz and Lynne Marks, no. 105 (Spring 1995).

11 National Archives [NA], Canadian Council on Social Development, MG 28, I–10, 'Child Welfare Council Inquiry into Mothers' Allowance Acts', 1927.

12 'First Annual Report of the OMA Commission, 1920–1921', 9.

13 *Toronto Star*, 26 March 1930, cited in Peter Oliver, *G. Howard Ferguson: Ontario Tory* (Toronto: University of Toronto Press, 1977):footnote #120, 368.

14 'First Annual Report of the OMA Commission, 1920–21', 10.

15 According to the policy, children were considered those under sixteen years of age. For the initial flat rate, see 'First Annual Report of the OMA Commission, 1920–21', 10, and 'Second Annual Report of the OMA Commission, 1921–22', *Ontario Sessional Papers* LV, Part VIII (1923):9–10.

16 Archives of Ontario [AO], Department of Labour, RG 7 12–0–21, 'Report on Mothers' Allowance, Prepared by W.A. Riddell, Superintendent Trades and Labour, 1919', 23.

17 AO, Lanark County Mothers' Allowance Board Minutes, 1920–38, F 1734–23, 'Meeting January 8, 1921', as cited in James Struthers, *The Limits of Affluence: Welfare in Ontario, 1920–1970* (Toronto: University of Toronto Press, 1994):Ch. 1, footnote #51, 38.

18 This provincial minimum wage was established for women eighteen years or over with at least one year's experience who worked in drug, confectionery, paper, box, textile, and needles trades or retail stores. AO, RG 7, series VII-1, vol. 5, file: Miscellaneous, 1921–25, 'Information Requested by the Canadian Government Trade Commissioner, February 1923', 4.

19 Michael Piva, *Condition of the Working Class in Toronto, 1900–1921* (Ottawa: University of Ottawa Press, 1979):31.

20 For a more detailed discussion of the Canadian Patriotic Fund, see Margaret McCallum, 'Assistance to Veterans and Their Dependants: Steps on the Way to

the Administrative State, 1914–1929', in *Canadian Perspectives on Law and Society: Issues in Legal History*, edited by W. Wesley Pue and Barry Wright (Ottawa: Carleton University Press, 1988):157–77.

21 AO, Legislative Office, RG 49, reel #588, press clippings, 1902–1934, 'Mothers' Allowances', Editorial, *Albertan*, 1 September 1923.

22 'First Annual Report of the OMA Commission, 1920–21', 22–3.

23 'Second Annual Report of the OMA Commission, 1921–22', 56.

24 'First Annual Report of the OMA Commission, 1920–21', 23.

25 'Second Annual Report of the OMA Commission, 1921–22', 61.

26 The number of beneficiaries is calculated at the end of each fiscal year. This is a portion of a chart provided by 'Minister of Public Welfare, 1946', *Ontario Sessional Papers* LXXVII, Part III, 17. Please note that the provincial population in 1930 is not known and is substituted with the 1931 census figure. Given that Ontario had entered a recession, it is presumed that the population did not change substantially between 1930 and 1931. *Sixth Census of Canada, 1921*, vol. 2 (Ottawa: King's Printer, 1925):241, and *Seventh Census of Canada, 1931*, vol. 2 (Ottawa: King's Printer, 1933):295.

27 'Seventh Annual Report of the OMA Commission, 1928', *Ontario Sessional Papers* LX, Part V (1928):16.

28 The Drury UFO electoral campaign platform had promised to 'stamp-out' favouritism and patronage and the administrative structure of OMA attempted to reflect this. Johnston, *E.C. Drury*, 151.

29 The year 1922–3 was a typical year when the chair or vice-chair of the provincial commissioners visited a total of thirty-four local boards. 'Third Annual Report of the OMA Commission, 1922–23', *Ontario Sessional Papers* LVI, Part VI (1924):5.

30 The Manitoba Mothers' Allowance Act stipulated that one of the provincial commission appointments should be a Roman Catholic. NA, Canadian Council on Social Development, 'Inquiry into Mothers' Allowance, 1927'.

31 'Appointment of New Chairman Was Resented By Mrs. Shortt?', *Toronto Telegram*, 29 September 1927, 33. Also, see 'Miss Thompson's Appointment Caused Commission Crisis', *Toronto Telegram*, 29 September 1927, 33; and 'Retires from Mothers' Allowances Board and Indicates That Minister of Health Had Given Way to Party Pressure: No Complaint of Colleagues: Alleges That Appointment Made Recently and Naming of Successor to Miss Farncombe Were Sources of Trouble', *Toronto Globe*, 29 September 1927.

32 AO, RG 49, reel #588, press clippings, 1902–1934, 'Claim Civil Service Powerless to Curb Mothers' Allowance Appointments: Demand "Showdown": Former Chief Investigator Hastens to Support Mrs. Shortt in Complaints', *Toronto Star*, 29 September 1927.

33 AO, RG 49, reel #26, press clippings, 1927–1928, 'Mrs. Adam Shortt's Resignation', Editorial, *Toronto Star*, 30 September 1927; 'Patronage at Queen's Park', Editorial, *Toronto Globe*, 30 September 1927; 'The Bane of Patronage', Editorial, *Toronto Star*, 1 October 1927; 'Mothers' Allowance', Editorial, *Brantford Expositor*, 1 October 1927; and 'Silence at Queen's Park', Editorial, *Toronto Globe*, 19 October 1927; 'Miss Belle Thompson Succeeds Mrs. Shortt:

Predecessor Describes the Appointment as "Abominable and Inconceivable"',
Toronto Star, 6 January 1928.

34 When a local board member was unavailable, application could be made to a
municipal clerk or, in case of an Indian reserve, to the Indian agent. 'Second
Annual Report of the OMA Commission, 1921–22', 61.

35 City of London Records Retention [LRR], OMA Local Board Minutes,
1920–47, 'February 15, 1926'.

36 This assumption that one had to be a societal leader to be appointed to the
local board was borne out by my father, a fourth-generation farmer in Peel
County, who keenly follows local politics. According to him, it was generally
understood that 'you had to be a reeve or deputy reeve to be on the [OMA]
board'. Interview with Newton J. Little, 22 December 1990.

   With regard to the table, the lone professor was eminent political scientist W.A. Mackintosh of Queen's University. These ratios remained virtually
unchanged at the end of the decade. It was impossible to trace those societal
leaders who did not have titles except for the Toronto case. The backgrounds
of the first Toronto local board are as follows: Miss Jane Barclay and P.S.
Paterson, the nominees of the city council; Miss Gertrude Lawler, president of
the Catholic Women's League of Canada and former head of the Department
of English at Harbord Collegiate; Frank Morgan, a member of the Railway
Men's Union, who was a member of the committee that brought the matter
of mothers' allowance before the government and a prominent labour
spokesperson; F.N. Stapleford, general secretary of the Neighbourhood
Workers' Association, and Mrs A.M. Huestis, a member of the executive of the
Local Council of Women, who was also a member of the committee that
brought the question of mothers' allowances before the government. See 'First
Annual Report of the OMA Commission, 1920–21', 36–50; 'Seventh Annual
Report of the OMA Commission, Fiscal Years 1925–26 and 1926–27', 33–42;
and AO, RG 49, reel #588, 'Toronto Members of Pensions Board:
Representative People Who Will Look After the Interests of Women', *World*,
11 October 1920.

37 Lang Pioneer Village [LPV], Keene, Ontario, Peterborough County Local
Mothers' Allowance Board Minutes, 1921–46, 'Meeting, February 1, 1936'.

38 This was a charge made to both the Prince Edward County and Toronto local
boards. County of Prince Edward Archives [CPEA], Picton, Ontario, Old Age
Pension and Mothers' Allowance Board Minutes, 'Meeting, December 29,
1926', and NA, John J. Kelso Collection, MG 30, C97, vol. 24, file: Newspaper
Clippings, Mothers' Allowances, 1925–27, 1933, 'Mothers' Allowances
Authorities "Too Niggardly" in Making Grants', *Toronto Telegram*, 10
December 1926.

39 A local board member complained at length in the local newspaper that the
local board had no power over provincial commission decisions. Peterborough
Centennial Museum and Archives [PCMA], Peterborough, Ontario, Dobbin
Files, 'How Mothers' Allowance Works Out in Peterboro', by F.H. Dobbin,
secretary of local board, *Peterborough Examiner*, 24 March 1921.

40 'Third Annual Report of OMA Commission, 1922–23', 10.

41 NA, Kelso Papers, vol. 24, file: Newspaper Clippings, Mothers' Allowance, 1925–27, 1933, 'Mothers' Allowances Authorities "Too Niggardly" in Making Grants', *Toronto Telegram*, 10 December 1926.

42 'Eighth Annual Report of the OMA Commission, 1927–28', *Ontario Sessional Papers* LXI, Part V (1929):6; LRR, OMA Local Board Minutes, 1920–47, 'Meeting, November 1, 1920'. Simcoe County Archives [SCA], Simcoe County Local Mothers' Allowance Board Minutes, 1920–1957, 'Meeting, November 25, 1920'; AO, Ferguson Papers, box 91, series 03–06–0–1184, Mothers' Allowance Commission, General Correspondence, 1926, 'Letter from the Central Council of the Neighbourhood Workers' Association', 11 January 1927; and AO, RG 49, reel #588, 'Pension Still Necessary: Change Should Be Made to Care for Families Where There Is Dependent Child—Apply the Ruling to a Given Case and It Looks Like Plain Injustice', *Stratford Herald*, 27 December 1927.

43 Johnston, *E.C. Drury*, 152.

44 'First Annual Report of the OMA Commission, 1920–21', 18.

45 'Second Annual Report of the OMA Commission, 1921–22', 30.

46 Andrew Armitage, *Social Welfare in Canada: Ideals and Realities* (Toronto: McClelland and Stewart, 1975):272.

47 During the first decade, the number and title of investigators were:

Title	1920–1 Number	1925–7 Number
Miss	11	12
Mrs	5	5
Mr	1	2
Total	**17**	**19**

'First Annual Report of the OMA Commission, 1920–21', 15–16, and 'Seventh Annual Report of the OMA Commission, Fiscal Years 1925–26, 1926–27', 23.

48 'Second Annual Report of the OMA Commission, 1921–22', 21.

49 Elgin County Library [ECL], St Thomas, Ontario, Mothers' Allowance Case Files, Elgin County, box 55, file 1, 'Letter from Helen Bapty to Mrs. Graham, enroute to Windsor', Spring 1933.

50 'First Annual Report of the OMA Commission, 1920–21', 17.

51 In 1921 there were 2,660 OMA beneficiaries and seventeen investigators; therefore the average case-load was 156 families. By 1922 the number of beneficiaries had increased by 33.8 per cent, but the number of investigators remained constant, with a case-load of approximately 209 cases. In 1929 the chairman claimed that the average case-load was 300 families. The calculations for 1921 and 1922 were made by Carol Cole, 'An Examination of the Mothers' Allowance System in Ontario, 1914–1940', MA thesis, Department of History, University of Waterloo, 1989, 85; and 'Ninth Annual Report of the OMA Commission, 1928–1929', 5.

52 One local board member charged that the investigators 'seem to be working from a distinctly holier-than-thou point of view and as a result are bringing

mixed feelings of fear and gratitude to hundreds of benefactors'. NA, Kelso Papers, vol. 24, file: Newspaper Clippings, Mothers' Allowances, 1925–27, 1933, 'Letter to the Editor', *Toronto Star*, 13 December 1926.

53 Letter from Mrs E. Nolan to the *Toronto Star*, 3 February 1926.

54 NA, Kelso Papers, vol. 24, file: Newspaper Clippings, Mothers' Allowances, 1925–27, 1933, 'Widowed Waitress Stoutly Defended by Local Laborites: Allegation Rouses Officials to Ask for Government Explanation', *Toronto Globe*, 13 December 1926.

55 'First Annual Report of the OMA Commission, 1920–21', 12.

56 'Fourth Annual Report of the OMA Commission, 1923–24', *Ontario Sessional Papers* LVII, Part V (1925):5–6.

57 NA, Canadian Council on Social Development, file #52, Mothers' Allowances 1929, 'Letter from Harry Bentley, Chief Investigator, OMA Commission to Miss Elizabeth King, Assistant Secretary, Canadian Council on Child Welfare', 29 July 1929.

58 D.B. Weldon Library [DBW], Western Regional Collection, London, Ontario, Mothers' Allowance Case Files, City of London, 1920–1940, 'Local Report Attached to Application, May 31, 1939'.

59 For more details on the 1928 trial, see Karen Dubinsky, *Improper Advances: Rape and Heterosexual Misconduct in Ontario, 1880–1929* (Chicago: University of Chicago Press, 1993):56–7.

60 DBW, Mothers' Allowance Case Files, London, 'Letter from Mrs. Regina Wise to Secretary, Mothers' Allowance Board, London, April 26, 1934'; 'Letter from Secretary, Local OMA Board, to Chairman and Members of the Local OMA Board, October 19, 1933'; 'Copy of Declaration by Mrs. Regina Wise, October 18, 1933'; 'Letter from Chairman, Provincial Commission to Acting Secretary, Local OMA Board, February 13, 1936'.

61 LRR, Mothers' Allowance Local Board Minutes, City of London, 'Meeting, January 9, 1928'.

62 'Second Annual Report of the OMA Commission, 1921–22', 10.

63 DBW, Mothers' Allowance Case Files, London, 'Letter from Beatty Brothers Manufacturing to Local OMA Board, November 15, 1937'.

64 SCA, Simcoe County Local Mothers' Allowance Board Minutes, 1920–1957, 'Meeting, August 7, 1924'.

65 ECL, Mothers' Allowance Case Files, Elgin County, 'Letter to Mrs. B. Graham, Investigator, October 26, 1926'.

66 This letter includes signatures from two reeves, three councillors, a treasurer, and a superintendent. ECL, Mothers' Allowance Case Files, Elgin County, 'Letter from Several Rate-payers of the Township of Bayham, June 1922'. There are, however, several examples of ratepayers, such as the Danforth Park Ratepayers Association, demanding that the provincial government be more restrictive in OMA administration. AO, RG 49, reel #588, file: Mothers' Pensions, 1920–1926, 'Government Is Asked to Revise Widows' Act', *Toronto Star*, 28 October 1926.

CHAPTER 3

1 The Ontario Mothers' Allowances Act, 1920, section 3, subsection (f) reads: A monthly allowance may be paid towards the support of the dependent children of a mother who '(f) Is a fit and proper person to have the care and custody of her children' (The Ontario Mothers' Allowance Act, 1920, *Statutes of Ontario*, First Session of the 15th Legislature of Ontario, Chapter 89). In contrast, the BC government chose to name its policy a mothers' *pension* rather than a mothers' *allowance* because it wanted to ensure a notion of entitlement. The Ontario lobbyists and the Drury government were well aware of the BC debate. For a comparative analysis of the British Columbia and Ontario Mothers' Allowance policies, see Margaret H. Little, 'Claiming a Unique Place: The Introduction of Mothers' Pensions in B.C.', *B.C. Studies*, Special Issue entitled Women's History and Gender Studies, edited by Annalee Golz and Lynne Marks, no. 105 (Spring 1995):80–102.

2 Archives of Ontario [AO], Ministry of Community and Social Services, RG 29, series 36, Mothers' Allowance Case Files, box 2.

3 'Tenth Annual Report of the OMA Commission, 1929–30', *Ontario Sessional Papers* LXIII, Part V (1931):5–6.

4 This was still the case in the 1940s when my grandmother, Margaret Hillyard, applied for an allowance. She wished to keep the $6,000 she had from the sale of the farm for the education of her four young children after her husband died. The regulators insisted that she buy a house when she preferred to bring her family to live with her aunt in a large house in the town of Caledon. Because she refused to purchase a house, she received only a small portion of the allowance. Interview with Lorna Margaret Little, 22 December 1990.

5 SCA, Simcoe County Local Mothers' Allowance Board Minutes, 'Meeting, June 7, 1923'.

6 James Struthers, *The Limits of Affluence: Welfare in Ontario, 1920–1970* (Toronto: University of Toronto Press, 1994):38.

7 AO, RG 29, series 36, box 2.

8 Acknowledged in the first report and subsequently articulated in almost every annual report of the decade. 'First Annual Report of the OMA Commission, 1920–21', 21; quote cited in 'Fourth Annual Report of the OMA Commission, 1923–24', 17.

9 'Second Annual Report of the OMA Commission, 1921–22', 29.

10 'First Annual Report of the OMA Commission, 1920–21', 23.

11 'Third Annual Report of the OMA Commission, 1922–23', 21.

12 Ibid., 21.

13 'First Annual Report of the OMA Commission, 1920–21', 24.

14 AO, RG 29, series 36, box 1.

15 'First Annual Report of the OMA Commission, 1920–21', 28.

16 'Fifth Annual Report of the OMA Commission, 1924–25', *Ontario Sessional Papers* LVIII, Part V (1926):13.

17 Table 2.7 indicates that widows initially accounted for 84 per cent of all OMA cases and declined throughout the decade to a low of 67 per cent in 1929–30.

The administrators were quite concerned about this decline, associating it with a general decline in moral values.

18 See James Snell for further discussion of the class distinctions between divorce and desertion. James G. Snell, *In the Shadow of the Law: Divorce in Canada, 1900–1939* (Toronto: University of Toronto Press, 1991):esp. Chs 1 and 2.

19 DBW, Mothers' Allowance Case Files, London, 'Letter from the Chairman of the Local Board to the Provincial Mothers' Allowances Commission, May 19, 1921'.

20 SCA, Simcoe County Local Mothers' Allowance Board Minutes, 'Meeting, November 25, 1920'. 'First Annual Report of the OMA Commission, 1920–21', 11.

21 'Eighth Annual Report of the OMA Commission, 1927–28', 5.

22 'First Annual Report of the OMA Commission, 1920–21', 28–9.

23 DBW, Mothers' Allowance Case Files, London, 'Letter Written to the London City Clerk, April 26, 1926'.

24 'Fifth Annual Report of the OMA Commission, 1924–25', 12.

25 DBW, Mothers' Allowance Case Files, London, 'London City Clerk's Account of Case', n.d.

26 'Seventh Annual Report of the OMA Commission, 1925–26 and 1926–27', 19.

27 AO, RG 29, series 36, box 1.

28 DBW, Mothers' Allowance Case Files, London, 'Letter from Inspector from Relief Department to City Clerk, August 19, 1926'.

29 DBW, Mothers' Allowance Case Files, London, 'Letter from the Juvenile Court Chambers to the City Clerk, September 8, 1933'.

30 DBW, Mothers' Allowance Case Files, London, 'Letter from the Local Board to the Provincial Mothers' Allowance Commission, March 3, 1924'.

31 'Second Annual Report of the OMA Commission, 1921–22', 24.

32 DBW, Mothers' Allowance Case Files, London, 'Letter from City Clerk to Relief Department Inspector, May 24, 1926'.

33 There is nothing other than Mrs Carpenter's attitude to explain this three-month trial period. DBW, Mothers' Allowance Case Files, 'Report from Local Children's Aid Society to Local Board, 1928'.

34 DBW, Mothers' Allowance Case Files, London, 'Letter from Mother to Local Board, May 10, 1927'; and 'Letter from City Clerk to Investigator, September 23, 1926'.

35 DBW, Mothers' Allowance Case Files, London, 'Letter from City Clerk to the Provincial Mothers' Allowance Commission', n.d.

36 DBW, Mothers' Allowance Case Files, London, 'Letter from City Clerk to Investigator, January 31, 1930'.

37 According to historian Don Avery, 'British immigration to Canada only amounted to about 50,000 a year or about 45 per cent of prewar levels.' For further discussion of the racial concerns of this era, see Don Avery, *'Dangerous Foreigners': European Immigrant Workers and Labour Radicalism in Canada, 1896–1932* (Toronto: McClelland and Stewart, 1979):Ch. 4, quotation cited on p. 96.

38 It is difficult to determine the precise immigration rate in Ontario during the

1920s. According to the 1921 census, Canadian and British-born citizens represented 93 per cent of the Ontario population, with 6.2 per cent foreign born. The 1931 census did not calculate racial questions according to place of birth but rather according to 'racial origin'. This latter census stated that 74 per cent of the Ontario population was Canadian or British in racial origin with 26 per cent of foreign origin. See *Census of Canada, 1921*, vol. 2, 240–1; and *Census of Canada, 1931*, vol. 2, 294–7.

39 The annual reports often mentioned that 'very few Indians have become beneficiaries', but failed to question why. 'First Annual Report of the OMA Commission, 1920–21', 9.

40 There is scant evidence to illustrate the experience of Aboriginal women on OMA. This case began in 1929, but the outcome is not known, according to the case file evidence. DBW, Mothers' Allowance Case Files, London, box 160, 'Application Form, August 1930'; 'Letter from City Clerk, on Behalf of the Local OMA Board, to Dr. Jamieson, OMA Commission, November 30, 1931'; 'Letter from Dr. Jamieson, OMA Commission, to Mr. S. Baker, Mothers' Allowance Local Board, December 7, 1931'; 'Letter from Local Board to Provincial Commission, December 29, 1931'; and 'Letter from Provincial Commission to Local Board, January 6, 1932'.

41 I have not found literacy a criterion for WASP applicants. LRR, Mothers' Allowance Local Board Minutes, London, 'Meeting, May 18, 1921'.

42 DBW, Mothers' Allowance Case Files, London, 'Letter from Investigator to Provincial Commission, June 27, 1928'.

43 DBW, Mothers' Allowance Case Files, London, 'Letter from Relief Department Inspector to City Clerk, April 24, 1931'.

44 DBW, Mothers' Allowance Case Files, 'Letter from The Canadian League for the Advancement of Colored People to the City Clerk and Local Board, April 27, 1927'.

45 DBW, Mothers' Allowance Case Files, n.d.

46 DBW, Mothers' Allowance Case Files, London, 'Letter from the Relief Inspector to the Local Board of Mothers' Allowance, April 18, 1929' and 'Letter from the Secretary, Mothers' Allowance Local Board to Mrs. Graham, Provincial Investigator, May 30, 1933'.

47 DBW, Mothers' Allowance Case Files, London, 'Letter from the Local Board to the Provincial Commission', n.d.

48 More historical research needs to be conducted regarding the lives of ethnic-minority women in Canada. From what little is known, it appears that some ethnic-minority women in both Canada and the United States formed their own benevolent associations because they could not expect much help from the state or society in general. See Dionne Brand, *No Burden to Carry: Narratives of Black Working Women in Ontario 1920s to 1950s* (Toronto: Women's Press, 1991):11–36; and Linda Gordon, 'Black and White Visions of Welfare: Women's Welfare Activism, 1890–1945', Discussion Paper no. 935–91 (Madison: Institute for Research on Poverty, University of Wisconsin-Madison, February 1991).

49 'First Annual Report of the OMA Commission, 1920–21', 11.

50 According to the annual reports, it was the third most common cause of death among widowed cases and the most common cause of death among foster parent and incapacitation cases. 'Fourth Annual Report of the OMA Commission, 1923–24', 13.

51 'Third Annual Report of the OMA Commission, 1922–23', 14.

52 TB represented the following percentages of the total OMA budget. (Note: Tuberculosis figures were not given for 1928–9.)

1921–2	10 per cent
1922–3	13 per cent
1923–4	13.21 per cent
1924–5	12.82 per cent
1925–6	13.44 per cent
1926–7	13.55 per cent
1927–8	13.12 per cent
1929–30	13.20 per cent

53 'Seventh Annual Report of the OMA Commission, 1925–26 and 1926–27', 19.

54 'Second Annual Report of the OMA Commission, 1921–22', 35.

55 In 1927–8 the commission stated that 'the number of applicants under the incapacitation conditions shows a very large increase and the Commission has given these cases the most careful consideration, and has been obliged to refuse a large percentage as not being totally and permanently disabled within the meaning of the Act'. 'Eighth Annual Report of the OMA Commission, 1927–28', 5.

56 'Seventh Annual Report of the OMA Commission, 1926–27', 21.

57 'Fourth Annual Report of the OMA Commission, 1923–24', 15.

58 For a more detailed discussion regarding education as a part of nation-building, see Bruce Curtis, 'Representation and State Formation in the Canadas, 1790–1850', *Studies in Political Economy* 28 (Spring 1989):59–88.

59 'Second Annual Report of the OMA Commission, 1921–22', 23.

60 Ibid., 26.

61 Ibid., 23.

62 'First Annual Report of the OMA Commission, 1920–21', 19.

63 'Eighth Annual Report of the OMA Commission, 1927–28', 5–6.

64 DBW, Mothers' Allowance Case Files, London, 'Letter from the Local Board, January 20, 1925'.

65 'Eighth Annual Report of the OMA Commission, 1927–28', 14.

66 DBW, Mothers' Allowance Case Files, London, 'Letter from Mother to Local Mothers' Allowance Board, September 1935'.

67 DBW, Mothers' Allowance Case Files, London, 'Letter from Chief Investigator, OMA Provincial Commission to Rev. T.D. McCullough, Chairman of London OMA Local Board, January 19, 1924'.

68 DBW, Mothers' Allowance Case Files, London, 'Letter from Relief Inspector to City Clerk, March 24, 1930' and 'Letter from Chief Investigator to Mother, June 4, 1930'.

69 DBW, Mothers' Allowance Case Files, London, 'Letter by Investigator, January 1931'.

70 DBW, Mothers' Allowance Case Files, London, 'Letter from Medical Superintendent to Provincial Commission, October 31, 1924' and 'Letter from the Local Board to the Provincial Commission, November 13, 1924'.

71 The term 'powers of the weak' was initially introduced by Elizabeth Janeway. Whereas Janeway associates these powers with all women, Linda Gordon discusses the many ingenious ways in which women have struggled as survivors of family violence. See Elizabeth Janeway, *Powers of the Weak* (New York: Knopf, 1980); and Linda Gordon, *Heroes of Their Own Lives: The Politics and History of Family Violence* (New York: Penguin Books, 1989):esp. Chs 8 and 9.

CHAPTER 4

1 In 1930, the first year of the Depression, there were fewer strikes and lockouts than ever in the previous twelve years. See John Herd Thompson and Allen Seager, *Canada 1922–1939: Decades of Discord* (Toronto: McClelland and Stewart, 1985):Table XII, 349.

2 Bryan Palmer, *Working-Class Experience: The Rise and Reconstitution of Canadian Labour, 1800–1980* (Toronto: Butterworths, 1983):206.

3 Charlotte Whitton, Canadian Welfare Council report, cited in Palmer, *Working-Class Experience*, 207.

4 James Struthers, 'A Profession in Crisis: Charlotte Whitton and Canadian Social Work in the 1930s', in *The 'Benevolent' State: The Growth of Welfare in Canada*, edited by Allan Moscovitch and Jim Albert (Toronto: Garamond Press, 1987):112.

5 Michiel Horn, *The League for Social Reconstruction: Intellectual Origins of the Democratic Left in Canada, 1930–1942* (Toronto: University of Toronto Press, 1980):9.

6 Ibid., 3–16.

7 The CCF consisted of an alliance of non-communist labour parties in all provinces west of Quebec, the Socialist Party of Canada, and three farm organizations: the United Farmers of Alberta, the United Farmers of Canada, and the United Farmers of Ontario. Thompson and Seager, *Canada 1922–1939*, 229–37.

8 All three authors illustrate how the Depression affected men's and women's roles in society and within the family. Margaret Hobbs documents a broadly based antifeminist sentiment that emerged in Canada during the 1930s and had devastating results for working women. See Ruth Roach Pierson, 'Gender and the Unemployment Insurance Debates in Canada, 1934–1940', *Labour/Le Travail* no. 25 (Spring 1990):78; Margaret Hobbs, 'Women, Work, and Unemployment in Canada During the Depression', Ch. 1, Ph.D. thesis, Department of History and Philosophy, Ontario Institute for Studies in Education; and Linda Gordon, *Pitied But Not Entitled: Single Mothers and the History of Welfare* (New York: Free Press, 1994):Ch. 7.

9 Hobbs, 'Women, Work and Unemployment', Chs 1, 26; For a historical analysis of how the Depression era affected Canadian men, see Michiel Horn, ed.,

The Dirty Thirties: Canadians in the Great Depression (Toronto: University of Toronto Press, 1972); A.E. Safarian, *The Canadian Economy in the Great Depression* (Toronto: University of Toronto Press, 1970); and H. Blair Neatby, *The Politics of Chaos: Canada in the Thirties* (Toronto: Macmillan, 1972).

Scholars have only begun to illustrate the relationship between work and masculinity. See Mark Rosenfeld, ' "It Was a Hard Life": Class and Gender in the Work and Family Rhythms of a Railway Town, 1920–1950', *Historical Papers*, Windsor (1988):237–79; Steven Maynard, 'Rough Work and Rugged Men: The Social Construction of Masculinity in Working-Class History', *Labour/Le Travail* 23 (Spring 1989):159–69; Cynthia Cockburn, *Brothers: Male Dominance and Technological Change* (London: Pluto Press, 1983) and *Machinery of Dominance: Women, Men and Technical Know-How* (London: Pluto Press, 1985); and Stan Gray, 'Sharing the Shop Floor', in *Beyond Patriarchy: Essays By Men on Pleasure, Power and Change*, edited by Michael Kaufman (Toronto: Oxford University Press, 1987):216–34; and Paul Willis, 'Shop Floor Culture, Masculinity and the Wage Form', in *Working-Class Culture: Studies in History and Theory*, edited by J. Clarke, C. Critchen, and Paul Willis (New York: St Martin's Press, 1979):196–7.

10 Leonard Marsh of McGill University warned that one of every ten Canadians was becoming part of the chronically unemployable. Leonard Marsh, *Canadians In and Out of Work* (1940):367–8, 371–2, cited in Horn, *The League for Social Reconstruction*, 10.

11 Letters to R.B. Bennett during this period reflect these racist attitudes. L.M. Grayson and Michael Bliss, eds, *The Wretched of Canada: Letters to R.B. Bennett 1930–1935* (Toronto: University of Toronto Press, 1971):18–19, 23, and 75–6. For a letter protesting these deportations, see p. 66 in Grayson and Bliss. Also see Barbara Roberts, *Whence They Came: Deportation from Canada 1900–1935* (Ottawa: University of Ottawa Press, 1988).

12 There has been a great deal of discussion lately among feminist scholars as to whether masculine and feminine identities are relational or semi-autonomous constructs. In other words, is it possible for the practices of femininity to change without provoking changes in masculinity? During the Depression, it was clear that both masculinity and femininity were interdependent, with both men and women experiencing changes in their prescribed roles as a result of a rapid decline in male employment and a simultaneous rise in female employment. See Hobbs, 'Women, Work and Unemployment', 32, for a detailed discussion of this point. Also see Joan Wallace Scott, 'Gender: A Useful Category of Historical Analysis', *American Historical Review* 91, Issue #5 (December 1986); and Michael Kimmel, 'The Contemporary "Crisis" of Masculinity in Historical Perspective', in *The Making of Masculinities: The New Men's Studies*, edited by Harry Brod (Boston: Allen and Unwin, 1987).

13 Series D8–85, *Historical Statistics of Canada*, 2nd edn, edited by F.H. Leacy (1983), as cited in Veronica Strong-Boag, *The New Day Recalled: Lives of Girls and Women in English Canada, 1919–1939* (Markham, Ontario: Penguin, 1988):43; and *Seventh Census of Canada, 1931*, vol.VII, Table 27, 38, as cited in Hobbs, 'Women, Work and Unemployment', 41.

14 Fertility rates in Canada dropped 22.3 per cent from 1921 to 1931 and the decline was greatest among urban dwellers and British and native-born

Canadians. Ellen Gee, 'Fertility and Marriage Patterns in Canada 1851–1971', Ph.D. dissertation, University of British Columbia (1978):45, cited in Strong-Boag, *The New Day Recalled*, 146–7. Regarding desertion, see Hobbs, 'Women, Work and Unemployment', 31.

15 The history of the Canadian women's movement during the 1930s remains virtually unexplored except for the work of Margaret Hobbs, Linda Kealey, and Joan Sangster. See Hobbs, 'Women, Work and Unemployment', and several articles in Linda Kealey and Joan Sangster, eds, *Beyond the Vote: Canadian Women and Politics* (Toronto: University of Toronto Press, 1989).

16 For example, the City of London fired all married women workers and the City of Ottawa fired forty women social workers and hired eleven male detectives in their relief department, arguing that women were good for caring jobs, but men made better welfare police. The Trades and Labour Congress passed a resolution in 1931 demanding that provincial and federal governments crack down on their employees whose wives also had jobs. The National Council of Women was divided on the issue, but the Toronto Local Council of Women passed a resolution in 1932 urging all wives whose husbands could support them to resign from their jobs. Both the provincial and federal governments discriminated against women in the civil service during this period. For further discussion of this issue, see Hobbs, 'Women, Work and Unemployment', 10–12; Pierson, 'Gender and Unemployment', 82; Jim Struthers, *Through No Fault of Their Own: Unemployment and the Canadian Welfare State 1914–1941* (Toronto: University of Toronto Press, 1983):149–50; Strong-Boag, *The New Day Recalled*, Ch. 2; and Archives of Ontario [AO], Office of the Premier, Hepburn Papers, RG 3, box 230, 'Letter from Eva Birss to Hepburn', 3 October 1934.

17 Hobbs explores this vocal group, which included members from a cross-section of society, through an analysis of newspaper debates, government policies, and magazine advertisements during the Depression. See Hobbs, 'Women, Work and Unemployment', Ch. 1.

18 This emergency relief aid ended in 1941. Dennis Guest, *The Emergency of Social Security in Canada* (Vancouver: University of British Columbia Press, 1980):86.

19 Struthers, 'A Profession in Crisis', 112.

20 Guest, *The Emergence of Social Security*, 94–5.

21 The maternal mortality rate rose to 5.8 per 1,000 live births in 1930 and was at 5.3 in 1936. National Archives [NA], Charlotte Whitton Papers, MG 30, vol. 19, All Subjects, file: Canada's Problems in Welfare and Assistance, 1936, 'Address Given by Whitton Before the Empire Club of Canada, Toronto, Friday, March 20, 1936', 2; Strong-Boag, *The New Day Recalled*, 153; and NA, Records of the Department of National Health and Welfare, RG 29–2, vol. 991, file 499–3–2, part 4, Child and Maternal Health Division, Canadian Welfare Council Nov. 1935–Jan. 1939, 'Canadian Welfare Council Annual Report of the Executive Director for the Year Ending March the 31st, 1936'.

22 See Cynthia R. Comacchio, *'Nations Are Built of Babies': Saving Ontario's Mothers and Children, 1900–1940* (Montreal: McGill-Queen's University Press, 1993):Ch. 4; Strong-Boag, *The New Day Recalled*, 151; and Kathy Arnup, 'Educating Mothers: Government Advice for Women in the Inter-War Years', in *Delivering Motherhood*, edited by K. Arnup et al. (New York: Routledge, 1990):190–20.

23 NA, Canadian Council on Social Development Records, MG 28, vol. 62, file no. 497, Mothers' Allowances 1935–40, 'Letter from Whitton to John Appleton, Secretary-Treasurer, The Canadian Life Insurance, Toronto, April 18, 1935'.

24 NA, MG 28, I-10, vol. 10, file: Mothers' Allowances 1932, 'Letter from Charlotte Whitton to Hon. W.G. Martin, Minister of Public Welfare, Ontario, January 20, 1932'.

25 NA, Whitton Papers, vol. 19, file: Canada's Problems in Welfare and Assistance, 1936, 'Address to the Empire Club of Canada, Toronto, Friday, March 20, 1936', 2, 5–6; NA, MG 28, vol. 10, file: Mothers' Allowances 1933–34, 'Letter from Charlotte Whitton to Ernest Blois, Director of Child Welfare, Dept. of Public Health, Province of Nova Scotia, September 5, 1934'; NA, MG 28, vol. 62, file no. 497, Mothers' Allowances 1935–40, 'Letter from C. Whitton to Harry Bentley, OMA Commissioner, March 11, 1935'; and NA, MG 28, vol. 62, file no. 497, Mothers' Allowances 1935–40, 'Letter from C. Whitton to John Appleton, Secretary-Treasurer, The Canadian Life Insurance, Toronto, April 18, 1935'.

26 Struthers, 'A Profession in Crisis', 112.

27 Clifford J. Williams, *Decades of Service: A History of the Ontario Ministry of Community and Social Services, 1930–1980* (Toronto: Ontario Government, 1984):22.

28 Ibid., 2–3.

29 AO, Commissions and Inquiries, RG 18, B-75, 'Royal Commission on Public Welfare, August 13, 1930', Report, 5–107; and Williams, *Decades of Service*, 6.

30 Henry rejected such programs as provincial unemployment insurance but instead established the unsuccessful back-to-the-land movement in 1932, which financed the return of farmers to the land as a solution to urban relief lists. For a careful examination of Henry's political life, see Don Spanner, ' "The Straight Furrow": In Search of George S. Henry, Ontario's Unknown Premier, 1930–1934', paper presented at the Canadian Historical Association, Learneds' Conference, Charlottetown, PEI, 31 May 1992.

31 Williams, *Decades of Service*, 7.

32 AO, Henry Papers, RG 3, box 162, series 03–08–0–354, 'Letter from the Toronto District Labour Council to Premier, August 5, 1933'.

33 Mitchell Hepburn was no ordinary farmer. He managed a 950-acre farm and was proprietor of Hepburn Co-operative Cheese Factory. AO, Ministry of Community and Social Services, RG 29, series 74, 'A History of the Department of Public Welfare'.

34 AO, Legislative Offices, RG 49, reel #49, Press Clippings, 1935, 'Mothers' Allowances: Amendment to Act Extends Benefits', *Globe*, Toronto, 6 April 1935.

35 Williams, *Decades of Service*, 39.

36 'Report of the Minister of Public Welfare, 1938–39', *Ontario Sessional Papers* LXXII, Part IV (1940):16.

37 'Report of the Minister of Public Welfare, 1936–37', *Ontario Sessional Papers* LXX, Part IV (1938):14.

38 AO, RG 49, reel #49, Press Clippings, 1935, 'Bill Is Read Second Time: Mother With One Child Also Will Be Given Allowance: Little Opposition', *Border Cities Star*, Windsor, 11 April 1935.

39 'Mr. Hepburn had promised to extend provisions of the Mothers' Allowance to widows with one daughter . . .', according to the *London Free Press* during the 1934 electoral campaign. AO, RG 49, reel #46, Press Clippings, 1934, 'Henry Nominated: Will Set Ontario Voting Date Today', *London Free Press*, 14 May 1934.

40 Simcoe County Archives [SCA], Simcoe County Mothers' Allowance Local Board Minutes, 1920–1957, 'Meeting, September 14, 1934'.

41 'Report of the Minister of Public Welfare, 1935–36', *Ontario Sessional Papers* LXIX, Part IV (1937):13.

42 Ibid., 13.

43 City of London Records Retention Room [LRR], City of London Mothers' Allowance Local Board Minutes, 'Meeting, June 15, 1938'.

44 AO, RG 49, reel #36, Press Clippings, 1931, 'Changes Suggested in Allowances Act: York County Deputation to Approach Welfare Minister', *Globe*, 31 January 1931.

45 Resolutions urging the provincial government to raise the age of children eligible were passed by the municipalities of East Windsor, Kitchener, St Thomas, Walkerville, Welland, North Bay, Stratford, and Kitchener. AO, Henry Papers, RG 3, box 160, series 03–08–0–326: 'Letter from Assistant Clerk C.G. Hays, Corporation of the City of East Windsor to Premier Henry', 3 January 1933; 'Letter from St. Thomas City Council', 9 January 1933; 'Letter from Walkerville Town Clerk's Office', 12 January 1933; 'Letter from Corporation of Welland City Clerk', 16 January 1933; 'Letter from City of North Bay, City Clerk', 17 January 1933; 'Letter from City of Stratford, City Clerk', 17 January 1933; and 'Letter from Kitchener', no date.

46 In 1934 mothers in the towns of Leaside, Mimico, New Toronto, and Weston; the villages of Forest Hill, Swansea, and Long Branch; and the townships of East York, York, Etobicoke, Scarborough, and North York were granted the same rates as mothers in Toronto. It was believed that this would benefit 450 widows. AO, RG 49, reel #36, Press Clippings, 1931, 'Changes Suggested in Allowances Act: York County Deputation to Approach Welfare Minister', *Globe*, 31 January 1931; AO, RG 49, reel #46, Press Clippings, 1934, 'Mothers' Allowance Increased in Suburbs: Beneficiaries in Five Centres Placed on City Rates: Effective on May 1', *Mail and Empire*, 16 May 1934, and 'Higher Mothers' Allowance Declared Election Stunt: "Political Move to Gain Votes," Declares Wm. J. Noble', *Daily Star*, 16 May 1934; and AO, Henry Papers, box 160, series, 03–08–0–326, 'Letter from Corporation of the Town of Mimico, Mayor to Premier, January 23, 1933', and 'Letter from Municipal Corporation of the County of York, Clerk to Premier, February 21, 1933'.

47 AO, RG 49, reel #49, Press Clippings, 1935, 'Government Share Not to Be Altered', *Fort William Daily Times Journal*, 10 July 1935, and reel #55, 1936, 'Ontario Urged Reduce Power School Boards: Mayors Would Give Municipal Councils Tighter Hold of Tax Expenditures', *Telegram*, 13 June 1936.

48 AO, RG 49, reel #58, Press Clippings, 1937, 'New Tax Plan Gets Approval from Ontario: Municipal Heads Expect Saving as Social Costs Paid by Province', no date.

49 AO, Henry Papers, box 153, series 03–08–0–241, 'Letter from the Corporation of the County of Kent to Premier, June 9, 1932'.

50 AO, RG 49, reel #64, Press Clippings, 1938, 'Allowance Increase For Mothers Urged', *Toronto Daily Star*, 10 February 1938.

51 AO, Henry Papers, box 162, series 03–08–0–354, 'Letter from Fanny Stewart, Orillia, July 19, 1935'.

52 AO, Ministry of Labour, RG 7, series 7–1–0–295, General Correspondence 'M' 1939, 'Letter from Allan McNeil, Arnprior, Ontario to Hon. H.A. Hipel, Minister of Labour, June 5, 1939'.

53 AO, Hepburn Papers, box 230, 'Letter from Eva Birss, London', 3 October 1924.

54 The quotation reflects the misspellings in the original letter. AO, Hepburn Papers, box 190, series 8, 'Letter from Harold Reynolds, Maberly, September 6, 1935'.

55 AO, Hepburn Papers, box 190, series 8, 'Letter from R.M. Teall, Vienna to Premier Hepburn, June 18, 1935'. AO, Hepburn Papers, box 209, 'Letter from Fred Wakely to Premier, June 23, 1937'; and 'Memorandum to Mr. G.S. Tattle, General Secretary, Department of Public Welfare, from Secretary of Mothers' Allowance Commission, June 29, 1937'. Quotation cited in AO, RG 49, reel #52, Press Clippings, 1935, 'Chisels On Pension Says It Legitimate: Vienna Man Goes to Jail—Took Commission', *Toronto Daily Star*, 6 November 1935.

56 An intense rivalry existed between the Toronto local board and the provincial commission during the early part of the decade, and the provincial commission replaced the provincial appointees on the Toronto local board. AO, RG 49, reel #36, Press Clippings, 1931, 'Allowances Board Serving Toronto to Be Reorganized: Four Members Told They Are Out of Office: To Name Successors: Prominent Conservatives Get the Axe from Provincial Headquarters', *Globe*, 17 April 1931; 'Allowances Board Assertions Denied', *Globe*, 18 April 1931; 'Citizens Ask Harmony on Mothers' Board', *Daily Star*, 7 May 1931; 'Say Cooperation Lacking in Mothers' Allowance Board: Central Council of Ratepayers Thinks Mayor and Controllers Should Step in Help Harmony', *Telegram*, 7 May 1931; 'Charge Denied by Jamieson Who Hits Back: Mothers' Allowances Are Paid, He Says, But City 3 Months in Arrears For Share', *Telegram*, 24 June 1931; 'Mothers' Allowance Investigation Asked', *Mail and Empire*, 5 November 1931.

57 'Annual Report of Public Welfare, 1935–36', 5.

58 The amount spent on OMA during the first five years of the Depression, fiscal year ending 31 October, were as follows:

1929	$2,324,388.00
1930	$2,394,088.00
1931	$2,394,088.00
1932	$2,251,886.41
1933	$2,819,111.20
1934	$3,026,155.07

'Seventh Annual Report of the Minister of Public Welfare, 1935–36 and 1936–37', *Ontario Sessional Papers* LX, Part V (1928):16.

59 'Second Annual Report of the Minister of Public Welfare, 1931–32', *Ontario Sessional Papers* LXV, Part IV (1933):3.

60 The annual report for 1931–2 even gave a breakdown of the amount saved from these discontinued allowances:

Allowances discontinued:	
Automatic	$703
Result of Supervision	$630
Average allowance	$37.00
Monthly reduction in disbursements	$23,310.00
Yearly reduction in disbursements	$279,720.00
Total Saving	$279,720.00

'Second Annual Report of the Minister of Public Welfare, 1931–32', 12 and 52.

61 AO, Lincoln County, Old Age Pension and Mothers' Allowance Records, 1937–1949, F 1741–30, box 3, 'Case File, May 1930'.

62 AO, F 1741–30, box 3, 'Third Application Form, November 1932'.

63 D.B. Weldon Library [DBW], Western Regional Collection, London, Ontario, Mothers' Allowance Case Files, 1920–1940, box 160, 'Application Form, November 1936'.

64 The story continues to include an itemized account of her weekly costs:

> She is paying, roughly, about $6.41 for her food. Soap, toilet needs and sundry items bring up her costs to around $7. She pays $1.32 for meat, hamburger, stewing meat and cheap sausages—at least she pays that when she has it or can get any further credit. Her milk comes to $2.04 and her bread to 90 cents. She tries to get the equivalent of 43 cents in vegetables each week, not counting potatoes which costs her about 25 cents. Cereal is another 25 cents. They eat butter one meal a day. It comes up to about 38 cents a week.
>
> Her basic shelter requirements cost $21.13 per month, and are divided as follows: Rent $17; electric light 80 cents; water 80 cents; gas $1.53; laundry $1.00. She gets her fuel free.
>
> Of pressing bills she has: Grocer $16.75; butcher $7, and milk $8.26. She is trying to pay off $2.42 on her grocery bills, which is properly added to the $21.13 bringing her monthly budget to this point up to $23.55. This leaves her $31.45 or $7.86 a week, out of her $55 allowance, based on $35 for a mother and one child and $5 for each succeeding child. . . .
>
> Even a relief budget for a family of five, 2 adults and 3 children, for goods purchased on the open market, is brought to $6.46 although with the special allowances on milk and bread, it actually is listed at $5.95 per week.
>
> And according to the minimum scale produced by the Ontario Medical Association, the minimum for a family of five is placed at today's valuations at $8.11.

AO, RG 49, reel #64, Press Clippings, 1938, 'Mothers' Allowance Scale Held Below Relief', *Globe*, 15 February 1938.

65 AO, F 1741–30, box 3, 'Application Form, March 1938'.

66 Elgin County Library and Archives [ECL], St Thomas, Ontario, Mothers' Allowance Case Files, Elgin County, box 42, file 1: 'Letter from Miss Ethel McKellar to Mrs. Bridgeman, March 23, 1933'.

67 Lynne Marks, Plate 32: New Approaches to Disease and Public Dependency, 'Mothers' Allowance and Old Age Pension, 1939: Patterns of Inadequacy', *Historical Atlas of Canada, Volume III: Addressing the Twentieth Century, 1891–1961*, edited by Donald Kerr and Deryck Holdsworth (Toronto: University of Toronto Press, 1990).

68 AO, RG 49, reel #64, Press Clippings, 1938, 'Mothers' Allowance Scale Held Below Relief', *Globe*, 15 February 1938.

69 AO, F 1741–30, box 3, Gertrude Willis's application form (December 1935) and Millie Tales's application form (February 1937).

70 In Lincoln County especially, single mothers often did seasonal fruit picking or other farm work to earn a little extra money. While the pay was very poor, this type of work allowed mothers to bring their children to the job site. Other types of work available for those who lived in towns were part-time and seasonal jobs at canneries and mills. These latter jobs paid better (12.5¢ an hour in 1934 at a canning factory in St David's, Lincoln Co.), but this would be deducted from their allowance cheques, and often these mothers were criticized for being away from their children. AO, F 1740–30, box 3.

71 AO, Henry Papers, box 142, series 03–08–0–120, 'Letter from Mrs. Caroline Mullen to Premier, October 30, 1931'.

72 In fact, on departmental letters sent to OMA recipients in the mid-1930s appeared the following sticker:

> WANTED—Jobs for qualified workmen.
> EMPLOYERS—Call your nearest Employment Office
> when help is wanted.
> DEPARTMENT OF LABOR
> ONTARIO

AO, Hepburn Papers, box 203. There was no campaign to find work for poor, unemployed women.

73 According to a report of the Factory Inspection Branch of the provincial department of labour: '[In] 1930 . . . only 8 children under 14 years of age were found in factories, shops, etc. and dismissed and that only 317 adolescents between 14 and 16 years were employed. During the year 1933, only 2 children under 14 years had to be dismissed and only ten between the ages of 14 and 16 were found to be regularly employed.' AO, RG 7, series 7–12–0–210, 'Notes re: Child Labour in Ontario, March 20, 1934'.

74 One mother complained to the premier that her daughter, who was older than sixteen, was 'hired out' but did not earn enough to help the family. AO, Henry Papers, box 162, series 03–08–0–354, 'Letter from Mrs. Ethel Doern to Premier, May 2, 1933'.

75 In Peterborough County, many mothers complained that their children would have found jobs if they lived in town, but none were available in rural areas. Lang Pioneer Village [LPV], Keene, Ontario, Peterborough County Local Mothers' Allowance Board Minutes, 1921–46.

76 'Annual Report of the Minister of Public Welfare, Fiscal Year 1935–36', 14.

77 AO, Henry Papers, box 153, series 03–08–0–241, 'Letter from Miss Amie G. Meighen to Premier Henry, August 26, 1932'.

78 'Report of the Mothers' Allowance Commission, 1930–31', *Ontario Sessional Papers* LXIV, Part IV (1932):44.

79 Other than tuberculosis, which was noted, it is impossible to explore whether certain types of incapacitation cases were more eligible than others and which were increasingly eligible during the 1930s since the annual reports changed the categories for reporting different types of incapacitation throughout the decade.

80 'Second Annual Report of the Minister of Public Welfare, Fiscal Year 1931–32', 55; 'Report of the Minister of Public Welfare, Fiscal Year 1935–36', 65. Percentages were not kept after the 1935–6 report.

81 During 1936–7 Dr Faulkner replaced H. Bentley as chairman. Bentley remained on the commission as commissioner. 'Report of the Minister of Public Welfare, 1936–37', 15.

82 ECL, box 55, medical form for one patient, 1929.

83 Remarks on the application form of one applicant stated: 'I read in the "Report of the Minister of Public Welfare 1937–38" in the Medical Officer's Report, in the last paragraph on Page 15 that "Cases where a man is admitted to hospital because of addition to alcohol are not considered eligible".' AO, F 1741–30, box 3, 'Application Form, October 1939'.

84 'Fourth Annual Report of the Minister of Public Welfare, 1933–34', *Ontario Sessional Papers* LXVII, Part IV (1935):48.

85 In one case, a family with an incapacitated breadwinner applied in July 1937 and was told that the man could not be considered totally incapacitated even though he had not been examined by the provincial medical officer. The local board repeatedly appealed to the medical officer to examine this case. Finally, in March 1940 the family was granted the allowance. AO, F 1741–30, box 3, application and supporting documents beginning July 1937.

86 AO, F 1741–30, box 3, 'Letter from City Clerk, St. Catharines to Mr. Walter Sheppard, Reeve, Niagara Township, September 19, 1938'.

87 DBW, box 160, 'Letter from Provincial Commission to City Clerk, February 19, 1937'.

88 DBW, Mothers' Allowance Case Files, London, 'Letter from Reverend J.A. Cook to Federation of Catholic Charities, Montreal, April 5, 1933'.

89 DBW, Mothers' Allowance Case Files, London, 'Letter from City Clerk to Reverend J.A. Cook, May 5, 1933'.

90 ECL, Mothers' Allowance Case Files, Elgin County, 'Medical Certificate by Provincial Medical Examiner, March 27, 1941'; the provincial commission declares the case ineligible in its written correspondence of 5 June 1939, 3 October 1939, 19 February 1940, 27 January 1941, 25 August 1941, and 6 January 1944. ECL, Mothers' Allowance Case Files, Elgin County.

91 AO, RG 29, series 74, box 9, file 1.9, 'The Tuberculosis Problem in Ontario as of 1937', 2–4.

92 The percentage of OMA recipients with tuberculosis was 13 per cent during the early 1930s; 20 per cent in 1934–5; 24 per cent of new cases and 32 per cent of reinstated cases in 1935–6. 'Report of the Department of Public Welfare, 1930–31', 45; 'Report of the Department of Public Welfare,

1932–33', 65; 'Report of the Department of Public Welfare, 1934–35', 61; and 'Report of the Department of Public Welfare, 1935–36', 41.

93 DBW, Mothers' Allowance Case Files, London, Ontario, 'Investigator's Report, September 29, 1933'.

94 DBW, Mothers' Allowance Case Files, London, Ontario, 'Letter from the Provincial Commission to the Local Board, June 30, 1933'.

95 ECL, Mothers' Allowance Case Files, Elgin County, 'Letter from Chief Investigator to Mrs. Spratt, April 11, 1933'.

96 ECL, Mothers' Allowance Case Files, Elgin County, 'Letter from Provincial Commission, April 26, 1940'.

97 There were many who believed that desertion was a social evil. The Canadian Council on Social Development opposed the inclusion of deserted mothers in the allowance, arguing that 95 per cent of these women were incapable of providing a decent home life for their children. 'Report of the Provincial Welfare Department, 1930–31', 10; and NA, MG 28, I–10, vol. 10, file 52, 'Some Underlying Principles of Mothers' Allowances', 2.

98 This figure was calculated from the annual reports regarding new applications received, granted, or found ineligible. 'Second Annual Report of the Minister of Public Welfare, 1931–32', 55; 'Fourth Annual Report of the Minister of Public Welfare and Municipal Affairs, 1933–34', 72; 'Report of the Minister of Public Welfare, 1934–35', 9; 'Report of the Minister of Public Welfare, 1935–36', 65; 'Report of the Minister of Public Welfare, 1938–39', 52.

99 DBW, Mothers' Allowance Case Files, London, Ontario, 'Letter from Investigator to Local Mothers' Allowance Board, August 27, 1940'.

100 One mother wrote the premier asking for an allowance and stated that she was a proper candidate as 'their [sic] is neither whisky nor tobacco comes into our home in any shape or form'. AO, Henry Papers, box 153, series 03–08–0–241, 'Letter to Premier Henry, February 24, 1932'.

101 'An Act to Amend the Mothers' Allowances Act', *Statutes of Ontario*, First Session of the 19th Legislature of Ontario, 1935, Ch. 42, 207.

102 ECL, Mothers' Allowance Case Files, Elgin County, sworn declaration from the man who hired the husband on board the ship, 26 July 1939, and declaration from the deserted wife, 13 June 1937.

103 AO, RG 49, reel #55, Press Clippings, 1936, 'Family Is in Direct Need, Red Tape Bars Allowance: Can't Get Government Help Because Father's Whereabouts Is Known: Star Fund Can Aid', *Toronto Daily Star*, 6 June 1936.

104 AO, RG 29, series 74, box 1, file 1.5, 'Unemployment Relief Branch, Activities in Public Assistance, 1934'.

105 AO, RG 29, series 74, box 9, 'Memorandum to Relief Inspectors and District Administrators from E.A. Horton, Deputy Minister, January 3, 1939', 2–4.

106 DBW, box 159, 'Letter from Acting Relief Inspector to City Clerk, May 22, 1931'.

107 DBW, box 159, 'Letter from Children's Aid Society to City Clerk, July 10, 1931'.

108 DBW, box 160, investigator's remarks on application form, dated 1936.

109 Given that there was very little immigration during the Depression era, this census figure for 1931 is the most accurate statistic available to reflect the pop-

ulation for the decade. *Seventh Census of Canada, 1931*, vol. 2 (Ottawa: King's Printer, 1933):295.

110 AO, Henry Papers, box 142, series 03–08–0–120, 'Letter from Mrs. Caroline Truro, October 30, 1931'.

CHAPTER 5

1 See Veronica Strong-Boag, 'Home Dreams: Women and the Suburban Experience in Canada, 1945–60', *Canadian Historical Review* LXXII, no. 4 (1991):471–504; Franca Iacovetta, *Such a Hard-working People* (Kingston: McGill-Queen's University Press, 1992); Ruth Roach Pierson, *'They're Still Women After All': The Second World War and Canadian Womanhood* (Toronto: McClelland and Stewart, 1986); and Beth Light and Ruth Pierson, eds, *No Easy Road: Women in Canada, 1920s to 1960s* (Toronto: New Hogtown Press, 1990); and more recently: Mary Louise Adams, *The Trouble With Normal: Postwar Youth and the Construction of Heterosexuality* (Toronto: University of Toronto Press, 1997); Karen Dubinsky, 'Sex, Class and the Postwar Honeymoon', unpublished paper presented at the Canadian Sociology and Anthropology Association, Ottawa, 1993; Julie Guard, 'Fair Play or Fair Pay? Gender Relations, Class Consciousness, and Union Solidarity in the Canadian UE', *Labour/Le Travail* 37 (Spring 1996):149–77; and Douglas Owram, *Born at the Right Time: A History of the Baby-Boom Generation* (Toronto: University of Toronto Press, 1976).

2 Wilfred Eggleston, 'Canada at the End of the War', *Queen's Quarterly* 12 (1945):360, as cited in Dennis Guest, *The Emergence of Social Security in Canada* (Vancouver: University of British Columbia, 1980):104.

3 For a detailed discussion of these reports, see Annalee Golz, 'Family Matters: The "Canadian Family" and the State in the Post–World War II Period', *Left History* 1, no. 2 (1993); Donald Smiley, ed., *The Rowell-Sirois Report*, Book 1 (Toronto: Macmillan, 1963); Guest, *The Emergence of Social Security*, 104–15; Keith Banting, *The Welfare State and Canadian Federalism* (Kingston: McGill-Queen's University Press, 1982):83–107; and Jane Ursel, *Private Lives, Public Policy: 100 Years of State Intervention in the Family* (Toronto: Women's Press, 1992):175–227.

4 For a more detailed discussion of the influence of Harry Cassidy, see James Struthers, *The Limits of Affluence: Welfare in Ontario, 1920–1970* (Toronto: University of Toronto Press, 1994):127–9.

5 Guest, *The Emergence of Social Security*, 117–21.

6 Ibid., 107.

7 For a more thorough discussion regarding family allowances, see Brigitte Kitchen, 'The Introduction of Family Allowances', in *The 'Benevolent' State: The Growth of Welfare in Canada*, edited by Allan Moscovitch and Jim Albert (Toronto: Garamond Press, 1987):222–41; and Dominique Jean, 'Family Allowances and Family Autonomy: Quebec Families Encounter the Welfare State, 1945–1955', in *Canadian Family History: Selected Readings*, edited by Bettina Bradbury (Mississauga: Copp Clark, 1992):401–37.

8 The Blind Persons Act (1951) and the Disabled Persons Act (1954). Guest, *The Emergence of Social Security*, 145.

9 This section merely details how these federal welfare proposals and policies affected Ontario Mothers' Allowance. For a more complete understanding of the emergence of these federal welfare programs, see Harry Cassidy, *Social Security and Reconstruction in Canada* (Toronto: Ryerson Press, 1948); J.L. Granatstein, *Canada's War: The Politics of the Mackenzie King Government, 1939–1945* (Toronto: Oxford University Press, 1975); Leonard C. Marsh, *Report on Social Security for Canada* (Toronto: University of Toronto Press, 1975); Charlotte Whitton, *The Dawn of Ampler Life* (Toronto: Macmillan, 1943); Dennis Guest, 'World War II and the Welfare State in Canada', in Moscovitch and Albert, eds, *The 'Benevolent' State* , 205–21; Donald Smiley, 'The Rowell-Sirois Report, Provincial Autonomy and Post-War Canadian Federalism', in *Canadian Federalism: Myth or Reality*, edited by J. Peter Meekison (Toronto: Methuen, 1968); Ursel, *Private Lives*, 175–282. For family allowances, see Kitchen, 'The Introduction of Family Allowances', 222–41; and Golz, 'Family Matters'. For unemployment insurance, see James Struthers, *No Fault of Their Own: Unemployment and the Canadian Welfare State, 1914–1941* (Toronto: University of Toronto Press, 1983):Ch. 6.

10 Ursel carefully studies this transition from direct control over the family and women's labour to an indirect, almost benevolent approach. While she argues that this was a trend experienced by both the federal and provincial states, I would argue that at least in the case of Ontario Mothers' Allowance, the provincial government did not relinquish direct intervention into the homes of its poorer citizens. Ursel, *Private Lives*, 175–282.

11 'Annual Report of the Ontario Department of Public Welfare, 1943–44', 16.

12 'Annual Report of the Ontario Department of Public Welfare, 1940–41', and 'Annual Report of the Ontario Department of Public Welfare, 1941–42'.

13 This letter also cites a number of other single mothers in Middlesex County who were forced to seek paid employment because the OMA rate was too low to live on. Archives of Ontario [AO], Hepburn Papers, RG 3, box 331, Welfare-Mothers' Allowances 1941, 'Letter from Helen Lordan, St. Thomas to Bob Gaskin, August 25, 1942'.

14 Quotation cited in Jonathan Manthorpe, *The Power and the Tories: Ontario Politics—1943 to the Present* (Toronto: Macmillan, 1974):20. Also see Neil McKenty, *Mitch Hepburn* (Toronto: McClelland and Stewart, 1967):249.

15 Manthorpe, *The Power and the Tories*, 32.

16 Ibid., 31; and Robert J. Williams, 'The Social Policy Field', in *The Government and Politics of Ontario*, 4th edn, edited by Graham White (Toronto: Nelson, 1990):339.

17 Struthers, *The Limits of Affluence*, 119.

18 AO, Lincoln County Old Age Pension and Mothers' Allowance Records, F 1741–30, box 3, 'Application Form, January 1943'.

19 AO, Hepburn Papers, box 216, 'Letter from Council of the City of London, Ontario, Endorsed by the St. Thomas City Council, to Hon. Mitchell Hepburn, July 11, 1941'.

20 National Archives [NA], Canadian Council on Social Development, MG 28 I–10, vol. 63, file 497, quote cited in 'Mothers' Allowances', Editorial, *Ottawa Citizen*, 1 November 1941. Also see 'Changes Are Sought in Mothers' Allowances', *Ottawa Citizen*, 1 November 1941.

21 NA, MG 28, I–25, vol. 79, file 19: Resolutions and Correspondence, 1940–41, 'Ontario Bill Would Increase Amount Going to Widows: Letters from Women's Groups Urging Passage of Measure', newspaper and date not cited.

22 NA, MG 28, I–10, vol. 63, file 497, 'Mothers' Allowances', Editorial, *Ottawa Citizen*, 1 November 1941.

23 AO, Hepburn Papers, box 331, 'Letter from Alexander Macdonald to Premier Hepburn, September 9, 1942'.

24 AO, Hepburn Papers, box 218, 'Letter from Toronto Municipal Employees' Association, Local 79, to Hon. Gordon D. Conant, December 7, 1942'.

25 City of London Records and Retention Room [LRR], Ontario Mothers' Pensions Commission, Local Board Minutes, 'Meeting, August 28, 1942'.

26 AO, Legislative Offices, RG 49, MS 755, reel #92, 'The "Increase" in Mothers' Allowances', Editorial, *Toronto Daily Star*, 8 February 1946.

27 AO, MS 728, Ministry of Community and Social Services, Minister's Correspondence, 1937–49, reel #1, microdex #3, 'Brief Submitted to R.P. Vivian, Minister of Health and Public Welfare by Fred Conboy, Mayor of Toronto, September 29, 1943', cited in Struthers, *The Limits of Affluence*, footnote #11, 121; and AO, RG 29–01, box 62, file #2435, Mothers' Allowance Commission, 'Budget for a Mother and Three Children over 13 Years of Age, January 22, 1943', cited in Struthers, *The Limits of Affluence*, footnote #13, 121.

28 The *Toronto Daily Star* complained that, 'The attitude in the department [of public welfare] we are told has been that this increase should be allowed to as few families as possible and supervisors were advised not to recommend it on a broad scale. . . . In other words, the increase is not provided—as we think was the impression created by the [1943 election] promise—as a right to Mothers' Allowance families generally.' AO, RG 49, MS-755, reel #92, 'The "Increase" in Mothers' Allowances', Editorial, *Toronto Daily Star*, 8 February 1946.

29 In 1954 the provincial mothers' allowance rates across the country were as follows:

Province	Rate for Mother with One Child
Newfoundland	$25.00
PEI	$25.00
Nova Scotia	No set maximum
New Brunswick	$35.00
Quebec	$40.00 (for population of 5,000 or more)
Ontario	$50.00
Manitoba	$51.00
Saskatchewan	$35.00
Alberta	$50.00
BC	$69.50

Note: Average (not including Nova Scotia): $42.28

30 Clifford J. Williams, *Decades of Service: A History of the Ontario Ministry of Community and Social Services, 1930–1980* (Toronto: The Ministry of Community and Social Services, 1984):53 and 71.

31 Manthorpe, *The Power and the Tories*, 44.

32 During this postwar period more than 2 million immigrants arrived in Canada. These 'New Canadians' accounted for two-thirds of the labour force growth in the early 1950s and another one-third during the less prosperous latter half of the decade. Bryan Palmer, *Working-Class Experience: The Rise and Reconstitution of Canadian Labour, 1800–1980* (Toronto: Butterworths, 1983):255–6.

33 AO, RG 49, MS 755, reel #119, 1949. Quote cited in 'They Served Faithfully', Editorial, *Stratford Beacon-Herald*, 18 January 1949. Regarding the dissolution of the local boards, see AO, RG 49, MS 755, reel #119, 'Pension Board Has Been Discontinued', *Pembroke Bulletin*, 17 January 1949; 'New Welfare Unit to Be Formed Here', *Oshawa Daily Times-Gazette*, 18 January 1949; and 'Old Age Pensions Boards Disbanded', *Tweed News*, 3 February 1949.

34 Metro Toronto Records and Archives [MTRA], Commission of Public Welfare for Toronto, RG 5.1, Correspondence Subject Files, box 43, file 47A, 'Letter from Minister of Public Welfare to Mothers' Allowance Toronto Board', 10 December 1941.

35 Williams, *Decades of Service*, 52.

36 'Annual Report of the Ontario Department of Public Welfare, 1952–53', 9–11, and 'Annual Report of the Ontario Department of Public Welfare, 1953–54', 24.

37 These areas were districts of Essex, Kent, and Lambton counties; districts of Elgin, Middlesex, Norfolk, and Oxford counties; districts of Brant, Haldimand, Lincoln, Welland, and Wentworth counties; districts of Bruce, Huron, and Perth counties; districts of Halton, Peel, Waterloo, and Wellington counties; districts of Dufferin, Grey, and Simcoe counties; districts of Durham, Haliburton, Ontario, Peterborough, and Victoria counties; districts of Hastings, Lennox and Addington, and Northumberland counties; districts of Dundas, Frontenac, Leeds, and Grenville counties; districts of Glengarry, Prescott, Russell, and Stormont counties; District of York; districts of Carleton, Lanark, and Renfrew counties; districts of Nipissing, Parry Sound, and Muskoka; districts of Sudbury and Manitoulin Island; districts of Cochrane and Temiskaming; District of Algoma; District of Thunder Bay, Kenora, and Rainy River. 'Annual Report of the Ontario Department of Public Welfare, 1952–53', 31–2.

38 'Annual Report of the Ontario Department of Public Welfare, 1948–49', 24.

39 Old age assistance required eighty days and disabled persons' allowances fifty days. 'Annual Report of the Ontario Department of Public Welfare, 1954–55', 5.

40 '*Reasoning* will follow the various steps in [new] paper-work processing', the annual report explained [my emphasis]. Ibid., 5.

41 'Annual Report of the Ontario Department of Public Welfare, 1955–56', 45.

42 'Annual Report of the Ontario Department of Public Welfare, 1953–54', 7.

43 The first provincial conference on social welfare was held in June 1947. Ontario Department of Public Welfare, 'Annual Report, Fiscal Year 1955–56', 121; and AO, Ministry of Community and Social Services, RG 29, series 74, box 2, file 2.3, 'The Ontario Council on Social Welfare, [address written by] Mr. James Cassidy, Secretary to the [Provincial] Prime Minister', 13 June 1947.

44 The two schools of social work in Ontario were at St Patrick's College in Ottawa and the University of Toronto. 'Annual Report of the Ontario Department of Public Welfare, 1961–62', 18; AO, Ministry of Community and Social Services, RG 29, series 74, box 2, file 2.7, 'Province Sets Up Welfare Bursaries', *London Free Press*, 31 May 1951; and 'Annual Report of the Ontario Department of Public Welfare, 1961–62', 19.

45 'Annual Report of the Ontario Department of Public Welfare, 1960–61', 2–3.

46 Ibid., 3.

47 'Annual Report of the Ontario Department of Public Welfare, 1955–56', 2.

48 Franca Iacovetta studies one private welfare agency's attempts to Canadianize non-British immigrants. Franca Iacovetta, 'Making "New Canadians": Social Workers, Women and the Reshaping of Immigrant Families', in *Gender Conflicts: New Essays in Women's History*, edited by Franca Iacovetta and Mariane Valverde (Toronto: University of Toronto Press, 1992):261–303, quotation cited on p. 270.

49 MTRA, RG 5.1, series 12.2, 'Interview with Judge Kenneth M. Langdon' by Lloyd M. Lockhart, *Chatelaine* (June 1964).

50 'The Mothers' and Dependent Children's Allowances Act, 1957', *Statutes of Ontario*, Fourth Session of the 26th Legislature of Ontario, Ch. 73, p. 572, section 2, clause (a), subclause (vi). The resolution at the Northwestern Ontario Municipal Association conference read: '7. That the Minister of Welfare be urged to introduce legislation to amend the Mothers' Allowance Act to permit of assistance to children of persons committed to extended terms of imprisonment; thereby removing the persecution of innocent children.' AO, RG 49, MS 755, reel #119, 'Municipal Association Approves 13 Resolutions at Recent Convention', *Fort Frances Times*, 29 October 1949.

51 AO, RG 29, series 74, box 3, file 3.2, Dorothy Howarth, 'Is Law Being Tricked on "Babies for Sale"?' *Toronto Telegram*, 24 November 1956.

52 NA, Charlotte Whitton Papers, MG 30, E 256, vol. 19, 'The Freedom of Mankind, 1940–41'.

53 AO, RG 3, box 333, 'Mothers' Allowances', Editorial, *News*, n.d.; 'On Illegitimacy', *Fort Erie Times-Review*, 28 January 1943; 'Unmarried Mother Victim of Legalism', *Globe and Mail*, 13 February 1943; 'Help Is Refused to Unwed Mother', *Globe and Mail*, 26 January 1943; 'Letter to the Editor from Mrs. A Nelson, R.N.', *Fort Erie Times-Review*, 28 January 1943; 'Letter from L.B.D. to Judge Plett, February 1, 1943', *Fort Erie Times-Review;* and 'Letter from G.D. Conant to John Flett, January 16, 1942', *Fort Erie Times-Review*.

54 My thanks to Mariana Valverde for introducing me to this study. Toronto Welfare Council, *A Study of the Adjustment of Children of Unmarried Mothers* (1943):1–32, esp. 11, 13, and 24.

55 For an excellent discussion of the transformation in the treatment of unwed mothers, see Rickie Solinger, *Wake Up Little Susie: Single Pregnancy and Race Before Roe v. Wade* (New York: Routledge, 1992):14–18 and Ch. 3. AO, RG 29, series 74, box 3, file 3.2, Dorothy Howarth, 'Unhappy Homes Behind Many Unwed Mothers', *Toronto Telegram*, 19 November 1956; and 'Defiantly Tried to Be Bad—Succeeded, Too', *Toronto Telegram*, 20 November 1956.

56 'Annual Report of the Ontario Department of Public Welfare, 1955–56', 42.

57 AO, Ministry of Labour, RG 7, series VII–1, Research Branch, Senior Investigator, General Files, box 4, file: Labour Legislation, 1922–1940, 'Legislative Programme Submitted to the Ontario Government by the Trades and Labour Congress of Canada', 17 January 1940.

58 In 1951 this group had to wait one year to apply for the allowance; in 1955 this requirement was waived for long-time Ontario residents who were temporarily outside the province. 'Annual Report of the Ontario Department of Public Welfare, 1951–52', 11.

59 'Annual Report of the Ontario Department of Public Welfare, 1962–63', 19.

60 There were a few separation cases reported in the case files, including one in AO, F 1741–30, box 3, 'Application Form, May 1948'.

61 AO, F 1741–30, box 3, 'Mothers' Allowance Application Form, December 1939'; and 'Decision from Ontario Mothers' Allowance, March 1940'.

62 'Annual Report of the Ontario Department of Public Welfare, 1959–60', 7.

63 Ibid., 20.

64 AO, RG 49, MS 755, reel #109, 'Demand Aid—When Wed', *Globe and Mail*, 25 February 1948.

65 NA, MG 28, I–10, vol. 63, file 497, 'Letter from Bessie Touzel, Executive Secretary, the Welfare Council of Toronto and District, to the Hon. Harold J. Kirby, Minister of Health and Welfare, Ontario, March 31, 1943'.

66 AO, RG 29, series 74, box 2, file 2.7, 'Community Welfare Council of Ontario', 21 April 1951.

67 'Annual Report of the Ontario Department of Public Welfare, 1957–58', 16, and 'Annual Report of the Ontario Department of Public Welfare, 1960–61', 10.

68 Williams, *Decades of Service*, 79.

69 Ibid.

70 With regard to the free medical service, see 'Annual Report of the Ontario Department of Public Welfare, 1941–42', *Ontario Sessional Papers* LXXV, Part III (1943):6. For free dental care, the province paid a monthly premium to the Royal College of Dental Surgeons of Ontario for each eligible child. This service was only available to children of OMA recipients; the single mothers themselves and other provincial welfare recipients were not eligible. See 'Annual Report of the Ontario Department of Public Welfare, 1957–58', 5.

71 AO, RG 29, series 74, box 2, file 2.5, 'Minister Praises Law Society', *Globe and Mail*, 18 November 1950; and 'Legal Aid Plan', *Sudbury Daily Star*, 12 November 1950.

72 According to the census figures, women's labour force participation in Canada was 17.7 per cent in 1921, 19.4 per cent in 1931, 22.9 per cent in 1941, 24.4 per cent in 1951, and 29.3 per cent in 1961. Light and Pierson, eds, *No Easy Road*, 252.

73 'Annual Report of the Ontario Department of Public Welfare, 1955–56', 44.

74 'Annual Report of the Ontario Department of Public Welfare, 1943–44', 16.

75 'Annual Report of the Ontario Department of Public Welfare, 1950–51', 10 and 12; and 'Annual Report of the Ontario Department of Public Welfare, 1962–63', 19.

76 Elaine May's work on postwar American families has made an enormous contribution to our understanding of this period. She demonstrates a strong relationship between political and familial values, arguing that the political ideology of the period provoked a desire for domestic security within the family home. Elaine Tyler May, *Homeward Bound: American Families in the Cold War Era* (New York: Basic Books, 1988):16–36.

77 'Annual Report of the Ontario Department of Public Welfare, 1955–56', 44.

78 Until 1948 the act had stipulated that an applicant must be 'a fit and proper person'. This wording was replaced with the qualification that she must be 'a suitable person to receive an allowance'. See 'An Act to Amend the Mothers' Allowances Act', *Statutes of Ontario*, Third Session of the 23rd Legislature of Ontario, 1951, Ch. 52, p. 290, section 2, clause (1), subclause (g); and 'The Mothers' and Dependent Children's Allowances Act', *Statutes of Ontario*, Fourth Session of the 26th Legislature, 1957, Ch. 73, p. 573, section 2, clause (1), subclause (x).

79 'Annual Report of the Ontario Department of Public Welfare, 1939–40', 28.

80 'Annual Report of the Ontario Department of Public Welfare, 1942–43', 21.

81 The average percentages of successful applicants for this period are as follows:

1939–40	50%
1941–2	57%
1942–3	51%
1943–4	59%
1944–5	54%
1945–6	49%
1946–7	51%
1953–4	47%
1954–5	61%
1955–6	61%
1956–7	58%
1957–8	61%
1958–9	60%

Statistics are not available for 1940–1, 1947–53, and after 1959. 'Annual Reports of the Ontario Department of Public Welfare, 1939–1959'.

82 'Annual Report of the Ontario Department of Public Welfare, 1954–55', 3–4. 'Multi-problem family' discussed in 'Annual Report of the Ontario Department of Public Welfare, 1961–62', 2.

83 'Annual Report of the Ontario Department of Public Welfare, 1954–55', 6.

84 Ibid., 10.

85 'Annual Report of the Ontario Department of Public Welfare, 1961–62', 5.

86 Gordon's study of family violence in Boston, Mass., also found that postwar social work emphasis on Freudian psychology 'resulted in treatment that de-emphasized material aid in favor of therapy. . . .' Linda Gordon, *Heroes of Their Own Lives: The Politics and History of Family Violence, Boston 1880–1960* (New York: Penguin Books, 1988):164. For a discussion of the end of poverty, see 'Annual Report of the Ontario Department of Public Welfare, 1954–55', 10.

87 For a more detailed discussion of sexuality in war and postwar Canada, see Adams, *The Trouble With Normal*; Dubinsky, 'Sex, Class and the Postwar Honeymoon'; Gary Kinsman, '"Character Weaknesses" and "Fruit Machines": Towards an Analysis of the Social Organization of the Anti-Homosexual Purge Campaign in the Canadian Civil Service', *Labour/Le Travail* 35 (Spring 1995):133–62; and Mariana Valverde, '"Building Anti-Delinquent Communities": Youth, Gender and Morality in the Post-War City', in *A Diversity of Women: Ontario, 1945–1980*, edited by Joy Parr (Toronto: University of Toronto Press, 1995).

88 'Annual Report of the Ontario Department of Public Welfare, 1953–54', 23–4.

89 'Annual Report of the Ontario Department of Public Welfare, 1949–50', 15.

90 AO, RG 29, series 74, box 2, file 2.7, 'Social Services Centralization Promotes Welfare State', *Stratford Beacon Herald*, 6 June 1951.

91 AO, RG 29, series 74, box 2, file 2.5, 'Deserted Families: Our Secret Shame', *Saturday Night*, 1 December 1951; AO, RG 29, series 74, box 3, file 3.7, 'Spouse Hunt', *Brantford Examiner*, 1 April 1961; AO, RG 49, 'Runaway Husbands Leave Behind Them Major Social Problem', *Toronto Telegram*, 15 February 1956.

92 AO, RG 49, reel #123, Charlotte Whitton, 'A Woman on the Line', *Guelph Mercury*, 21 March 1950.

93 AO, RG 29, series 74, box 2, file 2.5, 'Deserted Families: Our Secret Shame', *Saturday Night*, 1 December 1951.

94 AO, RG 49, reel #119, 'Town Seeks 30 Miners Left Wives', *Toronto Telegram*, 12 December 1949.

95 Ibid.

96 AO, RG 49, reel #119, 'Deserted Wives and Children', Editorial, *The Windsor Star* [reprinted in *Timmins Daily Press*], 19 December 1949.

97 Both Dubinsky's study of sexual crime and Forestell's case-study of Timmins have explored the relationship between region and moral reputation with regard to northern Ontario. Karen Dubinsky, *Improper Advances: Rape and Heterosexual Misconduct in Ontario, 1880–1929* (Chicago: University of Chicago Press, 1993):Ch. 6; and Nancy Forestell, 'All That Glitters Is Not Gold: The Gendered Dimensions of Work, Family and Community Life in the Northern Ontario Goldmining Town of Timmins, 1909–1950', thesis, Department of History, Ontario Institute for Studies in Education, 1993. For the Timmins case, see AO, RG 49, reel #119, 'Town Seeks 30 Miners Left Wives', *Toronto Telegram*, 12 December 1949; 'Deserted Wives and Children', Editorial, *Timmins Daily Press*, 19 December 1949; 'Desertion Habit Province Wide Says Goodfellow', *Timmins Daily Press*, 16 December 1949; and 'Toronto Reports 419 Desertions', *Toronto Telegram*, 12 December 1949.

98 *Ontario Legislature Debates*, 14 April 1964, Kenneth Bryden, Woodbine, MPP.

99 NA, MG 28, I–25, vol. 92, file 3, Provincial Councils of Women: Reports, Correspondence, 1950–51, 'Resolution from West Algoma to the Ontario Provincial Council of Women, Semi-Annual Meeting, May 29–30, 1951'.

100 AO, RG 29, series 74, box 3, file 3.7, 'Spouse-Hunt', *Brantford Examiner*, 1 April 1961.

101 For further information on the long association of James S. Band with public welfare, see Williams, *Decades of Service*, 69–70.

102 'Annual Report of the Ontario Department of Public Welfare, 1959–60', 6–7.

103 'Annual Report of the Ontario Department of Public Welfare, 1958–59', 18.

104 'Annual Report of the Ontario Department of Public Welfare, 1959–60', 20.

105 MTRA, RG 5.1, series 12.1, Investigations—Special Investigation Unit, December 1960—December 1963.

106 AO, RG 49, reel #240, 'Husbands Tracked Down', *Globe and Mail*, 22 January 1964.

107 AO, RG 49, reel #240, 'Seek Separation Statistics', *Toronto Telegram*, 25 March 1964. For a more detailed discussion regarding societal concerns about desertion and divorce, see James Snell, *In the Shadow of the Law: Divorce in Canada, 1900–1939* (Toronto: University of Toronto Press, 1991); and Dorothy Chunn, *From Punishment to Doing Good: Family Courts and Socialized Justice in Ontario, 1880–1940* (Toronto: University of Toronto Press, 1992).

108 'Annual Report of the Ontario Department of Public Welfare, 1955–56', 43.

109 Ontario Legislature Debates, 11 March 1958, Ross Mackenzie Whicher, MPP, Bruce County.

110 AO, RG 29, series 74, box 3, file 3.2, 'Mothers Are Not Unhappy', *Toronto Telegram*, 22 November 1956.

111 AO, RG 29, series 74, box 3, file 3.5—1959, 'Never Fared So Well as on Welfare', *The Glengarry News*, 28 October 1959.

112 AO, RG 29, series 74, box 3, file 3.2, Dorothy Howarth, 'Is Law Being Tricked on "Babies For Sale"?' *Toronto Telegram*, 24 November 1956.

113 AO, RG 29, series 74, box 3, file 3.6, 'Illegitimacy a World Low in Ontario', *Toronto Telegram*, 3 February 1960.

114 'Annual Report of the Ontario Department of Public Welfare, 1943–44', 16.

115 Elgin County Library [ECL], boxes 42 and 55, 'Letter from Mrs. Isabelle T. Watson to Clerk, St. Thomas, January 24, 1940 and August 19, 1940'.

116 AO, RG 3, box 213, 'Resolution from the Municipal Corporation of the Town of Kenora to Premier Hepburn, June 11, 1940'.

117 AO, F 1741–30, box 3, Application Form, February 1937.

118 AO, F 1741–30, box 3, 'Letter from Neighbour to Mrs. Montgomery, OMA, February 13, 1941'.

119 AO, F 1741–30, box 3, 'Letter from Neighbour to Mrs. Montgomery, OMA, March 7, 1941'.

120 AO, F 1741–30, box 3, OMA letter, 3 July 1941.

121 AO, F 1741–30, box 3, 'Letter from Local Board to Provincial Commission, December 17, 1940'.

122 'Annual Report of the Ontario Department of Public Welfare, 1953–54', 23.

123 'Annual Report of the Ontario Department of Public Welfare, 1960–61', 21.

124 'Annual Report of the Ontario Department of Public Welfare, 1956–57', 25.

125 'Annual Report of the Ontario Department of Public Welfare, 1960–61', 8.

126 'Annual Report of the Ontario Department of Public Welfare, 1957–58', 3 and 36.

CHAPTER 6

1 Archives of Ontario [AO], Legislative Offices, RG 49, reel #260, 'Ottawa $25 Million to Aid 200,000 needy', *Toronto Daily Star*, 7 April 1965.

2 Janine Brodie, 'New State Forms, New Political Spaces', in *States vs. Markets: the limits of globalization*, edited by Robert Boyer and Daniel Drache (London: Routledge, 1996):386.

3 Ramesh Mishra, 'The Welfare of Nations', in Boyer and Drache, eds, *States vs. Markets*, 319.

4 Ian Adams, William Cameron, Brian Hill, and Peter Penz, eds, *The 'Real' Poverty Report* (Edmonton: Hurtig Ltd, 1971):171.

5 Ibid.

6 John Robarts won a majority government in the 1967 election. The results were: Progressive Conservatives (sixty-nine seats), Liberals (twenty-eight seats), New Democratic Party (twenty seats). William Davis was even more successful during the 1971 election: Progressive Conservatives (seventy-eight seats), Liberals (twenty seats), NDP (nineteen seats). Claire Hoy, *Bill Davis* (Toronto: Methuen, 1985):44 and 92–4.

7 Clifford Williams, *Decades of Service: A History of the Ontario Ministry of Community and Social Services, 1930–1980* (Toronto: Ministry of Community and Social Services, 1984):72.

8 Other programs included under FBA were unemployment assistance, old age assistance, blind persons' allowances, and disabled persons' allowances. 'An Act to Provide Benefits to Persons and Families in Need' [The Family Benefits Act, 1966], *Statutes of Ontario*, Ch. 54, 203–11.

9 The FBA stipulated that: 'Any applicant or recipient may request a hearing and review by the board of review of a decision, order or directive of the Director affecting the applicant or recipient, as the case may be.' The board of review has the power to direct the director and the board's decision is final. Initially called the Board of Review, this was renamed the Social Assistance Review Board in 1974. 'An Act to Amend the Family Benefits Act, 1974', *Statutes of Ontario*, Ch. 98, p. 723, section 1, clause (da); section 11, clause (2), (3), and (4), with quote from clause (2). With regard to morality, there was a brief omission of moral criteria in the 1948 OMA amendments, but this was reinstated by 1951 (see Chapter 4 for details).

10 'Annual Reports of Community and Social Services Ministry, 1965–66 to 1990–91'.

11 'FBA, 1966', *Statutes of Ontario*, Ch. 54, section 1, clause (e), subclause (i), (ii), and quote from (iii).

12 Ibid., Ch. 54, section 7, clause (1).

13 According to census statistics, widows maintained a similar percentage of the provincial population during this decade, whereas the number of unwed mothers as heads of households doubled and the number of divorced women as heads of households quadrupled. Please note that these statistics only indi-cate who is head of the household; they do not indicate the presence or absence of children.

Head of Household	1966	1976
Widowed women	167,382 (8.9%)	236,930 (8.9%)
Unwed women	62,137 (3.3%)	135,035 (5.1%)
Divorced women	10,609 (.5%)	53,655 (2%)

Source: Census of Canada, 1966, vol. II, Table 37; (1976), Table 93–809.

14 Williams, Decades of Service, 72.

15 Ibid., 102.

16 Keith G. Banting, The Welfare State and Canadian Federalism, 2nd edn (Kingston: McGill-Queen's University Press, 1987):Table 30, 114–15.

17 Ontario Legislature Debates, 28 June 1966, Stephen Lewis, 5365.

18 Ibid., Louis Cecile, 5365.

19 Metropolitan Toronto Records and Archives [MTRA], Investigation by the Special Investigations Unit, Provincial, RG 5.1, series 12.1, January 1969—December 1970, case: Mrs Susan Billings.

20 In 1971 the provincial government wrote a letter to the general welfare administrators explaining that 'the decision whether or not to make a Declaration of Paternity, or to visit the Children's Aid Society or to state who is the father is, in the final analysis, at the discretion of the unwed mother, not at the discretion of the welfare administration.' MTRA, RG 5.1, series 12.2—Investigations—Deserted and Separated Wives, Unmarried Mothers, February 1967 to November 1972, 'Letter from the Provincial Department of Social and Family Services to Municipal Welfare Administration, Indian Band Welfare Administrations and Regional Administrations, March 8, 1971'.

21 AO, RG 49, reel #260, 'Why I Became a Prostitute—Girl, 16', Toronto Telegram, 15 November 1965.

22 In 1965 it was reported that one-third of unwed mothers were keeping their babies. AO, RG 49, reel #260, 'One Third of Girls Now Keep Babies and in Future More Will Have To', Toronto Daily Star, 20 December 1965, and 'Some Unmarried Mothers "Good for Baby"', Toronto Daily Star, 21 December 1965; ibid., reel #285, 'Problems of Illegitimacy Frightening, CAS Is Told', Welland Evening Tribune, 21 April 1966; ibid., reel #314, 'Rise in Illegitimacy Boosts CAS Caseload by 20% in Metro', Globe and Mail, 27 January 1967, and 'Unwed Mothers Increase: She May Have to Keep Her Baby', Toronto Telegram, 21 March 1967; ibid., reel #349, 'More Unmarried Mothers Keep Children, Report Says', Ottawa Journal, 24 January 1968; ibid., reel #388, 'Rate of Illegitimacy Rising Even as Births Fall', 12 March 1969, and 'Miniskirts Blamed for Illegitimate Births', 21 March 1969; and ibid., reel #389, 'Officials Puzzled as Ontario's Illegitimate Birth Rate Doubles', 8 July 1969, and 'The Unwed Mothers' Dilemma', 5 November 1969.

23 AO, RG 49, reel #260, quote cited in 'A Study of Canadian Poverty', Peterborough Examiner, 14 April 1965. Also see ibid., 'Rural Poverty Report: Some Subsist on $11.71 Each Month', Ottawa Journal, 8 December 1965.

24 Ibid., 'Poverty: Million Can't Read or Write', Toronto Telegram, 8 December 1965.

25 Andrew Armitage, Social Welfare in Canada: Ideals, Realities and Future Paths, 2nd edn (Toronto: McClelland and Stewart, 1988):277.

26 Adams et al., *The 'Real' Poverty Report*, Preface.

27 This is the first and only evidence I discovered of a group of single mothers writing the prime minister. National Archives [NA], Pearson Papers, MG 26, vol. 208, file 641-L, 'Letter from Mrs. Mary Firston, Sarnia to Prime Minister, November 4, 1966'.

28 These were the words on one of its first flyers. Cited in Howard Buchbinder, 'The Just Society Movement', in *Community Work in Canada*, edited by Brian Wharf (Toronto: McClelland and Stewart, 1979):134. Also see 'Just Society Movement: Toronto's Poor Organize', *Canadian Dimension* (June–July 1970):19–22. Another antipoverty group that emerged during the late 1960s and early 1970s was Women Against Soaring Prices, a group of women opposed to rising inflation. See 'Women Against Soaring Prices News Release', 30 April 1971, and 'Housewives Winning Price Skirmishes', *Toronto Star*, 2 August 1979. Many thanks to David Kidd for allowing me to 'raid' the activist files in his archival closet.

29 Interview with David Kidd, Toronto, 10 December 1993.

30 Buchbinder, 'The Just Society Movement', 132–3.

31 AO, RG 49, reel #388, 'Toronto Women Organize Action Group by the Poor for the Poor', 22 May 1969; 'Welfare Mothers Post Protest Signs at $4.75 Luncheon', 27 June 1969; 'How the Poor Rate the Social Workers', 28 June 1969; 'Mother, 2 Children Move into City Hall', 4 July 1969; 'Metro's Poor Form Their Own Union', 5 July 1969; 'Just Society Opens First Office', 22 July 1969.

32 The details of the JSM as an organization remain sketchy and are based on newspaper clippings and interviews with people associated with the group. For a more detailed discussion of JSM's actions, see Howard Buchbinder, 'Social Planning or Social Control: An Account of a Confrontation with the Social Welfare Establishment', in *The City: Attacking Modern Myths*, edited by Alan Powell (Toronto: McClelland and Stewart, 1972).

   For theoretical discussions on the topic of community control during this period, see Gerry Hunnius, ed., *Participatory Democracy for Canada* (Montreal: Black Rose, 1971):esp. Buchbinder, 49–51; Joan Kuyek, 78–82; and Hunnius, 83–7. Interview with Howard Buchbinder, 3 December 1991. Also see AO, RG 49, reel #349, 'Two Angry "Clients" Crash Welfare Experts' Meeting', 20 June 1968; 'Client Power', 13 July 1968; ibid., reel #389, 'United Appeal Ignores Poor, Says Just Society', 28 October 1969; ibid., reel #440, 'The Day They Routed the Social Planning Council', 23 March 1970; 'Militant Poor Crash Welfare Meeting', 22 April 1970; 'Angry Mothers Storm Office', 27 August 1970; and ibid., reel #491, 'Poor People and Reformers Desert the Social Planning Council', 17 April 1972.

33 Interview with Buchbinder.

34 Michael Valpy, 'Reunion Recalls Glory Days of CYC', *Globe and Mail*, 9 October 1991, A11.

35 David Kidd, a long-time antipoverty activist in Toronto, recalls a number of low-income people who were able to use the CYC to meet their own personal and political goals. Interview with David Kidd.

36 AO, RG 49, reel #389, '150 in Halifax Jeer Senate Poverty Probe', 5 November 1969.

37 Ibid., 'Senate Probers Avoid Halifax Poverty Areas', 5 November 1969, and 'Poor Can't Wait for Band-Aids', 10 December 1969.

38 Ibid., reel #440, 'Poverty Hearings in a Ballroom', 10 March 1970.

39 Cited in Buchbinder, 'The Just Society Movement', 139–40.

40 Adams et al., *The 'Real' Poverty Report*, Preface.

41 Ibid., 187.

42 Much of the documentation concerning the preparation of this conference was lost as a result of the suspicious bombing of the Praxis office. Interview with Buchbinder.

43 Interview with Buchbinder.

44 Interview with John Clarke, provincial organizer, Ontario Coalition Against Poverty, Toronto, 18 November 1991.

45 Frances Fox Piven and Richard A. Cloward, *Poor People's Movements: Why They Succeed, How They Fail* (New York: Random House, 1979):1–37.

46 Mishra, 'The Welfare of Nations', 316–17.

47 Ramesh Mishra presents these three strategies in his book, *The Welfare State in Capitalist Society: Politics of Retrenchment and Maintenance in Europe, North America and Australia* (Toronto: Harvester Wheatsheaf, 1990):77.

48 Gosta Esping-Andersen, 'The Three Political Economies of the Welfare State', *Canadian Review of Sociology and Anthropology* 26, no. 1 (February 1989):10–36.

49 For further discussion of the federal limit to CAP spending and its impact on social programs, see Canada, *The Canada Assistance Plan: No Time For Cuts* (Ottawa: National Council of Welfare, Winter 1991).

50 John Clarke, 'Ontario's Social Movements—the Struggle Intensifies', in *Culture and Social Change: Social Movements in Quebec and Ontario*, edited by Colin Leys and Marguerite Mendell (Montreal: Black Rose Books, 1993):217.

51 Hoy, *Bill Davis*, 128–32. Citation quoted on p. 128.

52 The 1975 election results were: Progressive Conservatives (fifty-one seats); New Democratic Party (thirty-eight seats); Liberals (thirty-six seats). Ibid., 133.

53 Williams, *Decades of Service*, 78.

54 Interview with John Stapleton, former acting director, Special Projects, Social Assistance and Employment Opportunities Division, Ministry of Community and Social Services, 17 September 1993.

55 Ibid.

56 Ibid.

57 Lorna Hurl claims that 9.2 per cent of all FBA recipients were dependent fathers. This figure does not distinguish between incapacitated and healthy sole-support fathers. Lorna Hurl, 'The Nature of Policy Dynamics: Patterns of Change and Stability in a Social Assistance Program', unpublished paper presented at the Fourth National Conference on Social Welfare Policy, Toronto, October 1989, 15.

58 When FBA recipients across the province met to discuss changes to the policy, it was noted that sole-support fathers did not experience the same intrusive and moralistic investigation by social workers and community members that

single mothers endured. *Speaking Out: Final Report of the New Social Assistance Legislation Consumer Focus Group Project* (Toronto: Queen's Printer for Ontario, February 1992):77–8.

59 The 1985 election results were: Progressive Conservatives (fifty-two seats); Liberals (forty-eight seats); NDP (twenty-five seats). The most recent coalition in Ontario had been between 1919 and 1923 when the Independent Labour Party helped the United Farmers to form a government in exchange for two cabinet positions. For election results, see *Canadian Parliamentary Guide* (Toronto: Globe and Mail Publishing, 1993):828. Regarding coalition governments, see Rosemary Speirs, *Out of the Blue: The Fall of the Tory Dynasty in Ontario* (Toronto: Macmillan, 1986):135.

60 George Ehring and Wayne Roberts, *Giving Away a Miracle: Lost Dreams, Broken Promises and the Ontario NDP* (Oakville: Mosaic Press, 1993):211.

61 Ibid.

62 Ibid.

63 The report stated: 'Ontario's present reliance upon categories of eligibility reinforces old notions that some poor people are more "deserving" than others. The use of defined categories was heavily criticized in submissions to this committee on the grounds that it is confusing and complex, provides widely differing entitlements on the basis of factors other than need, results in an over-reliance on discretion, and reinforces the social stigma that attaches to seeking assistance.' Ministry of Community and Social Services, *Transitions: Report of the Social Assistance Review Committee* (Toronto: Queen's Printer, 1988):29. Also see p. 121.

64 The report states, 'Yet by any standard—including those set by poverty lines, market baskets, or public perceptions of how much money people need to live—the rates are inadequate. They provide too little for shelter, too little for food, and too little for other necessities. . . . Not one submission concluded that social assistance rates were adequate. . . . None argued that the current rates met real needs.'

The market-basket approach would include: food (supermarket and occasional restaurant), clothing, shelter, personal needs (toiletries), household supplies, transportation (basic and some recreational), health care (prescription and patent remedies including vitamins), basic recreation, basic reading and education, basic miscellaneous items (telephone and children's allowances), plus a small life insurance policy. This list is neither expected to raise the recipient to general community standards nor provide a minimum that allowed for any contingencies. *Transitions*, 127; for national comparison, 54–8; market-basket recommendation, 182 and 193.

65 *Transitions*, 527–8.

66 This opportunity planner would help the recipient 'develop an action plan that builds on the recipient's existing skills and strengths and is in keeping with the resources and opportunities in the community. The jointly developed plan will take into consideration the recipient's longer-term goals and aspirations and will identify the activities, services, or programs that might enable the recipient to attain his or her personal goals. Clearly, if it is to succeed, this kind of assistance must be tailored to the individual to the greatest extent possible.' *Transitions*, 206.

67 Clarke, 'Ontario's Social Movements', 218.

68 Ehring and Roberts, *Giving Away a Miracle*, 246.

69 Interview with Clarke; and Ehring and Roberts, *Giving Away a Miracle*, 213.

70 Interview with Stapleton.

71 Interview with Nancy Vander Plaats, community legal worker, Scarborough Community Legal Services, Toronto, 15 September 1993.

72 Interview with Stapleton.

73 Judy Wolfe was economic policy adviser to the Ontario Women's Directorate from 1986 to 1990. Interview with Judy Wolfe, executive coordinator, Cabinet Committee on Economic Development, Cabinet Office, Toronto, 14 September 1993.

74 Stapleton actually helped to write the cabinet submission that changed the legislation from 'not living as a single person' to the three-year cohabitation rule. Interview with Stapleton.

75 For further discussion of the spouse-in-the-house rule from 1970 to 1984, see Jane Haddad, 'Sexism and Social Welfare Policy: The Case of Family Benefits in Ontario', Occasional Papers in Social Policy Analysis, no. 8 (Toronto: Ontario Institute for Studies in Education, 1985):10.

76 Interview with Ian Morrison, Toronto, 18 March 1997.

77 Interview with Stapleton; interview with Vander Plaats.

78 Interview with Vander Plaats.

79 Previously the largest majority government was formed after the Progressive Conservative's electoral win of ninety-one seats in 1929. The 1987 election results were Liberals (ninety-five seats); NDP (nineteen seats); Progressive Conservatives (sixteen seats). *Canadian Parliamentary Guide*, 828.

80 Ehring and Roberts, *Giving Away a Miracle*, 394.

81 Ibid., 239–40.

82 Ibid., 278, 313, and 362.

83 OCAP worked closely with Ontario Coalition for Social Justice, the provincial arm of the Action Canada Network, during the provincial election.

84 Interview with Carole Silliker, past president, Mothers and Others Making Change, Kitchener, 19 November 1991.

85 As of the end of November, LIPI had already served 2,570 people to date that year. In the month of September, a total of 601 people asked for their services. Interview with Patsy Turcotte, LIPI, North Bay, 28 November 1991.

86 Interview with Laurie Hannah, founder and coordinator for Citizens for Action, Belleville, 10 December 1991.

87 Interview with Clarke.

88 Interview with Chandra Pala, acting manager, Policy Development Section, Policy Development and Program Design Branch, Social Assistance and Employment Opportunities Division, Ministry of Community and Social Services, Toronto, 13 September 1993.

89 Interview with Charles Pitchford, program analyst, Policy and Program Development Branch, Social Assistance and Employment Opportunities Division, Ministry of Community and Social Services, 13 September 1993.

Ministry of Community and Social Services, *Back on Track: First Report of the Advisory Group on New Social Assistance Legislation* (Toronto: Queen's Printer for Ontario, 1991):Action 28, p. 12.

90 Following a lengthy discussion and support statistics, one study of poverty concludes, 'This evidence suggests a disturbing and indisputable conclusion: social assistance recipients in Ontario not only have incomes below any acceptable community standard, but they are significantly below the poverty line as well . . . [and] in the last five years, the adequacy of social assistance incomes has deteriorated sharply.' Metropolitan Toronto Social Planning Council, *And the Poor Get Poorer: A Study of Social Welfare Programs in Ontario*, 2nd edn (Toronto: Metropolitan Toronto Social Planning Council, 1981):passim, quote cited on p. 23. For an earlier report, see Metropolitan Toronto Social Planning Council, *Social Allowances in Ontario: An Historical Analysis of General Welfare and Family Benefits 1961–1976* (Toronto: Metropolitan Toronto Social Planning Council, 1977).

91 Supplementary aid is cost-shared by the provincial and municipal governments at an 80/20 rate and covers extra fuel, shelter costs, and other 'extraordinary needs'. Special assistance is cost-shared on a 50/50 basis between these two levels of government and is for those in financial need in the following circumstances: moving, dental services, prosthetic appliances, drugs, funerals, and burials.'Annual Report of the Ministry of COMSOC, Fiscal Year 1978–79', regarding Income Maintenance Branch.

92 Metro Toronto Social Planning Council, *And the Poor Get Poorer*, 28.

93 For a full discussion of the inadequacy of spousal support, see E. Diane Pask and Marnie L. McCall, *How Much and Why? Economic Implications of Marriage Breakdown: Spousal and Child Support* (Calgary: Canadian Research Institute for Law and the Family, 1989).

94 The increase for basic necessities was 1 per cent. There was a shelter allowance increase of 1 per cent, but not all recipients were deemed worthy of this increase. This was the first welfare rate cut since 1975 under Progressive Conservative Premier William Davis.
    'Ontario Welfare Payments to Rise by 1 Per cent', *Globe and Mail*, 28 January 1993,A5, and 'Ontario Hasn't Always Had Best Rates', *Globe and Mail*, 23 March 1994, A9.

95 *Welfare Reform*, report by the National Council of Welfare (Ottawa: Ministry of Supply and Services Canada, Summer 1992):27–8.

96 'Welfare Cuts an "option" If Federal Funding Frozen', *Toronto Star*, 17 December 1993, A11.

97 'Refugees Accused of Fraud', *Globe and Mail*, 28 October 1993, A32. For further discussion of the treatment of immigrants on welfare, see Ian Morrison, ' "Looking After Our Own": Immigrants and Welfare in Canada', paper presented at the Canadian Political Science Association, St John's, Newfoundland, June 1997.

98 E. (Rico) Sabatini, with Sandra Nightingale. *Welfare—No Fair: A Critical Analysis of Ontario's Welfare System, 1985–1994,*(Vancouver: The Fraser Institute, 1996): 163.

99 'Welfare Check on Children's School Records Causes Uproar', *Globe and Mail*, 1 June 1994, A10.

100 As a whole, fraud has accounted for approximately 2.59 to 3.66 per cent of total payments. The approximate breakdown for fraudulent cases is as follows: unreported 'spouse in the house' providing support (60 per cent); unreported income (20 per cent); undisclosed liquid assets in excess of allowable limits, unreported changes in circumstances, or cashing duplicate cheques (20 per cent). See Peat Marwick and Partners, 'Welfare Fraud and Overpayment', SARC background paper, September 1987, 19 and 54.

Transitions did, however, open the door for the possibility of a fraud squad: 'We have no evidence to suggest that fraud in the social assistance system is greater than it is in the tax system or the unemployment insurance system. Nevertheless, because public confidence in the social assistance system depends in large part on the belief that the funds are being well spent and that abuse is being kept to a minimum, we accept that some of the measures adopted to control social assistance fraud may need to be more extensive than they are in other systems.' Transitions, 384.

101 'Ontario's Expenditure Control Plan', Minister of Finance, Queen's Park, April 1993.

102 According to Transitions, 'nearly 50% of single parents receiving FBA who receive no support payments at all averaged between 3.5 and 4 years in the program. The 11% receiving between $10 and $100 per month averaged 2.5 to 3 years, while those receiving between $100 and $200 per month averaged 2 to 2.5 years. Finally, the mere 6% receiving in excess of $200 per month averaged less than 2 years in the program.' Transitions, 44–5.

103 'ID Card Proposal Attacked as Degrading', Toronto Star, 18 February 1994, A18.

104 'Major Welfare Foulups Revealed', Toronto Star, 22 September 1994, A1 and A28; Thomas Walkom, 'The Welfare Fraud Shocker That Wasn't', Toronto Star, 24 September 1994, B4. For a detailed analysis of the report and welfare fraud generally, see Ian Morrison, 'Facts About Social Assistance Administration That Criminal Lawyers Ought to Know', paper presented to the Department of Continuing Legal Education, the Law Society of Upper Canada, 25 March 1995.

105 Hurl, 'The Nature of Policy Dynamics', 23.

106 'Annual Report of the Department of Social and Family Services, Fiscal Year 1968–69', Ontario.

107 Among the strategies attempted were phase-out grants for recipients who were beginning either full-time work or retraining programs. For more discussion of these early programs, see 'Annual Report of the Department of Social and Family Services, Fiscal Year 1970–71', 26; 'Annual Report of the Ministry of Community and Social Services, Fiscal Year 1975–76', Provincial Benefits Branch; Patricia Evans and Elaine McIntyre, 'Welfare, Work Incentives and the Single Mother: An Interprovincial Comparison', in The Canadian Welfare State: Evolution and Transition, edited by Jacqueline Ismael (Edmonton: University of Alberta Press, 1987):101–25.

108 'Annual Report of the Ministry of Community and Social Services, Fiscal Year 1979–80', deputy minister's report.

109 For an overview of the program, see 'Survey of Provincial/Municipal Integration Sites', Ministry of Community and Social Services, Toronto, June 1986.

110 Patricia Evans argues that there are three major work-incentive strategies employed by industrialized nations: monetary rewards, the provision of services to reduce barriers to employment, and an enforcement strategy that relies upon regulatory measures and administrative practices to compel recipients to find work. See Patricia Evans, 'Targeting Single Mothers for Employment: Comparisons from the United States, Britain, and Canada', *Social Service Review* 66, no. 3 (September 1992):381.

111 Studies of ESI suggest that participants had difficulties finding employment, particularly long-term jobs, and generally were no better off. See *Employment Opportunities Program Evaluation Report*, vol. 11 (Toronto: Ministry of Community and Social Services, 1988); and Patricia Evans, 'Work Incentives and the Single Mother: Dilemmas of Reform', *Canadian Public Policy* 14, no. 2 (June 1988):125–36.

112 Ministry of Community and Social Services, *Time for Action* (Toronto: Queen's Printer for Ontario, 1992):79.

113 Ibid., 84–5.

114 I was fortunate to receive the document from a concerned civil servant in December 1992 and immediately sent the document to a number of antipoverty activists, including John Clarke of OCAP. An ad hoc coalition of concerned antipoverty activists and labour representatives called a press conference and released the document in early January 1993. 'Social Assistance Reform—Proposed Program Model', draft III, leaked document from the Ministry of Community and Social Services, 25 November 1992, 33; 'NDP Eyes Making Welfare Recipients Work', *Toronto Star*, 29 January 1993.

115 Ehring and Roberts, *Giving Away a Miracle*, 320.

116 Quotation by Ruth Mott cited ibid.

117 Ibid.

118 Informal discussion with a provincial civil servant who wished to remain anonymous. Also verified by Josephine Grey, antipoverty activist and single mother, who has worked closely with the Ministry of Community and Social Services on welfare reform. Interview with Grey, Toronto, September 1993.

119 The mini-budget included reductions to STEP and to moving expenses; deductions for home-owners and those with interest from savings accounts, and significant cuts to transfer payments for municipal welfare benefits. 'Ontario's Expenditure Control Plan'.

120 Accompanying the July FBA cheques was the following statement: 'Workers will help sole support parents of children over the age of 12 to explore retraining and employment opportunities.' See 'Communication to Family Benefits Recipients', Ministry of Community and Social Services, July 1993.

121 *Turning Point: New Support Programs for People with Low Incomes*, Ministry of Community and Social Services, July 1993.

CHAPTER 7

1 Kenora Legal Clinic spokesperson at the Social Assistance Review Committee hearings, cited in Ministry of Community and Social Services, *Transitions: Report of the Social Assistance Review Committee* (Toronto: Queen's Printer, 1988):125.

2 For the most part, scholars have concentrated on the role agents of the state have played in the moral regulation of citizens. This is most notably seen in the work of Philip Corrigan and Derek Sayer. Education historian Bruce Curtis has argued that there is considerable moral direction conducted through the school system by workers who may be at arm's length from the state, but who are still paid and held accountable by state regulations. Mariana Valverde, on the other hand, has concentrated on social reformers at the turn of the century, namely, charitable and religious leaders. These individuals, for the most part, worked outside of the state apparatus, but were influential and committed to the moral regulation of citizens. See Philip Corrigan and Derek Sayer, *The Great Arch: English State Formation as Cultural Revolution* (Oxford: Basil Blackwell, 1985); Bruce Curtis, 'Representation and State Formation in the Canadas, 1790–1850', *Studies in Political Economy* 28 (Spring 1989):59–88; and Mariana Valverde, *The Age of Light, Soap, and Water: Moral Reform in English Canada, 1885–1925* (Toronto: McClelland and Stewart, 1991).

3 Josephine Grey, Democracy Conference, 'Session 5: Democratic Administration, Reforms and Civil Service Unions', York University, 18 April 1991.

4 Both Dennis Guest and Richard Splane argue that moral concerns have withered with the introduction of the post–Second World War welfare state. See Dennis Guest, *The Emergence of Social Security in Canada* (Vancouver: University of British Columbia Press, 1980):esp. 1–2, 203; and Richard Splane, *Social Welfare in Ontario* (Toronto: University of Toronto Press, 1965).

5 In her insightful book, Elizabeth Janeway explores, from a feminist perspective, the many different types of power that the weak may utilize. Quotation cited in Elizabeth Janeway, *Powers of the Weak* (New York: Alfred A. Knopf, 1980):21. Also for a discussion of the 'powers of the weak', see Linda Gordon, *Heroes of Their Own Lives: The Politics and History of Family Violence* (New York: Penguin, 1989):Ch. 9.

6 For a discussion of popular educational techniques and their utility for social science research, see William Foote Whyte, ed., *Participatory Action Research* (Newbury Park, Calif.: Sage Publications, 1991). The approach I have found most helpful is the Ah-hah! workshop technique: GATT-Fly, *Ah-hah! A New Approach to Popular Education* (Toronto: Between the Lines, 1983).

7 For discussions of oral history practices, see Paul Thompson, *The Voice of the Past: Oral History* (Oxford: Oxford University Press, 1978); Derek Reimer, ed., *Voices: A Guide to Oral History* (Victoria: Government of British Columbia, 1984); and Thad Sitton, George Mehaffy, E.L. Davis, Jr, eds, *Oral History: A Guide for Teachers* (Austin: University of Texas Press, 1983). More recently feminists have added to this issue. See in particular Sherna Berger Gluck and Daphne Patai, eds, *Women's Words: The Feminist Practice of Oral History* (New York: Routledge, 1991).

8 The only group that did not respond is Low Income People Involvement (LIPI). This is a very active group that has been extensively involved in the Ontario government's welfare reform activities. Given that they were asked to respond if they had any difficulties with the project, I can only assume that they were otherwise occupied but did not object to any of the content.

9 Interview with Mothers and Others Making Change (MOMC), Kitchener, 19

November 1991. Bank accounts are also regularly checked in Belleville. Interview with Citizens for Action, Belleville, 10 December 1991.

10 Interview with MOMC.

11 Interview with Nick di Salle, former FBA worker, Ontario Public Service Employees Union, Toronto, 22 November 1991.

12 Interview with MOMC.

13 Interview with LIPI, North Bay, 28 November 1991.

14 Interview with Hannah, Citizens for Action.

15 Single Mothers Workshop, Fight-back Metro Coalition Event, 11 April 1992.

16 Interview with LIPI.

17 While a single mother may win a little extra cash through bingo, it will be eventually taxed back through a regressive tax measure.

18 My thanks to Becki Ross for this quotation. Becki Ross, 'A Feminist Reconceptualization of Women's Work and Leisure: A Study of Kingston Mother Workers', MA thesis, Department of Physical Education, Queen's University, Kingston, 1984, 212.

19 Interview with LIPI.

20 Interview with Richard D'Arcy, community legal worker, Community Outreach Programs of Elgin County, 22 November 1991.

21 My thanks to Brigitte Kitchen and Michael Shapcott for their knowledge of the Canadian taxation system.

22 Interview with MOMC.

23 Interview with MOMC and interview with Women's Weekly, Toronto, 11 December 1991.

24 Interview with LIPI.

25 Interview with MOMC.

26 Interview with LIPI.

27 Ibid.

28 Ibid.

29 Women's Weekly, May 1990; and *Speaking Out: Final Report of the New Social Assistance Legislation Consumer Focus Group Project* (Toronto: Queen's Printer for Ontario, 1992):68.

30 Interview with LIPI.

31 This was one of the major complaints made by numerous recipients who participated in the SARC Consumer Focus Group Project, which met seventeen groups across the province. *Speaking Out*, 60–75.

32 *Transitions*, 289.

33 Ibid., 291.

34 Interview with LIPI.

35 Interview at Women's Weekly, 19 June 1991.

36 Interview at Women's Weekly, May 1990.

37 Ibid.

38 Interview at Women's Weekly, 19 June 1991.

39 Ibid.

40 Interview with Women's Weekly, 11 December 1991.

41 For further discussion of the restrictions concerning cohabitation, see Chapter 5.

42 Interview with John Clarke, provincial organizer, Ontario Coalition Against Poverty, Toronto, 18 November 1991.

43 John Stapleton also admits that the questionnaire was indeed designed to 'trip up' the respondents so the nature of the relationship could be firmly established and reduce the number of legal battles between recipients, legal clinics, and the Ministry of Community and Social Services concerning particular cases. Interview with Nancy Vander Plaats, community legal worker, Scarborough Community Legal Services, Toronto, 15 September 1993; and interview with John Stapleton, former acting director, Special Projects, Social Assistance and Employment Opportunities Division, Ministry of Community and Social Services, 17 September 1993.

44 Interview with D'Arcy. For further discussion of the spouse-in-the-house rule from 1970 to 1984, see Jane Haddad, 'Sexism and Social Welfare Policy: The Case of Family Benefits in Ontario', Occasional Papers in Social Policy Analysis, no. 8 (Toronto: Ontario Institute for Studies in Education, 1985):10.

45 Interview with Women's Weekly, 11 December 1991.

46 The bathroom investigation was a very common experience shared by women from the Women's Weekly, MOMC, and LIPI. Quote from interview with Women's Weekly, 11 December 1991.

47 Interview with LIPI.

48 All of these examinations were printed in the manual for FBA workers in London, Ontario. Parking lot stake-outs have been practised in London and North Bay. Interview with Clarke; interview with Gunness; and interview with LIPI.

49 Interview with Women's Weekly, 11 December 1991.

50 Ibid.

51 Ibid.

52 Interview with LIPI.

53 Interview with Women's Weekly, 11 December 11, 1991. Nick di Salle confirmed that FBA workers often wrote 'the place was filthy' on the client's form. Interview with di Salle.

54 *Speaking Out*, 34.

55 Ibid., 89.

56 Ibid., 86–98.

57 Interview with LIPI.

58 There is little documentation of Aboriginal single mothers' stories. I was able to interview only one woman who identified herself as Aboriginal. This is also based on interviews I conducted for a youth community project that included workshops at the First Nations School and at Anduylan, a shelter for Aboriginal women in downtown Toronto. Also see Heather Ross, 'First Nations Self-Government: A Background Report', prepared for the Social Assistance Review Committee, Toronto, September 1987, 136.

59 Interview with Carolann Wright, Toronto, 3 December 1991.

60 Interview with di Salle.

61 These deductions were based on Regulation 8 of the FBA, which allows a social worker to deduct money from the recipient's benefit if the worker believes that the recipient has not made a reasonable effort to obtain child support. Lawrence explored the cases of 311 single mothers, two-thirds of whom were White, to determine her findings. She made her complaint to the Ontario Human Rights Commission, but the commission did not address it. Later the Ministry of Community and Social Services conducted a provincial study on the matter and found many deduction charges were inappropriate, but did not address the question of race. See Kathleen Lawrence, 'Systemic Discrimination: Regulation 8—Family Benefits Act: Policy of Reasonable Efforts to Obtain Financial Resources', *Journal of Law and Social Policy* 6 (Fall 1990):57–76.

62 *Transitions*, 244–5.

63 Allan Moscovitch, 'Session 4: The Bureaucrat and the Street: Controlling or Empowering Citizens', Democracy Conference.

64 Interview with di Salle.

65 Ibid.

66 Ibid.

67 Interview with Gunness.

68 The Ministry of Community and Social Services estimated that the average case-load for fieldworkers delivering FBA in 1986–7 was 332 cases. Welfare workers and community legal workers have suggested that this was still the average case-load in the early and mid-1990s. *Transitions*, 241.

69 For a broader discussion of the contradictions of social work, see Ben Carniol, *Case Critical: The Dilemma of Social Work in Canada* (Toronto: Between the Lines, 1987):esp. Chs 4 and 5.

70 Jennifer Dale and Peggy Foster, *Feminists and State Welfare* (London: Routledge and Kegan Paul, 1986):96.

71 *Transitions*, 245.

72 Interview with Women's Weekly, 11 December 1991.

73 Confirmed during interview with di Salle and interview with Women's Weekly, May 1990 and 11 December 1991.

74 Interview with LIPI.

75 Interview with MOMC.

76 Interview with Women's Weekly, 11 December 1991.

77 Interview with LIPI.

78 Josephine Grey, Democracy Conference.

79 Interview with LIPI.

80 Interview with MOMC.

81 Carole Silliker, from a MOMC flyer entitled, 'What It Means to Be Poor'.

82 Several single mothers told me this during an interview with Women's Weekly, 19 June 1991. This was also verified by Carolann Wright: 'Yes, MTHA let FBA workers into your apartment without your permission. Absolutely.' Interview with Wright.

83 There has been a trend in the United States to intensify the connection between welfare benefits and school attendance. In reaction, the SARC report recommended that a child's attendance no longer be considered grounds for ineligibility. *Transitions*, 143.

84 Interview with Women's Weekly, 11 December 1991.

85 Ibid.

86 Interview with Women's Weekly, May 1990. I also observed this during my volunteer work at Bridge House, Kingston, 1983–5.

CONCLUSION

1 C. Wright Mills, 'On Intellectual Craftsmanship', *Sociological Imagination* (New York: Oxford University Press, 1959).

2 While Bill 142 does not recognize parents' child-rearing responsibilities, the Harris government has suggested that single parents with very young children may be exempt from some of the employment activities required of other welfare recipients. 'Bill 142: An Act to Revise the Law Related to Social Assistance By Enacting the Ontario Works Act and the Ontario Disability Support Program Act, By Repealing the Family Benefits Act, the Vocational Rehabilitation Services Act and the General Welfare Assistance Act and By Amending Several Other Statutes', First Session, 36th Legislature of Ontario.

3 For further discussion of this theme, see Margaret Little, 'The Blurring of Boundaries: Private and Public Welfare for Single Mothers in Ontario', *Studies in Political Economy* 47 (Summer 1995):89–110.

4 The latter phrase is borrowed from Linda Gordon, *Heroes of Their Own Lives: The Politics and History of Family Violence, Boston 1880–1960* (New York: Viking, 1988).

5 To date, provincial governments have maintained their welfare appeal boards, but several governments, including Ontario, have dramatically reduced legal aid spending.

6 The Ontario figures are for the number of sole-support parents, but according to government studies, more than 95 per cent of sole-support parents on welfare are mothers. National Council of Welfare, *Poverty Profile 1994* (Ottawa: Supply and Services Canada, 1996):17; Ministry of Community and Social Services, *Transitions: Report of the Social Assistance Review Committee* (Toronto: Queen's Park Printer, 1988):31; Melodie Mayson, 'Welfare Reform and Single Mothers', Ontario Social Safety NetWork Backgrounder, 1.

7 The disabled have been exempted from this welfare cut. The impact of these cuts is only beginning to be documented. See 'Report from Evictions Subcommittee of Metro Advisory Committee on Homeless and Socially Isolated Persons', Toronto, 1 May 1996; 'Impacts of General Welfare Assistance Rate Reductions', report to Metro Toronto Human Services Committee, Toronto, 27 May 1996; 'Impact of Ontario Government Funding Cuts', Ontario Association of Social Workers, February 1996; 'Welfare Rate Cuts: The Real Issues', Ontario Social Safety NetWork, June 1995; 'Creating Hunger: Impact of Ontario Government Welfare Reforms', Daily Bread Food Bank, Summary of 1996 Survey of People Accessing Emergency Food Programs in the Greater

Toronto Area, 30 July 1996; 'Parkdale Community Audit', vol. 2, Metropolitan Toronto Social Planning Council, Toronto, Spring 1997; and 'Social Change in Hamilton-Wentworth, 1997', Hamilton Social Planning Council, Hamilton, March 1997.

8 Affidavit of Kevin Costante, assistant deputy minister, Ministry of Community and Social Services, *Falkiner v. Ontario*, paragraphs 93 and 94. For a more detailed discussion of this spousal amendment, see Margaret Little and Ian Morrison, 'The Pecker Detectors Are Back: Changes to the Spousal Definition in Ontario Welfare Policy', paper presented to the Canadian Political Science Association, St John's, Newfoundland, 8 June 1997.

9 'Welfare Fraud Control Database', as cited by Ian Morrison, 'Welfare Reform and Welfare Fraud: The Real Issues', Ontario Social Safety NetWork Backgrounder, 5–6.

10 In 1992 less than half the people reported to the Metro Toronto welfare fraud line were on assistance. 'Social Assistance Caseload Characteristics', Metro Toronto Social Services, Community Services and Housing Division Presentation, 23 November 1993, as cited by Morrison, 'Welfare Reform and Welfare Fraud', 3.

11 Community legal workers in Kingston and Toronto are aware of a number of cases where single mothers have had their allowances cancelled as a result of an anonymous call to the fraud line. Interview with Sharon Lee, Kingston Community Legal Clinic, Kingston, 10 March 1996. Interview with Ian Morrison, executive director, Clinic Resource Office, Toronto, 8 March 1996.

12 Michael Ornstein, 'A Profile of Social Assistance Recipients in Ontario' (Toronto: Institute for Social Research, York University, June 1995):57.

13 *Speaking Out: Final Report of the New Social Assistance Legislation Consumer Focus Group Project* (Toronto: Queen's Printer for Ontario, February 1992):68. For a more general discussion regarding the trends of women and work, see Marcy Cohen, 'The Feminization of the Labour Market: Prospects for the 1990s', in *Getting on Track: Social Democratic Strategies for Ontario*, edited by Daniel Drache (Kingston: McGill-Queen's University Press, 1992):105–23.

14 Declining labour force participation for single mothers is also occurring in Britain and United States. For Canadian data, see Martin D. Dooley, 'Changes in the Market Work of Married Women and Lone Mothers with Children: 1973–1986', paper presented at the meetings of the Canadian Population Society, May 1989, cited in Patricia Evans, 'Targeting Single Mothers for Employment: Comparisons from the United States, Britain and Canada', *Social Services Review* 66, no. 3 (September 1992), footnote #53, 393.

15 For a more detailed discussion of how Bill 142 increases the policing of welfare recipients, see Morrison, 'Welfare Reform and Welfare Fraud', 1–15.

16 Bill 142, Schedule A, Ontario Works Act, 1997, section 1, subsection b.

Bibliography

PRIMARY SOURCES

Archival Collections

Archives of Ontario

a) Manuscript Groups:

Toronto Local Council of Women, F805-1-0-1 to F805-1-0-3, and F805-10-0-10.

b) Government Records:

Brant County Mothers' Allowance Local Board Minutes, 1920–37, F 1551-14.

Lanark County Mothers' Allowance Local Board Minutes, 1920–38, F 1734-23 to F 1734-32.

Legislative Offices, RG 49, series 1-7-E, and MG-755, Press Clippings 1934–73.

Lincoln County Mothers' Allowance Case Files, 1937–49, F 1741-30, boxes 1 and 3.

Lincoln County Mothers' Allowance Local Board Minutes, 1920–37, F 1741-30, box 1.

Ministry of Community and Social Services, RG 29, series 36 and 74; MS-728, reels 1-3.

Ministry of Labour, RG 7-1-0-148, 7-1-0-229, 7-1-0-295, 7-1-0-347, 7-1-0-625, 7-12-0-1 to 7-12-0-33, 7-12-0-52, and 7-12-0-55.

Ontario Commission on Unemployment, 1916, RG 18, B-40.

Ontario County Mothers' Allowance Local Board Minutes, 1920–45, F 1839-33 and 1839-35.

Premiers' Office, RG 3, boxes 35, 69, 91, 100, 104, 107–8, 142, 146, 153, 160, 162, 190, 203, 209, 213, 216, 218, 228, 230, 247–8, 317, 331, 333, and 422.

Provincial Board of Health, RG 62, series F-1-a.

Provincial Secretary, RG 8, series I-1-B-1.

Royal Commission on the Care of the Feeble-Minded and Mentally Defective and the Prevalence of Venereal Disease, 18 October 1919, RG 18, B-49.

Royal Commission on Prison and Reformatory System of Ontario, 1891, RG 18, B-10.

Royal Commission on Public Welfare, 13 August 1930, RG 18, B-75.

Select Committee on Child Labour, 25 March 1907, RG 18, D-I-20.

City of London Records Retention, London

City of London Mothers' Allowance Local Board Minutes, 1920–47.

D.B. Weldon Library, Western Regional Collection, London

City of London Mothers' Allowance Case Files, 1920–40, boxes 159 and 160.

Middlesex County Old Age Pensions and Mothers' Allowance Local Board Minutes, 1938–48.

Elgin County Library, St Thomas

Elgin County Mothers' Allowance Case Files and Correspondence, 1920–48, boxes 42 and 55.

Elgin County Mothers' Allowance and Old Age Pension Local Board Minutes, 1935–45, vol. 2.

Port Stanley Mothers' Allowance Case Files, 1946–52.

Lang Pioneer Village, Keene

County of Peterborough Mothers' Allowance Local Board Minutes, 1921–48.

Metropolitan Toronto Records and Archives, Toronto

Commission of Public Welfare, City of Toronto, RG 5.1, series 4, 9, 12, 17, 20, 24, 27, 29, 33, 36, 43, 45, 47, and 48.

Community Services Department, Social Service Commission, City of Toronto, RG 5.6.

National Archives of Canada

a) Manuscript Groups:

Canadian Council on Social Development, MG 28, I-10, vols 10, 37, 43, 58, 62, 63, and 110.

David Croll Papers, MG 32, C49, vol. 24.

John J. Kelso Papers, MG 30, C 97, vols 5 and 24.

Lester Bowles Pearson Papers, MG 26, N3, vols 208, 225, and 226.

National Council of Women Collection, MG 28, I-25, vols 66, 67, 68, 72, 73, 76, 79, 81, 89, 92, 105, 106, 107, 108, 151, and 152.

b) Government Records:

Department of Labour, RG 79, vol. 1906.

Department of National Health and Welfare, RG 29, vols 31, 32, 51, 97, 413, 989, 990, 991, 992, 993, 2112, 2114, 2115, and 2116.

Norwich and District Archives, Norwich

Oxford County Mothers' Allowance Local Board Minutes, 1920–39, RG 2, boxes 636, 637, 643, and 705.

Oxford County Mothers' Allowance Unprocessed Case Files, RG 2.

Prince Edward County Archives, Picton

Prince Edward County Old Age Pension and Mothers' Allowance Board Minutes, 1920–47.

Region of Peel Archives

Peel County Old Age Pension and Mothers' Allowance Local Board Minutes, 1938–48.

Queen's University Archives, Kingston

Social Welfare Department of the City of Kingston.

Simcoe County Archives, Minesing

Simcoe County Mothers' Allowance Local Board Minutes, 1920–42.

INTERVIEWS

a) Single mothers interviewed:

Women's Weekly, a low-income single mothers group,

Toronto, May 1990	10
Women's Weekly, Toronto, 19 June 1991	12
Women's Weekly, Toronto, 11 December 1991	11
Citizens for Action, Belleville	1
Low Income Families Together, Toronto	1
Low Income People Involvement, North Bay	5
Mothers and Others Making Change, Kitchener	20
Women for Economic Justice, Toronto	1
Total	**61**

b) Community legal workers interviewed: Richard D'Arcy, Community Outreach Programs of Elgin County; Patty Gunness, Neighbourhood Legal Services, London and Middlesex County; Nancy Vander Plaats, community legal worker, Scarborough Community Legal Services.

c) Antipoverty activists interviewed: John Clarke, Ontario Coalition Against Poverty, Toronto; Josephine Grey, Low Income Families Together, Toronto; David Kidd, Workers Information and Action Centre, Toronto; Ruth Mott, Women for Economic Justice (WEJ), Toronto; Carolann Wright, WEJ, Women's Health and Women's Hands, Toronto.

d) Social workers interviewed: Nick di Salle, OPSEU, former FBA worker, Toronto; one former FBA worker, Toronto, who requested anonymity.

e) Senior Ontario government bureaucrats interviewed: Charles Pitchford, program analyst, Policy and Program; Development Branch, Social Assistance and Employment; Opportunities Division, Ministry of Community and Social Services; Chandra Pala, acting manager, Policy Development Section, Policy Development and Program Design Branch, Social Assistance and Employment Opportunities Division, Ministry of Community and Social Services; John Stapleton, former acting director, Special Projects, Social Assistance and Employment Opportunities Division, Ministry of Community and Social Services; Judy Wolfe, executive coordinator, Cabinet Committee on Economic Development, Cabinet Office; two senior officials with the Ministry of Community and Social Services who requested anonymity.

PUBLISHED SOURCES

Newspapers

Border Cities Star, Windsor

Brockville Recorder and Times, Brockville

Chatham Daily News, Chatham

Farmers' Sun, Toronto

Fort William Daily Times-Journal, Thunder Bay

Hamilton Herald, Hamilton

Hamilton Spectator, Hamilton

Kingston Whig-Standard, Kingston

London Advertiser, London

London Free Press, London

North Bay Nugget, North Bay

Ottawa Citizen, Ottawa

St Catharines Standard, St Catharines

Sault Daily Star, Sault Ste Marie

Toronto Globe, Toronto

Toronto Mail and Empire, Toronto

Toronto Star, Toronto

Toronto Telegram, Toronto

St Thomas Times-Journal, St Thomas

PROCEEDINGS, ANNUAL REPORTS, AND GOVERNMENT DOCUMENTS

Agard, Ralph. 'Access to the Social Assistance Services Delivery Systems by Various Ethno-Cultural Groups'. Manuscript prepared for the Social Assistance Review Committee, vol. 3, 1988.

Canada. *Canadian Council on Social Development Papers.* Manuscript group 28, National Archives of Canada, Ottawa.

————. *Census of Canada, 1921.* Ottawa: King's Printer, 1925.

————. *Labour Gazette.* Ottawa: Department of Labour, 1900–20.

————. *One in a World of Two's.* A report on one-parent families in Canada. Report by the National Council of Welfare. Ottawa: Ministry of Supply and Services Canada, April 1976.

————. *Poor People's Groups,* a report of the National Council of Welfare Seminar on Self-Help Problem Solving by Low-Income Communities. Ottawa: Ministry of Supply and Services Canada, February 1973.

————. *The Canada Assistance Plan: No Time for Cuts.* Report by the National Council of Welfare. Ottawa: Ministry of Supply and Services Canada, winter 1991.

_____. *Welfare in Canada: The Tangled Safety Net*. Report by the National Council of Welfare. Ottawa: Ministry of Supply and Services Canada, November 1987.

_____. *Welfare Incomes 1989*. Report by the National Council of Welfare. Ottawa: Ministry of Supply and Services Canada, winter 1990–1.

_____. *Welfare Reform*. Report by the National Council of Welfare. Ottawa: Ministry of Supply and Services Canada, summer 1992.

_____. *Women and Poverty Revisited*. Report by the National Council of Welfare. Ottawa: Ministry of Supply and Services Canada, summer 1990.

Drea, Frank. Remarks by the Minister of Community and Social Services at the annual convention of the Ontario Municipal Social Services Association, 1981.

Hogan, Mary. 'Immigrants and Social Assistance'. Manuscript prepared for Social Assistance and Review Committee, vol. 26, 1988.

International Labour Office. *International Survey of Social Services*, series M, no. 11. Geneva: International Labour Office, 1933.

_____. *The Law and Women's Work: A Contribution to the Study of the Status of Women*, series 1, no. 4. Geneva: International Labour Office, 1939.

_____. *Women's Work under Labour Law: A Survey of Protective Legislation*, series 1, no. 2. Geneva: International Labour Office, 1932.

Irving, Allan. 'From No Poor Law to the Social Assistance Review: A History of Social Assistance in Ontario, 1791–1987'. Manuscript prepared for the Social Assistance Review Committee, vol. 44, 1988.

James, Jean M. *Family Benefits Mothers in Metropolitan Toronto*. Toronto: Ministry of Community and Social Services, 1973.

Lang, Vernon. *The Service State Emerges in Ontario*. Toronto: Ontario Economic Council, 1974.

Ministry of Community and Social Services. *Back on Track: First Report of the Advisory Group on New Social Assistance Legislation*. Toronto: Queen's Printer for Ontario, 1991.

_____. *Speaking Out: Final Report of the New Social Assistance Legislation Consumer Focus Group Project*. Toronto: Queen's Printer for Ontario, February 1992.

_____. *Time for Action*. Toronto: Queen's Printer for Ontario, 1992.

_____. *Transitions: Report of the Social Assistance Review Committee*. Toronto: Queen's Printer, 1988.

_____. *Turning Point: New Support Programs for People with Low Incomes*. Toronto: Queen's Printer for Ontario, July 1993.

Ontario. Department of Social and Family Services Annual Reports. Toronto: Queen's Printer, 1966–71.

_____. *Legislature Debates*. Toronto: Queen's Printer, 1951–92.

_____. Ministry of Community and Social Services Annual Reports. Toronto: Queen's Printer, 1972–84.

_____. Report of the Minister of Public Welfare, Ontario. Toronto: Queen's Printer, 1930–66.

_____. 'Report on the Spouse in the House Rule'. Manuscript prepared for the Social Assistance Review Committee, January 1987.

_____. Sessional Papers, Annual Reports of the Ontario Mothers' Allowance Commission. Toronto: Queen's Printer, 1920–30.

Ontario Social Service Council of Canada. *Social Welfare*. Toronto: Ontario Social Service Council of Canada, October 1918.

Ross, David P. 'Benefit Adequacy in Ontario'. Manuscript prepared for the Social Assistance Review Committee, vol. 43, 1988.

Ross, Heather. 'First Nations Self-Government: A Background Report'. Manuscript prepared for the Social Assistance Review Committee, vol. 52, 1988.

Social Development Council. . . . *And the Poor Get Poorer: A Study of Social Welfare Programs in Ontario*, rev. edn. Toronto: Social Development Council, September 1983.

Status Review Committee. *Survey of Provincial/Municipal Integration Sites*. Toronto: Ministry of Community and Social Services, June 1986.

Willems, Harry, and Michael Benjamin. *Project Report on Best Interest of Child and Alternative Care Linkage in Respect of Family Benefits Act Work Expectation Program*. Toronto: Ministry of Community and Social Services, 4 December 1981.

Williams, Clifford J. *Decades of Service: A History of the Ontario Ministry of Community and Social Services, 1930–1980*. Toronto: Government of Ontario, 1984.

_____. 'The Social Service Story in Ontario, 1970 to 1987: A History of the Ministry of Community and Social Services of the Government of Ontario from 1970 to 1987'. Manuscript, Ministry of Community and Social Services.

SELECTED SECONDARY SOURCES

Abramovitz, Mimi. *Regulating the Lives of Women: Social Welfare Policy from Colonial Times to the Present*. Boston: South End Press, 1988.

Adams, Ian, William Cameron, Brian Hill, and Peter Penz, eds. *The 'Real' Poverty Report*. Edmonton: Hurtig Limited, 1971.

Adams, Mary Louise. *The Problem with Normal: Postwar Youth and the Construction of Heterosexuality*. Toronto: University of Toronto Press, 1997.

Albo, Greg, and Jane Jenson. 'A Contested Concept: The Relative Autonomy of the State'. In *The New Canadian Political Economy*, edited by Wallace Clement and Glen Williams, 180–211. Kingston: McGill-Queen's University Press, 1989.

_____, David Langille, and Leo Panitch, eds. *A Different Kind of State? Popular Power and Democratic Administration*. Toronto: Oxford University Press, 1993.

Allan, Richard. *The Social Passion: Religion and Social Reform in Canada, 1914–1929.* Toronto: University of Toronto Press, 1971.

Andrew, Caroline. 'Women and the Welfare State'. *Canadian Journal of Political Science* 17 (December 1984):667–83.

Armitage, Andrew. *Social Welfare in Canada: Ideals and Realities.* Toronto: McClelland and Stewart, 1975.

Armstrong, Pat. *Labour Pains: Women's Work in Crisis.* Toronto: Women's Press, 1984.

_____, and Hugh Armstrong. *The Double Ghetto: Canadian Women and Their Segregated Work.* Toronto: McClelland and Stewart, 1978.

Arnup, Katherine, Andrée Lévesque, and Ruth Roach Pierson. *Delivering Motherhood: Maternal Ideologies and Practices in the 19th and 20th Centuries.* New York: Routledge, 1990.

Avery, Don. *'Dangerous Foreigners': European Immigrant Workers and Labour Radicalism in Canada, 1896–1932.* Toronto: McClelland and Stewart, 1979.

Bacchi, Carol. *Liberation Deferred?: The Ideas of English-Canadian Suffragists, 1877–1918.* Toronto: University of Toronto Press, 1983.

Bakker, Isabella. *Rethinking Restructuring: Gender and Change in Canada.* Toronto: University of Toronto Press, 1996.

Baldock, Cora V., and Bettina Cass. *Women, Social Welfare and the State in Australia.* Sydney: Allen and Unwin, 1983.

Banting, Keith. *The Welfare State and Canadian Federalism.* Kingston: McGill-Queen's University Press, 1982.

Barrett, Michele. *Women's Oppression Today.* London: New Left Review, 1980.

_____, and Mary McIntosh. 'The Family Wage: Some Problems for Socialists and Feminists'. *Capital and Class* no. 11 (1980):51–72.

_____, and _____. *The Anti-social Family.* London: Verso, 1982.

Baxter, Sheila. *No Way To Live: Poor Women Speak Out.* Vancouver: New Star Books, 1988.

Bell, D. *The Cultural Contradictions of Capitalism.* New York: Basic Books, 1978.

Bell, Winifred. *Aid to Dependent Children.* New York: Columbia University Press, 1965.

Block, F. 'The Ruling Class Does Not Rule'. *Socialist Review* 7 (May–June 1977):6–28.

_____, Richard A. Cloward, Barbara Ehrenreich, and Frances Fox Piven. *The Mean Season: The Attack on the Welfare State.* New York: Pantheon, 1987.

Blouin, Barbara. 'Women and Children Last: Single Mothers on Welfare in Nova Scotia'. Halifax: Institute for the Study of Women, Mount Saint Vincent University, February 1989.

Bock, Gisele, and Pat Thane, eds. *Maternity and Gender Policies: Women and the Rise of the European Welfare States, 1880s–1950s.* London: Routledge, 1991.

Bothwell, Robert, Ian Drummond, and John English. *Canada Since 1945: Power, Politics and Provincialism*. Toronto: University of Toronto Press, 1981.

Bowles, S., and H. Gintis. *Democracy and Capitalism*. New York: Basic Books, 1986.

Boyer, Robert, and Daniel Drache, eds. *States vs. Markets: The Limits of Globalization*. London: Routledge, 1996.

Bradbury, Bettina, ed. *Canadian Family History: Selected Readings*. Mississauga, Ontario: Copp Clark, 1992.

Brandt, Gail Cuthbert. 'Pigeon-holed and Forgotten: The Work of the Subcommittee on Post-war Problems of Women, 1943'. *Social History* 15, no. 29 (May 1982):239–59.

Brodie, Janine. *Women and Canadian Public Policy*. Toronto: Harcourt Brace and Company, 1996.

Brown, Wendy. 'Finding the Man in the State'. *Feminist Studies* 18, no. 1 (Spring 1992):7–33.

Bryce, Peter. 'Mothers' Allowance'. *Social Welfare* 1, no. 6 (1925):131–2.

Bryden, Penny. *The Welfare State in Canada: Past, Present and Future*. Concord, Ontario: Irwin, 1997.

Bullen, John. 'J.J. Kelso and the "New" Child-Savers: The Genesis of the Children's Aid Movement in Ontario'. *Ontario History* LXXXII, no. 2 (June 1990):107–28.

Burstyn, Varda, Dorothy Smith, and Roxanna Ng. *Women, Class, Family and the State*. Toronto: Garamond, 1985.

Cameron, D. 'The Expansion of the Public Economy: A Comparative Analysis'. *American Political Science Review* 4 (1978):1243–61.

Capponi, Pat. *Dispatches from the Poverty Line*. Toronto: Penguin Books, 1997.

Carniol, Ben. *Case Critical: The Dilemma of Social Work in Canada*. Toronto: Between the Lines, 1987.

Carroll, William, ed. *Organizing Dissent: Contemporary Social Movements in Theory and Practice*. Toronto: Garamond, 1992.

Cassidy, Harry. *Social Security and Reconstruction in Canada*. Toronto: Ryerson Press, 1943.

Christie, Nancy, and Michael Gauvreau. *A Full-Orbed Christianity: The Protestant Churches and Social Welfare in Canada, 1900–1940*. Kingston: McGill-Queen's University Press, 1996.

Chunn, Dorothy. *From Punishment to Doing Good: Family Courts and Socialized Justice in Ontario, 1900–1940*. Toronto: University of Toronto Press, 1992.

Clarke, John. 'Ontario's Social Movements—the Struggle Intensifies'. In *Culture and Social Change: Social Movements in Quebec and Ontario*, edited by Colin Leys and Marguerite Mendell, 213–24. Montreal: Black Rose Books, 1993.

Cohen, J.L. *Mothers' Allowance Legislation in Canada: A Legislative Review and Analysis with a Proposed 'Standard' Act*. Toronto: Macmillan, 1927.

Comacchio, Cynthia R. *'Nations Are Built of Babies': Saving Ontario's Mothers and Children, 1900–1940*. Montreal: McGill-Queen's University Press, 1993.

_____.' "The Infant Soldier":The Great War and the Medical Campaign for Child Welfare'. *Canadian Bulletin of Medical History* 5, no. 2 (Winter 1988):99–119.

_____. ' "The Mothers of the Land Must Suffer": Child and Maternal Welfare in Rural and Outpost Ontario, 1918–1940'. *Ontario History* LXXX, no. 3 (September 1988):183–205.

Concoran, Mary, Greg Duncan, and Marth Hill. 'The Economic Fortunes of Women and Children: Lessons from the Panel of Income Dynamics'. *Signs* 10 (Winter 1984):232–47.

Cook, Ramsay. *The Regenerators: Social Criticism in Late Victorian English Canada*.Toronto: University of Toronto Press, 1985.

Corrigan, Philip, ed. *Capitalism, State Formation and Marxist Theory*. London: Quartet, 1980.

_____. 'On Moral Regulation: Some Preliminary Remarks'. *Sociological Review* 29, no. 2 (1981):313–37.

_____, and Derek Sayer. *The Great Arch: English State Formation as Cultural Revolution*. Oxford: Basil Blackwell, 1985.

Curtis, Bruce. *Building the Educational State: Canada West, 1836–1871*. London: Althouse Press, 1988.

_____. 'Representation and State Formation in the Canadas, 1790–1850'. *Studies in Political Economy* 28 (Spring 1989):59–88.

Dale, Jennifer, and Peggy Foster. *Feminist and State Welfare*. London: Routledge and Kegan Paul, 1986.

Dally, Ann. *Inventing Motherhood: The Consequences of an Ideal*. New York: Schocken Books, 1983.

Davies, Megan. 'Services Rendered, Rearing Children for the State: Mothers' Pensions in British Columbia, 1919–1931'. In *Not Just Pin Money: Selected Essays on the History of Women's Work in British Columbia*, edited by Barbara Latham and Roberta Pazdro, 249–64.Victoria: Camosun College, 1984.

D'Emilio, John. 'The Homosexual Menace:The Politics of Sexuality in Cold War America'. In *Passion and Power: Sexuality in History*, edited by Kathy Peiss and Christina Simmons, 226–40. Philadelphia: Temple University Press, 1989.

Dickinson, James, and Bob Russell, eds. *Family, Economy and State: The Social Reproduction Process under Capitalism*.Toronto: Garamond, 1987.

Drache, Daniel, ed. *Getting on Track: Social Democratic Strategies for Ontario*. Montreal: McGill-Queen's University Press, 1992.

_____, and Meric Gertler, eds. *The New Era of Global Competition: State Policy and Market Power*. Kingston: McGill-Queen's University Press, 1991.

Drover, Glenn, and Patrick Keirans, eds. *New Approaches to Welfare Theory*. Aldershot: Edward Elgar, 1993.

Drury, E.C. *Farmer Premier: Memoirs of the Honourable E.C. Drury*. Toronto: McClelland and Stewart, 1966.

Dubinsky, Karen. *Improper Advances: Rape and Heterosexual Conflict in Ontario, 1880–1929*. Chicago: University of Chicago Press, 1993.

Duffy, Ann, Nancy Mandell, and Norene Pupo. *Few Choices: Women, Work and Family*. Toronto: Garamond, 1989.

Durkheim, Emile. *Moral Education: A Study in the Theory and Application of the Sociology of Education*. New York: Free Press, 1961.

Dwork, Deborah. *War Is Good for Babies and Other Young Children: A History of the Infant and Child Welfare Movement in England, 1898–1918*. London: Tavistock Publications, 1987.

Ehrenreich, Barbara. *The Hearts of Men: American Dreams and the Flight from Commitment*. New York: Anchor Books, 1983.

Ehring, George, and Wayne Roberts. *Giving Away a Miracle: Lost Dreams, Broken Promises and the Ontario NDP*. Oakville, Ontario: Mosaic Press, 1993.

Eichler, Margrit. *Families in Canada Today: Recent Changes and Their Policy Consequences*. Toronto: Gage, 1983.

Eisenstein, Zillah. *Capitalist Patriarchy and the Case for Socialist Feminism*. New York: Review Press, 1979.

———. *The Radical Future of Liberal Feminism*. New York: Longman, 1981.

Elshtain, Jean Bethke. *Public Man, Private Woman: Women in Social and Political Thought*. Princeton: Princeton University Press, 1984.

Esping-Andersen, Gosta. 'Citizenship and Socialism: Decommodification and Solidarity in the Welfare State'. In *Stagnation and Renewal*, edited by G. Esping-Andersen, M. Rein, and L. Rainwater, 78–101. New York: M.E. Sharpe, Armonk, 1987.

———. *Politics against Markets*. Princeton: Princeton University Press, 1985.

———. 'Power and Distributional Regimes'. *Politics and Society* 14 (1985):223–56.

———. 'The Three Political Economies of the Welfare State'. *Canadian Review of Sociology and Anthropology* 26, no. 1 (February 1989):10–36.

———, and R. Friedland. 'Class Coalition in the Making of West European Economies'. *Political Power and Social Theory* 3 (1982):1–52.

Evans, Patricia M. 'Eroding Canadian Social Welfare: The Mulroney Legacy, 1984–1993'. *Social Policy and Administration* 28, no. 2 (June 1994):107–119.

———. 'Targeting Single Mothers for Employment: Comparisons from the United States, Britain and Canada'. *Social Service Review* 66 (September 1992):378–98.

———. 'Work Incentives and the Single Mother: Dilemmas of Reform'. *Canadian Public Policy* 14, no. 2 (June 1988):125–36.

———, and Eilene L. McIntyre. 'Welfare, Work Incentives, and the Single Mother: An Interprovincial Comparison'. In *The Canadian Welfare State:*

Evolution and Transition, edited by Jacqueline S. Ismael, 101–25. Edmonton: University of Alberta Press, 1987.

Evans, Peter B., Dietrich Rueschemeyer, and Theda Skocpol, eds. *Bringing the State Back In*. Cambridge: Cambridge University Press, 1985.

Falk, J.T.H. 'Mothers' Allowance'. *Social Welfare* 1, no. 6 (1919):131.

Fildes, Valerie, Lara Marks, and Hillary Marland, eds. *Women and Children First: International Maternal and Infant Welfare, 1870–1945*. London: Routledge, 1992.

Flora, Peter, and Jens Alber. 'Modernization, Democratization and the Development of Welfare States in Europe'. In *The Development of Welfare States in Europe and America*, edited by Flora Heidenheimer and Arnold J. Heidenheimer, 37–80. London: Transaction Books, 1981.

Folbre, Nancy. 'The Pauperization of Motherhood: Patriarchy and Public Policy in the United States'. *Review of Radical Political Economics* 16 (Winter 1984):72–88.

Foucault, Michel. *A History of Sexuality*, vols 1 and 2, translated by Robert Hurley. New York: Pantheon Books, 1978.

Fox Piven, Frances, and Richard A. Cloward. *Poor People's Movements: Why They Succeed, How They Fail*. New York: Random House, 1979.

_____, and _____. *Regulating the Poor: The Functions of Public Welfare*. New York: Pantheon Books, 1971.

Frager, Ruth. 'Women Workers and the Canadian Labour Movement, 1870–1940'. In *Union Sisters: Women in the Labour Movement*, edited by Linda Briskin and Lynda Yanz, 44–66. Toronto: Women's Press, 1983.

Fraser, Nancy. *Unruly Practices: Power, Discourse and Gender in Contemporary Social Theory*. Minneapolis: University of Minnesota Press, 1989.

Gagnon, Georgette, and Dan Rath. *Not Without Cause: David Peterson's Fall from Grace*. Toronto: HarperCollins, 1992.

Ginzberg, Lori D. ' "Moral Suasion Is Moral Balderdash": Women, Politics, and Social Activism in the 1850s'. *Journal of American History* 73 (December 1986):601–22.

_____. *Women and the Work of Benevolence: Morality, Politics and Class in the 19th Century United States*. New Haven: Yale University Press, 1990.

Golz, Annalee. 'Family Matters: The "Canadian Family" and the State in the Post-World War II Period'. *Left History*, forthcoming.

Goodwin, Joanne. 'An American Experiment in Paid Motherhood: The Implementation of Mothers' Pensions in Early Twentieth-Century Chicago'. *Gender and History* 4 (1992):323–42.

_____. *Gender and the Politics of Welfare Reform: Mothers' Pensions in Chicago, 1911–1929*. Chicago: University of Chicago Press, 1997.

Gordon, Linda. 'Black and White Visions of Welfare: Women's Welfare Activism, 1890–1945'. *Journal of American History* 78 (September 1991):559–90.

_____. *Heroes of Their Own Lives: The Politics and History of Family Violence, Boston, 1880–1960*. New York: Penguin Books, 1989.

_____. *Pitied But Not Entitled: Single Mothers and the History of Welfare*. New York: Free Press, 1994.

_____. 'Single Mothers and Child Neglect, 1880–1920'. *American Quarterly* 37 (Summer 1985):173–92.

_____. 'What Does Welfare Regulate? A Review Essay on the Writings of Frances Fox Piven and Richard A. Cloward'. *Social Research* 55 (Winter 1988):609–30.

_____, ed. *Women, the State, and Welfare*. Madison: University of Wisconsin Press, 1990.

Gough, Ian. *The Political Economy of the Welfare State*. London: Macmillan, 1979.

Gourevitch, P. *Politics in Hard Times*. New York: Cornell University Press, 1986.

Graham, Roger. *Old Man Ontario: Leslie M. Frost*. Toronto: University of Toronto Press, 1990.

Granatstein, J.L. *Canada's War, the Politics of the Mackenzie King Government, 1939–1945*. Toronto: Oxford University Press, 1975.

Grayson, L.M., and Michael Bliss, eds. *The Wretched of Canada: Letters to R.B. Bennett, 1930–1935*. Toronto: University of Toronto Press, 1971.

Guest, Dennis, *The Emergence of Social Security in Canada*. Vancouver: University of British Columbia Press, 1980.

Haddad, Jane. 'Sexism and Social Welfare Policy: The Case of Family Benefits in Ontario'. *Occasional Papers in Social Policy Analysis*, no. 8. Toronto: Department of Sociology, OISE, 1985.

_____, and Stephen Milton. 'The Construction of Gender Roles in Social Policy: Mothers' Allowances and Day Care in Ontario before World War II'. *Canadian Woman Studies* 7, no. 4 (Winter 1986):68–70.

Hall, Stuart, Dorothy Hobson, Andrew Lowe, and Paul Willis. *Culture, Media, Language*. London: Hutchinson, 1980.

Hamilton, Roberta. *The Liberation of Women: A Study of Patriarchy and Capitalism*. London: Allen, 1978.

Heclo, Hugh. *Modern Social Politics in Britain and Sweden*. New Haven: Yale University Press, 1974.

Higonnet, Margaret Randolph, Jane Jenson, Sonya Michel, and Margaret Collins Weitz, eds. *Behind the Lines: Gender and the Two World Wars*. New Haven: Yale University Press, 1987.

Horn, Michiel, ed. *The Dirty Thirties: Canadians in the Great Depression*. Toronto: University of Toronto Press, 1972.

_____. *The League for Social Reconstruction: Intellectual Origins of the Democratic Left in Canada, 1930–1942*. Toronto: University of Toronto Press, 1980.

Houle, François. 'Economic Strategy and the Restructuring of the Fordist Wage-Labour Relationship in Canada'. *Studies in Political Economy*, no. 11 (Summer 1983):127–47.

Hoy, Claire. *Bill Davis*. Toronto: Methuen, 1985.

Humphries, Jane. 'Protective Legislation, the Capitalist State and Working Class Men: The Case of the 1842 Mines Regulation Act'. *Feminist Review* 7 (1981):1–33.

_____. 'The Working Class Family, Women's Liberation, and Class Struggle: The Case of Nineteenth Century British History'. *The Review of Radical Political Economics* 9, no. 3 (Fall 1977):25–41.

Hunnius, Gerry, ed. *Participatory Democracy for Canada*. Montreal: Black Rose, 1971.

Hurl, Lorna. 'Building a Profession: The Origin and Development of the Department of Social Service in the University of Toronto 1914–1928'. Working Papers on Social Welfare in Canada, School of Social Work, University of Toronto.

Iacovetta, Franca, and Mariana Valverde, eds. *Gender Conflicts: New Essays in Women's History*. Toronto: University of Toronto Press, 1992.

Ismael, J.S., ed. *Canadian Social Welfare Policy: Federal and Provincial Dimension*. Kingston: McGill-Queen's University Press, 1985.

Jenson, Jane. 'Gender and Reproduction: Or, Babies and the State'. *Studies in Political Economy* 20 (Summer 1986):9–46.

_____. 'Paradigms and Political Discourse: Protective Legislation in France and the United States Before 1914'. *Canadian Journal of Political Science* 22 (June 1989):235–58.

Jessop, B. *The Capitalist State*. Oxford: Martin Robertson, 1982.

Johnston, Charles M. *E.C. Drury: Agrarian Idealist*. Toronto: University of Toronto Press, 1986.

Jones, Andrew, and Len Rutman. *In the Children's Aid: J.J. Kelso and Child Welfare in Ontario*. Toronto: University of Toronto Press, 1981.

Kamerman, Sheila B., and Alfred J. Kahn. *Privatization and the Welfare State*. Princeton: Princeton University Press, 1989.

Katz, Michael B. *Improving Poor People: The Welfare State, the 'Underclass', and Urban Schools as History*. Princeton: Princeton University Press, 1995.

Katzenstein, P. *Small States in World Markets*. Ithaca: Cornell University Press, 1985.

Kaufman, Michael, ed. *Beyond Patriarchy: Essays by Men on Pleasure, Power and Change*. Toronto: Oxford University Press, 1987.

Kealey, Linda, ed. 'Canadian Socialism and the Woman Question, 1900–1914'. *Labour/Le Travailleur* 13 (Spring 1984):77–100.

_____. *A Not Unreasonable Claim: Women and Reform in Canada 1880s–1920s*. Toronto: Women's Press, 1979.

_____, and Joan Sangster. *Beyond the Vote: Canadian Women and Politics*. Toronto: University of Toronto Press, 1989.

Kennedy, Col. T.L. *Tom Kennedy's Story*. Toronto: University of Toronto Press, 1960.

Kinsman, Gary. *The Regulation of Desire: Sexuality in Canada*. Montreal: Black Rose, 1987.

Kitchen, Brigitte. 'Wartime Social Reform: The Introduction of Family Allowances'. *Canadian Journal of Social Work Education* 7, no. 1 (1981):29–54.

Klein, Anne, and Wayne Roberts. *Women at Work, Ontario, 1850–1930*. Toronto: Canadian Women's Education Press, 1974.

Koven, Seth, and Sonya Michel. 'Report: Gender and the Origins of the Welfare State'. *Radical History Review* 43 (1989):112–19.

_____, and Sonya Michel, eds. *Mothers of a New World: Maternalist Politics and the Origins of Welfare States*. New York: Routledge, 1993.

Ladd-Taylor, Molly. *Mother Work: Women, Child Welfare, and the State, 1890–1930*. Urbana: University of Illinois Press, 1994.

Lawrence, Kathleen. 'Systemic Discrimination: Regulation 8—Family Benefits Act: Policy of Reasonable Efforts to Obtain Financial Resources'. *Journal of Law and Social Policy* 6 (Fall 1990):57–76.

Laxer, Gordon. 'Social Solidarity, Democracy and Global Capitalism'. *Canadian Review of Sociology and Anthropology* 32, no. 3 (1995):287–313.

Laxer, Robert. *Canadian Unions*. Toronto: Lorimer, 1976.

Leman, Christopher. *The Collapse of Welfare Reform: Political Institutions, Policy, and the Poor in Canada and the United States*. Cambridge: MIT Press, 1980.

Lewis, Jane, ed. *Women's Welfare, Women's Rights*. London: Croom Helm, 1983.

Luxton, Meg. *More Than a Labour of Love: Three Generations of Women's Work in the Home*. Toronto: Women's Press, 1980.

McBride, Stephen, and John Shields, eds. *Dismantling a Nation: Canada and the New World Order*. Halifax: Fernwood, 1993.

McCallum, Margaret. 'Assistance to Veterans and Their Dependants: Steps on the Way to the Administrative State, 1914–1929'. In *Canadian Perspectives on Law and Society: Issues in Legal History*, edited by W. Wesley Pue and Barry Wright, 157–77. Ottawa: Carleton University Press, 1988.

McConnachie, Kathleen. 'Methodology in the Study of Women in History: A Case Study of Helen MacMurchy, M.D.'. *Ontario History* LXXV, no. 1 (March 1983):61–70.

McDougall, A.K. *John P. Robarts: His Life and Government*. Toronto: University of Toronto Press, 1986.

McIntosh, Mary. 'The State and the Oppression of Women'. In *Feminism and Materialism: Women and Modes of Production*, edited by Annette Kuhn and Ann Marie Wolpe, 254–89. London: Routledge and Kegan Paul, 1978.

McKenty, Neil. *Mitch Hepburn*. Toronto: McClelland and Stewart, 1967.

MacKinnon, Catharine. *Toward a Feminist Theory of the State*. Cambridge, Mass.: Harvard University Press, 1989.

McLaren, Angus. *Our Own Master Race: Eugenics in Canada, 1885–1945*. Toronto: McClelland and Stewart, 1990.

_____. *Reproductive Rituals: The Perception of Fertility in England from the Sixteenth Century to the Nineteenth Century.* London: Methuen, 1984.

_____, and Arlene Tigar McLaren. *The Bedroom and the State: The Changing Practices and Politics of Contraception and Abortion in Canada, 1880–1980.* Toronto: McClelland and Stewart, 1986.

MacPherson, Ian. *Each for All: A History of the Cooperative Movement in English Canada, 1900–1945.* Toronto: Macmillan of Canada/Institute of Canadian Studies, Carleton University, 1979.

Mahon, Rianne. 'From "Bringing" to "Putting": The State in Late Twentieth-Century Social Theory'. *Canadian Journal of Sociology* 16, no. 2 (Spring 1991):119–44.

Manthorpe, Jonathan. *The Power and the Tories: Ontario Politics—1943 to the Present.* Toronto: Macmillan, 1986.

Marsh, Leonard C. *Report on Social Security for Canada.* Toronto: University of Toronto Press, 1975.

Marsh, Margaret. *Suburban Lives.* New Brunswick: Rutgers University Press, 1990.

May, Elaine T. *Homeward Bound: American Families in the Cold War Era.* New York: Basic Books, 1988.

Maynard, Steven. 'Rough Work and Rugged Men: The Social Construction of Masculinity in Working-Class History'. *Labour/Le Travail* 23 (Spring 1989): 159–69.

Miliband, Ralph. *The State in Capitalist Society.* London: Quartet, 1969.

Mills, C. Wright. *Sociological Imagination.* New York: Oxford University Press, 1959.

Milwaukee County Welfare Rights Organization. *Welfare Mothers Speak Out: We Ain't Gonna Shuffle Anymore.* New York: W.W. Norton and Co., 1972.

Mishra, Ramesh. *The Welfare State in Capitalist Society: Politics of Retrenchment and Maintenance in Europe, North American and Australia.* Toronto: Harvester Wheatsheaf, 1990.

_____. *The Welfare State in Crisis: Social Thought and Social Change.* Brighton, UK: Harvester Press, 1984.

Mort, Frank. *Dangerous Sexualities: Medico-Moral Politics in England Since 1830.* London: Routledge and Kegan Paul, 1987.

Morton, Suzanne. *Ideal Surroundings: Domestic Life in a Working-class Suburb in the 1920s.* Toronto: University of Toronto Press, 1995.

Moscovitch, Allan, and Jim Albert, eds. *The 'Benevolent' State: The Growth of Welfare in Canada.* Toronto: Garamond, 1987.

_____, and Glenn Drover, eds. *Inequality: Essays on the Political Economy of Social Welfare.* Toronto: University of Toronto Press, 1981.

Mosse, George. *Nationalism and Sexuality: Middle-Class Morality and Sexual Norms in Modern Europe.* Madison: University of Wisconsin Press, 1985.

Myles, J. *Old Age in the Welfare State.* Boston: Little, Brown, 1984.

Naylor, Jim. *The New Democracy: Challenging the Social Order in Industrial Ontario, 1914–25.* Toronto: University of Toronto Press, 1991.

Nelson, Barbara J. 'The Origins of the Two-Channel Welfare State: Workmen's Compensation and Mothers' Aid'. In *Women, the State and Welfare*, edited by Linda Gordon, 123–51. Madison: University of Wisconsin Press, 1990.

Ng, Roxana, Gillian Walker, and Jacob Muller, eds. *Community Organization and the Canadian State.* Toronto: Garamond, 1990.

O'Connor, James. *The Fiscal Crisis of the State.* New York: St Martin's Press, 1973.

Offe, Claus, 'Advanced Capitalism and the Welfare State'. *Politics and Society* 4 (1972):479–88.

_____. *Contradictions and the Welfare State.* London: Hutchinson, 1984.

_____. *Disorganized Capitalism.* Cambridge: MIT Press, 1985.

Oliver, Peter. *G. Howard Ferguson: Ontario Tory.* Toronto: University of Toronto Press, 1977.

Orloff, Ann Shola. *The Politics of Pensions: A Comparative Analysis of Britain, Canada, and the United States, 1880–1940.* Madison: University of Wisconsin Press, 1993.

Owram, Douglas. *Born at the Right Time: A History of the Baby-boom Generation.* Toronto: University of Toronto Press, 1996.

Palmer, Bryan. *Working-Class Experience: The Rise and Reconstitution of Canadian Labour, 1800–1980.* Toronto: Butterworths, 1983.

Panitch, Leo, ed. *The Canadian State.* Toronto: University of Toronto Press, 1977.

Parr, Joy, ed. *Childhood and Family in Canadian History.* Toronto: McClelland and Stewart, 1982.

_____. *The Gender of Breadwinners: Women, Men and Change in Two Industrial Towns, 1880–1950.* Toronto: University of Toronto Press, 1990.

Pask, E. Diane, and Marnie L. McCall. *How Much and Why? Economic Implications of Marriage Breakdown: Spousal and Child Support.* Calgary: Canadian Research Institute for Law and the Family, 1989.

Pateman, Carole. *The Disorder of Women: Democracy, Feminism and Political Theory.* Stanford: Stanford University Press, 1989.

_____. 'The Patriarchal Welfare State: Women and Democracy'. In *Democracy and the Welfare State*, edited by Amy Gutman, 231–60. Princeton: Princeton University Press, 1988.

Pearce, Diana. 'Welfare Is Not *for* Women: Why the War on Poverty Cannot Conquer the Feminization of Poverty'. In *Women, the State and Welfare*, edited by Linda Gordon, 265–79. Madison: University of Wisconsin Press, 1990.

_____. 'Women, Work and Welfare: The Feminization of Poverty'. In *Working Women and Their Families*, edited by K. Feinstein, 103–24. London: Sage Publications, 1979.

Pearson, Carol Lyn. *One of the Seesaw: The Ups and Downs of a Single-Parent Family.* New York: Random House, 1988.

Pedersen, Susan. 'The Failure of Feminism in the Making of the British Welfare State'. *Radical History Review* 43 (1989):105.

_____. *Family, Dependence and the Origins of the Welfare State: Britain and France, 1914–1945.* Cambridge, NY: Cambridge University Press, 1993.

_____. 'Gender, Welfare, and Citizenship in Britain During the Great War'. *American Historical Review* 95 (October 1990):983–1006.

Penner, Norman. *The Canadian Left.* Scarborough: Prentice-Hall, 1977.

Pierson, Ruth Roach. 'Gender and the Unemployment Insurance Debates in Canada, 1934–1940'. *Labour/Le Travail* 25 (Spring 1990):77–103.

_____, and Beth Light, eds. *No Easy Road: Women in Canada, 1920s to 1960s.* Toronto: New Hogtown Press, 1990.

Piva, Michael. 'The Workmen's Compensation Movement in Ontario'. *Ontario History* LXVII, no. 1 (March 1975):39–56.

Piven, Frances Fox, and Richard A. Cloward. *Regulating the Poor: The Functions of Public Welfare.* New York: Pantheon Books, 1971.

_____, and _____. 'Humanitarianism in History: A Response to the Critics'. In *Social Welfare or Social Control? Some Historical Reflections on Regulating the Poor,* edited by Walter Trattner, 114–48. Knoxville: University of Tennessee Press, 1983.

_____, and _____. 'Welfare Doesn't Shore Up Traditional Family Roles: A Reply to Linda Gordon'. *Social Research* 55 (1988):631–47.

Polanyi, Karl. *The Great Transformation.* New York: Farrar & Rinehart, 1944.

Porter, Marion, and Joan Gullen. 'Sexism in Policy Relating to Welfare Fraud'. In *Taking Sex into Account,* edited by Jill Vickers, 209–18. Ottawa: Carleton University Press, 1984.

Poulantzas, N. *Political Power and Social Classes.* New York: New Left Books, 1973.

Powell, Alan, ed. *The City: Attacking Modern Myths.* Toronto: McClelland and Stewart, 1972.

Prentice, Alison, and Susan Houston, eds. *Family, School and Society in Nineteenth-Century Canada.* Toronto: Oxford University Press, 1975.

Prentice, Susan. 'Workers, Mothers, Reds: Toronto's Postwar Daycare Fight'. *Studies in Political Economy* 30 (Autumn 1989):115–42.

Pryor, F. *Public Expenditures in Communist and Capitalist Nations.* London: Allen and Unwin, 1969.

Przeworski, A. *Capitalism and Social Democracy.* Cambridge: Cambridge University Press, 1985.

_____. 'Material Bases of Consent: Politics and Economics in a Hegemonic System'. *Political Power and Social Theory* 1 (1980):21–66.

Pumphrey, Muriel W., and Ralph E. Pumphrey. 'The Widows' Pension Movement, 1900–1930: Preventive Child-Saving or Social Control?' In *Social Welfare or Social Control? Some Historical Reflections on Regulating the*

Poor, edited by Walter I. Trattner, 51–66. Knoxville: University of Tennessee Press, 1983.

Quadagno, Jill. *The Color of Welfare: How Racism Undermined the War on Poverty*. New York: Oxford University Press, 1994.

_____. 'Race, Class and Gender in the U.S. Welfare State: Nixon's Failed Family Assistance Plan'. *American Sociological Review* 55 (February 1990):11–28.

Ralph, Diana, André Regimbald, and Nerée St-Amand, eds. *Open for Business: Closed to People—Mike Harris's Ontario*. Halifax: Fernwood, 1997.

Ramkhalawansingh, Ceta. 'Women During the Great War'. In *Women at Work, 1850–1930*, edited by J. Acton et al., 261–308. Toronto: Canadian Women's Educational Press, 1974.

Roberts, Wayne. 'Besieged Innocence: The "Problem" and the Problems of Working Women—Toronto 1896–1914'. In *Women at Work, 1850–1930*, edited by J. Acton et al., 21–59. Toronto: Canadian Women's Educational Press, 1974.

Rooke, P.T., and R.L. Schnell. 'Making the Way More Comfortable: Charlotte Whitton's Child Welfare Career'. *Journal of Canadian Studies* 17, no. 4 (Winter 1983):33–45.

Rose, Sonya. *Gender, Labor, and Capital: The Creation of a Segregated World of Work and Its Consequences in 19th Century Britain*. Forthcoming.

Rosenberg, Rosalind. *Divided Lives: American Women in the Twentieth Century*. New York: Noonday Press, 1992.

Ruggie, Mary. *The State and Working Women: A Comparative Study of Britain and Sweden*. Princeton: Princeton University Press, 1984.

Rutman, Len. 'Importation of British Waifs into Canada: 1868 to 1916'. *Child Welfare* 53, no. 3 (March 1973):158–66.

Sabatini, E. Rico, with Sandra Nightingale. *Welfare—No Fair: A Critical Analysis of Ontario's Welfare System, 1985–1994*. Vancouver: The Fraser Institute, 1996.

Sangster, Joan. *Dreams of Equality: Women on the Canadian Left, 1920–1950*. Toronto: McClelland and Stewart, 1989.

Sargent, L., ed. *Women and Revolution*. Boston: South End Press, 1979.

Sassoon, Anne Showstack, ed. *Women and the State: The Shifting Boundaries of Public and Private*. London: Hutchinson, 1987.

Schnell, R.L. 'Female Separatism and Institution-Building Continuities and Discontinuities in Canadian Child Welfare, 1913–1935'. *International Review of History and Political Science* 25, no. 2 (May 1988):14–46.

Scott, Joan W. 'Rewriting History'. In *Behind the Lines: Gender and the Two World Wars*, edited by Margaret Higonnet, Jane Jenson, Sonya Michel, and Margaret Weitz, 21–30. New Haven: Yale University Press, 1987.

Sheehan, Susan. *Welfare Mothers*. Boston: Houghton Mifflin, 1975.

Showalter, Elaine. *Sexual Anarchy: Gender and Culture at the Fin de Siècle*. New York: Viking, 1990.

Siim, Birte. 'Towards a Feminist Rethinking of the Welfare State'. In *The Political Interests of Gender*, edited by Kathleen Jones and Anna Jonasotlis, 160–86. Newbury Park: Sage Publications, 1988.

Simeon, Richard, ed. *Division of Powers and Public Policy*. Toronto: University of Toronto Press, 1985.

Skocpol, T. *Protecting Soldiers and Mothers: The Political Origins of Social Policy in the United States*. Cambridge, Mass.: Belknap Press of Harvard University Press, 1992.

———, and E. Amenta. 'States and Social Policy'. *Annual Review of Sociology* 12 (1986):131–57.

———, and J. Ikenberry. 'The Political Formation of the American Welfare State in Historical and Comparative Perspective'. *Comparative Social Research* 6 (1983):87–148.

Smart, Carol, ed. *Regulating Motherhood: Historical Essays on Marriage, Motherhood and Sexuality*. London: Routledge, 1992.

Smith, Allan. 'The Myth of the Self-Made Man in English Canada, 1850–1914'. *Canadian Historical Review* 59, no. 2 (June 1978):189–219.

Snell, James. *In the Shadow of the Law: Divorce in Canada, 1900–1939*. Toronto: University of Toronto Press, 1991.

Social Service Council of Canada. *Social Service Congress 1914: Report of Addresses and Proceedings*. Toronto: Social Service Council of Canada, 1914.

Speirs, Rosemary. *Out of the Blue: The Fall of the Tory Dynasty in Ontario*. Toronto: Macmillan, 1986.

Splane, Richard. *Social Welfare in Ontario*. Toronto: University of Toronto Press, 1965.

Stansell, Christine. *City of Women: Sex and Class in New York 1789–1860*. New York: Knopf, 1986.

Strange, Carolyn. *Toronto's Girl Problem: The Perils and Pleasures of the City, 1880–1930*. Toronto: University of Toronto Press, 1995.

Strong-Boag, Veronica. 'Canada's Early Experience with Income Supplements: The Introduction of Mothers' Allowance'. *Atlantis: A Women's Studies Journal* 4, no. 2 (Spring 1979):35–43.

———. 'The Girl of the New Day: Canadian Working Women in the 1920's'. *Labour/Le Travailleur* IV, no. 4 (1979):131–64.

———. 'Home Dreams: Women and the Suburban Experience in Canada, 1945-60'. *Canadian Historical Review* LXXII, no. 4 (December 1991):471–504.

———. *The New Day Recalled: Lives of Girls and Women in English Canada, 1919–1939*. Markham: Penguin Books, 1988.

———. *The Parliament of Women: The National Council of Women of Canada, 1893–1929*. Ottawa: National Museums of Canada, 1976.

———. 'Wages for Housework: Mothers' Allowances and the Beginnings of Social Security in Canada'. *Journal of Canadian Studies* 1 (Spring 1979):24–34.

_____. 'Working Women and the State: The Case of Canada, 1889–1945'. *Atlantis* 6, no. 2 (Spring 1981):1–9.

Struthers, Jim. 'How Much Is Enough? Creating a Social Minimum in Ontario, 1934-44'. *Canadian Historical Review* LXXII, no. 1 (March 1991): 39–83.

_____. *The Limits of Affluence: Welfare in Ontario, 1920–1970*. Toronto: University of Toronto Press, 1994.

_____. *Through No Fault of Their Own: Unemployment and the Canadian Welfare State, 1914–1941*. Toronto: University of Toronto Press, 1983.

Teeple, Gary. *Globalization and the Decline of Social Reform*. Toronto: Garamond Press, 1995.

Thompson, Brenda. 'The Single Mother Movement'. *Resources for Feminist Research*, Feminist Perspectives on the Canadian State, Special Issue (September 1988):124.

_____. *The Single Mothers' Survival Guide*, Halifax–Dartmouth Area edn. Halifax: Pandora Publishing, 1990.

_____. *The Single Mothers' Survival Guide*, Nova Scotia edn. Halifax: Dalhousie Public Interest Research Group, 1990.

Thompson, John Herd, and Allen Seager. *Canada 1922–1939: Decades of Discord*. Toronto: McClelland and Stewart, 1985.

Titmus, R. *Essays on the Welfare State*. London: Allen and Unwin, 1958.

Trattner, Walter. *From Poor Law to Welfare State: A History of Social Welfare in America*. New York: Free Press, 1984.

_____, ed. *Social Welfare or Social Control? Some Historical Reflections on Regulating the Poor*. Knoxville: University of Tennessee Press, 1983.

Tufte, E. *Political Control of the Economy*. Princeton: Princeton University Press, 1978.

Ursel, Jane. *Private Lives, Public Policy: 100 Years of State Intervention in the Family*. Toronto: Women's Press, 1992.

Valverde, Mariana. *The Age of Light, Soap, and Water: Moral Reform in English Canada, 1885–1925*. Toronto: McClelland and Stewart, 1991.

_____. ' "Building Anti-Delinquent Communities": Youth, Gender and Morality in the Post-War City'. In *Women in Ontario Since 1945*, edited by Joy Parr. Toronto: University of Toronto Press, forthcoming.

_____. 'The Rhetoric of Reform: Tropes and the Moral Subject'. *International Journal of the Sociology of the Law* 18, no. 1 (1990):61–72.

_____, and Lorna Weir. 'The Struggles of the Immoral: Preliminary Remarks on Moral Regulation'. *Resources for Feminist Research* 17, no. 3 (September 1988):31–4.

Weaver, John C. 'Tomorrow's Metropolis Revisited: A Critical Assessment of Urban Reform in Canada 1890–1920'. In *The Canadian City*, edited by G.A. Stetler and A.F.J. Artibise, 393–418. Toronto: McClelland and Stewart, 1977.

Weeks, Jeffrey. *Sex, Politics and Society: The Regulation of Sexuality Since 1800*. London: Longman, 1981.

Weiner, Lynn. *From Working Girl to Working Mother: The Female Labor Force in the United States 1820–1980*. Chapel Hill: University of North Carolina Press, 1985.

Weir, Margaret, Ann Shola Orloff, and Theda Skocpol, eds. *The Politics of Social Policy in the United States*. Princeton: Princeton University Press, 1988.

————, and T. Skocpol. 'State Structures and the Possibilities for "Keynesean" Responses to the Great Depression in Sweden, Britain and the United States'. In *Bringing the State Back In*, edited by P. Evans et al., 107–63. New York: Cambridge University Press, 1985.

West, Guida. *The National Welfare Rights Movement: The Social Protest of Poor Women*. New York: Praeger Special Studies, 1981.

Wharf, Brian, ed. *Community Work in Canada*. Toronto: McClelland and Stewart, 1979.

Whitaker, Reginald. *Double Standard: The Secret History of Canadian Immigration*. Toronto: Lester and Orpen Dennys, 1987.

White, Graham, ed. *The Government and Politics of Ontario*, 4th edn. Toronto: Nelson, 1990.

Whitton, Charlotte. *The Dawn of Ampler Life*. Toronto: Macmillan, 1943.

Wilson, Elizabeth. *Women and the Welfare State*. London: Tavistock, 1977.

THESES AND UNPUBLISHED PAPERS

Bain, Ian. 'The Role of J.J. Kelso in the Launching of the Child Welfare Movement in Ontario'. MSW thesis, University of Toronto, 1955.

Banting, Keith. 'Looking Back: The Political Economy of Social Policy in the 1980's'. Keynote address at the Fourth National Conference on Social Welfare Policy, Toronto, 24–7 October 1989.

Bass, Alan. ' "Their Natural Inclination": The Experience of Single Unemployed Women in Toronto During the Great Depression'. Manuscript, York University.

de la Cour, Lykke. 'Dr Helen MacMurchy on "Feeble-Minded" Women and Children: Examples of an Unconstrained Campaign'. Manuscript, Department of History, University of Toronto, December 1986.

————. 'Tis Not As It Should Be: The Regulation of Unwed Motherhood in Ontario, 1870s–1920s'. Manuscript, University of Toronto, January 1990.

Evans, Patricia M. 'Work, Welfare and the Single Mother: A Dual Labour Market Investigation'. Ph.D. dissertation, School of Social Work, University of Toronto, 1985.

Forestell, Nancy. ' "All That Glitters Is Not Gold": The Gendered Dimensions of Work, Family and Community in the Northern Ontario Goldmining Town of Timmins, 1909–1950'. Ph.D. dissertation, Department of History and Philosophy, Ontario Institute for Studies in Education, 1993.

Gavreau, Danielle. 'Broken Marriages in the Saguenay Region: Women's

Experiences before 1930'. Paper presented to the Social Science Historical Association Conference, Minneapolis, 18 October 1990.

Goodwin, Joanne. 'The Differential Treatment of Motherhood: Mothers' Pensions, Chicago 1900–1930'. Paper presented at the Conference on Gender and Social Policy in conjunction with the Social Science History Association Conference, Minneapolis, 18 October 1990.

Hamlet, L. 'Charlotte Whitton and the Growth of the Canadian Council on Child Welfare 1926–1942'. MSW research paper, School of Social Work, Carleton University, 1978.

Hurl, Lorna. 'The Nature of Policy Dynamics: Patterns of Change and Stability in a Social Assistance Program'. Paper presented at the Fourth National Conference on Social Welfare Policy, Toronto, 24–7 October 1989.

Jenson, Jane. 'Making Claims: Social Policy and Gender Relations in Postwar Sweden and France'. Paper presented at the Conference on Gender and Social Policy in conjunction with the Social Science History Association Conference, New Orleans, November 1991.

Koven, Seth, and Sonya Michel. 'Womanly Duties: Maternalist Politics and the Origins of Welfare States in France, Germany, Great Britain, and the United States, 1880–1920'. Paper presented at the Conference on Gender and Social Policy in conjunction with the Social Science History Association Conference, Minneapolis, 18 October 1990.

McInnis, Peter. ' "That Harmonious Balance": Labour-Government Co-operation During and After World War Two'. Paper presented at the Canadian Historical Association, Charlottetown, 6 June 1993.

Moore, Libba. 'Mothers' Pensions: The Origins of the Relationship Between Women and the Welfare State'. Ph.D. dissertation, University of Massachusetts, 1986.

Newton, Janice. 'Enough of Exclusive Masculine Thinking: The Feminist Challenge to the Early Canadian Left, 1900–1918'. Ph.D. dissertation, Department of Political Science, York University, 1987.

Owram, Doug. 'Home and Family at Mid-Century'. Paper presented at the Canadian Historical Association, Charlottetown, June 1992.

Riches, Graham. 'Child Poverty and Welfare Reform: Robbing the Poor to Pay the Poor'. Paper presented at the Fourth National Conference on Social Welfare Policy, Toronto, 26 October 1989.

Romo, Enrique. 'The Origins of Mothers' Allowance Legislation in Ontario'. MSW research paper, School of Social Work, Carleton University, 1979.

Ross, Becki. 'A Feminist Reconceptualization of Women's Work and Leisure: A Study of Kingston Mother Workers'. MA thesis, Department of Physical Education, Queen's University, 1984.

Tennyson, Brian D. 'The Political Career of Sir William Hearst'. MA thesis, Department of History, University of Toronto, 1963.

Valverde, Mariana. 'The Mixed Social Economy as a Canadian Tradition'. Manuscript, York University, 20 May 1993.

Index